From the Margins

From the Margins

Historical Anthropology and Its Futures

Edited by Brian Keith Axel

Duke University Press   Durham and London 2002

© 2002 Duke University Press

All rights reserved

Printed in the United States of America on acid-free paper ∞

Typeset in Trump Mediaeval by Keystone Typesetting, Inc.

Permissions and Library of Congress Cataloging-in-Publication Data

appear on the last printed page of this book.

Contents

Preface

After many years of working on the margins of their disciplinary homes and within disparate systems of institutional support, scholars and students of historical anthropology have begun to constitute a shared domain of conversation and debate. There may not necessarily be a consensus on what historical anthropology is or should be, nor is consensus necessarily sought after. However, at the beginning of the twenty-first century, historical anthropology has gained momentum as both a pedagogical practice and a way to interrogate the dynamics of emergent world orders. It is the challenging character of these sites of pedagogy and interrogation that we would like to explore in this book.

The idea to capture this moment in historical anthropology with a volume came out of a series of conversations I had during the Spring of 1999 at Emory University and was made possible by the unique collaborative opportunities afforded me as Emory's Mellon Postdoctoral Faculty Fellow in Ethnography and Historiography. As the title of the fellowship suggests, my two institutional homes—the Department of Anthropology and the Graduate Institute of Liberal Arts (ILA)—were interested in facilitating an interaction between anthropology and history. Toward this end, I was invited to work with Donald Donham to coordinate a semester-long historical anthropology program. Don and I planned a graduate workshop to be built around a series of presentations by guest speakers. We were fortunate to have several important scholars in the field visit Emory throughout the semester. And we were just as fortunate to enroll the participation of faculty and graduate students from several different departments and fields.

Historical anthropology is often defined as a form of knowledge production that is based on an exchange of methods and theories between history and anthropology. Understood as a mode of disciplinary exchange, this type of inquiry seems to bear all the signs of interdisciplinarity, an intellectual enterprise so celebrated these days. In fact, when first beginning to plan Emory's historical anthropology workshop, we very much saw our project in this light. We started with a pragmatic sense of working knowledge and hoped to establish a dialogue between the two disciplines of history and anthropology in order to refine modes of exchange for their respective methods and theories.

The workshop, indeed, represented only one example of a broader trend in supporting programs of interdisciplinary inquiry on campus. More generally, we have seen this kind of trend burgeoning all over the United States in response to epistemological crises engendered by the excitement (or alarm) of globalization, changing world orders, or sudden civilizational clashes. However, what we were proposing to investigate was not at first necessarily infused with this sense of newness or danger, and for some, it even seemed to be merely an extension of what was already in place. After all, had not historians been deploying anthropological methods for decades? And had not anthropologists made ample use of history? At the very least, the challenge was to persuade representatives of both fields to gather in the same room—no small feat, as many remarked, for a campus that, by its very architecture and landscape, kept the different departmental homes apart.

If anything, this challenge of forging institutional connections can be taken as symbolic of the dilemma of interdisciplinarity itself, and engaging it gave us an opportunity to reformulate our initial ideas of historical anthropology. As the semester unfolded, a workshop oriented toward shifting disciplinary distinctions often evoked hesitation in students and faculty trained in either history or anthropology who saw their departmental alliance called into question. For some of us, the possibility of transcending or bridging institutional boundaries—a prospect supposedly signified by "historical anthropology"—engendered a renewed effort to define and separate the sites transcended. At best, this disciplinary "unease" was not squelched but rather fueled by the presentations of our guests, whose papers tended to demonstrate diverse sites for the production of historical anthropology rather than defining the inquiry itself. Sometimes the speakers were challenged to accentuate or specify precisely how their work transformed or moved between conventional boundaries. Yet, at other times, they were met with questions that demanded they be better historians or more recognizable anthropologists. As Bernard Cohn once noted: "It is relatively simple to suggest and explore subject matters which are of joint interest to historians and anthropologists. It is much more difficult to delineate a common epistemological space which can be termed historical anthropology."

Cohn's words indicate a crucial distinction, wherein we may discern the limitations of interdisciplinarity. Uncannily mimetic of the university campus's architectural divisions, our interdisciplinary desires tend, more often than not, to rely upon and sustain the functioning of disciplinary divisions, leaving their frontiers and boundaries intact and therefore requiring a conception of knowledge production as exchange or borrowing. The papers that our guests presented to the workshop, however, questioned such divisions. Their work could be characterized more precisely as disruptive of institutionally defined strictures.

We might say, then, that our presenters prompted us to revise our understanding of the workshop's challenge: one that lay less in convincing participants to explore the features of what was already familiar—and more in seeing how we might recognize historical anthropology as *something other* than a way of structuring disciplinary exchange. For many of us, it became clear that this type of historical anthropology—as something other—called forth a certain ambivalence. In other words, the promise of historical anthropology as a powerful inquiry seemed also to be a kind of threat—to our training, our sense of property, or our disciplinary identifications. More generally, it may be argued that this is a tension around which we may discern the features of a new, critical historical anthropology emerging. The workshop as a whole became a valuable venue for expressing such vicissitude, and this book offers one way to consider the productivity of that ambivalence.

I should reiterate my gratitude to Emory University and the Mellon Foundation, as well as to Emory's Department of Anthropology and the ILA, for providing support to the Historical Anthropology Workshop in the Spring of 1999. Particular thanks go to Peter Brown, Chair of the Department of Anthropology, and Bobby Paul, Director of the ILA, who not only asked me to help structure the workshop during my first year as a Mellon Fellow, but gave me the opportunity to teach undergraduate courses related to historical anthropology throughout two years at Emory. I am grateful to Donald Donham for taking me on as a co-conspirator, and for a wonderful semester of debate about historical anthropology. The workshop, of course, and this book, would not have had its particular quality and character without our guest speakers: Jean Comaroff, Nicholas Dirks, J. D. Y. Peel, Irene Silverblatt, Paul Silverstein, and Ann L. Stoler. What made the workshop extremely stimulating was the participation of several faculty and graduate students, including, among faculty, Edna Bay, Carla Freeman, Bruce Knauft, Corinne Kratz, Kristin Mann, Randall Packard, Matthew Payne, Ellen Schattschneider, Debra Spitulnik, and Bob White; and, among graduate students, Yamini Nagaraja Atmavilas, Maria Marsilli Cardozo,

Joanna Davidson, Lara Deeb, Robert Goddard, Ben Junge, Steve Levin, Holly Maluk, Jeremy Pool, Jay Straker, and Sarah Willen.

With the exception of J. D. Y. Peel (whose very important paper unfortunately could not be included here), all of the workshop's guests provided contributions to this volume (but not, in each case, the same essay as originally presented). The remaining contributions come from scholars who, although not present at Emory during the Spring of 1999, have been very much a part of—or indeed have generated the possibility for—this continuing conversation: Talal Asad, John Comaroff (writing with Jean Comaroff), Bernard Cohn and Terri Silvio, and Michel-Rolph Trouillot.

I would like to thank my undergraduate students at Emory who gave me the opportunity to explore historical anthropology in its many guises over four semesters. They provided me with powerful challenges to think more clearly and seek the edges and limits of my own practice of knowledge production. Shifting between categories of student and teacher themselves, the following students offered me a unique tutorial in the vicissitudes of pedagogy: Jennifer Bagley, Christopher Barbie, Amy Bracewell, Whitney Cook, Blake Eno, Jeremy Hendon, Heather Hussey, Nicollette Monaco, Aaron Oeser, and Karla Waller.

Since I have left Emory, I have acquired new colleagues and a new structure of institutional support at Harvard University, without which this project could not have been completed. I express my thanks to my colleagues at the Harvard Academy, and to the Weatherhead Center more generally, as well as to my anthropology colleagues Steve Caton, Michael Herzfeld, and Randy Matory.

Ken Wissoker, my editor at Duke University Press, continues to be an engaged and critical interlocutor and I thank him again for supporting this project. Additionally, Duke's Leigh Anne Couch has made a great contribution to this volume. Two anonymous readers for Duke also provided invaluable commentary which has helped refine the text. Both Jean Comaroff and Paul Silverstein read through early drafts of my introductory essay and, via long distance from Cape Town to Chicago and Manhattan to Portland, took time to speak with me about it at length. Additionally, Nick Dirks and Ann Stoler have provided me with many a conversation, suggesting new ways to refocus and clarify the directions of this project. I owe a special acknowledgment to Jean Comaroff and Arjun Appadurai, whose pedagogy and friendship have been a constant source of inspiration and whose scholarship has had an extremely important impact on my own work and on the development of historical anthropology more generally. Finally, I can never express enough gratitude to Bernard S. Cohn who first introduced me (and many others) to this type of inquiry called historical anthropology and whose lessons in this field are far from exhausted.

From the Margins

Introduction: Historical Anthropology and Its Vicissitudes

Brian Keith Axel

Rethinking Historical Anthropology

Reflecting on what it meant to "rethink" his own discipline—and musing on the "heresy" of his own "unorthodox assumptions"—Edmund Leach (1961, v) commented on the play of citation and pedagogy in anthropological practices of knowledge production:

> The game of building new theories on the ruins of old ones is almost an occupational disease. Contemporary arguments in social anthropology are built out of formulae concocted by Malinowski, Radcliffe-Brown and Levi-Strauss who in turn were only "rethinking" Rivers, Durkheim, and Mauss, who borrowed from Morgan, McLennan, and Robertson-Smith—and so on. Sceptics may think that the total outcome of all this ratiocination adds up to very little; despite all our pedagogical subtleties, the diversities of human custom remain as bewildering as ever. But that we admit. The contemporary social anthropologist is all too well aware that he knows much less than Frazer imagined he knew for certain.

On many occasions—and with as much a sense of heresy and wit—Bernard Cohn also reflected on the powerful, though often banal, practice of conjuring the ghosts of our discipline's "theoretical guides" through the "exchange of irrelevant or widely known citations" (1987, 3); and with wry humour, he has noted the place of pedagogy in the perpetuation of this exchange: "Old debates never die; they just become enshrined in graduate curricula and text books" (1987, 67). Perhaps more to the point, however, Cohn (1987, 201; 1987, 168) has never tired of reminding us of the insidious manner by which the assumptions developed through more than 200 years of colonial rule have been insinuated "consciously or unconsciously" into our present analytical models (1987, 168, 201).

To rephrase Leach's and Cohn's insights, I might argue that historical anthropology proliferates within a forest of citations, and, if anything, rethinking the emergence of the field tends to stir up an uncanny sense of that iterable quality.[1] Citationality, however, indicates a double procedure. To the extent that it refers to—or, rather, constitutes—the "origins" of a field, our present work may occasionally be forestalled when we consciously or unconsciously accept the gifts of our predecessors. Yet, while our obsession with the origins of our field sometimes leaves us prone to the shortcomings of its founding figures and to its colonial provenance, we might note, in a more Derridean vein, that there is potential in citationality to introduce critical epistemological shifts and contextual transformations.

This doubleness of citationality notwithstanding, today's proliferation of gestures to *culture* and *history* or to *ethnography* and the *archive* all too often fall prey to the unmarked insinuation of our predecessors' disquieting limitations—and this more often than not from within work claiming interdisciplinary status. Such mainstream gestures, now seeming more and more naturalized, herald an unremarkable shift in disciplinary centers of gravity. Their attempts to maneuver both the historical turn and the anthropological turn seem not only taken for granted but untheorized. Against such work, what we are here calling historical anthropology remains a marked field—not because its practitioners mark out what they are doing as historical anthropology, but because their very analytic procedures threaten to reveal the fragile epistemologies and contexts of present scholarship's doxa. It is this quality that positions historical anthropology on the margins of conventional academic practice.

In this specific sense, it may be said that the textual practices of historical anthropology operate from the margins—hence the title of this book. With this, however, it should not be understood that either the topics under investigation, or the scholars involved in the inquiry, are marginal. In fact, in many cases, they are quite central. Nor should it be taken to imply that historical anthropology only studies marginal events or marginalized people—whether in terms of the underrepresented or the non-Western. On the contrary, historical anthropology, very powerfully, develops inquiries into the non-eventful, the colonizer, and the imaginaries of the West, Europe, and North America. Against the valorization of the diversity, or essentialized difference, of forgotten, subaltern, or past peoples, historical anthropology shows up the ways that the supposed margins and metropoles, or peripheries and centers, fold into, constitute, or disrupt one another (cf., Comaroff and Comaroff 1997, 17). In other words, historical anthropology constitutes new centers of inquiry, just as it demonstrates the powerful positionality of the margins right at the center.

In our rethinking of the field from the concerns of present imperatives, it is quite clear, then, that what distinguishes historical anthropology is not its effort (in more conventional terms) to account for social and cultural formations in "the past." Rather than the study of a people in a particular place and at a certain time, what is at stake in historical anthropology is explaining the production of a people, and the production of space and time. This orientation engenders a critical interest in seeking to understand the politics of living the ongoing connections or disjunctures of futures and pasts in heterogeneous presents. Pursuing an understanding of diverse presents leads historical anthropology toward the limits of its own procedures of knowledge production, in order to critically engage both its own provenance and the historical moments that gave rise to the social sciences and humanities. Here then is a more complex characterization of this field's work as from the margins. Historical anthropology reaches toward its own margins just as it works on the margins of institutional epistemologies to look at the problematic nature of history itself and to rethink the presumptions of social theory and disciplinarity.

In the next few pages, I cannot help but cite briefly some of the moments that have been called upon before in discussions of historical anthropology. Yet it is not my aim in this introduction to construct a genealogy of historical anthropology per se or to provide an exhaustive account of supposed interchanges between the two disciplines of history and anthropology. In order to avoid confusion, it may be helpful to spell out my goals: 1) to pinpoint a moment just after World War II (between 1950 and 1970 in England and the United States) where related inquiries with very different approaches emerged—and concurrently to differentiate that specific moment and those approaches from pre-World War II studies; 2) to spell out what history meant for each of these sites; and 3) to delineate objects of inquiry which have continued to occupy our attention, such as the nation, colonialism, time, space, ethnography, the archive.

For many of us, the 1950s and 1960s were key decades, known for instituting important practices of repetition and transformation that opened up new possibilities for historical anthropology. Before this period, debates about the interarticulation of history and anthropology (which included and harkened back to many of the figures cited by Leach above) were fixed upon dismissing evolutionism, questioning diffusionism, or rejecting functionalism. Within anthropology, the primary concern with history was in evaluating its use as a technique of reconstruction—the viability of which relied upon whether it might successfully yield an image of primitive society prior to the advent of colonialism.[2] With the end of the World Wars, however, and with the ascendance of America as a Cold War world power, early signs of historical anthropology underwent considerable alteration. New objects of study came into view, and new university programs began to produce more researchers. I would like to highlight three disparate sites within this two-decade period for discerning the emergence of distinct lines of inquiry, objects of study, and models of history—each of which, to varying degrees, continue to have relevance today.[3]

In the United States, supported by the government's effort to produce knowledge out of the promises of some of the world's "new" nations and the threats of others, both old and new, scholars began innovative projects based on unprecedented, interdisciplinary collaborations. One example—and our first important site—is provided by the team of researchers led by Margaret Mead to develop an approach to the study of "cultures at a distance" (for example, Japanese, Jewish, Chinese, Russian). Their work immediately extended the pioneering analytic introduced by Ruth Benedict (1946) in her study of Japan, accomplished through archival work and interviews conducted in the United States. Most importantly, however, these studies redeployed Boas' techniques ("memory ethnographies"), supplementing them with ideas from linguistics and Jungian psychology (Axel 1996b, 2001a; Stocking 1986). What was most novel about this work was its object of study, national culture. As Mead (1953, 4) wrote in the introduction to her manual:

> This focus on national cultures has been dictated by an interest in the role of nationally originating behavior in warfare, policy making, domestic educational and morale-building campaigns, and so on. The method is, however, equally suitable for the study of . . . a group like the East European Jews, whose communities stretched across several national boundaries. With appropriate redefinitions, the same methods can be used to explore . . . the regular behavior of members of a religious order distributed in many countries. The national emphasis in our studies has been the exigent one that they were studies designed to help national governments to deal with members of other nations who were also behaving nationally. . . . So this Manual is primarily a manual on interdisciplinary research practices as they apply particularly to the study of cultural character structure in cultures that are spatially or temporally inaccessible.

Mead's group had good reason to be concerned about the provenance of its theory and methodology, as well as the significance of its conclusions. It was not only the case that the U.S. government demanded and funded the production of theories of "culture at a distance" and national character, but the government also demanded their immediate use in policy making. The U.S. government was interested in the threat of the Soviet Union and Communist China. These cultures were spatially inaccessible because they could not be studied in person. Since the U.S. government necessitated a sketch of their national character for strategic purposes, this group of scholars needed to develop a theory of a constitutive relation between those places and Soviet or Chinese people living in the United States. Likewise, the U.S. government was interested in the problem of the displacement of Jews who were "behaving nationally" (those who were "un-American"). Since the places of origin of these populations may have ceased to exist, their national character was described as temporally inaccessible.

The significance of history for these American-made studies was very specific (Mead 1953). Oriented toward studying people who were "spatially distant" (whose places of origin were inaccessible to the researcher), Mead and her colleagues transposed the older notion of reconstruction into the "reconstructive imagination" (Mead 1953, 10–21). In this procedure, history was qualified as a means of measuring temporal distance, and pertained particularly to the temporal distance of a people's origin from its people. This kind of historical anthropology intended to define a relationship between a place of origin and a displaced people: it would depict not just the movement of a people through time, or from one place to another, but the embodiment of an origin within that people's contemporary linguistic and psychological characteristics (personality). History, in other words, for these postwar American scholars was a recitation and an expansion of the prewar model of diffusion (Axel 1996b, 2001a).

A second site for the elaboration of an emergent historical anthropology may be located in postwar Europe, where Evans-Pritchard (1962c), Leach (1954), Lévi-Strauss (1963, 1966), I. Schapera (1962), and Keith Thomas (1963, 1964) began asking a set of questions that would be repeated for decades to come. When, if ever, should anthropologists and historians make use of each other's techniques or methods? Is there a difference between the two disciplines? Will the successful development of one make the other redundant? Many, if not all, of these scholars were beginning to have a sense of how the changing world order (out of the dissipation of colonial regimes) affected the imperatives of their work—not to the extent, however, that they were willing to make explicit the relationship of their work to colonial violence, a problem already well criticized (Asad 1973; Clifford 1988; Clifford and Marcus 1986; Cohn 1987).[4] Not only were their objects of study former subjects of Empire, but those objects were now susceptible to the transformations of modernity and the desires of progress. As Evans-Pritchard (1962b, 147–48) remarked, "The problem here raised is becoming a pressing one because anthropologists are now studying communities which, if still fairly simple in structure, are enclosed in, and form part of, great historical societies. . . . They can no longer ignore history. . . . As anthropologists turn their attention more to complex civilized communities the issue will become more acute, and the direction of theoretical development in the subject will largely depend on its outcome."

After Radcliffe-Brown's condemnation of "conjectural history" and Malinowski's functionalist rejection of history *tout court*, Evans-Pritchard's statement may have seemed to some British scholars to stray quite far from the accepted trajectory of social anthropology. His essays and lectures on anthropology and history traced the emergence of what he characterized as a traumatic "breach" between two "sister" disciplines which he proposed were originally indissociable, or at least naturally intertwined in the hands of the "precursors and founders of our science" (1962b, 172). The problem, he claimed, was not that the likes of Westermarck, Hobhouse, Marrett, Durkheim, Maine, and Robertson-Smith did history, but that they did "bad history," and it was because of this confusion (of history as such with bad history) that the functionalist critics of both evolutionists and diffusionists wrongly abandoned history altogether. However, it seemed to Evans-Pritchard that functionalism had gotten the upper hand, and with dire consequences: "[The tendency] to overestimate what are called functional ethnographic studies of primitive societies at the expense of developmental studies, and even to ignore historical facts altogether, has prevented us from testing the validity of some of the basic assumptions on which our studies have long rested, that for example, there is an entity which can be labeled 'society' and that such an entity has something called a 'structure,' which can be further described as a set of functionally interdependent institutions or sets of social relations" (1962b, 181).

In actuality, Evans-Pritchard's exhortation of history was only an extreme instance of a more general, though perhaps more cautious, awareness in Britain of an intersection between anthropology and history. More contentious were Evans-Pritchard's two proclamations: that functionalist anthropologists displayed an antihistorical prejudice and that the difference between history and anthropology "is largely illusory" (1962b, 187). Evans-Pritchard received a prompt reply by I. Schapera (1962) in an article titled "Should Anthropologists Be Historians?" Quite simply, Schapera argued, Evans-Pritchard was wrong on both counts. First, functionalist ethnographers had been doing history all along, a proposition Schapera demonstrated by drawing heavily on examples from his own work and citing those of Firth, Hogbin, Wilson, Richards, Nadel, and Kuper, among others. Second, the difference between history and anthropology was quite clear, identifiable by the former's focus on the "social past" and the latter's concern to describe the "social present."

The debate between Evans-Pritchard and Schapera is significant not only because it indicates an explicit concern with history in anthropology, but because it identifies the emergence of a particular understanding of what history itself was for postwar British historical anthropology—an understanding seemingly distinct from the prewar fetish of precolonial purity and the postwar American fascination with the origins of displaced peoples.[5] Presaging a dawning postcolonial moment, British social anthropologists were aware of the effects of colonialism on their objects of study (yet again, as Asad was to point out, "the colonial system as such—within which the social objects studied were located—[was not] analyzed by the social anthropologist" [1973, 18]). Schapera seemed to be speaking for most of his colleagues when he commented that "the tribes they studied had been so greatly influenced by contact with Europeans that to ignore the resulting changes would have led to an incomplete and distorted view of present-day social life" (1962, 145).

History, then, indicated a technique to help explain social change and modern developments, both of which were correlates of "European influence." And while Schapera answered his own question, "Should Anthropologists Be Historians?" with a confident "no," he did agree with Evans-Pritchard that anthropologists can and should, if circumstances require, utilize the historian's tools. Concurrently, anthropologists could make use of the historian's methods to produce what would become future historical documents, and they could bring to the archive insights drawn from the anthropological experience of the field. Yet most importantly, history, or its appropriation within anthropology as historical anthropology (Evans-Pritchard 1962c), would provide a corrective to the problems of stasis that afflicted older structural-functionalist accounts, and it would add a dynamic sense of movement to revised models of social life—or so it would seem. Indications of European influence (that ever-present term) signify a problem. In this view of history, temporality—as natural, dynamic movement—came from the outside, from European influence, to jump-start social change and modern developments. Hence we see a return, in new guise, of the search for, or postulation of, what I have called a precolonial purity. In the words of Bernard Cohn: "There was a time, anthropologists argue, when the systems we want to study were stable or static, and the anthropologist studies change by studying what happened from the postulated period of stability" (1987, 168). Or, more succinctly, "Theories of change always involve a model of what society is 'really' like when it is stable" (1987, 190).

I invoke the work of Bernard Cohn again because his writings, during the

1955–1970 period, locate a third site for the production of an emergent historical anthropology—and this at a time prior to the ascendance of the University of Chicago's department of anthropology, as a kind of iconic locality for the proliferation of "dialogues" between history and anthropology.[6] Nevertheless, Cohn was certainly not working in a vacuum. Indeed, similar to Mead's environment at Columbia University, this version of historical anthropology developed within an interdisciplinary environment consisting of such Chicago scholars as McKim Marriott, Robert Redfield, Edward Shils, Milton Singer, Aristede Zolberg and others involved with the Committee on the Comparative Study of New Nations.[7] Likewise, Cohn's scholarship critically engaged that of British historians, as well as South Asianist and Africanist anthropologists. Emerging within this broad discursive field, Cohn's work offered an approach that was somewhat distinct from the reigning models of the post-Boasians and postwar British social anthropologists.[8] In Cohn's writings, we can discern a shared interest in questions of the nation, violent displacement, and the effects of colonialism, but the formulation of these problems is quite different.

As my previous citations have indicated, Cohn generated a project to deconstruct received empiricism and its categories of analysis, seeing them as remnants and embodiments of colonial modalities of rule. This critique was not merely a starting point, but rather an immanent aspect of what Cohn took as his object of study: the dynamic interaction of the colonizer and the colonized. Here we see an important difference from the foci in British social anthropology. Rather than attempting to conceive of the European influence on primitive social life, Cohn framed his questions in terms of a dialectical relation that constituted both metropole and colony, the European and the Other, as indissociable. He showed this dialectic most clearly in essays looking at interrelations between formations of Indian society, on one hand, and Orientalist, missionary, and census practices, on the other (1957). His later writing reflected on this orientation more succinctly (1987, 44):

> Anthropological "others" are part of the colonial world. In the historical situation of colonialism, both white rulers and indigenous peoples were constantly involved in representing to each other what they were doing. Whites everywhere came into other peoples' worlds with models and logics, means of representation, forms of knowledge and action, with which they adapted to the construction of new environments, peopled by new "others." By the same token these "others" had to restructure their worlds to encompass the fact of white domination and their powerlessness. Hence, one of the primary subject matters of an historical anthropology or an anthropo-

logical history is, to use Balandier's term, the colonial situation. This is not to be viewed as "impact," nor as "culture contact," nor is it to be viewed through a methodology that seeks to sort what is introduced from what is indigenous. It is rather to be viewed as a situation in which the European colonialist and the indigene are united in one analytic field.

According to Cohn, it was through the dynamics of the colonial world's united field that basic notions in anthropological and historical studies emerged: not just social change and modernization, but time, space, the people, region, the village, law, and land. Cohn's analytic, in other words, articulated a concern with the productive qualities of power and knowledge, and the contradictions or paradoxes of domination. This had broad implications for his approach to research and writing. I discuss these implications for South Asian studies specifically in chapter nine (see also Dirks 1996a; Guha 1987; Mathur 2000). But here, what is important to note is the reorientation from the British functionalist anthropological focus on small scale tribal or village societies and recent periods of social change to larger scale cultural phenomena and transformative processes over the long term. However, just as Cohn turned to the study of colonialism with a cultural perspective, his work argued that colonialism was itself a cultural project of control and that culture was likewise an effect of colonial history (Dirks 1992, 3).

Cohn's version of historical anthropology reconstituted particular notions of both history and anthropology. His work in the 1950s and 1960s began a relentless pursuit of unveiling both history and anthropology, with their relations to the archive and ethnography, as effects of and as complicit with colonial rule; and it offered a persistent critique of the legacies of colonialism in the formation of the modern nation-state and institutions of knowledge production like area studies. Such a position led Cohn not to abandon the projects of history or anthropology themselves, but rather to experiment critically (and playfully) with redeploying their procedures of knowledge production. Indeed, he developed a distinctive practice that would "treat the materials of history the way an anthropologist treats his field notes" (1987, 2), and this treatment of historical materials would return him to questions about the construction of culture.

In the same way that Leach saw himself and his generation rethinking and re-citing the work of prior generations, today we continue to reconstitute and transform the work produced during the 1950s and 1960s. The three sites I have isolated indicate one set of beginnings for understanding the inquiries of historical anthropology. These, of course, may be expanded to include others—for example, one may take the trajectory represented in the very important works of Wolf, Mintz, and Roseberry (Mintz 1956, 1974, 1985; Mintz and Price 1976; Mintz and Wolf 1989; Roseberry 1978, 1989; Wolf 1951, 1966, 1982; Wolf and Mintz 1957). This latter domain of knowledge production, highlighting the significance of political economy as a problem for historical anthropology, has been dealt with by other scholars, and their discussions may be read alongside the present volume. It is clear, however, that questions of ethnography, the archive, the colonial situation, the nation, origins, and displacement raised during the 1950s and 1960s are far from settled—and, as Leach never hesitated to remind us, we perhaps know far less about their nuances and vagaries than we often admit. My treatment in the following sections of this chapter—and discussions in the remaining chapters of this volume—return to these questions, showing also how the theoretical interventions of recent years have helped to shed new light on or redirect how we may conceptualize their challenges.

In many ways, then, the essays in this book may be taken as a response to some old disputes—without simply repeating the familiar terms of those debates and without presuming to answer their queries. What distinguishes the contributors to this book is how they engage the problems of our erstwhile "theoretical guides." They indeed stand somewhat to the side of historical anthropology's forest of citations, which I have all too briefly outlined here. Rather, their historical anthropology is, as I note in my preface, "something other," and it may, as such, generate frustration and ambivalence, particularly for those readers who see historical anthropology as a modality of disciplinary exchange.

Still, we cannot easily escape the architecture of the institutions that make our inquiries possible. Such structures, indeed, have long supported the separation of history and anthropology. The work brought together in this book comes from scholars positioned in a diversity of institutional departments, sometimes in both anthropology and history. Nevertheless, the essays do not presume the inquiries of historical anthropology to be easily separable (if at all) into the institutionally delimited domains of anthropology or history, no matter how much our institutional landscapes may sequester the two.[9] Yet they do demonstrate a concern to interrogate the epistemologies that those disciplinary distinctions have engendered: for example, the view that the past is foundational, or final authority, for interpreting the present. The work of historical anthropology, these essays suggest, is not about a closed set of determinations but about a rigorous, yet open, sense of contextualization—and about the production of time and space.[10]

Our conventional institutional structures not only support the separation of history and anthropology, they also encourage the development of theoretical models that are place-dependent or that presume regions to be naturally isolable.[11] We cannot help but associate ourselves with various area studies programs in our respective universities. The essays presented here, however, do not reproduce the geographic imaginary that has sustained many similar inquiries. Unlike the few other edited volumes published recently on historical anthropology (Biersack 1991; Siikala 1990; Silverman and Gulliver 1992), they move between a variety of different periods and geographic or areal foci. Represented together in this volume, the disparity of these sites for the production of historical anthropology prompt a more general questioning of the ways our disciplinary definitions and theoretical models have been determined by the cartographic distinctions of colonial regions or nation-states. These contributions illuminate the character of historical formations of domination, cultural reality, and knowledge production as constitutive of, and developing through, an emerging global field. Disrupting a conventional analytics of division and isolation, this inquiry specifies the logics of circulation and comparison that have brought together (and created) the interrelationship of histories typically seen as segregated.

Hence one of the book's basic aims: to develop a critical sense about the institutional worlds within which historical anthropology has evolved its characteristic styles and objects of study. This is a project spelled out by Nicholas B. Dirks and Talal Asad in the book's first section, "Ethnography and the Archive." For Irene Silverblatt, Paul Silverstein, and Ann L. Stoler—contributors to the second section, "Colonial Anxieties"—this kind of interrogation grounds a renewed exploration of colonialism and its enduring legacy. These chapters exemplify an approach that extends the earlier work of Bernard Cohn and Talal Asad (1973), as well as the later refinements by scholars taking up questions introduced by Foucault and Said (cf., Appadurai 1996a and b; Breckenridge and van der Veer 1993; Comaroff and Comaroff 1992; Cooper and Stoler 1997; Dirks 1992; Stoler 1995).[12] The explorations of "Marginal Contexts" by Michel-Rolph Trouillot and Bernard Cohn and Teri Silvio, take up explicitly an inquiry into our procedures of contextualization. Finally, the chapters by Axel and Jean Comaroff and John Comaroff in the "Archaeologies of the Fantastic" section, although certainly not sidestepping important questions of colonialism, are oriented toward the qualities and effects of postcoloniality and globalization.

Ultimately, this book looks toward the futures of historical anthropology. How can we develop new approaches to explore the articulation or intersections of historically specific local practices with processes of a world historical order? How can these processes illuminate, or provide the basis for, a reevaluation of basic categories of analysis like time and space, violence and sexuality, or people and the individual? To what extent can historical anthropology's position within specific institutional frameworks define possibilities for an investigation into, and the transformation of, disciplinary boundaries?

Ethnography and the Archive

In the following pages, I do not presume to summarize the book's chapters, or to represent the work of the different authors, particularly if that implies offering a transparent lens through which to view what they have supposedly accomplished. Rather, I am reconstituting the trajectories of the different contributions, I hope not unfairly, with the aim of making a specific argument about historical anthropology and its futures. The argument has two parts. The first, simply, is that it is not viable to think of historical anthropology as defined by an exchange of methods and theories, or of the relationship between history and anthropology as one characterized by dialogue. The second part is that historical anthropology may productively deploy the tensions and conflicts of the institutionally defined relationship between history and anthropology to generate a new, critical practice of knowledge production. The following sections of this introduction spell this argument out, and the contributors to this book elaborate it in different ways.

This book is not the first text to criticize normative understandings of a relationship between history and anthropology, but I feel that the critique needs to be restated, and that a clear alternative must be presented. We may note, however, that such a critique is not to be confused with Evans-Pritchard's originary fantasy of anthropology and history as "once upon a time," constituting a singular entity, which, like Plato's image of the original human, underwent a traumatic breach and forever-after sought reunion (Evans-Pritchard 1962, 172). Rather, what we are presenting may be related to a position articulated early on by John L. Comaroff: "The point has been lost that any substantive relationship between disciplines is determined *not* by the intrinsic nature of those disciplines—if any such thing exists—but by prior theoretical considerations. . . . In my own view, there ought to be no 'relationship' between history and anthropology, since there should be no division to begin with. . . . Existing disciplinary divisions are rooted in the establishment of positivist empiricism as the dominant scientific ideology of western culture" (1982, 143–44; emphasis mine). Taking John Comaroff's 1982 position in a slightly different direction, an important part of our project now is that we interrogate different disciplinary genealogies of what has, indeed, become a "relationship" between history and anthropology.[13]

Since the 1950s, of the many issues circulating within discussions of historical anthropology, questions of ethnography and the archive have been given the most attention. This is perhaps not without reason. Both appear to be indispensable portals providing access to the very realities with which anthropology and history are supposed to be concerned. And when, as is often the case, historical anthropology is conceived of as an inquiry that brings together the methodologies or techniques of two already established disciplines, then ethnography and the archive take center stage as either points of mediation or elements of exchange. However, in all the bustle to try to figure out how history and anthropology can use each other's techniques (and thus, supposedly, constitute a historical anthropology), what most often goes without comment is the presumption that history and anthropology are whole and complete in themselves. Here, we regard this presumption as a problem—one leading to the very common way of speaking about historical anthropology as exemplifying a dialogue between history and anthropology. And we may take as our starting point the epistemological status of ethnography and the archive, with their metonymical power to stand in for the imaginary totalities of anthropology and history.[14] How have anthropology and history come to be seen as attaining such unique pinnacles and positions of closure? What are the conditions needed for the assignment of ethnography and the archive as transparently privileged sites of knowledge production? Is it possible to constitute a historical anthropology not through an exchange of already extant techniques and methods but from a critique of those very terms?

One way to address these questions emerged within the debates of the 1950s and 1960s. During that time, scholars first began to scrutinize their approach to and use of the documents found in archives. Bernard Cohn (1987, 2) was the most articulate on this topic when, as I have already noted, he urged us to "treat the materials of history the way an anthropologist treats his field notes." In a different, and perhaps more rigorous, manner, the status of the archival document and historical narrativity was carefully explored by Barthes (1970) and Foucault (1972). By the 1980s, the importance of this kind of inquiry was amply demonstrated in the works of many scholars (Davis 1981, 1987; Dirks 1987; Ginzburg 1981, 1989; Stoler 1985; Silverblatt 1987). And of course, Ranajit Guha (1988), with the Subaltern Studies collective, generated an extremely influential technique not only for reading archival documents of the colonial period but also for distinguishing different types of documents and their relations to the forces of domination they purported to represent. The basic lesson we learn from this trajectory of scholarship is that we must be careful to regard archival documents not as repositories of facts of the past but as complexly constituted instances of discourse that produce their objects as *real*, that is, as existing prior to and outside of discourse.[15]

This is a lesson, which has by now become part of the common parlance for historical anthropology. Nevertheless, reiterating some of its implications may prove useful, not only because the project of theorizing the status of archival documents continues to have resonance today, but also because today's trajectory of historical anthropology pushes that project even further. We may enumerate the implications regarding the question of the archival document in the following, albeit truncated, way: 1) documents were generated through complex interactions between different agents of colonialism and colonized subjects—various categories of official and non-official individuals or bureaucrats interacting with "local assistants," each of whom had their own interests and agendas; 2) the generation of documents involved the transformation of practices through entextualization, a process constituting new forms of textual authority; 3) documents pertaining to precolonial history have never had a life outside of colonial history (the archivization of the putatively precolonial is itself a colonialized modality of knowledge production);[16] 4) demonstrating their inexorable historical embeddedness in the logics of colonial power, archival documents may be understood as simultaneously the outcome of colonial processes, integral to the continuing formation of such processes, and the condition for the production of historical knowledge (see Dirks's and Stoler's contributions to this volume). In short, we do not treat archival documents as fictions, but as signs signifying the effectivity of disparate forms of colonial practice to generate "truth."

One way that historical anthropology has begun to extend this basic lesson is by attending "not only to colonialism's archival content, but also to its particular and sometimes peculiar form" (Stoler, this volume, 157). This attention to the interrelation of form and content redescribes the notion of bringing an ethnographic sensibility to an archival object.[17] In the work of Comaroff and Comaroff (1991, 1992, 1997), Dirks (1987, 1992), Richards (1992, 1993), and Stoler (1992a and b, 1995), among others, this kind of theoretical intervention poignantly illuminates archival documents as domains of knowledge production that are rife with intertextuality, polysemia, and contradiction. As Stoler comments: "Colonial lexicons were unevenly appropriated, sometimes constraining what agents of empire thought, elsewhere delimiting the political idioms in which they talked, indicating not what they thought but only what they said" (1992a, 183).

This troubling of the referential epistemologies of archival documents, however, is only a beginning. We are reminded of the imperative to persistently question the historical foundations of the archive where we find these documents.[18] Following this imperative, "the task is less to distinguish fiction from fact than to track the production and consumption of those facticities themselves" (Stoler, forthcoming). As we know, ethnography was a basic modality of colonial knowledge production, and we may interrogate ethnography itself as a central means for that production. In other words, one of the important projects of historical anthropology today is to understand not just the status of archival documents but the position of ethnography within the archive, specifying how an emergent ethnographic enterprise not only supplied the archive with an ever growing number of texts but also, and concurrently, made possible the growth of the archive itself. This way of showing up ethnography and the archive as mutually constitutive indicates an important way of questioning their institutional separation. At the same time, it breaks up the monolith of both the archive and its colonial provenance, demanding not only that we distinguish changing practices and forms of documentation, record keeping, survey techniques, and the collection of artifacts, but also that we identify the fragile foundation of an archive built upon the products of colonial ethnography: knowledge about transformations in rights of ownership, extractions of revenue, intricacies of administration, strategies of trade, fluctuations of markets and industries, and forms of military or political expansion. Making these distinctions helps specify the intersection within the archive of diverse modalities of knowledge production with changing formations of power, with disjunct processes constitutive of sovereignty, and with emergent conceptions of the past and its habitations.

Investigating the position of ethnography within the archive provides a basis for generating an archive of ethnography itself. This important aspect of historical anthropology is exemplified by several contributions to this volume. Dirks's "Annals of the Archive" adds a unique inflection to this kind of inquiry, highlighting a historical moment when ethnography became a basic manner of producing archival documents of colonial South Asia. Concerned with British colonial rule in India and representations of India's precolonial past, Dirks locates a major transformation that began to emerge around 1857: "The foundational importance of historical argument for land policy yielded to . . . [a concern with identifying] those populations that were inherently loyal to the British, and . . . learn[ing] the customs of other populations in order to know and control them" (Dirks, this volume, 57). Embodied within the India Office archive is a shift between historiography and ethnography as a privileged modality of colonial domination. In the specific instance Dirks explores how this shift concerns not only the manner of ruling, or the formation of relations of power, but also ways of knowing. The movement between historiography and ethnography in the mid-nineteenth century inaugurated a process of entextualization, generating and positioning within the archive new categories of classification of different Indian identities of caste and religion (themselves apparently exempt from the progress of history). The processes that brought ethnography into the archive thus facilitated a perpetuation of the archive (a prospect taken up in Stoler's chapter more fully). In other words, the moment highlighted by Dirks shows the imbrication of the archive and ethnography both in the formation of the colonial state and in the constitution of an Indian people as a people struggling to reconcile modernity with its imputed precolonial past.

Talal Asad offers a different archive of ethnography, in this case through a critical comparison with statistical practice. Today, statistics may seem somewhat marginal to anthropology. Yet, as Asad attests, supplementing Stoler's and Dirks's discussions, both ethnography and statistics share a provenance in colonial administration as a political discipline. A central issue drawn from the historicizing of the conjunctions and ruptures between ethnography and statistics concerns the relation between experience and representation that ethnography valorizes—one in which representation is understood to stem from, and present an image of, an intimate experience with the real. In the history of critique of ethnography, most often what has been subject to analysis is either the bias of the representation or the partiality of the experience, whereas the realism of experience—assumed to be foundational for representation—has gone unquestioned (Clifford 1988; Clifford and Marcus 1986; Gupta and Ferguson 1997). Cohn (1987, 1996) and Foucault (1975) have quite clearly pointed out how this problematic quality of empiricism (with its relation to presentism) has been engendered by the disciplinary procedures of the human sciences. But Asad takes the account of anthropology in a different direction, discussing how the privilege accorded ethnographic experience proliferates two assumptions: 1) that publicly accessible writing does not connect directly with social life, but that memory of personal encounters does, and 2) that inscription is always a representation (either true or false) of social life but can never constitute social life itself. The crystallization of this foundationalism of experience within ethnography has had significant effects.[19] Not only has ethnographic fieldwork become anthropology's rite of passage, but its intimate impact on the "observer as a total human being" (to use Evans-Pritchard's words) has come to limit the scope of anthropology to an emphasis on the present, a preoccupation with local conditions, an attention to small scale events, and an identification of what is perceived to be typical within and representative of the field.

Indications of the typical and of the representative lead us not only to a more general inspection of the relation between representation and experience, but also to a consideration, once again, of ethnography and the archive as complexly conjoined enterprises. In the same way that we now find untenable the presumption of the archival document as a repository of the past, it is clear that we can no longer sustain an understanding of ethnography as a transparent representation of directly experienced facts and events. If we underscore the productivity of representation, then the foundationalism perpetuated by our conventional conception of ethnography becomes susceptible to a powerful critique, showing not how representation is born of experience but rather how representation produces modern society and "radically new conditions of experience" (Asad, this volume, 83; see also Axel 1998, 2001a). The possibility of representation constituting experience cannot be encompassed within an ethnographic epistemology, which, like that of the archive, posits a teleological movement from the "real" of experience to the transparency of representation, or from the intimate sanctity of sight to the distanced referentiality of the written.

We may now turn Cohn's phrase around, and consider treating our field notes as archival documents. In this case, anthropology must be forced to rethink its older distinctions of seeing and reading which have been integral to a search for a certainty of the real—a search which, after all, prompted early ethnographers to go to the field in the first place to do their own research. What at first may have seemed a solid division between the epistemologies of ethnography and the archive now appears to be quite fragile, if not specious. However, these considerations should not necessarily be taken as a temptation to abandon ethnography. Rather, they may lead us to generate new forms of ethnography that disrupt a prior fixation on the presentism of the small scale and to pursue the use of diverse kinds of data in comparative analyses of large scale phenomena. Such possibilities are discussed below, and demonstrated more thoroughly in John Comaroff and Jean Comaroff's chapter in this volume.

Colonial Anxieties

By taking an ethnographic approach to the archive, historical anthropology shows up ethnography within the archive and generates the possibility for a critical archivization of ethnography itself. Dialectically, this analytic illuminates the diverse modalities and motivations by which ethnography perpetuates the growth of the archive. A key element of historical anthropology, however, is not just that we understand ethnography and the archive as having a relation, one that is mutually constitutive, but that we seek to specify what that emergent and dynamic relation produces. The study of colonialism is an important means for such a project. Yet, from this standpoint, what is at issue is not a desire to uncover and narrate the oppression of an underrepresented or subaltern group, the existence of which seems to have been secure prior to colonial intervention. Rather, the analysis shifts to the production of disparate categories of people through the representational strategies of political discipline. In other words, historical anthropology offers not merely a critique of representation as such, or of its supposed inaccuracies, but, as Stoler says, an engagement with the "changing force fields in which these models were produced" (this volume, 157).

This engagement moves back and forth between the distillation of intricate local moments and the emergence of logics of circulation, politics of comparison, and global orders of power and knowledge. Within and between disparate colonial formations of archive and ethnography, the productions of categories of peoplehood—and concurrently of racialized and sexualized difference—take on the semblance of an obsession unfolding within the uncertain search for certainty and the dubious discovery of origins. These temporalizing procedures would infuse colonial archives with new ethnographies, genealogical charts, and theories of descent. Yet the obsessive and uncertain quality of these procedures is telling, and several chapters of this book (Silverblatt, Silverstein, Stoler) pause within that uneasy domain to carefully depict the fragile grounds of different colonial states' negotiations of an immanent trepidation. Writing from the very margins of the colonial archives, and thus, as Foucault might say, producing new centers for the analysis of marginal peoples, historical anthropology may reveal the constitutive power of colonial anxieties.

We must be clear that this notion of colonial anxiety signifies not just the perceived threat of enemies and incommensurable temporalities within the state, but the possibility of colonialism's recognition, within its own regulatory forms, of the tenuousness of the state and its futures.[20] At the most obvious level, we may see the effectivity of this anxious modality in colonialism's notorious procedures for conjuring the origins of a people and fixing there the essentialisms of identity. Such regulatory procedures, of course, founded one of the basic ironies of colonial rule: that it produced the possibility of its own demise while setting the ground for the emergence of national and ethnic identities, those seemingly contagious hallmarks of modernity.

What colonialism did not do, however, was constitute a simple form of difference in the figure of a singular Other, as has sometimes been suggested by theorists of colonialism. The contributions of Silverblatt, Silverstein, and Stoler demonstrate some of the ways that the colonial situation proliferated differences in the plural, some of which may have momentarily been conflated into a categorical enemy and others of which stood uneasily between a racialized colonial divide. For instance, in the colonial imagination of the Spanish Inquisition, as Irene Silverblatt shows, innumerable, chimerical populations of "crypto-Jews" moved undercover, as vehicles of global commerce, speaking multiple languages, and "cultivating subversive ties with the enemies within— indios and negros—as well as with Spain's foreign adversaries" (Silverblatt, this volume, 101). Yet, the Inquisition's inquiry into the origins of the crypto-Jews concurrently presented a problem for dominant understandings of the Spanish colonial state itself; after all, as one of her interlocutors muses, "the Spanish nation was [at one time] Jewish" (this volume, 112). Paul Silverstein's chapter illuminates an analogous procedure in French colonialism's modality of generating distinct types of originary difference and similitude between the categories Berber and Arab. Colonial ethnography produced the Arab people as a fanatical, nomadic religious population that was incommensurable with France's own identity and Christian morality. Simultaneously, however, those ethnographic procedures defined the difference of the Berber as one that was commensurate with a French identity, stemming from not only a similarity of livelihood and religiosity, but, indeed, a shared origin. The ambivalent qualities of the crypto-Jews and the Berber may be related to, and differentiated from, those of other peoples, like the *inlandsche kinderen* ("mixed blood," "European paupers," "descendants of European men and native women") discussed by Stoler. The inlandsche kinderen, however, were a people that sustained an altogether different sense of threat, for indeed their threat was only potential. Under certain circumstances, Dutch colonial authorities argued, they appear in the guise of blanken-haters ("white-haters"), but under proper tutelage they could be transformed into productive laborers and supporters of Dutch rule.

Despite their seeming isolation, within different times and localities, colonizers engaged with these disparate formations of people—whether crypto-Jew, Berber, or *inlandsche kinderen*—in terms of an emerging, transnational discourse, signifying an interaction between various colonial states. Indeed, models for dealing with the vicissitudes of a colonized people's promises and threats attained worldwide relevance and global circulation. Stoler refers to this problematic as the "production of transnational equivalencies and of an emergent colonial politics of comparison" (this volume, 157). In other words, at the intersection of colonialism's archive and ethnography, and between the logic of circulation and the logics of an emergent capitalism, when we turn our attention from the colonized to the colonizers, we must be careful to discern disparate modalities of colonial anxiety. Here, from the localization of diverse origins and peoples constituted within the dialectics of the colonial situation, were generated possibilities of comparativism and racialized commensurability. The anxious repetitions of these productions, of course, in their many forms, were facilitated and globally translated by a tribe of ethnographers, geographers, and linguists who "catalogued and racialized traits, language forms, sociopolitical traditions, and religious rites . . . along a continuum of progress from savagery to civilization" (Silverstein, this volume, 133). Positioned within the colonial archive, such ethnographic entextualizations constituted a mobile itinerary of contested knowledges that nevertheless made possible effective, though constantly changing, technologies of rule. What is at stake for the historical anthropology of colonialism, in short, is not merely understanding the formation of generalized identities and particular kinds of ethnicities within the colonial period, but also the interweaving of commensurability and comparison in subjectification's heralding of (and terror at) the incommensurable.

Analyzing colonialism's procedures for producing disparate peoples through ethnographic practice turns us again to the question of the archive. But what, precisely, is the archive? We should not be too quick to identify the archive with the physical structure. That structure, of course, does have a certain significance, but we may wish to question how the conventional understanding of the archive as a "repository of ultimate value" seduces us "by its appearance of the real" (Dirks, this volume, 48, 60). Bringing ethnography to bear on the archive and its presumed physical formation in a critical way, we may reflect on both the creation of the historian as subject and the effectivity of that subject's defining space. For indeed, whereas the arrival of the historian into the archive is often seen as a rite of passage constituting the historian as such, the monumentality of the archive's space—with its specialist inhabitants and its looming architectural distinctions—must be understood as a crucial element in constructing the ambivalent desire of history to seek in its documents authoritative embodiments of a past authenticity, or an authentic past.

This is a problematic pursued furthest in Stoler's chapter, which is less concerned with the inlandsche kinderen as such than with the peculiarity of the archive that produced these people as objects of knowledge. An ethnography of the archive, as Stoler's work has prodigiously demonstrated, is one that comes from a willingness to make strange our own society and its modes of knowing. Stoler fixes upon this strangeness. She, indeed, begins with the contents of the archival site and is impressed with the disquiet of the archive itself, indicated by the "sheer volume of documents, the unexpected profusion of proposals fashioned to deal with those who made up only a sliver of colonial society" (this volume, 156). The documents with which she works, however, do not report events or successfully implemented plans, but rather signify the shadows of the "non-eventful." Aside from a few experiments and failed programs, nothing was done with the proposals to deal with the inlandsche kinderen. The colonial archive is filled with rich ethnographic productions and typifications of an uncannily racialized people and its questionable origins, certainly. But rather than as a receptacle of the facts of events or colonialism's subjects, the archive itself may be seen as a process productive of an imaginary of the colonial state's pure past and a utopia of colonialism's future configured and stalled by what Stoler calls the 'horizons' of administrative anxiety" (this volume, 157). Thus Stoler presents an argument that may be more generally significant. Historical anthropology moves from colonialism's archival content to the vagaries of its form, just as it tracks the arrival of the historian onto the scene and the inauguration of that particular subject of desire into history itself. Between the fantasy of colonialism's apotheosis and the implausibility of its plans—against the monumental growth of the archive and the minutiae of its ethnographic detail and statistical calculations—the archive takes on a different quality, not as a container of truths or a place of originary knowledge, but as a signifier of colonial distress and an epistemological process of temporalization.

Marginal Contexts

On the site of the archive, where we see the obsessive production of peoples—a temporalizing process fixated on points of origin—we no doubt also discern a desire to put those people in what de Certeau (1984, 1988) would call their "proper place." This desire, with all its indications of stability and essentialism, shows up not only as a fixation on identifying a people's typical lifestyle and social habits but also as a quest for determining a context appropriate to those identifications, a site of closure and determination present to itself. Within the relation of ethnography and the archive, a science of context is born, along with dichotomies of colony and metropole, center and periphery, and us and them.

This science has been enthusiastically refined by over a century of theory production within the social sciences. Anthropologists have tested out the viability, variously, of the island model of Radcliffe-Brown and Malinowski, the segmentary society model of the Africanists, and the village model of the South Asianists, each designed to identify not just a well-defined field where we can do our work but the supposed boundedness and authenticity of the people we study (Cohn 1987). Linguists have rigorously distinguished an extra-linguistic context from an intra-linguistic context to capture the complex relationship between the determining features of a grammatical code and the immediate sur-roundings of an utterance (Mertz 1985). And ethnomethodologists, representing perhaps the pinnacle of contextual obsession, have attended to the minute de-tails of enunciation, bodily movement, and emergent meaning within minutely delineated "real-time" settings of social interaction. Thus we have carried on that spatializing task to frame, to circumscribe, and define "our" people, caught at the very places where they and their cultural forms are purported to originate.

Still, in order to make our work intelligible, we must ever ask: What is our context of analysis? How do we contextualize our inquiry? How are we to select our analytic frame?

These questions pose a challenge to historical anthropology, but they also may be somewhat misleading. Simply put, we must continue to remind ourselves that not only do we produce our object of study as subject, but we also generate that subject's context. Thus, the point is not to abandon the notion of context, but to generate a critical analysis of contextualization, from which we may illuminate disparate cultural forms of creativity, subversion, or collective identification. Two elements common to ethnographic practice present obsta-cles to this approach. First, is the manner in which studies continue to be seduced by the wonder of origins. Second, is the way ethnographic models al-most invariably strive to seize their objects as a totality. In such a modality of knowledge production, context—and its captivating allure of the actual—seems ever receding. Just out of grasp, its capture is always deferred. The ethnographic approach is just as interminable. In contrast, deploying an ethnographic mo-dality which brings acute attention to changing historical circumstances of our own procedures of subjectification (how we produce our object as subject), his-torical anthropology may explore the productive yet fragmentary character of any contextualization—which concurrently tells of the utterly fantastical qual-ity of origins and totalities. But turning to context and contextualization in this way does not signal a return to empiricism, with its idealization of the real. Rather it suggests a self-conscious procedure that admits the inevitability of its own abstraction.

How may we develop that process of abstraction purposively? Michel-Rolph Trouillot's contribution to this volume offers one demonstration, analyz-ing creolization's culture at the edges of the plantation. Thus Trouillot claims baldly: "*The* plantation, as such, never existed" (this volume, 201). He distin-guishes, rather, a disjunction between typologies—globally mobile models and logics which offered images of how a plantation should be structured—and the "daily exigencies masters and overseers had to face within individual units of production" (201). In light of this basic tension, Trouillot generates, or abstracts, three separate contexts through which to analyze creolization: a plantation context, an enclave context, and a modernist context. These heuristics allow him to address a common confusion about creolization based on the mirage image of its typological model, particularly the notion that creolization could not have occurred within the plantation. On the contrary, it may have been that creolization emerged as a specific effect of the disjunction between the model and its diversity of deployments, within and through its three contexts. Slaves developed a practice of poaching (to use de Certeau's word [1984]), which played upon and between, or rather within, what Trouillot calls the "interstices" of different contexts: "On the one hand acknowledging the system, on the other circumventing its actualization in carefully chosen instances—they solidified the *détour,* the social time and space that they controlled on the edges of the plantations" (202). Playing within the margins of the system and upon the plantation's own self-marginality, Trouillot argues, "creolization did not happen away from the plantation system, but within it" (202).

But an acute awareness of our own procedures of knowledge production and of their effectivity in constituting contexts is only one step in a larger process. Here we may ask with Derrida: "But are the prerequisites of a context ever absolutely determinable? Does not the notion of context harbor, behind a certain confusion, very determined philosophical presuppositions" (1982, 310)? In addressing this question, we may note again the close tie between the temporalizing desire of the archive (to isolate the real at some point in the past) and the spatializing desire of context (to delimit the qualities of a culture at its place of origin). Foucault's analysis of the Nietzschean genealogy is pertinent here: "What is found at the historical beginning of things is not the inviolable identity of their origin; it is the dissension of other things. It is disparity" (1977, 142). Or to take Derrida again: "A context is never absolutely determinable, or . . . its determination is never certain or saturated" (1982, 310). In other words, upon closer inspection, powerful procedures of displacement abound at the center of the "origin" wherein we are ever tempted to graft our theories of identity and the past. These are important considerations for historical anthropology, made that much more difficult to address when we discern how the interruptive elements of dissension, disparity, and displacement make any context marginal to itself and certainly never susceptible to closure.

Bernard Cohn and Teri Silvio's contribution to this volume demonstrate how historical anthropology may refine its notion of context from a critical engagement with marginality and displacement. They consider the American nation-state's landscape filled with monuments to the Revolutionary War and the Civil War. Such monuments certainly provide modes of creating collective

identity that are generated through discourses of kinship and logics of genealogy. Yet, the American landscape Cohn and Silvio depict is not one inhabited by
an Andersonian community sharing the daily ritual of newspaper consumption
(Anderson 1991), but more like a ghostly stage of corpses and abandoned or
forgotten icons, sequestered from the more readily recognizable monumentality of a Washington, D.C., or a New York City. Adding another dimension to
our awareness of the fetishization of origin and totality, Cohn and Silvio reconstitute the context of the nation as fetishism's very mise-en-scène. Here is a
national landscape saturated with memorabilia made to speak of glorious pasts.
What at first sight seems extremely obvious or for some even trivial appears
now, to use Marx's words, "a very strange thing abounding in metaphysical
subtleties and theological niceties" (1990, 163). Extrapolating from Cohn and
Silvio's discussion, we may underscore how an archival desire to excavate national origin is indissoluble from the nation-state's contextualizing desire to
construct monuments designed to keep the people in their place and protect
citizens against that procedure's discoveries. Historical anthropology may thus,
through an inquiry into the nation as a marginal context, see a point of con-
juncture between the Marxian analysis of a national "commodity and its secret"
(Marx 1990, 163) and a Freudian understanding of the visuality of "tokens of
triumph" (Freud 1977, 353). For like the Freudian story of the fetish, in which
the horror of violent dismemberment "sets up a memorial to itself" (1977,
353), national monuments ultimately stand in for, and disavow, the marginality of the nation's own center and the historical marginalization of what may
have been at the very heart of nation-formation: violence, displacement, and
disparity.

Archaeologies of the Fantastic

The final section of the book returns to what I noted in the first pages of
this introduction to be one of the marks of a new, critical historical anthropology (Dirks 1992, 11)—that is, an inquiry into the politics of living the ongoing
connections (or disjunctures) of pasts and futures in heterogeneous presents.
How might we characterize the living of these diverse temporalities? What is
the quality of experience in times (whether colonial or postcolonial) often defined by radical spatial transformation? In line with such questioning, John
Comaroff and Jean Comaroff offer historical anthropology a challenge that
stands against much of what we have learned from our training in the social
sciences: enchantment is everywhere on the rise. In each chapter of this volume
we see our contributors, more or less explicitly, setting the groundwork for

an engagement within this perplexing proposition—and making a clearing for what, indeed, will be a problem for historical anthropology's futures. Inscribing their objects of study through a willing recognition of the determinations and indeterminacies of their conditions of production, and through imaginative experiments in rigorous refinement, our contributors explore the enchantment of modernity in its multiplicity. Stoler and Dirks draw our attention to the seductions of the archive, to the monumentality of its structure, and to the power of its documents to conjure an aura of the real. Stoler likewise discerns within the archive the ubiquitous shadows of, in her felicitous phrase, a "colonial utopia obliquely expressed" (this volume, 157). Asad invokes the ethnographer's fascination with the fieldwork experience as a mysterious rite that effects the total human being, and Trouillot displaces the wonder of origins and totalities that the experience of ethnography inspires. Silverblatt fixes upon the anxiety generated around the chimerical figure of the crypto-Jew. Silverstein shows the contradictory processes by which the French colonial regime attempted to "dis-enchant the territory and chronology of the natives" while simultaneously working to "reanimate the imagination of 'national glory'" (this volume, 131, 128). And Cohn and Silvio trace features of captivation within a national landscape dotted with monuments of grandeur's past, yet haunted by ghosts of unsettling origins.

Following the lead of John Comaroff and Jean Comaroff, we may give a name to this type of analytic procedure: an archaeology of the fantastic. But the fantastic, and fantasy more generally, is here not indicative of a realm of illusions or visual fallacies, separating some internal world of imagination from an exterior realm of reality. And our work is not meant to capture and isolate the distressing features of shadows, ghosts, and chimeras as such. Rather we turn our attention to the disruptive though complexly interlinked forces which—often phantasmatic in themselves—have lifted those features into landscapes of actuality, making the intimate negotiation of their intimations very real. Hence our concern, to use the old phrase, with the social construction of reality (Berger and Luckmann 1966), which is illuminated within the interstices of colonialism and postcoloniality and between the formation of nation-states and the formative processes of globalization.

Fantasy redescribes many of the processes I have been elaborating in this introduction, allowing us, for example, to interrogate the spatializing assumptions of context and peoplehood which rely upon an arsenal of images of scenic frontiers and territorial boundaries. As an analytic category, fantasy concurrently shows up the diverse ways that the production of context operates fundamentally through various procedures of displacement—or, more precisely, how it plays upon a vicissitude of displacement and place. The process of fantasy, in other words, is one in which generalized sentiments of identity and affects of culture become instantiated in the local while local affiliations are disrupted (Berlant 1991, 5, 49). However, unlike Anderson's notion of imagination, this is a process that, while constitutive of a diversity of subjects, is not necessarily or always equally accessible to the experience of individuals. To put this more succinctly, fantasy designates a modality of subjectification.[21] As such, it draws attention to formations of temporality (not a "homogeneous empty time" but the obsessive fixing upon diverse origins), indicated by the postulation of a time before the emergence of the subject (e.g., the "birth of the nation") or a putatively causal anterior condition from which the subject is presumed to emerge (the abolition of prior forms of affiliation).[22]

The case of the Sikhs and Punjab discussed in my essay "Fantastic Community" offers an important instance of these broad considerations, not least because of the almost two decades of violent transnational struggle to create a Sikh homeland called Khalistan (Axel 2001a, 2002). Constituted as a marginal people living within a diasporic border zone—and as representatives indeed of a past enemy—these citizens have been repeatedly susceptible to judicial and extrajudicial procedures designed to simultaneously put them in their place and displace the power of their "fissiparious tendencies" (Axel 2001a, 2002). While Indian constitutional law pictures the birth of the nation in 1947 to have followed from a surrender of all prior affiliations of territoriality, caste, race, and class, the nation-state continues to set in motion procedures for the annihilation of, for example, regional alliance, which according to nationalist discourse perpetually haunts and threatens to disrupt the purity of the people. The figure of the Sikh—which in a national fantasy literally steps into the present from an incommensurable past and a diasporic elsewhere—takes on these ghostly qualities in the extreme. But what the analytic of fantasy helps discern is that any citizen may be identified as just such a threat at any time. Here, indeed, is a stronger argument that an analysis of national fantasy facilitates: the logic of citizenship relies upon, and is constituted through, this very ambivalence, thus positioning the limitations of sovereignty and the limits of territoriality at the very center of the formation of the modern nation-state's collective subject, the people.

If the figure of the diaspora seems to bring into clarity the ambivalent processes of national fantasy, which repeatedly assert the conditions of a nation's birth as a totality, then it may be of little surprise that globalization riddles the recent ascendance of the new South Africa with fantastic disequilibrium. Not least important is the manner in which the Rainbow Nation came into being at a time when the presumed cultural stability of the nation-state is threatened. As John Comaroff and Jean Comaroff comment: "The cruel irony of contemporary South Africa is that, as one of the world's last colonies, it won its right to secular modern nationhood just as global economic processes were seriously compromising the sovereignty and material integrity of the nation-state, sui generis" (this volume, 280). But the concern of John Comaroff and Jean Comaroff here is less with the threat to the nation-state and more with proliferation of new types of practices within its shifting frame: what they call "occult economies" or the deployment of magical means for material ends. These include, as is shown in rich detail, a wide range of phenomena, from ritual murder, the sale of body parts, and the putative production of zombies, to pyramid schemes and other financial scams. And they have often led to violent reactions against people accused of illicit accumulation. Yet these instances of the fantastic in the locality of the new nation only tend to indicate a world beyond themselves. Neither are "the stories of witchcraft, body parts, zombies, and the brutalization of children . . . peculiarly South African. Everywhere the confident contours and the boundaries of the human are being called more and more into question; hence the assertion of animal rights, the fear of invasion by aliens clothed in humdrum bodily form, the dangerous promise of cloning and genetic mutation" (this volume, 270).

More generally, then, a central problem for historical anthropology today is to account for the specific intersections of the banal and uncanny within the articulations and disarticulations of the local and the global. This analytic attends to the specific historical conditions which have given shape to the diverse, and often perverse, economies of an emerging globalization: the shifting between the colonial epoch and the postcolonial moment, the experience of moral and material deregulation, and the perception that business might deliver infinite wealth if only its magic could be tapped (John and Jean Comaroff 1999, 308).

This deployment of an archaeology of the fantastic as a modality of historical anthropology returns us, ultimately, to a critique of conventional ethnography's fixation on the present, on local conditions, and on small-scale events. This fixation has presented a problem for most anthropological studies of globalization. More often than not, the work we see within this emergent field ends up offering nothing other than old-style village studies with a new twist: within the village, certain commodities or symbolic objects come from elsewhere, and therefore we are told the village, which is located within the nation-state, is affected by all manner of things which not only remain unhindered by the myth of national integrity, but also threaten the basic tenets of the nation-form itself. More sophisticated studies, of course, spell out how their observations reflect something that has been going on for a long time, and that does not necessarily represent the end of the nation-state, but rather its dynamic, emergent, even constitutive relationship with processes of globalization (see Ong 1999).

I do not intend to dismiss these kinds of studies of globalization, particularly because they have provided such important beginnings and insights. But I would like to point out two issues that historical anthropology in general must address (see also Appadurai 1996a, 2000; Comaroff and Comaroff 1999, 2000). First, the challenge of globalization to historical anthropology is not merely that we must learn to supplement what we usually do with reflections on the way something global comes into and affects the lives of the local people, making them imagine themselves within a larger world of social and cultural life. Rather, the challenge is to generate a radical critique of ethnography. Second, our relationship to the important work within sociology and political science must be considered closely. Anthropologists, most often, have relied on these other disciplines to generate the big theory that can then be referenced or given nuance by the anthropologist who does what the anthropologist is usually expected to do and what our graduate programs teach our students to desire: deep, rich, thick, descriptive, and local ethnography. Historical anthropology, on the contrary, may critically engage other scholarship on globalization, and while we attempt to transform what ethnography can be, we may likewise form a grounding from which to collaborate on big theory.

In short, what we are here calling historical anthropology warns against a "romance [that] gestures back to an old form of anthropological patronization" (John and Jean Comaroff, this volume, 289). Against such romance, each of the essays in this volume demonstrates several sites for the production of a historical anthropology concerned with exploring the intersections of historically specific local practices with processes of a world historical order—for instance, millennial capitalism with the culture of neoliberalism (Appadurai 2000; Comaroff and Comaroff 2000).

Historical Anthropology and Its Vicissitudes

This is a historical anthropology from the margins, but in more ways than one. It is not merely that our contributors interrogate the marginal and the marginalized, as I have already noted. There is more. Their productions, while advancing toward the limits of our conventions and epistemologies, expose the margins at the center of our institutionally defined disciplines. That anthropology and history, with ethnography and the archive, have their provenance in colonial formations is perhaps a commonplace. What is rarely sought is the specific manner in which those colonial processes imbue and threaten both the celebratory ideals of postcolonial reason and the enlightenment of today's liberal practices in the social sciences and humanities. This book outlines the effects of that contradiction without presuming an easy escape from its dynamic strictures.

This type of historical anthropology, I have argued, is also something other, and as such, it calls forth a certain ambivalence. It calls forth an ambivalence but it also emerges out of just that vicissitude. This vicissitude takes many shapes and may be referred to in many ways: the shifting between anthropology and history, the sequestering of ethnography and the archive, the unstable postulation of origins and the hopeful hailing of futures, the displacements of contexts and contextualizations, and the stark reality of fantastical formations. The diverse textures of these shapes and names with the dubious formalism of their separations provide us with the basic terms of our critique and the starting points of our inquiry. Thus this book's contributors offer an ethnography of the archive that shows up the position of ethnography within the archive; and they generate an archive of ethnography that illuminates an archival desire immanent to ethnography. While their procedures supply new ways for understanding the complicity of history and anthropology in the production of colonial peoples and the colonial state, our contributors nevertheless seek ways to redeploy those basic terms and tools. For example, Stoler finds in the archive not an event history, but the historical negatives of the non-eventful. Trouillot spells out a patient ethnographic approach intentionally designed not to explore the experience of the present, but to generate new abstractions and trace their histories. John Comaroff and Jean Comaroff point to the possibilities of anthropology's futures in the analysis of the global.

The work of our contributors aside, however, the ambivalence of a historical anthropology has, in the not so recent past, met with less welcoming gestures. During the 1970s, for example, attempts at creating a historical anthropology often met rejoinders filled with warning and sometimes unequivocal animosity—not least from within the few disciplinary corners of history which hoisted an anthropological banner (Macfarlane 1970; Thomas 1971). E. P. Thompson commented famously on some historians' perceptions of anthropology: "In some eyes, the 'systematic indoctrination' of historians 'in the social sciences' conjures up a scene of insemination, in which Clio lies inert and passionless (perhaps with rolling eyes) while anthropology or sociology thrust their seed into her womb" (1972, 46). Fox-Genovese and Genovese, wanting to separate all remnants of anthropology from history, stated plainly: "By now, it ought to be obvious that . . . the current fad of 'anthropology' in social history [is] a bourgeois swindle" (1976, 215). In the 1980s, Taussig, himself an influential scholar of historical anthropology, remained skeptical about the fetishization of history. In a scathing critique of Mintz (1985) and Wolf (1982), he claimed, "the contemporary revivalist enthusiasm for History in American Anthropology was—to say the least—naive, untheorized, and unself-critical" (1989, 23).[23] Sahlins, perhaps less scandalously, generated a highly theorized project to "explode the concept of history by the anthropological experience of culture" (1985).[24] And, most recently, Clifford Geertz, who had participated in delimiting the terms of *dialogue* between anthropology and history over several decades, replaced the fireworks of warning and rapprochement with subdued, or perhaps resigned, reflection. Here he posited an uneasy identification of disparate desires: "The anthropological desire to see how things fit together sits uneasily with the historical desire to see how they are brought about" (1995, 259).

Against these various protestations, I reiterate the point that it is no longer—indeed, never has been—viable to see historical anthropology as defined by an exchange of methods and theories. Rather, we may strive to understand how historical anthropology emerges out of the tensions and conflicts of the institutionally defined relationship between history and anthropology. However, if, instead of following a Geertzian isolationism, we are to argue that historical anthropology's ambivalence is generative of the inquiry itself, it remains to submit that vicissitude to analysis. Evans-Pritchard, one of historical anthropology's first interlocutors, provides us with one site from which to interrogate this ambivalence. Here, he depicts the anthropologist confronting the unsettling unspeakability of archival documents; yet, he can barely pause within the ambivalence that his own enunciation projects. Rather, turning away from the posited indissociability of history and anthropology that he wishes to herald, Evans-Pritchard reiterates more familiar, conventional proclamations of the power of experience to generate more accurate representations: "The questions we have learnt to ask ourselves and our informants, arising from personal contact with social reality, questions forced on us, as it were, by the pressure of recurrent situations, are not asked and the answers not given. Nor in any case do the documents yield the abundant material we possess on such topics as I have mentioned, partly because the societies we study are so rich in it, and partly because we can observe behaviour directly and ask questions which elicit replies, whereas the historian can only observe behaviour in documents, and *when he questions them they are often dumb*" (1962, 185; emphasis mine).

Dirks's ethnographic narrative of archival arrival, found in this volume, provides another instance of discourse that may help isolate the quality I am noting. However, unlike Evans-Pritchard, Dirks pauses within that uncanny confrontation of archive and field:

> I walked into the archive for the first time with all the excitement that my fellow anthropology students had reserved for the moment they arrived in a "field of their own." My excitement soon merged with terror when I realized that I hadn't a clue what to do next. . . . I panicked, feeling a bizarre envy for the traditional research historian who was assigned a topic on the basis of a specific collection of records or documents their supervisor had preselected for them, at the same time wondering if I should just discard history and go to the field instead, trying my hand at anthropology, the flip side of my disciplinary formation and training. (this volume, 50–51)

Most, if not all, historians, and even anthropologists who have ventured into the archive, can identify with this strange mixture of emotions. The generalizability of this identification, I think, is telling. I recall this with particular acuteness, perhaps because of my own experiences in the India Office. I have felt, to use Dirks's word, "keen" to find documents from a prior time, yet worried about the provenance of the archive. I am familiar with the fear and embarrassment, excitement and terror, dissatisfaction and envy. Yet, if this vicissitude is a generalized aspect of the experience of historians, or of anthropologists entering the archive, it is also something that anthropologists know well as they enter their privileged site of knowledge production, the field. At least my own experience has taught me this. The archive and the field are both monuments to the contradictions of history and anthropology—monuments which we aspire to translate and describe. No matter how much we wish otherwise, they provide us with the fantasy scenario where we go in search of something that is always just out of our reach, where we feel our own inadequacy, where we sense our power, and perhaps a thrill in transgression.

Let me offer one possibility for understanding how this formation of ambivalence and fantasy relates to the imbrication of colonialism and postcoloniality. For this, let me remind you of, and take in a slightly different direction, Dirks's discussion of a historical moment that witnessed a shift in colonial practice between historiography and ethnography. What if we understand this shift between history and anthropology, by which "anthropology supplanted history as the principle colonial modality of knowledge" (Dirks, this volume, 56), as incomplete, indeed as one effect of a colonial fantasy of disciplinarity? What if we understand this incompleteness to signify not only the impossibility of a complete transition from history to anthropology, but the impossibility of an isolation of either history or anthropology from each other—a quality that might itself prompt or locate a certain anxiety that moves between the two? This incompleteness and anxiety, I would argue, shows us some of colonialism's enduring legacies: that is, the constitution of a desire to isolate history and anthropology, the formation of a fantasy of their independence, and a continual or persistent repetition of that rift.

These effects may be clarified through an example from work on South Asia, the field and archive most familiar to me (see essays on pages 47 and 233 for more detailed discussion). Within South Asianist scholarship, questions of land tenure and caste have maintained a central position; they have been, in other words, fetishized in South Asian Studies. They do not merely signify certain kinds of practices and attachments. They provide different ways of constituting both an Indian People and a Colonial Sovereignty (and, needless to say, an Indian Nation). I would suggest that they accomplish this by generating a specific form of temporality that is associated with, and indeed constitutive of, that people. Particularly through genealogy and through the identification of an essentialized structural hierarchy, they generate a specific anteriority, a time before colonial rule, a time from which the Indian people must emerge into the domain of Empire as subjects and into the nation-state as citizens. Within colonialist discourse, this time before points to the fantasy origins of a people's practices and beliefs and identifies that people as somehow premodern. South Asian Studies today also justifies the study of modernization, of changing or unchanging tradition, of the village, of religious heritage, and on and on. Indications of this anteriority presume to explain why the Indian people have not yet entered modernity, or have done so, at least, with great difficulty.

These formations of temporality within colonial India and postcolonial studies of India are indicative of something more general. In the shift between history and anthropology, here is what moves between the two: not just an anxious recognition of the impossibility of their isolation, but the desire to identify that anteriority. Bernard Cohn calls this temporality "the before," and he suggests that its effectivity stems from an academic practice caught within colonialism's disavowal (1987, 19, 27, 56). He relates the desire of the before to what he calls our "dreaming" of a people's boundedness and authenticity (1987, 21). The before and the dreaming, more often than not, serve as epistemological references by signifying the "real" that is postulated to exist prior to and outside of our disciplines' textual procedures. Put another way, the archive and the field provide the mise-en-scène within which the desire of anteriority may be played out (thus Geertz's isolation of an "anthropological desire" and a "historical desire" seems somewhat perverse). Historical anthropology's ambivalence indicates both the unsettled relation to that fantasy and the incomplete shift between history and anthropology which has made the repetition of that fantasy possible.

The central point, I should emphasize again, is that the identification of a historically emergent, yet iterable, moment of shift between the putatively isolated domains of history and anthropology has very important implications for understanding colonialism, studies of colonialism and postcoloniality, and historical anthropology itself. As regards the latter, it may very well be that we can strive to base the practice of historical anthropology on the dynamic tensions and contradictions which the name implies, rethinking our practices of knowledge production through a critical elaboration of ethnography and the archive, colonial anxieties, marginal contexts, and archaeologies of the fantastic. This book attempts to locate a point of citation and transformation for the futures of historical anthropology—which we may call a historical anthropology from the margins.

Notes

1   With the language of "citation" and "iteration," I intentionally allude to theories of performativity, which I hope to consider in a future work to develop a critique of what might be called the subject of historical anthropology. The analytic of performativity calls to mind not only the work of Austin (1999), but also Benveniste (1971), Barthes (1970), Butler (1990, 1993, 1997), and Bhabha (1994). One of the important moments of performativity within historical anthropology is the repetitive conjuring of Maitland's implied warning or threat (an "impure" performative in Austin's terms): "By and by anthropology will have the choice between being history and being nothing" (1936, 249). This phrase has been recited and transformed innumerable times. However, Maitland is almost never cited (and one wonders whether his text has been read); rather Evans-Pritchard is cited, captured, as it were, in his own moment of citation. Evans-Pritchard complicates this iterability by citing himself. In the initial instance, he repeats Maitland word for word (1962a, 152); in the second instance, he claims: "Maitland has said that anthropology *must choose* between being history and being nothing" (1962b, 190; emphasis mine). Later, we find many variations on this theme—for example Silverman and Gulliver (1992, 12), who very much demonstrate the thickets of this forest of citations: "In 1961, Evans-Pritchard reaffirmed Maitland's century-old assertion that anthropology *had to choose* between *becoming* history *or being* nothing" (1992, 12; emphasis mine). Nevertheless, the effectivity of this process of citation, I would venture, has constituted Maitland as a kind of originary text, the performative threat of which has not necessarily lost its power, but rather gained.

2   In his famous essay on "The Genealogical Method of Anthropological Inquiry," W. H. R. Rivers was ultimately concerned with people "suffering from the effects of

European influence." As is well known, his genealogical method—embodying the reconstructionist desire—was designed to "[take] us back to a *time before* this influence [European] has reached them [primitives]" (Rivers 1968, 109; emphasis mine). Boas, who had developed methods for studying the cultures of people who were considered all but extinct, stated quite plainly: "As a matter of fact, all the history of primitive peoples that any ethnologist has ever developed is reconstruction and cannot be anything else" (1936, 139). Malinowski (1922, 155–56), who was seen to be quite clearly "anti-historical," nevertheless lamented that the carefully recorded details of his ethnography reflected only a shadow of the Trobriandor's "original condition" prior to colonial rule. And Radcliffe-Brown—who stood against Rivers' "conjectural history" not because it was history but because it was conjectural—commented at length on the impossibility, not of history, but of reconstructing the pre-colonial pasts of primitives: "For scientific study of primitive societies in conditions in which they are free from the domination by more advanced societies, we have unfortunately an almost complete lack of authentic historical data. We cannot study, but only speculate about, the processes of change that took place in the past of which we have no record. Anthropologists speculate about former changes in the societies of the Australian aborigines, or the inhabitants of Melanesia, but such speculations are not history and can be of no use in science" (1952, 202–3).

3 One significant area of neglect is that I make no mention of the very important topic of "ethnohistory" in the U.S. and its place within these debates. For the latter, I direct the reader to Krech's (1991) lucid discussion. For a variety of examples and considerations of historical anthropology more generally, see Asad (1973, 1993), Axel (1996a, 1996b, 1998, 2001a, 2001b, 2002), Brow (1978), Burke (1987), Cannadine and Price (1987), Cohen and Odhiambo (1989), Cohen and Roth (1995), John L. Comaroff (1982), Comaroff and Comaroff (1991, 1992, 1997), Cohn (1987, 1996), Cooper and Stoler (1997), Coronil (1997), D'Agostino, et al. (1995), Dirks (1987, 1992), Faubion (1993), Fay, Pomper, and Van (1998), Kelly and Kaplan (1990), Lewis (1968, 1999), Lindholm (1996), McDonald (1996), Macfarlane (1970), Ohnuki-Tierney (1990), Pels (1997, 1999), Roseberry (1989), Segalen (1986), Silverblatt (1987), Stoler (1985), Thompson (1977), Trouillot (1988), Wilentz (1985).

4 In Britain, not least important were the "big schemes" envisioned for the social sciences during the War, as Fortes records: "Economic, political and especially military necessities aroused a new and lively public interest in the African and Asiatic dependencies of Britain and her allies. The plans for postwar economic and social development in these areas generated under pressure of wartime experiences included big schemes of research in the natural and social sciences" (in Asad 1973, 14).

5 I do not here intend to ignore Leach's important contribution to these debates or to the formation of a trajectory of historical anthropology. The significance of his work is discussed at length in J. L. and J. Comaroff (1992).

6 The specificity of this period (1955–1970) is crucial for my discussion. I certainly do not intend to neglect the impact of other scholars whose names are associated with the University of Chicago, particularly Marshall Sahlins, Raymond Smith, and George Stocking. My intention here is to illuminate a specific period and not to elaborate a genealogy of historical anthropology at the University of Chicago. The

impact of such scholars as Sahlins, Smith, and Stocking (among others) may be more precisely discussed as pertinent to the period after the one examined here (not that these scholars did not produce important work in the 1960s, but that their pedagogy and scholarship came to the fore in the 1970s most powerfully).

7   We might note that Cohn was only occasionally in residence at the University of Chicago during the 1950s (he was also appointed at the University of Rochester), and did not become a permanent member of the faculty until 1964.

8   During the 1950s, Cohn also took part in interdisciplinary research as part of the Korean War effort. Yet, while he was certainly influenced by Kroeber (a Boasian of sorts), Cohn, as Ranajit Guha has discussed, extended only one aspect of the Kroeberian analytic, while sidestepping its "metaphysics of holism, 'patternism,' acculturation and universalism" (Guha 1987, xiii).

9   This aspect distances our work from Geertz's image of historical anthropology, the disciplinary ideals of which he envisions as akin to a nation-state's "natural" indications of territoriality: "What has undermined [these professional ideals] has been a change in the ecology of learning that has driven historians and anthropologists, like so many geese, onto one another's territories: a collapse of the natural dispersion of feeding grounds that left France to the one and Samoa to the other" (Geertz 1995, 251).

10 In regard to the production of time and space, what is presented here may be taken as an investigation of the inquiry opened by several scholars, of which only a few examples are Appadurai (1981, 1986, 1988, 1996a, 1996b), Bloch (1977), de Certeau (1984), Fabian (1983), Feld and Basso (1996), Harvey (1990), Lefebvre (1991), Massey (1994), and Munn (1992).

11 For discussions of how social and cultural theories have relied upon a geographic imaginary, see Appadurai (1986, 1988, 1996a, 2000), Axel (2001a, 2002), Clifford (1997), Cohn (1987), de Certeau (1984), Gupta and Ferguson (1997). See also the collections of essays in Boyarin (1994), Lavie and Swedenburg (1996), and Yaeger (1996).

12 Stoler (1995) provides an extremely important discussion of the significance of Foucault to colonial studies, one that powerfully engages both the possibilities and limitations of Foucault's work to the kinds of inquiries proposed here. The reader is also advised to consult Cooper and Stoler (1997) for citations to, and discussions of, the voluminous literature in historical anthropology and other fields that take up colonialism.

13 This is not a criticism of John Comaroff's work, but rather an extension of his quite prescient exploration.

14 In different ways, the works of Cohn (1957, 1987, 1996), Derrida (1996), de Certeau (1984, 1988), Guha and Spivak (1988), and Richards (1992, 1993)—and needless to say Foucault (1972, 1977) and Nietzsche (1969, 1997)—may also be seen to contribute to this inquiry.

15 Indicating one of the effects of positivist empiricism (noted by Comaroff in his 1982 article), this point suggests one way to answer two of the questions noted above: "How have anthropology and history come to be seen as attaining such unique separable pinnacles and positions of closure?" and "What are the conditions of possibility for the

assignment of ethnography and the archive as transparently privileged sites of knowledge production?" By positing a real object that exists prior to and outside of our
textual strategies, the disciplinary positions of history and anthropology, seen as
separate and isolable, are set into place. Each, thus, supposedly offers a unique tool for
analyzing that posited object, which, according to whether it exists in the past or the
present, may be merely described through archival or ethnographic textual strategies.
This answer however, truncates a longer discussion developed in the following pages.

16 On the notion of "entextualization," see Bauman and Briggs (1990), Hanks (1989),
and Silverstein and Urban (1996). Processes of entextualization signal yet another
site—delimited through an inquiry into linguistic structure, pragmatics, and ideology—for the production of historical anthropology that calls for further elaboration.
A closer reading, especially of the contributions by Silverblatt, Silverstein, and
Trouillot in this volume shows the obsession of diverse colonialisms with not
merely the nature of language, as putative indices of origins, but the threat of language, as surreptitious means for communicating amongst the colonized. Needless to say, colonialism's various *discoveries* of linguistic difference and similitude
brought together and grounded the twinned productions of a "command of language"
and a "language of command" (Cohn 1996). Said (1978) and Cohn (1996) have commented on such intersections at length (see also Dharwadker 1993; Inden 1990; Lele
1993; Lelyveld 1993; Pollack 1993; Spivak 1993). See Benveniste (1971) for reflections
on the relation between Saussure's notion of the arbitrariness of the sign and late-
nineteenth-century relativist and comparativist thought. Elizabeth Povinelli (2002)
provides a very important analysis of colonialism, aboriginal subjectification, and
the development of both metapragmatic and ethical linguistic phenomena.

17 With unprecedented rigor and creativity, Ann Laura Stoler has taken powerful steps
toward rethinking the epistemologies of ethnography and the archive, specifically in
the context of colonialism. In her contribution to this volume (which I discuss more
fully in the following section), as well as in her other work (e.g., Stoler 1992a and b,
1995), we are provided with several productive approaches that interweave an inquiry into epistemology with colonial critique.

18 As I have already noted, the 1950s and 1960s saw the initial conceptualizations of
such an approach, particularly in the work of Cohn and Evans-Pritchard, both of
whom recommended ethnographic studies of historical practice. More recently, understandings of the complex relations between ethnography and the archive have
been refined by a burgeoning literature, several of the authors of which are included
in the present volume (e.g., Comaroff and Comaroff 1992; Dirks 1993; Trouillot
1995). See also, for example, Amin (1995), Appadurai (1996a), de Certeau (1988),
Davis (1987), Dening (1995), Derrida (1995), Echevarria (1990), Ginzburg (1989),
Guha (1983), Hamilton (forthcoming), Rappaport (1994), Thomas (1963), and White
(1987).

19 For important critical engagements with the notions of experience and representation along similar lines, see Derrida (1982) and Scott (1992).

20 In a way that is not unrelated to the chapters in this section, Sara Suleri (1992) writes
eloquently of the intersections of colonial anxiety, subject formation, ethnography,
chronology, and the constitution of origins.

21 One might thus be tempted to use this terminology to redescribe the production of, for example, inlandsche kinderen, the New Christian, the Berber, or the slave.

22 Although using a different analytical model, Segal (1994) offers an insightful discussion of Trinidad and Tobago that demonstrates many of the same procedures of temporalization. See also Axel 1998, 2001a, 2002; Berlant 1991; Bhabha 1994; Burgin 1986; Laplanche and Pontalis 1973, 1986; Rose 1996.

23 Mintz and Wolf (1989) reply to Taussig in the same volume of *Critique of Anthropology.*

24 See Dirks for a reiteration of this phrase in his *The Hollow Crown* (1987), which he later inverts in a rigorous critique of Sahlins, claiming to explode culture through a turn to history (1996b). For another critical engagement with Sahlins, see Webster (1989).

References

Adams, John W. 1981. "Consensus, Community, and Exoticism." *Journal of Interdisciplinary History* 12, no. 2 (autumn): 253–65.

Amin, Shahid. 1995. *Event, Metaphor, Memory: 1922–1992.* Berkeley: University of California Press.

Anderson, Benedict. 1991. *Imagined Communities: Reflections on the Origins and Spread of Nationalism.* London: Verso.

Appadurai, Arjun. 1981. "The Past as a Scarce Resource." *Man* 16: 201–19.

——. 1986. "Theory in Anthropology: Center and Periphery." *Comparative Studies in Society and History* 28, no. 2: 356–61.

——. 1988. "Putting Hierarchy in Its Place." *Cultural Anthropology* 3, no. 1 (February).

——. 1996a. *Modernity at Large: Cultural Dimensions of Globalization.* Minneapolis: University of Minnesota Press.

——. 1996b. "Sovereignty Without Territoriality: Notes for a Postnational Geography." In *The Geography of Identity,* edited by Patricia Yaeger. Ann Arbor: University of Michigan Press.

——. 2000. *Globalization.* A special issue of the journal *Public Culture* 30.

Asad, Talal, ed. 1973. *Anthropology and the Colonial Encounter.* Atlantic Highlands, N.J.: Humanities Press.

——. 1993. *Genealogies of Religion: Discipline and Reasons of Power in Christianity and Islam.* Baltimore: Johns Hopkins University Press.

Austin, John. 1962. *How to do Things with Words.* Edited by M. S. and J. O. Urmson. Cambridge, Mass.: Harvard University Press.

Axel, Brian Keith. 1996a. "Time and Threat: Questioning the Production of the Diaspora as an Object of Study." *History and Anthropology* 9, no. 2: 415–443.

——. 1996b. "Notes on Space, Cartography, and Gender." In *The Transmission of Sikh Heritage in the Diaspora,* edited by Pashaura Singh and N. Gerald Barrier. New Delhi: Manohar.

——. 1998. "Disembodiment and the Total Body: A Response to Enwezor on Contemporary on South African Representation." *Third Text* no. 43 (summer).

—. 2001a. *The Nation's Tortured Body: Violence, Representation, and the Formation of a Sikh "Diaspora."* Durham, N.C.: Duke University Press.

—. 2001b. "Who Fabled: Joyce and Vico on History." *New Vico Studies* 17.

—. 2002. "The Diasporic Imaginary." *Public Culture,* 14, no. 2.

Barthes, Roland. 1970. "Historical Discourse." In *Introduction to Structuralism,* edited by M. Lane. New York: Basic Books.

Bauman, Richard and Charles L. Briggs. 1990. "Poetics and Performance as Critical Perspective on Language and Social Life." *Annual Review of Anthropology* 19: 59–88.

Benedict, Ruth. 1946. *The Chrysanthemum and the Sword.* Boston: Houghton Mifflin.

Benveniste, Emile. [1966] 1971. *Problems in General Linguistics.* Coral Gables, Fla.: University of Miami Press.

Berger, Peter L., and Thomas Luckmann. 1966. *The Social Construction of Reality: A Treatise in the Sociology of Knowledge.* Garden City, N.Y.: Doubleday.

Berlant, Lauren Gail. 1991. *The Anatomy of National Fantasy: Hawthorne, Utopia, and Everyday Life.* Chicago: University of Chicago Press.

Bhabha, Homi K., ed. 1990. *Nation and Narration.* London: Routledge.

—. 1994. *The Location of Culture.* New York: Routledge.

Biersack, Aletta, ed. 1991. *Clio in Oceania: Toward a Historical Anthropology.* Washington, D.C.: Smithsonian Institute Press.

Bloch, Maurice. 1977. "The Past and The Present in the Present." *Man* 12: 278–292.

Boas, Franz. 1940. "The Limitations of the Comparative Method of Anthropology." In *Race, Language, and Culture.* New York: Macmillan.

Boyarin, Jonathan, ed. 1994. *Remapping Memory: The Politics of Timespace.* Minneapolis: University of Minnesota Press.

Breckenridge, Carol A. and Peter van der Veer, eds. 1993. *Orientalism and the Postcolonial Predicament: Perspectives on South Asia.* Philadelphia: University of Pennsylvania Press.

Brow, James. 1978. *Vedda Villages of Anuradhapura: The Historical Anthropology of a Community in Sri Lanka.* Seattle: University of Washington Press.

Burke, Peter. 1987. *The Historical Anthropology of Early Modern Italy: Essays on Perception and Communication.* Cambridge: Cambridge University Press.

Butler, Judith. 1990. *Gender Trouble: Feminism and the Subversion of Identity.* New York: Routledge.

—. 1993. *Bodies that Matter: On the Discursive Limits of "Sex."* New York: Routledge.

—. 1997. *Excitable Speech: A Politics of the Performative.* New York: Routledge.

Cannadine, David and Simon Price, eds. 1987. *Rituals of Royalty: Power and Ceremonial in Traditional Societies.* New York: Cambridge University Press.

Clifford, James. 1988. *The Predicament of Culture: Twentieth-Century Ethnography, Literature, and Art.* Cambridge: Harvard University Press.

—. 1997. *Routes: Travel and Translation in the Late Twentieth Century.* Cambridge, Mass.: Harvard University Press.

Clifford, James, and George E. Marcus, eds. 1986. *Writing Culture: The Poetics and Politics of Ethnography.* Berkeley: University of California Press.

Cohen, David William. 1994. *The Combing of History*. Chicago: University of Chicago Press.

Cohen, David William, and E. S. Atieno Odhiambo. 1989. *Siaya: The Historical Anthropology of an African Landscape*. Athens, Ohio: Ohio University Press.

Cohen, Ralph and Michael S. Roth, eds. 1995. *History and . . . Histories Within the Human Sciences*. Charlottesville: University Press of Virginia.

Cohn, Bernard S. 1957. "India as a Racial, Linguistic, and Cultural Area." In *Introducing India in Liberal Education*, edited by Milton Singer. Chicago: University of Chicago Press.

——. 1987. *An Anthropologist Among the Historians and Other Essays*. Delhi: Oxford University Press.

——. 1996. *Colonialism and Its Forms of Knowledge: The British in India*. Princeton: Princeton University Press.

Comaroff, John L. 1982. "Dialectical Systems, History and Anthropology: Units of Study and Questions of Theory." *Journal of Southern African Studies* 8, no. 2 (April): 143–172.

Comaroff, Jean, and John L. Comaroff. 1991. *Of Revelation and Revolution: Christianity, Colonialism, and Consciousness in South Africa, Volume 1*. Chicago: University of Chicago Press.

——. 1992. *Ethnography and the Historical Imagination*. Boulder, Colo.: Westview Press.

——. 1997. *Of Revelation and Revolution: The Dialectics of Modernity on a South African Frontier, Volume 2*. Chicago: University of Chicago Press.

——. 1999. "Second Thoughts." *American Ethnologist* 26, no. 2: 307–9.

——. 2000. "Millennial Capitalism: First Thoughts on a Second Coming." *Public Culture* 12, no. 2: 291–343.

Cooper, Frederick, and Ann Laura Stoler. 1997. *Tensions of Empire: Colonial Cultures in a Bourgeois World*. Berkeley: University of California Press.

Coronil, Fernando. 1997. *The Magical State: Nature, Money, and Modernity in Venezuela*. Chicago: University of Chicago Press.

de Certeau, Michel. 1984. *The Practice of Everyday Life*. Berkeley: University of California Press.

——. 1988. *The Writing of History*. New York: Columbia University Press.

D'Agostino, Mary Ellin, Elizabeth Prine, Eleanor Casella and Margot Winer, eds. 1995. *The Written and the Wrought: Complementary Sources in Historical Anthropology, Essays in Honor of James Deetz*. Berkeley: Kroeber Anthropological Society Papers.

Davis, Nathalie Z. 1981. "The Possibilities of the Past." *Journal of Interdisciplinary History* 12, no. 2 (autumn): 267–75.

Davis, Natalie. 1987. *Fiction in the Archives: Pardon Tales and their Tellers in Sixteenth-Century France*. Stanford, Calif.: Stanford University Press.

Dening, Greg. 1995. *The Death of William Gooch: A History's Anthropology*. Honolulu: Hawaii University Press.

Derrida, Jacques. 1982. *Margins of Philosophy*. Chicago: University of Chicago Press.

——. 1995. *Archive Fever: A Freudian Impression*. Chicago: University of Chicago Press.

—. 1996. *Archive Fever: A Freudian Impression, Religion and Postmodernism.* Chicago: University of Chicago Press.

Dharwadker, Vinay. 1993. "Orientalism and the Study of Indian Literatures." In *Orientalism and the Postcolonial Predicament: Perspectives on South Asia,* edited by Carol Breckenridge and Peter van der Veer. Philadelphia: University of Pennsylvania Press.

Dirks, Nicholas B. 1987. *The Hollow Crown: Ethnohistory of an Indian Kingdom.* Chicago: University of Chicago Press.

—, ed. 1992. *Colonialism and Culture.* Ann Arbor: University of Michigan Press.

—, ed. 1993. "Colonial Histories and Native Informants: Biography of an Archive." In *Orientalism and the Postcolonial Predicament: Perspectives on South Asia,* edited by Carol Breckenridge and Peter van der Veer. Philadelphia: University of Pennsylvania Press.

—. 1996a. "Introduction." In *Colonialism and Its Forms of Knowledge: The British in India,* edited by Bernard S. Cohn. Princeton: Princeton University Press.

—. 1996b. "Is Vice Versa? Historical Anthropologies and Anthropological Histories." In *The Historic Turn in the Social Sciences,* edited by Terence J. McDonald. Ann Arbor: University of Michigan Press.

Echevarria, Roberto Gonzalez. 1990. *Myth and Archive: A Theory of Latin American Narrative.* Cambridge: Cambridge University Press.

Evans-Pritchard, E. E. 1962a. "Social Anthropology: Past and Present." In *Social Anthropology and Other Essays.* New York: The Free Press of Glencoe.

—. 1962b. "Anthropology and History." In *Social Anthropology and Other Essays.* New York: The Free Press of Glencoe.

—. 1962c. *Social Anthropology and Other Essays.* New York: The Free Press of Glencoe.

Fabian, Johannes. 1983. *Time and the Other: How Anthropology Makes Its Object.* New York: Columbia University Press.

Faubion, James D. 1993. "History in Anthropology." *Annual Review of Anthropology* 22: 35–54.

Feld, Steven, and Keith H. Basso, eds. 1996. *Senses of Place.* Santa Fe, N. Mex.: School of American Research Press.

Foucault, Michel. 1972. *The Archaeology of Knowledge and the Discourse on Language.* New York: Pantheon Books.

—. 1975. *The Birth of the Clinic: An Archaeology of Medical Perception.* New York: Vintage Books.

—. 1977. *Language, Counter-Memory, Practice: Selected Essays and Interviews.* Ithaca, N.Y.: Cornell University Press.

Fox-Genovese, Elizabeth, and Eugene D. Genovese. 1976. "The Political Crisis in Social History." *Journal of Social History* 10, no. 2 (winter): 205–220.

Freud, Sigmund. [1928] 1977. "Fetishism." In *On Sexuality: Three Essays on the Theory of Sexuality and Other Works.* New York: Penguin.

Geertz, Clifford. 1995. "History and Anthropology." In *History and . . . Histories Within the Human Sciences,* edited by Ralph Cohen and Michael S. Roth. Charlottesville: University Press of Virginia.

Ginzburg, Carlo. 1981. "A Comment." *Journal of Interdisciplinary History* 12, no. 2 (autumn): 277–78.

—. 1989. *Clues, Myths, and the Historical Method*. Baltimore: Johns Hopkins University Press.

Guha, Ranajit. 1983. *Elementary Aspects of Peasant Insurgency in Colonial India*. Delhi: Oxford.

—. 1983. *Writings on South Asian History and Society*. Delhi, N.Y.: Oxford University Press.

Guha, Ranajit. 1987. "Introduction." In *An Anthropologist Among the Historians and Other Essays*, edited by Bernard S. Cohn. Delhi: Oxford University Press.

Guha, Ranajit, and Gayatri C. Spivak, eds. 1988. *Selected Subaltern Studies*. New York: Oxford University Press.

Gupta, Akhil, and James Ferguson. 1997. *Anthropological Locations: Boundaries and Grounds of a Field Science*. Berkeley: University of California Press.

Hanks, William F. 1989. "Text and Textuality." *Annual Review of Anthropology* 18: 95–127.

Harvey, David. 1990. *The Condition of Postmodernity: An Enquiry into the Origins of Cultural Change*. Oxford: Blackwell.

Inden, Ronald B. 1990. *Imagining India*. Oxford, UK: Basil Blackwell.

Kelly, John D., and Martha Kaplan. 1990. "History, Structure, and Ritual." *Annual Review of Anthropology* 19: 119–150.

Krech, Shepard III. 1991. "The State of Ethnohistory." *Annual Review of Anthropology* 20: 345–375.

Lavie, Smadar, and Ted Swedenburg, eds. 1996. *Displacement, Diaspora, and Geographies of Identity*. Durham: Duke University Press.

Leach, Edmund Ronald. 1954. *Political Systems of Highland Burma: A Study of Kachin Social Structure*. London: Bell.

—. 1961. *Rethinking Anthropology*. London: The Athlone Press.

Lefebvre, Henri. 1991. *The Production of Space*. Oxford: Blackwell.

Lele, Jayant. 1993. "Orientalism and the Social Sciences." In *Orientalism and the Postcolonial Predicament: Perspectives on South Asia*, edited by Carol Breckenridge and Peter van der Veer. Philadelphia: University of Pennsylvania Press.

Lelyveld, David. 1993. "The Fate of Hindustani: Colonial Knowledge and the Project of a National Language." In *Orientalism and the Postcolonial Predicament: Perspectives on South Asia*, edited by Carol Breckenridge and Peter van der Veer. Philadelphia: University of Pennsylvania Press.

Lévi-Strauss, Claude. 1963. *Structural Anthropology*. New York: Basic Books.

—. 1966. *The Savage Mind*. Chicago: University of Chicago Press.

Lewis, Ioan M., ed. 1968. *History and Social Anthropology*. London: Tavistock Publications.

—. 1999. *Arguments with Ethnography: Comparative Approaches to History, Politics and Religion*. London: The Athlone Press.

Lindholm, Charles. 1996. *The Islamic Middle East: An Historical Anthropology*. Oxford: Blackwell Publishers.

McDonald, Terence J., ed. 1996. *The Historic Turn in the Social Sciences*. Ann Arbor: University of Michigan Press.

Macfarlane, Alan. 1970. *The Family Life of Ralph Josselin, A Seventeenth-Century Cler-*

gyman: An Essay in Historical Anthropology. Cambridge: Cambridge University Press.

Maitland, Frederic William. 1936. *Selected Essays.* Edited by H. D. Hazeltine et al. Cambridge: Cambridge University Press.

Malinowski, Bronislaw. 1922. *Argonauts of the Western Pacific; An Account of Native Enterprise and Adventure in the Archipelagoes of Melanesian New Guinea.* New York: E. P. Dutton & Co.

——. 1948. *Magic, Science, and Religion and Other Essays.* Boston: Beacon Press.

Marx, Karl. 1990. *Capital: A Critique of Political Economy, Volume 1.* London: Penguin Books.

Massey, Doreen. 1994. *Space, Place, and Gender.* Minneapolis: University of Minnesota Press.

Mathur, Saloni. 2000. "History and Anthropology in South Asia: Rethinking the Archive." *Annual Review of Anthropology* 29: 89–106.

Mead, Margaret, ed. 1953. *The Study of Culture at a Distance.* Chicago: University of Chicago Press.

Mertz, Elizabeth, ed. 1985. *Semiotic Mediation.* Chicago: University of Chicago Press.

Mintz, Sidney W. 1956. "Canamelar: The Subculture of a Rural Sugar Plantation Proletariat." In *The People of Puerto Rico,* edited by Julian Steward et al. Urbana: University of Illinois Press.

——. 1974. *Caribbean Transformations.* Chicago: Aldine.

——. 1985. *Sweetness and Power: The Place of Sugar in Modern History.* New York: Viking Penguin.

Mintz, Sidney W., and Richard Price. 1976. *An Anthropological Approach to the Afro-American Past: A Caribbean Perspective.* Philadelphia: Institute for the Study of Human Issues.

Mintz, Sidney W., and Eric R. Wolf. 1989. "Reply to Michael Taussig." *Critique of Anthropology* 9, no. 1: 25–31.

Munn, Nancy D. 1992. "The Cultural Anthropology of Time: A Critical Essay." *Annual Review of Anthropology.* 21: 93–123.

Nietzsche, Friedrich Wilhelm. 1956. *The Birth of Tragedy, and, The Genealogy of Morals.* Garden City, N.Y.: Doubleday.

——. [1887] 1969. *On the Genealogy of Morals.* N.Y.: Vintage Books.

——. 1997. *Untimely Meditations.* Translated by R. J. Hollindale. Cambridge: Cambridge University Press.

Nuttall, Sarah, and Carli Coetzee, eds. 1998. *Negotiating the Past: The Making of Memory in South Africa.* Capetown: Oxford University Press.

Ohnuki-Tierney, Emiko. 1990. *Culture Through Time: Anthropological Approaches.* Stanford: Stanford University Press.

Ong, Aihwa. 1999. *Flexible Citizenship: The Cultural Logics of Transnationality.* Durham: Duke University Press.

Pels, Peter. 1997. "The Anthropology of Colonialism: Culture, History, and the Emergence of Western Governmentality." *Annual Review of Anthropology.* 26: 163–183.

Pollack, Sheldon. 1993. "Deep Orientalism? Notes on Sanskrit and Power Beyond the Raj." In *Orientalism and the Postcolonial Predicament: Perspectives on South Asia,* edited by Carol Breckenridge and Peter van der Veer. Philadelphia: University of Pennsylvania Press.

Povinelli, Elizabeth. 2002. *The Cunning of Recognition.* Durham: Duke University Press.

Radcliffe-Brown, A. R. 1952. *Structure and Function in Primitive Society.* New York: The Free Press.

Rappaport, Joanne. 1994. *Cumbe Reborn: An Andean Ethnography of History.* Chicago: University of Chicago Press.

Richards, Thomas. 1992. "Archive and Utopia." *Representations* 37 (winter): 104–135.

———. 1993. *The Imperial Archive: Knowledge and the Fantasy of Empire.* London: Verso.

Riley, Carroll L., and Walter W. Taylor, eds. 1967. *American Historical Anthropology: Essays in Honor of Leslie Spier.* Carbondale: Southern Illinois University Press.

Rivers, W. H. R., Raymond William Firth, and David Murray Schneider. 1968. *Kinship and Social Organization.* New York. Humanities Press.

Roseberry, W. 1978. "Historical Materialism and The People of Puerto Rico." *Social Anthropology in Puerto Rico* 8: 26–36.

———. 1989. *Anthropologies and Histories: Essays in Culture, History, and Political Economy.* New Brunswick: Rutgers University Press.

Sahlins, Marshall. 1985. *Islands of History.* Chicago: University of Chicago Press.

Said, Edward W. 1978. *Orientalism.* New York: Pantheon Books.

Schapera, I. 1962. "Should Anthropologists Be Historians?" *Journal of the Royal Anthropological Institute* 92, no. 2: 198–221.

Scott, Joan W. 1992. " 'Experience.' " In *Feminists Theorize the Political,* edited by Judith Butler and Joan W. Scott. New York: Routledge.

Segal, Daniel A. 1994. "Living Ancestors: Nationalism and the Past in Postcolonial Trinidad and Tobago." In *Remapping Memory: The Politics of Timespace,* edited by Jonathan Boyarin. Minneapolis: University of Minnesota Press.

Segalen, Martine. 1986. *Historical Anthropology of the Family.* Cambridge: Cambridge University Press.

Siikala, Jukka, ed. 1990. *Culture and History in the Pacific.* Helsinki: Finnish Cultural Anthropological Society.

Silverblatt, Irene. 1987. *Moon, Sun, and Witches: Gender Ideologies and Class in Inca and Colonial Peru.* Princeton: Princeton University Press.

Silverman, Marilyn, and P. H. Gulliver, eds. 1992. *Approaching the Past: Historical Anthropology Through Irish Case Studies.* New York: Columbia University Press.

Silverstein, Michael, and Greg Urban, eds. 1996. *Natural Histories of Discourse.* Chicago: University of Chicago Press.

Smith, Bonnie G. 1995. "Gender and the Practices of Scientific History: The Seminar and Archival Research in the Nineteenth Century." *American Historical Review* 100, nos. 4–5: 1150–76.

Spivak, Gayatri Chakravorty. 1993. "The Burden of English." In *Orientalism and the Postcolonial Predicament: Perspectives on South Asia,* edited by Carol Breckenridge and Peter van der Veer. Philadelphia: University of Pennsylvania Press.

———. 1999. *A Critique of Postcolonial Reason: Toward a History of the Vanishing Present.* Cambridge, Mass.: Harvard University Press.

Stocking, George W. 1986. *Malinowski, Rivers, Benedict, and Others: Essays on Culture and Personality.* Madison, Wis.: University of Wisconsin Press.

Stoler, Ann Laura. 1985. *Capitalism and Confrontation in Sumatra's Plantation Belt, 1870–1979.* New Haven: Yale University Press.

———. 1989. "Rethinking Colonial Categories: European Communities and the Boundaries of Rule. *Comparative Studies in Society and History* 31: 134–161.

———. 1992a. "In Cold Blood: Hierarchies of Credibility and the Politics of Colonial Narratives." *Representations* 37: 151–189.

———. 1992b. "Sexual Affronts and Racial Frontiers." *Comparative Studies in Society and History* 34, no. 3: 514–51.

———. 1995. *Race and the Education of Desire: Foucault's* History of Sexuality *and the Colonial Order of Things.* Durham: Duke University Press.

———. 1997. "Racial Histories and Their Regimes of Truth." *Political Power and Social Theory.* 11: 183–255.

Stoler, Ann Laura, and Karen Strassler. 2000. "Castings for the Colonial: Memory Work in 'New Order Java.'" *Comparative Studies in Society and History* 42, no. 1: 4–48.

Suleri, Sara. 1992. *The Rhetoric of English India.* Chicago: University of Chicago Press.

Taussig, Michael. 1989. "History as Commodity: In Some Recent American (Anthropological) Literature." *Critique of Anthropology.* 11, no. 1 (spring): 7–23.

Thomas, Keith. 1963. "History and Anthropology." *Past and Present* 24 (April): 3–24.

———. 1964. "Work and Leisure in Pre-Industrial Society: A Conference Paper." *Past and Present* 29 (December): 50–62.

Thompson, E. P. 1972. "Anthropology and the Discipline of Historical Context." *Midland History* 1: 45–55.

———. 1977. "Folklore, Anthropology, and Social History." *The Indian Historical Review* 3: 247–266.

Trouillot, Michel-Rolph. 1988. *Peasants and Capital: Dominica in the World Economy.* Baltimore: Johns Hopkins University Press.

Yaeger, Patricia, ed. 1996. *The Geography of Identity.* Ann Arbor: University of Michigan Press.

Webster, Steven. 1989. "Some History of Social Theory in Sahlins' Structuralist Culture History." *Critique of Anthropology.* 9, vol. 3: 31–58.

White, Hayden. 1987. *The Content of the Form: Narrative Discourse and Historical Representation.* Baltimore: Johns Hopkins University Press.

Wilentz, Sean, ed. 1985. *Rites of Power: Symbolism, Ritual, and Politics Since the Middle Ages.* Philadelphia: University of Pennsylvania Press.

Wolf, Eric R. 1951. "The Social Organization of Mecca and the Origins of Islam." *Southwestern Journal of Anthropology* 7: 329–356.

———. 1966. *Peasants.* Englewood Cliffs, N.J.: Prentice Hall.

———. 1982. *Europe and the People Without History.* Berkeley: University of California Press.

Wolf, Eric R. and Sidney W. Mintz. 1957. "Haciendas and Plantations in Middle America and the Antilles." *Social and Economic Studies* 6: 380–411.

1 Ethnography and the Archive

Annals of the Archive: Ethnographic Notes on the Sources of History

Nicholas B. Dirks

History is the work expended on material documentation (books, texts, accounts, registers, acts, buildings, institutions, laws, techniques, objects, customs, etc.) that exists, in every time and place, in every society . . . in our time, history is that which transforms documents into monuments . . . in our time, history aspires to the condition of archaeology, to the intrinsic description of the monument.—Michel Foucault, *Archaeology of Knowledge*

It is the state which first presents subject matter that is not only adapted to the prose of History, but involves the production of such history in the progress of its own being.—G. F. W. Hegel, *The Philosophy of History*

Ethnography of the Archive

The first time I entered an archive, I panicked. My historical zeal inexplicably vanished as I desperately stemmed a welling desire to exit immediately and search for the nearest pub. I saw before me the thousands of documents I could indent, the books I could read, the files I had to wade through. I tried to imagine which index to consult, what department to decipher, how best to control the chaos of what seemed an infinite chain of documents. My proposal for research, so lucid a minute before, seemed inappropriate, unwise, impossible. I felt embarrassed to expose my ignorance in front of professional archivists anxious to discern a research topic that might bear some relationship to the archive itself. Alas, my interest in the small voices and contradictory ruptures of history was not designed for easy access. My proposal to understand the essential relationship between political authority and social relations could take me to any fragment, and yet I knew that all fragments were not equal, that most documents by themselves were mere reminders of the quotidian tedium of history, that I not only needed to start somewhere, I needed to start somewhere promising. The archive is a glorious monument of history, but the documents within are simply the sedimented detritus of a history that from the inside had seemed both endless and banal.

Most historians write history before they enter the archive, beginning their professional apprenticeship by using those secondary sources in libraries that are already contaminated by interpretation and selection. But even at the beginning, such sources establish their authenticity through referencing an archive that demarcates the partial and secondary nature of all sources from outside. The archive is constituted as the only space that is free of context, argument, ideology—indeed history itself. Accordingly, historians can only really become historians or write history once they have been to the archive. The originary arrival of the historian in the archive is much like the arrival of the anthropologist in the field—that threshold of disciplinary certification—the magical moment when the scientist-scholar sets down upon a shore that beckons with the promise that one can finally engage in the act of discovery, at last come face to face with truth and the realm of unmediated facts. But while anthropologists have subjected their arrival stories to historical and critical scrutiny, the historian's arrival story is largely untold, shielded by the fact that while the archive has often seemed mystical, it has never appeared exotic. Travelers' tales and adventurers' yarns have never rendered the archive a major source of narrative, and yet the monumentality of the archive is enshrined in a set of assumptions about truth that are fundamental both to the discipline of history and to the national foundations of history. While these assumptions about truth and history have been critiqued in relation to historical writing (and the use of sources), they have rarely been examined in relation to the sources themselves, except inside the very historical footnotes that summon the greatest respect for the archive as a repository of ultimate value (Grafton 1997).[1] The archive is simultaneously the outcome of historical process and the very condition for the production of historical knowledge. The time has come to historicize the archive.[2]

My own archive arrival story was prefaced by several years of working with original documents that themselves preceded the establishment of the modern archive. Intrigued as I was by the character of the premodern state in southern India, I began my professional career as a historian by reading epigraphical series and reports, transcriptions and translations of inscriptions that were for the most part etched into either stone or copper surfaces. Stone inscriptions typically recorded endowments to temples and were inscribed on the stone walls of the shrines where worship was to be conducted, or on the walls surrounding the centers of worship. Copper-plate inscriptions were typically held by the descendants of kings, landlords, and various other magnates whose entitlements to land, tribute, office, and honor were itemized, publicly declared, and permanently instantiated by the presentation of the material text. In addition to recording details of landholding rights and relations, political positions and perquisites, ritual emoluments and entailments, and so on, these inscribed surfaces provided occasions for textual performances of various kinds, most significantly when the pedigree of the presenter became the basis for historical narrations of the exploits and exemplariness of certain families and their forebears. Inscriptions thus provided the stuff of history—the details of property and politics, identity and institutions—at the same time that they were themselves historical texts, recording in genealogical form the claims made by history itself for and about authority. History was already monumental, most particularly in the elaborate and sometimes enormous temple complexes that yielded surface after surface for textual inscription, but also in the use of precious metals to insure the permanence of the text (though its very preciousness meant there was always the temptation for textual meltdown). In one sense history was only monumental, for the myriad other texts that must have been etched on the surfaces of palmyra palm were consigned to certain obsolescence in ways that meant that if history was to last, it had to be written on or as a monument.

But if the temple complex was itself an archive, it was an archive of a very different kind than we imagine when we contemplate the contemporary institution. The walls of the temple complex served in one sense as a local record room, the origins of most modern archives; however, the records were attached to a preexisting monument, and functioned in effect to secure the monument as well as the authoritative relations and figures whose own power was symbolized and deployed through the institutional formation of the temple. And despite the ample epigraphical record, the actual record is slight compared to any modern paper archive, and with all the textual efflorescence of preambles and genealogical histories, the details of administrative procedure were few, far between, and only rarely cross-referenced in ways that betrayed the constant surveillance and custodianship of a bureaucratic managerial elite that would seem the sine qua non of modern archives and states.

Nevertheless, the temple complex was an archive of sorts. It preserved records necessary for the maintenance of a polity, even as the polity itself relied heavily on the institutional relations of the temple. And it preserved these records for reference use as well as in ways that worked to monumentalize both history and its documents. The inscriptional texts themselves appear emblematic of a particular kind of archival history, combining the most banal of details with the most glorious panegyrics in praise of kingly dynasties, local rulers, and institutional arrangements (ranging from the banking functions of temples or the maintenance of ritual performances to the memorialization of property relations and honorific offices). At the same time, neither historians nor "history" proper was necessary for the transformation of documents into history, as happened later when the myriad record offices of government still had to be monumentalized into archives in order to transit from the realm of governmentality to the domain of history. In southern India, documents began their careers as monuments.

It was with this experience of history that I set off on my journey to the archive. Even though by then I had shifted my own historical interests from the eighth and ninth centuries to the eighteenth and nineteenth, I was still ambivalent about the modern archive. Given my interest in precolonial state and society—specifically in charting out the nature of kingly authority and caste relations in southern India immediately before the onset of British colonial rule and then tracing transformations over the first colonial century—I was keen to find documents that existed before the modern colonial state and its documentation apparatus. At best, the archive might have admitted documents from an earlier age as an expression of the colonial state's need to know how things really were before the British arrived. But I worried that the archive was at least in part about the contamination of the west, or the modern, or both. At the same time, I walked into the archive with all the trepidation of the academic apprentice, worried that I would never penetrate the secrets of the archive, and worse that the secrets of the archive were impenetrable not because of the daring originality of my line of research but because of my fundamental ignorance of the archival structure of the conditions of historical knowledge.

The archive that inaugurated my experience as a historian was the India Office Library in London. Originally the library and record room of the India Office, the agency of the British government that oversaw Britain's colonial relationship with India until independence in 1947, it had been moved into a separate archive in the early 1970s, subsequently placed under the management of the British Library, and has now been moved to and amalgamated with the archival and library holdings of the new British Library in St. Pancras. Despite the shabby postwar high-rise that housed the miles of shelves, I walked into the archive for the first time with all the excitement that my fellow anthropology students had reserved for the moment they arrived in a "field of their own." My excitement soon merged with terror when I realized that I hadn't a clue about what to do next—whether I should look at the index for the political, public, or home departments, what the mechanisms might be for genealogical research, and how to access either Tamil or English manuscript collections. I remember spending the first day paging through the index of one particular department with a key word that failed to appear for anything more than the most trivial of documents. In frustration, I handcopied one very long letter that seemed vaguely important (only to realize later that I had already photocopied a passage from a government manual where all the good bits had already been excerpted). I wondered why the archive seemed far less satisfying than a basic university library. I panicked, feeling a bizarre envy for the traditional research historian who was assigned a topic on the basis of a specific collection of records or documents their supervisor had preselected for them, at the same time wondering if I should just discard history and go to the field instead, trying my hand at anthropology, the flip side of my disciplinary formation and training.[3] At the same time, I realized I would have to do extensive fieldwork on the archive itself,[4] learning both about the history of British governmental rule at the concrete levels of yearly bureaucratic organization and interaction, and about the history of various kinds of collections and record keeping.

Little by little, step by step, I learned about the nature, classifications, and institutional investments of some of the records and collections that were to become the primary documentation for my thesis. I also began to learn about the complex relationship between archives in Britain and archives in India—what sorts of files, what levels of detail, and what manner of departments were to be found and could be found to organize materials at the India Office Library in London, the National Archives of India in New Delhi, and the Tamil Nadu Record Office in Madras. The London and Delhi offices paid particular interest to the Princely States of India, one of which came to be the primary historical and ethnographic site for my research on state and society. At the same time, to find out much in the way of detail about the actual land settlements that implemented the introduction of new forms of property and new relations between "cultivators" and the state, I learned that I had to look at the "settlement registers" that were housed in Madras itself. So daunted was I by the stacks of settlements when I first encountered them that I found it difficult to anticipate that I would later come to relish these records; as it happened, I spent much of my thesis research period looking at records of tax-free land settlements, gradually coming to realize the extent to which these "inam" land classifications revealed much about the way the history of political privileges from precolonial times was sedimented into landed privileges under the early colonial regime.

My first experience of the archive was thus frustrating for several major reasons, quite apart from the myriad frustrations that any scholar working in archives in the 1970s took for granted, such as the absence of photocopy machines, the now unimaginable absence of the computer, and the often highly personalized contingencies of archival access. I was frustrated not only because I felt buried under the weight of archival excess, but because this excess seemed to signify (indeed amplify) the distortions of a colonial regime, one that either sought to eradicate the past, or to represent it in ways that seemed at best mobilized as evidence for unreliable arguments in favor of one or another colonial rhetorics of rule. I was, after all, determined to discover what I could about the nature of state and society in the immediate precolonial period, and the more I looked in colonial archives, the more I felt the impossibility of the project. And so I began to spend increasing numbers of hours away from the archive in a library of "Oriental Manuscripts" that housed, among other things, the manuscript collection of Colin Mackenzie.

Colin Mackenzie, an engineer and mathematician by training, went to India as an army man and soon became known for his extraordinary cartographic talents, first designing plans of military assault then plans for surveying and mapping newly conquered territories. His surveying skills were recognized as he was designated as the Surveyor-General of Madras in 1810, only to become the first Surveyor-General of India in 1815. Mackenzie, a Scot from the outer Hebrides who, like many other educated Scots of his time, went to India to find a more flourishing career than would have been available in Scotland, was also an avid antiquarian and became vitally committed to the collection of historical materials about peninsular India. On his own initiative and with his own resources he hired and trained a group of local assistants who helped him collect local histories of kingly dynasties, chiefly families, castes, villages, temples, and monasteries, as well as of other local traditions and religious and philosophical texts in a variety of Indian languages. He also took rubbings of stone and copper-plate inscriptions, collected coins, images, and antiquities, and made extensive plans and drawings wherever he went. By the time of his death in 1821, he had amassed a collection of 3,000 inscriptions, 1,568 literary manuscripts, 2,070 local tracts, and large portfolios and collections of drawings, plans, images, and antiquities (Dirks 1993).

The Mackenzie archive promised unmediated access to the historical mentalities and genres of the late precolonial period. As I attempted to understand the nature of the holdings of the archive through a range of indexes and annotations that were compiled as early as 1828 in the still canonical account of the collection by H. H. Wilson (1828), I came to be especially interested in historical texts that were generally called "vamcavali," or dynastic histories of kingly/chiefly families. These texts are genealogies of a sort, both in that they list the entire line of the family, and in that genealogy acts as the narrative frame of the text. What chronology is to modern historical narrative, genealogy is to the vamcavali—it provides both sequence and structure. Typically, each episode consists of some action performed by a hero-ancestor, which is then followed by an account of gifts made by a great king to that of a chiefly ancestor. For example, the hero may kill a tiger that has been plaguing villagers in the king's domain or set off to do battle against some enemy of the king's. The king then calls the chief to court where he presents him with gifts consisting of titles, emblems, and rights over land. The basic structure of the texts often seems repetitive, albeit conveying little in the way of "social historical" information. Rather, historical events that lead to the establishment or reestablishment of a special relationship between the chief and a king are elevated to narrative significance and serve to herald the accomplishments of each noteworthy ancestor. Further, the royal family is seen to have the accumulated merit of these discrete historical events, inheriting the full measure of royal perquisites and entitlements that reflect the heroic history of the family (Dirks 1993b).

However, even as I took these texts as the record not just of particular histories but also of particular kinds of history, I became aware that they were not positioned fully outside colonial history. Many of the chiefly family histories concluded with petitions for recognition, reinstatement, or some other claim for authority and position. Some of the most glorious family histories were of kingly families that had participated in the late eighteenth-century wars against the British (sometimes in collaboration with the French), leaving the contemporary kings in disgrace. Other family histories turned out to be claims on behalf of the branch of the family that had been bested by another in internecine struggles for landlord status/privileges under the new terms of British rule. Even as old regime logics of heroism, gift exchange, and royal relationship were clearly in evidence in the old histories, these texts also demonstrated their inexorable historical embeddedness in new logics of colonial power and command.

In subsequent research, I further learned that the Mackenzie collection itself was part of the history of early colonial conquest. Mackenzie collected texts while mapping and surveying newly conquered territories of southern India. Even though he never conducted a revenue survey, scrupulously avoiding direct inquiries about production and revenue, there was no way to promise that knowledge about local lineages or tenures might not be used by an imperial power that was at this very point establishing itself as a revenue state. Indeed, virtually all of the information collected by Mackenzie turned out to concern the rights and privileges of kings, chiefs, headmen, Brahmans, and religious institutions. There was good reason for what one of Mackenzie's assistants characterized as "friendless suspicion." Additionally, the collection of materials was actually conducted by a variety of local assistants, many though not all learned Brahmans, who had multiple agendas, interests, and locations of their own. Mackenzie's assistants were invested in certain kinds of representations of India, at the same time that they sought assiduously to please their "master" and satisfy his endless ambition to collect local histories and texts.

Even when traces of precolonial voices, genres, and forms survive in the Mackenzie archive, they do so in the context of colonial interest. Certainly the different voices, agencies, and modes of authorization that were implicated in the production of the archive were substantially lost once they inhabited the colonial archive. Distinctions between types of texts (e.g. texts that derived from ancient authorship or the hastily transcribed remarks from a local source) and concerns about the use-value of knowledge (how textual knowledge might be used to de-authorize and de-legitimate) became blurred and increasingly dissolved at each stage of collection, transcription, translation, and canonization. And the role of Mackenzie's native assistants became relegated to the position of technical mediation, their diaries and letters rarely included with the textual material. The early colonial archive was itself a form of colonization, reproduced even in the conceits of antiquity and authenticity that characterize the Mackenzie collection.

Nevertheless, colonial interests in knowledge changed over time and did so dramatically in the period between the late eighteenth and the mid-nineteenth centuries. If the Mackenzie collection reflects early colonial interests, it is also the case that within a decade of Mackenzie's death in 1821 the collection changed from seeming a significant resource to becoming a historical burden. The distinguished Orientalist H. H. Wilson almost abandoned his cataloguing project when he realized the growing lack of interest in Mackenzie's work; the materials in the collection seemed neither historical enough to satisfy any genuine historical interest in the reconstruction of precolonial Indian history, nor classical enough to provide a respectable basis for an Orientalist's reputation or labor. At the same time that we acknowledge the early colonial mediations that produced the very textual forms and forms of knowledge enshrined in the Mackenzie collection, we must also realize that Mackenzie's texts occupy a marginal position, both in the archive and in the colonial state project that archived the documents. The histories that Mackenzie had collected had already been overtaken by a different kind of history.

What survives instead at the center of the early colonial archive are the land records that became so fundamental to the debates over land tenure and settlement in the initial years of British rule. These documents—used so extensively by historians of agrarian relations—turn out to be far more than assessments of different land parcels and their potential (or actual) productivity, as at first they seemed. Rather, they acted as interventions in the way the colonial state worked to constitute land relations as the basis of the state's ultimate right of ownership and more generally land records intervened in the colonial state's delineation of relationships between state and society. The early colonial state after it shed its initial formation in the mercantilist origins of the East India Company was above all an agrarian state that used various representations of Oriental despotism to justify its legitimacy and bolster its claims to ultimate power through the bureaucratic regulation of and extraction of revenue from landed property. Building on arguments between those who argued that the East India Company was inheriting the king's right of ownership over all property and those who used a Ricardian theory of rent to claim for the Company the right to set revenue rates and collect taxes as fundamental to the custodial project of the state, the British (all the while ceding sovereignty at a formal level to the Mughal rulers) gradually established a state bureaucracy, focusing primarily on land revenue, that acted as if it had sovereign authority over all of India. Decisions about whether the bureaucracy should accord proprietary rights to landlords (*zamindars*), village brotherhoods, or principal cultivators (*ryots*) became critical interventions in the relationship between state and society, at the same time that these decisions both produced, and were produced by, a variety of different histories of India that were important parts of early colonial rhetorics of rule.

When I first waded through settlement land records, I did so to determine the nature of agrarian relations in different parts of southern India and also to assess arguments made by different administrators about the nature of the precolonial village community. The arguments were complex and robustly documented and always assumed that historical forms were necessary predicates for colonial policies. Intellectual histories of some of the key players of the period have revealed how much historical argument was tied to political ambition and European experience. Cornwallis was influenced by the physiocrats and driven by his ambition to recreate in India the authority and position of the landed gentry in Britain (already under major assault and in considerable defensiveness given the events of the revolution in France); Munro and Elphinstone were captured by Burkean rhetorics of paternal responsibility and a Scottish sense of the folk heroism of the yeoman cultivator. But despite my sense of the intellectual genealogies of land policy, I only realized little by little how much the documentation project of the early colonial state around matters of land and revenue was fundamental to the formation of that very state. Indeed, during the period heralded by Warren Hasting's disgrace (at the hands of Edmund Burke) in the late eighteenth century and brought to a chastened conclusion around the events of the Great Rebellion of 1857, the colonial state formed around the relationship of revenue to land itself. The commercial enterprises of the East India Company yielded steadily in importance to the arguments of free traders who saw in landed wealth the development of a new market for British goods, at the same time that economic activity was progressively yoked to the grand imperial project of political and military expansion.

The Archive of Ethnography

By the second half of the nineteenth century the colonial state had to transform itself once again. If land and the revenue and authority that accrued from its relationship with the state were so fundamental to the formation of the early colonial state, the fact that the rebellions of 1857 quickly led to agrarian revolt and the steadily diversifying economic character of imperial power (propelled by the building of railways in the 1850s) made it clear that things had to change. Land tax was still an important source of revenue in the late nineteenth century, but imperial ambition moved to an altogether new level. The steady absorption of new lands through the aggressive policies of Lord Dalhousie, that in the taking of Oudh in 1856 had led directly to the Great Rebellion of 1857, were brought abruptly to a halt, and policies of indirect rule were mobilized to accommodate and ultimately appropriate the incomplete project of colonial conquest (one third of India remained under princely control at the time of the rebellion). Concurrently, the rebellion made it clear that some communities in India could be counted as loyal, as others became doomed to perpetual suspicion. Bengalis were no longer to be recruited to the armed forces, which were now to be stocked only by the loyal "martial" races, as Macaulay's hyperbole was translated into state policy. In the new rhetorical economy of colonial rule, political loyalty replaced landed status. And the form of knowledge and argument that seemed most appropriate to assess matters of loyalty rather than histories of land control was knowledge of peoples and cultures. To put the matter in bold relief, after 1857 anthropology supplanted history as the principal colonial modality of knowledge. The colonial state changed from a "revenue state" to an "ethnographic state" (Dirks 2001).

I am not referring here to disciplines of knowledge in the modern sense; anthropology had not yet been invented as an academic discipline in any case (though its invention was certainly tied to its rising significance for colonial rule), and Indian history for Europe was not only written outside the academy but usually in the corridors of colonial bureaucracy—or as the work of colonial bureaucrats, as in the case of Mill and Elphinstone. Rather, I am suggesting that the foundational importance of historical argument for land policy yielded to another overriding concern, namely to identify those populations that were inherently loyal to the British and to learn the customs of other populations in order to know and control them in a grand effort to avoid the humiliating and near fatal calamity of the rebellion. In part the product of strategic repression, in part the product of the ebullient illusion of permanence characteristic of late-nineteenth-century "high" imperial rule, this was an age in which the history of conquest was virtually erased; the Cambridge historian Seeley noted in his imperial history lectures that India had been conquered in a "fit of absent-mindedness." In place of this history, an anthropology of the peoples and cultures of India became the canonical knowledge of empire. The decennial census, begun in 1871, became the apotheosis of the new ethnographic imperative of the colonial state.

At the heart of this new knowledge, caste was viewed as the primary institution—and sphere of social relations—that articulated the legacies of tradition, standing in place of the historical-mindedness that was seen as absent from Indian sensibilities. Colonial historiography increasingly conceded to anthropology the study of historical subjects which had not yet entered modernity. Anthropology grew out of modern history, becoming the history of those without history as well as the prehistory of those now mired in history. By the late nineteenth century, anthropology became quite literally the history of the colonized. In this division of disciplinary labor, anthropology, whether of a physical body or a body politic, was less a complement than an extension of modern history, spatialized by the logic of colonial conquest and rule, linked directly to the interests and forms of the state. And in the global imperial order of things, history was to the modern metropolitan state what anthropology was to the colonial state, reflecting both the similarities and the differences between state systems at home and in the colonies. History constructed a glorious past for the nation in which the present was the inevitable teleological frame; anthropology assumed histories that necessitated colonial rule. History told the story of the nation; anthropology explained why a nation had not yet emerged—as for example in Risley's understanding of caste as an impediment to national mobilization (Risley 1909).

If the British failed to see history as a fundamental attribute of Indian culture, it is no coincidence that they established their rule on the ruins of a political (and historical) order that they had aggressively conquered, destroyed, and replaced. Mackenzie had been one of the last colonial savants to exercise himself primarily in the collection of local, indigenous histories. James Mill propounded instead that whatever past India might have could be left in the dustbin of history, arguing with liberal intention that all that was good in India would be imported from Britain (Mehta 1999). Colonial history was generally overtaken by the concern to document not simply land tenures but the relationships between land and the state. But by the middle of the century history was at best irrelevant, at worst an embarrassment, and colonial anthropology took on growing importance. Thus the late nineteenth century witnessed the first experiments in ethnographic surveys, even as the records in the archives increasingly reflected a colonial preoccupation with the customs and social relations of the people of India. I can only assert this argument here, but I have written elsewhere about the way in which late-nineteenth-century arguments about social policy tended increasingly to reflect anthropological sensibilities—as for example in British concerns, mobilized in part by missionary pressure to regulate forms of religious expression that appeared to be particularly backward or barbarous (Dirks 1997). At the same time, there was an explosion of writing—in books, treatises, and administrative files—about caste. Caste was used to explain and to classify, to predict and contain the potential unruliness and recalcitrance of colonial subjects; indeed caste became an alternative colonial civil society that made other kinds of civic institutions, let alone political rights, seem either unnecessary, or foreign, or both. As a result, the state and the archive became increasingly ethnographic.

Reflections on the Archive

I have suggested elsewhere the need for anthropologists engaged in the study of their own history to approach the colonial archive both as the repository of sources for their research and in terms of larger historical contexts that document the genealogical entailments of colonial knowledge for contemporary scholarship (Dirks 1999). And yet I would also advocate the need for historians to engage in an ethnography of the archive, for the archive itself reflects the forms and formations of historical knowledge that have been so markedly shaped by their implication in the history of the state whose past it is meant to enshrine. To engage in an ethnography of the archive entails going well beyond seeing it as an assemblage of texts, a depository of and for history. The archive is a discursive formation in the totalizing sense that it reflects the categories and operations of the state itself—in the case presented here, of the colonial state.

The state literally produces, adjudicates, organizes, and maintains the discourses that become available as the primary texts of history.

When I did historical research on the late nineteenth century, I consulted the records of the "Public" Department, the "Political" Department, and the "Home" Department, among many others. I paged through indexes of documents that reflected the quotidian procedures of government, files that considered and then ruled on issues ranging from the appointment of a particular individual to a position (such as Superintendent of Ethnography) to his salary and his official duties, both of which were scaled in relation to the other positions, financial needs, and political requirements of government. When I found materials about so-called barbaric practices such as hookswinging, I read through files that responded to widespread pressure from missionaries and others regarding the suppression of an activity that brought no grievous bodily harm and little in the way of significant social unrest to the attention of district administrators, who nevertheless had to worry about the representation of governmental activities both within India and back in Britain itself. When I began to correlate the interest of official ethnography in native bodily practices with the Torture Commission Report of 1855, I had to rely on my own archival experience of working with land and settlement records as early as the late eighteenth century in order to dismantle the character of official self-congratulation in relation to the deployment of horror stories around brutality and violence in the south Indian countryside. Each record in the archive references previous records, both as precedent and as paper trail; archival research itself invariably proceeds genealogically—record by record, decision by decision, trace by trace. Although documents are frequently scripted with posterity in mind, history in one sense is an afterthought, only incidentally related to the sources that are fetishized as so fundamental to the craft of history itself. And yet history is encoded on the surfaces of the very files—the numbering systems, the departmental structures, and classificatory rubrics—as well as in the reports, letters, decisions, and scribbles within that make up the archive. The archive contains primary sources at the same time that it is always already a secondary trace of historical discourse.

The archive encodes a great many levels, genres, and expressions of governmentality. Commissions of Inquiry have very different histories from routine papers that surface in the government orders of everyday official practice; government manuals and gazetteers have very different uses from occasional notes or office correspondence that move in haphazard circuits of official (and semi-official) exchange. Historical research can reveal connections that become effaced by the effects of history itself: for example, the connection between the proliferation of land records and debates over the proper way to introduce a proprietary economy into India and the need of the colonial state for a form of revenue and political authority that would circumvent the rising power of commercial elites; between the anxiety over agrarian and military revolt and the social classifications that became hardened into late-colonial views of caste; between the concerns of the police to apprehend habitual criminals and the general criminalization of colonial populations in the early development of anthropometry; and between the modern career of anthropology (as well as general social scientific thought about such issues as tradition and modernity) and the legacies of the colonial past. Even as the connections never completely come full circle—never foreclosing the possibilities of other connections and frequently displacing other possible ones—they move us well away from the certainties of linear and autonomous textual histories of anthropology and history, dissolving texts into contexts even as contexts constantly become reabsorbed by other texts and historical traces. While the archive has no transparency of its own—its facts can be construed in any number of ways, and the historical record alone can by no means explain why we write the way we do—it is nevertheless the field within which we all conduct our research, pushing us by its recalcitrance, limiting us by its aggravating absences, fascinating us by its own patterns of intertextuality, and seducing us by its appearance of the real.

The colonial archive has a peculiar opacity. While all archives reflect their particular origins as state records, colonial archives betray the additional contradictions of colonial governmentality. In the case of India, the early colonial state was officially answerable to the British Parliament and Crown through a cumbersome process that required a minimum of six months for the exchange of correspondence by sea. In fact, the East India Company, a monopoly joint stock firm, ran the day to day affairs of the colony, only yielding provisional authority after a century of incomparable corruption, giving way completely after a military mutiny and agrarian revolt virtually brought the empire to its knees in 1857–58. But even after the assumption of Crown rule, the subjects of empire were governed by imperial fiat with none of the demands of public representation and accountability encountered by the metropolitan state. Revenue records might have debated the high points of Mughal history in order to find precedents for Ricardian theories of rent, but the question of legitimation was balanced only by threats of disorder rather than by the checks of dissent and debate. Perhaps even more critically, the accumulation of an ethnographic archive in the late nineteenth century worked not just to displace colonial sovereignty but to proclaim the colonial subject as lacking both in political capabilities and in historical understanding. As a result, the archive reflects the shift of state anxiety from the political and juridical to the social and cultural. Caste identity, for example, became not just the object of knowledge but the end of knowledge, eclipsing political persuasion, class position, or regional interests as the basis for state concerns about control and containment. The ethnographic state produced ethnographic subjects, not political ones. The colonial archive resisted the onset of modern history.

Modern history could only develop in the metropole, on the interior ruins of eschatological conventions that were anchored in theological temporalities and religious institutions. But with the eighteenth-century recognition that history had an open future came the steady appropriation of this enlightenment sensibility by the apparatus of the state. The state became the measure for nascent temporalities as surely as it provided the boundaries for nationally conceived social spaces (Koselleck 1985). The state also became the instrumentality through which historical documents became meaningful as the primary and authentic record of the past. History served as a principal form of governmentality at the same time that governmentality expressed itself through the categories of historical thought and writing. In more prosaic terms, history was organized theoretically in narratives that made the state (and, when not arrested by colonial rule, ultimately the nation) into the subject and the object of temporal consequence; it also became primarily located within the formal ambits and agencies of state power. History was written by the state to educate and justify political policies and practices, and it was produced and preserved by the state for future historical reference in the archive. The archive, that primary site of state monumentality, was the very institution that canonized, crystallized, and classified the knowledge required by the state even as it made this knowledge available for subsequent generations in the cultural form of a neutral repository of the past.[5]

Many commentators, from Hegel to Koselleck, have noted that modern history—or rather the modern idea of history—was born with the French Revolution. It is perhaps even more true to say that the modern archive was born with the French Revolution, and, as befits that tumultuous event, the modern archive was as much about the destruction as it was about the preservation of the past (Posner 1984). The Archives Nationales of Paris was created by the Decree of September 12, 1790, and open access to the archives was declared a right of citizenship rather than a perquisite of state power (or scholarly interest) (Panitch 1996). Older archives had been in the possession of kings and courts and were placed only at the disposition of those in power, largely for the preservation of titles to rights, privileges, honors, and land. The modern archive was born in the violence of revolution precisely because of the way documents had supported the privilege of the old regime; according to Philippe Sagnac, in many acts of rural rebellion, the French peasant, "took his own Bastille, invaded the chateaux, ran straight to the seigneurial archives, held at last in his hands the charters, monuments of his own servitude, and delivered them to the fire" (Sagnac 1973, 85). More centrally, the new government itself initiated the wholesale destruction of records as part of its revolutionary program. State-sponsored bonfires consigned papers of the nobility, orders of knighthood, and other documents of the old regime to ashes in the years between 1789 and 1793, a policy extolled by none other than Condorcet: "It is today that, in the capital, Reason burns, at the foot of the statue of Louis XIV, 600 folio volumes attesting to the vanity of this class whose titles will at last disappear in smoke" (Panitch 1996, 34).

The new French State did not maintain the full openness of the archive, as the imperatives of the postrevolutionary nation-state had to accommodate new forms of privilege and secrecy (Milligan). In England, where no revolution produced such a dramatic archival history, the modern archive developed directly out of the records of the Chancery Department, most of which were housed in the Tower of London until the Public Record Office was built in the middle of the nineteenth century.[6] Unlike in France, where the new archives were established as part of a new revolutionary state with the specific purpose of undermining the old regime, in England the archives embodied the rights and privileges that had been appropriated by the British aristocracy over centuries (Schellenberg 1964). The establishment of the Public Record Office roughly coincided with the electoral reforms that sought to enlarge the voting public and open the procedures of government to the new, increasingly urban and mercantile bourgeoisie. But colonial records remained in the India Office, tied as they were directly to protocols of governance, until the end of empire itself. Unsurprisingly, the idea of public access for colonial records required the emergence of a postcolonial public (although the principal public for the India Office Record Room is still the British ex-colonial). The contradictions of colonial governmentality extended both to history and to the archives, exemplifying the limits of representation and accountability that were so fundamental to the colonial relationship.

In reflecting briefly on the history of archives, and in retelling the history of the archives of my own research career, I have attempted to call attention to some of the ways in which the archive not only contains documents but is itself the primary document of history. At the same time, I have commented on the particular character of the colonial archive. From the beginning of colonial conquest, long before historical narratives had given way to ethnographic accounts, colonial governmentality produced a different kind of relationship to the past, and to its collection, preservation, and destruction, than had been the case in the imperial metropole. In many ways, the archive was the literal document that expressed the rupture between nation and state engendered by the colonial form. The colonial archive was not just the record of the colonial state but also the repository of the sources for an imperial history whose public was in the metropole rather than the colony. Thus it was that anticolonial nationalist movements had to struggle not just to narrate alternative histories but to find different sources and authorities for the development of their national historiographies (Dirks 1990; Guha 1997).

The archive is the instantiation of the state's interest in history. It survives as the remains of the record rooms of everyday governmental business, and it is monumentalized by the state to preserve its own history in the assumed name of the nation (or colony) rather than the state (or metropole). The monument preserves much of its sacred legacy—with its hierarchical structures, its labyrinthine procedures, its professional cabals—enshrining the secularized state with the full solemnity of the past. As critics of history and historiography we must therefore chip away at the history of this monument, at the same time that we recognize the monumentality of all historical evidence and by implication the monumental limits and conditions of all historical writing. Historians may make their own history, but they cannot always make it as they choose. Historians make history in archives that already sediment an archaeology of the state—indeed an archaeology of history—that, perhaps necessarily, remains to this day largely unwritten.

Notes

This paper was originally prepared for a conference entitled "Early Modern History and the Social Sciences: Braudel's Mediterranean Fifty Years After," which took place in Bellagio, June 23–27, 1997. I am grateful to Naveeda Khan for research assistance concerning the history of European archives.

1   Grafton's fine book both traces the history of the footnote in modern historical writing and treats the complex and contested history of the documentary source for historical research. Grafton also notes that while Leopold Ranke proclaimed and propounded the place of the archive for history, he was neither the first to do so, nor by any means solely, if even principally, reliant on archival sources.

2   What follows in this chapter is mostly personal reflection about my own research based in the history of South Asia, hardly an adequate basis for the historicizing of the archive. Indeed, such a project would entail, at the very least, comprehensive and comparative historical research on different national archives, combined with reflec-

tion and critique, drawing from recent debates in the philosophy of history as well as methodological concerns of practicing historians. Unfortunately, historians often betray a serious reticence to combine these registers. I will comment on preliminary efforts in this direction in the final section of this paper.

3   Although I did my Ph.D. in a department of history, my advisor, Bernard S. Cohn, had originally been trained as an anthropologist and thus exposed his history students both to anthropology and its adherents.

4   I took my inspiration from Bernard Cohn, not only because of his witty and perceptive account of his fieldwork among historians (see Cohn, 1962), but because he questioned the nature and history of the colonial archive in terms of what he called a "colonial sociology of knowledge."

5   Archival science has been born out of the generally accepted mandate that the modern archive maintain records that satisfy two conditions, first that they were records of state administration, and second that they can be demonstrated to serve historical and administrative purposes distinct from the original one. See Jenkinson (1984).

6   As a result of the Public Records Act of 1838.

References

Cohn, Bernard. 1962. "An Anthropologist among the Historians: a Field Study." *The South Atlantic Quarterly* 61, no. 1 (winter).

Dirks, Nicholas B. 1990. "History as a sign of the Modern." *Public Culture* 2, no. 2.

—. 1993a. "Colonial Histories and Native Informants: Biography of an Archive." In *Orientalism and the Postcolonial Predicament*, edited by P. van der Veer and C. Breckenridge. Philadelphia: University of Pennsylvania Press.

—. 1993b. *The Hollow Crown: Ethnohistory of an Indian Kingdom*. Ann Arbor: University of Michigan Press.

—. 1997. "The Policing of Tradition: Colonialism and Anthropology in India." *Comparative Studies in Society and History* (January).

—. 1999. "The Crimes of Colonialism: Anthropology and the Textualization of India." In *Colonial Subjects: Essays on the Practical History of Anthropology*, edited by Peter Pels and Oscar Salemink. Ann Arbor: University of Michigan Press.

—. 2001. *Castes of Mind: Colonialism and the Making of Modern India*. Princeton: Princeton University Press.

Grafton, Anthony. 1997. *The Footnote: A Curious History*. Cambridge: Harvard University Press.

Guha, Ranajit. 1997. *Dominance without Hegemony: History and Power in Colonial India*. Cambridge: Harvard University Press.

Jenkinson, Hilary. 1984. "Reflections of an Archivist." In *A Modern Archives Reader: Basic Readings on Archival Theory and Practice*, edited by M. Daniels and Timothy Walch. Washington, D.C.: National Archives and Records Services.

Koselleck, Reinhart. 1985. *Futures Past: On the Semantics of Historical Time*. Cambridge: MIT Press.

Mehta, Uday. 1999. *Liberalism and Empire*. Chicago: University of Chicago Press.

Milligan, Jennifer E. n.d. "The Problem of the Public in the Archives of the Second Empire." Unpublished paper.

Panitch, Judith. 1996. "Liberty, Equality, Posterity? Some Archival Lessons from the Case of the French Revolution." *American Archivist* 59, no. 1.

Posner, Ernst. 1984. "Some Aspects of Archival Development Since the French Revolution." In *A Modern Archives Reader: Basic Readings on Archival Theory and Practice,* edited by M. Daniels and Timothy Walch. Washington, D.C.: National Archives and Records Services.

Risley, H. H. 1915. *The People of India.* Edited by W. Crooke. London: W. Thacker and Co.

Sagnac, Philippe. [1898] 1973. *La Legislation civile de la Revolution francaise (1789–1804).* New York: AMS Press.

Schellenberg, T. 1964. *Modern Archives: Principles and Techniques.* Chicago: University of Chicago Press.

Wilson, H. H. 1828. *Catalogue of the Mackenzie Collection.* Madras.

Ethnographic Representation, Statistics, and Modern Power

Talal Asad

I

Much has been written recently on how the anthropologist's experience in the field comes to be inscribed as authoritative ethnography. Although, in this effort, the rhetorical structures of ethnographic representation have been usefully explored, my main interest here is different. I ask how the problem of representation is addressed when the mode of inquiry is fieldwork, how this compares with representation in social statistics, and what the political implications of this contrast might be. My answers to the questions are inevitably sketchy as they offer preliminary attempts to explore the idea of Western hegemony from an anthropological standpoint. I am not concerned about the merits and demerits of qualitative versus quantitative methods in reaching the truth about social reality. In fact, I want to examine the role statistical representation has played in creating the world of modern power that anthropologists inhabit.

The juxtaposition of ethnography and statistics engenders rich contrasts: First, unlike the real cultural wholes of ethnography, the statistical universe, as well as the categories out of which that universe is created, are the products not of experience but of enumerative practices. Second, statistical universes can be expanded or contracted, segmented or merged, depending entirely on pragmatic rather than veridical considerations. Third, sampling techniques in statistical practice allow one to move from representing social types (which is a characteristic of ethnographic representation) toward representing the variational patterns of a population.

In making these contrasts I do not want to be understood as saying that anthropologists never employ statistics. They do, and many anthropologists have long advocated that they should do so more systematically. Statistical inference in the service of evolutionary theory, as exemplified in the attempts by Tylor (1889) and Murdock (1949), may have virtually disappeared in social and cultural anthropology, but social surveys and other forms of quantification have not. Nearly sixty years ago Malinowski regretted that he had not collected quantitative data more systematically: "Were I able to embark once more on field-work I would certainly take much greater care to measure, weigh and count everything that can be legitimately measured, weighed and counted" (1935, 159). And many anthropologists since then have proposed that statistics are indispensable in determining social norms. Clyde Mitchell, for example, suggested that statistical methods should be seen as a complement to qualitative information collected on the basis of field experience: "Quantitative methods are essentially aids to description. They help to bring out in detail the regularities in the data the field-worker has collected. Means, ratios, and percentages are ways of summarizing the features and relationships in data. Statistical measures based on the theory of probability go beyond the mere quantitative data and use devices to bring out the association between the various social facts the observer has collected" (Mitchell 1967, 20; see also Nadel 1951, 114). But in general, statistical reasoning has remained relatively marginal to the discipline.

My purpose here is not to press for a greater use of quantification in anthropology. Still less do I intend to attack the value of interpretive understanding (although I think it is necessary to remind some anthropologists that such understanding is not necessarily linked to ethnographic fieldwork). My aim is to explore the idea that ethnographic fieldwork characteristically invokes a conception of knowledge modeled on subjective vision but statistics does not. (I use the term "statistics"—following historians of the subject—to refer both to social surveys and to probability theory because the two are connected.)[1] I argue that statistical concepts and practices are essential to the systematic manipulation of complex social formations and time series.

II

Fieldwork has not always been a central concern of anthropologists. In the nineteenth century anthropologists addressed themselves to the history of institutions and ideas without themselves ever doing ethnographic fieldwork. Even in the twentieth century some anthropologists have attempted to compare structures of behavior or systems of belief, but usually only after having established their credentials by doing original ethnographic fieldwork.

The definition of anthropology in terms of ethnographic fieldwork has had two interesting consequences which have often been noted: (1) a heavy emphasis on the present but also on the past as a symbolic construction in the present; and (2) a preoccupation with local conditions as an experiential whole. In considering what is relevant, the field-worker is encouraged not only to direct her attention at small-scale events and structures, but also to identify events that are typical within the field under investigation. This last point is especially important.

Personal field research—in which the anthropologist observes and participates in the activities of the people being studied—was originally justified as the basic method in ethnography on the grounds that the societies anthropologists studied were "simple" and "small."[2] But it was as a consequence of fieldwork that the anthropologist's object of study was limited in particular ways. In other words, many spatio-temporal complexities and variations were excluded from the object of study because they were not directly observable in the field. For example, the systematic force of European economic, military, and ideological powers in non-European regions was and still is often conceptualized as being external to locally observable behavior and discourse, or as being an abstract system having little to do with the belief and conduct of people "on the ground."[3]

Anthropological investigation into the contrasts between historically diverse institutional practices and modes of reasoning also tends to get marginalized. In the late fifties, Franz Steiner complained that comparative work in social anthropology had all but disappeared owing partly to the emphasis on intensive fieldwork—given the time and energy that it demanded—and partly to the functionalist doctrine of social integration, which discouraged the separation of beliefs and practices from their full context (Steiner 1958).[4] Since Steiner spoke, the great wave of Lèvi-Straussian structuralism has come and gone, and one consequence is that comparative work is not quite as exceptional as it once was. And partly due to the growth of Marxist anthropology, studies based on historical texts have become more common.[5]

Anthropological research, novices are told, is based on fieldwork, which means that ethnographers must live with the people being studied. Of course, while they are in the field ethnographers observe, ask questions, conduct surveys, and read local documents. It would be a mistake to suppose that anthropologists depend on a single method. However, the primary foundation of anthropological research as a distinctive form of inquiry is *a particular kind of experience*. In the words of G. Condominas, "The most important moment of our professional life remains fieldwork: at the same time our laboratory and our *rite de passage,* the field transforms each of us into true anthropologists. Of course, before undertaking one's fieldwork, one needs a solid intellectual background, but intelligence and training alone are insufficient. A minimum of human warmth and a certain openness are necessary in order to establish contact with others, and to maintain it" (1973, 2).

E. Evans-Pritchard put the matter of ethnographic experience thus: "What comes out of a study of a primitive people derives not merely from intellectual impressions of native life but from its impact on the entire personality, on the observer as a total human being. . . . The work of the anthropologist is not photographic. He has to decide what is significant in what he observes and by his subsequent relation of his experiences to bring what is significant into relief" (1951, 82).

How did experience come to be so central to the definition of anthropology as an academic discipline?

In 1951, Evans-Pritchard recounted a neat little story which is probably still accepted in its essentials by most anthropologists today. I reproduce it here not to invoke its authority for real history but to examine its reasoning. "Between the heyday of the moral philosophers and the earliest anthropological writings in the strict sense, between, that is, the middle of the eighteenth century and the middle of the nineteenth century," writes Evans-Pritchard, "knowledge of primitive peoples and of the peoples of the Far East was generally increased. European colonization of America had been widely expanded, British rule had been established in India, and Australia, New Zealand, and South Africa had been settled by European emigrants. The character of ethnographic description of the peoples of these regions began to change from travelers' tales to detailed studies by missionaries and administrators who not only had better opportunities to observe, but were also men of greater culture than the gentlemen of fortune of earlier times" (1951, 67).[6]

The accumulation of this ethnographic information based on extended stays by sophisticated missionaries and colonial administrators allowed for speculation and new hypotheses by men, such as Morgan, McLennan, and Tylor, who devoted themselves to the study of "primitive societies." About this move, Evans-Pritchard tells us that "it became apparent that if the study of social anthropology was to advance, anthropologists would have to make their own observations" (71). How did this become apparent?

In the nineteenth century, Evans-Pritchard notes, anthropologists were generally lawyers, biblical scholars, or classicists, and consequently they were accustomed to dealing with texts that had been composed by someone else. But the next generation was recruited largely from the natural sciences. Thus Boas was a physicist and geographer, Haddon a marine zoologist, Rivers a physiologist, Seligman a pathologist, Elliot Smith an anatomist, Balfour a zoologist, Malinowski a physicist, and Radcliffe-Brown an experimental psychologist. "These men," Evans-Pritchard explains, "had been taught that in science one tests hypotheses by one's own observations. One does not rely on laymen to do it for one" (72). The significance of experience, at this point in the story, lies in its being close to the idea of laboratory experimentation.[7] That is to say, the experience that is invoked here is conceptual (involving classifications, hypotheses, explanations) and active (involving the systematic manipulation of data and manufacture of events). It has nothing to do with empathy.

So it was—the story goes—that anthropological fieldwork came into being, and anthropological analysis and explanation were thus provided with a sounder basis than they could have had in the nineteenth century. However, we are given to understand that although the scientific attitude to research was introduced into anthropology by trained natural scientists, its full benefits were not obtained until much later because most of the early scientific field-workers were largely ignorant of the languages of the peoples they studied and did not stay long enough among them. This deficiency, Evans-Pritchard relates, was eventually put right by the pioneers of anthropological fieldwork, Boas and Malinowski.

"We have now," concludes Evans-Pritchard, "reached the final, and natural, stage of development, in which observations and the evaluation of them are made by the same person and the scholar is brought into direct contact with the subject of his study. Formerly the anthropologist, like the historian, regarded documents as the raw material of his study. *Now the raw material was social life itself*" (74; emphasis mine). Evans-Pritchard stresses that this raw material can be collected only through an appropriate command of the relevant language and long periods of stay in the society studied, so that the ethnographer "lives, thinks, and feels in their culture" (79). Here the anthropologist's experience has become something she undergoes; it is by exposing herself to it that the ethnographer can spontaneously reproduce the thoughts and feelings of her subjects, understanding and interpreting things as they do.

According to this conception of fieldwork, direct access to "social life itself" does not preclude interpretation and analysis—hence the phrase "raw material." But it does presuppose the representation of social life as a real, experiential whole, which is one reason why anthropologists even today accept that fieldwork calls for extended periods of residence and sound knowledge of the language. "It is impossible," says Evans-Pritchard, "to understand clearly and comprehensively any part of a people's social life except in the full context of their social life as a whole" (80). In other words, social life as a whole is not only real and representable, it is representable *because* it is accessible as a totality to the ethnographer's living experience, to the ethnographer as knowing subject.

Evans-Pritchard's notion of social life itself as raw material is an interesting fusion of two quite different metaphors. On the one hand it suggests that the anthropologist's account is taken from the experience of social life; so the emphasis is on the contrast between experience and its representation. On the other hand it refers to the process by which experience is transformed from one form (raw data) into another (finished text). Here experience is thought of as being capable of modification and directly open to public inspection.[8] It is the former, however, that seems to give the dominant sense to the idea of fieldwork. In this sense "social life itself" is experienced and represented through the device of *typification*. The "typical" is what the investigator comes to recognize in the field and writes about in the ethnography. But to the extent that her personal experience is offered as the foundation for that knowledge, others with a different experience may reasonably receive it with skepticism. This fact becomes especially critical when, as in our day, ethnography is consciously planted in the domain of identity politics. It is then that the experiential basis of ethnographic representation is directly challenged—not by analyzing the latter, but by confronting one experience with another.

In her essay on anthropological fieldwork published in 1939, Audrey Richards explained and justified ethnographic method in what had become a standard formula: "The student of primitive societies enjoys certain advantages in observation. The communities he observes are for the most part so small that they can be investigated as functioning wholes, and not merely as subdivisions of a larger society. He is therefore able to collect data to show the working of all the fundamental institutions of a particular tribe, and is not limited, as in the case of a complex civilization, to a study of one particular aspect, such as the economic or the educational" (1939, 293). The object of study as a functioning whole is thus defined in terms of the activities and relationships that are seen and heard by the anthropologist in the field. More precisely, that object is constituted by what the anthropologist's personal experience yields. But equally important, the ethnographer of a small community (or locality) generalizes on the basis of case studies in which she has learnt to identify social types. When she writes up her ethnography, these social types often appear as representative samples of the community.

Richards's earlier article on the village census dealt with the use of case histories for comparing social types classified according to generation and area.

In it she explained that the information she had collected about a large number of individuals could be tabulated to yield systematic information about historical change and local differences. "It will be clear," Richards declared, "that any set of village case-histories can be used in two ways—to give information about individual types, if the entries are read horizontally; and to throw light on the structure of the group by comparing the entries in any one column vertically. For instance, the marriage and divorce rates of one village could be compared with those of another in a different part of the area, or the customs of two different generations in a village could be compared by examining the histories of the old men with those of the middle-aged men and boys" (1935, 28). Richards thus advocates that anthropologists carry out social surveys of the locality being studied, but the purpose of the survey seems to be to construct social types.

Although Richards's method of deploying case histories may not be very common among ethnographers today, the recording of case studies is still regarded as central to anthropological fieldwork. In his introduction to *The Interpretation of Cultures* (1973), Geertz explains the value of case studies for ethnography as follows:

> The essential task of theory building . . . is not to codify abstract regularities but to make thick description possible, not to generalize across cases but to generalize within them.
>
> To generalize within cases is usually called, at least in medicine and depth psychology, clinical inference. . . . In the study of culture the signifiers are not symptoms or clusters of symptoms, but symbolic acts or clusters of symbolic acts, and the aim is not therapy but the analysis of social discourse. But the way in which theory is used—to ferret out the unapparent import of things—is the same. (26)

The drawing of parallels between ethnography and psychoanalysis is a favorite theme among anthropologists.[9] Whatever we may think of Geertz's resort to that parallel here, there is, it will be noted, an implicit acknowledgment that "generalization within cases" depends on and helps to construct social types—medical, psychiatric, or ethnographic. The recording of case histories can merge into the reportage of life histories. But whether it is constructed through case history or through life history, the type stands for a universe of the same.

In ethnographic sociology—as distinct from social anthropology—there is a tendency to construct representative types directly in the form of individualized characters, thus self-consciously writing ethnography as a form of literature. "The 'heroes' of life-histories and ethnographic monographs," P. Atkinson claims of this genre,

> provide the reader with two parallel sets of potentially satisfying experiences. On the one hand they furnish the sense of intimate acquaintance with characters that most readers themselves would not encounter at first hand in their everyday lives. On the other hand, these characters illuminate a range of settings in which, again, the respectable reader may have no direct involvement. The individual character may thus embody opportunities for social exploration and discovery . . . [as in] Matza's deviant, Paul Cressey's taxi-dancer, Donald Cressey's embezzler, Sutherland's professional thief, Marvin Scott's jockey and Becker's marihuana user are assembled and then set free to bring back intelligence about the nature of social life. . . . The detailed portrayal of individuals—usually through a mixture of their own words and the observations of the ethnographer—thus helps to establish the warrant for credibility and authority in the text. (1999, 133)

According to Atkinson, character is richer, more "real" than type; its depiction in ethnography is not only based on direct experience but can recreate that experience for the reader.

Etymologically, *character*—like *type*—is an inscription (in Arabic characters, in boldfaced type) which is made to be read. As such, character and type are visible differences that are infinitely reproducible and also part of a set by means of which a continuous reading and writing is made possible. A creative selection of readable signs, in which a continuous exchange takes place between reading and being read, character is often taken to represent both itself and the essence expressed by it. It is at once Atkinson's "sense of intimate [personal] acquaintance" and the "range of [social] settings" illuminated by that acquaintance; both Geertz's visible "symbolic acts" and their "unapparent import." For Geertz, in particular, character embraces the individual human being and the individualized collectivity to which he belongs: "It is perhaps as true for civilizations as it is for men that however much they may later change, the fundamental diversions of their character, the structure of possibilities within which they will in some sense always move, are set in the plastic period when they first are forming" (1986, 11).[10] Of course, this concept of character (or type) is necessary to an understanding of social life. But it becomes problematic when it is regarded as expressing an irreducible essence that is apprehended by the ethnographer's experience.

In the empiricist tradition, the ethnographer may encounter characters in the field but she typifies them by way of a system in her ethnography. They become brother and sister, husband and wife, affines, clan members, etc., with specifiable rights and obligations. I quote from Richards yet again: "The individual characters, all with their temperamental and physical peculiarities and the dramatic incidents of everyday life, seem to stand out in bold relief, while the formal patterns of kinship, which we have just described, fade from view. We are watching a number of people who like or hate to share their food, or to prepare it in common, and not plotting a system of relationships on a kinship chart. But this is, of course, how the scene appears in the context of everyday life" (1939, 160). Here typification consists not in an inevitable simplification of experiential complexity but in the imposition by the anthropologist of an idealized cultural system on remembered and recorded data.

It should be stressed that in social anthropology the emphasis on observation in the field did not necessarily commit the ethnographer to a naive empiricism. Certainly, despite Radcliffe-Brown's methodological pronouncements, many of his followers insisted that the local social structures which they attempted to study and describe were not accessible to direct observation. As M. Fortes put it in an essay published in 1949, "Structure is not immediately visible in 'concrete reality.' . . . When we describe structure we are already dealing with general principles far removed from the complicated skein of behavior, feelings, beliefs, &c., that constitute the tissue of *actual social life*. We are, as it were, in the realm of grammar and syntax, not of the spoken word" (1949, 56; emphasis mine). According to Fortes, the ethnographer's consciousness of "actual social life" needs to be distanced, sifted, and analyzed, a process that reveals local appearances to be the varying expressions of an enduring essence. He therefore regarded the problem of ethnographic representation as the explanation of types (or recurring social events) in terms of the statistical variants of a single underlying form—the cultural whole.[11] Five years after Fortes's essay, Leach developed a more complex version of this argument in non-quantitative terms.[12] Yet in spite of their sophisticated approach to ethnographic representation, anthropologists like Fortes and Leach retain the empiricist distinction between observation and theorization as two linked but separate moments in the ethnographic enterprise. There is supposed to be actual social life one observes in the field, and then there is theory one is expected to apply when one returns home with the data. And yet, if pressed, such anthropologists would concede that observation is informed by theoretical concepts (of which typification is one) and that theorization is scarcely more than the organization of observational and textual data in ethnographic form.

There is an awareness of this complexity in a recent collection of essays by John and Jean Comaroff. Although they begin by reaffirming the centrality of the observer's eye in the ethnographic enterprise, they go on immediately to register the urgent "need of a methodological apparatus to extend its range" (1992, x). The extension they advocate is clearly metaphoric: "Indeed, we would argue that no humanist account of the past or present can (or does) go very far without the kind of understanding that the ethnographic gaze presupposes. To the extent that historiography is concerned with the recovery of meaningful worlds, with the interplay of the collective and the subjective, it cannot but rely on the tools of the ethnographer" (xi). In this conception, it is not the observer's eye that is actually extended in range (as in observing with interference microscopes and radar telescopes [Hacking 1983]), but something within the subject—"the mind's eye"—that simulates its function. "The eye," now transposed onto an imaginary plane, is able to inhabit freely the categories of time and space, like any good story teller and listener. In other words, the "ethnographic gaze" is taken to be the source of a knowledge because it is rooted in the researcher's ability to observe human subjects, then to imagine a meaningful world around what is witnessed, and finally to present a verbal image[13] corresponding to that partly-imagined, partly-witnessed world. Existing texts are admitted to be important for the ethnographic researcher, but they play a supplementary part. It is the directly visible and locatable field that remains the privileged foundation. But the precise connection of that empiricist foundation to the extended world of the ethnographer's imagination is obscure in the Comaroffs' presentation—obscure because the historian, who can have no such privileged foundation, is also said to depend on the ethnographic gaze. Yet the historian's field is not, like the ethnographer's, a visible ground on which people live, but a conceptual space within which she interacts with texts. This obscurity may be resolved if by the ethnographic gaze we take the Comaroffs to mean the construction of a discursive universe inhabited by human types who are capable of being understood because, like them, they are human.

So the ethnographer's attempt to represent a real cultural universe is, in the final analysis, rooted in the experience of fieldwork and mediated by an imaginative act by which the ethnographer can occupy the consciousness of his ethnographic subjects. The ethnographer knows what she has experienced once she has learnt to interpret a culture from within; her task is to communicate that knowledge in textual form.[14] She may concede that her success has been only partial, because the qualitative character of her personal experience is difficult to translate into language. Yet that concession does not disprivilege her experience. Thus the gap between experience and representation parallels the notorious gap between incommensurable cultures. As such, that double gap has political implications which I will take up by contrasting statistical representation and ethnographic representation.

III

In the interviews with Raymond Williams published under the title *Politics and Letters* (1982), there is an arresting passage in which Williams attempts to reformulate his views on the question of experience. The interviewer urges him to reflect on the limited character of experience as a foundation of social knowledge. Williams agrees and responds as follows:

> It is very striking that the classic technique devised in response to the impossibility of understanding contemporary society from experience, the statistical mode of analysis, had its precise origins within the [1840s]. For without the combination of statistical theory, which in a sense was already mathematically present, and arrangements for collection of statistical data, symbolized by the foundation of the Manchester Statistical Society, the society that was emerging out of the industrial revolution was literally unknowable. . . . After the industrial revolution the possibility of understanding an experience in terms of the available articulation of concepts and language was qualitatively altered. There were many responses to that. New forms had to be devised to penetrate what was rightly perceived to be to a large extent obscure. Dickens is a wonderful example of this, because he is continually trying to find fictional forms for seeing what is not seeable. . . .
>
> From the industrial revolution onwards, qualitatively altering a permanent problem, there has developed a type of society which is less and less interpretable from experience—meaning by experience, a lived contact with the available articulations, including their comparison. The result is that we have become increasingly conscious of the positive power of [statistical] techniques of analysis, which at their maximum are capable of interpreting, let us say, the movements of an integrated world economy, and of the negative qualities of a naive observation which can never gain knowledge of realities like these. (170–1)

Williams's remarks in this passage parallel the distinction I indicated at the beginning of this essay when I referred to ethnographic and statistical modes of representation. His primary concern is to defend experience as a legitimate basis of knowledge against Althusserians who had sought to dismiss it. For Williams as a democratic socialist, the experience of living in a particular society is a necessary basis for responsible politics. But it is only one basis, because an understanding of historical structures and movements that are inaccessible to experience is also essential to an informed politics. It is this political commitment that sets Williams's interest in experience apart from the ethnographer's dedication to fieldwork experience as a source of disinterested knowledge—and also (more latterly) from experimental ethnographers in the service of identity politics.

However, in *Keywords,* an earlier work, Williams had made a summary distinction which seems partly to overlap the contrast he notes in the passage I have quoted between "experience past" (in the sense of lessons learnt) and "experience present" (meaning a full and active awareness). Although it is apparently more carefully constructed, this distinction is conceptually and politically less clear than the one employed casually in the interview. Less clear because the two kinds of experience are conceptualized at one and the same time partly as types of authorized knowledge-material (personal/unsystematic or impersonal/systematic), partly as knowledge-purviews (more inclusive or less so), and partly as knowledge-stances (reflective or unreflective). The distinction in Williams's *Keywords* is also politically more troubling than the formulation in *Politics and Letters* because of its conclusion: "In the deepest sense of experience all kinds of evidence and its consideration should be tried" (1983, 170). This recommendation might be open to the charge that it is either vacuous (of course one should search for all evidence relevant to the problem in hand) or a recipe for chaos (the obligation to try everything makes a sustained and responsible politics highly problematic). However, one could defend Williams by reformulating this sense of experience as a continuously self-correcting process, guided by specific standards, through which a particular practical learning takes place. In such a process there is no epistemological foundation—neither subjective experience nor objective social life itself.[15] Both ethnographic and statistical representations are part of the material for learning and teaching certain kinds of practice—including the practices of a nonfoundational anthropology, which are not to be confused with active politics.

But there is something else that must be said about Williams's comments. When Evans-Pritchard gave his account of the fieldwork revolution in anthropology, he spoke approvingly of the shift from reliance on reading reports (compiled by others with experience of the object of study) to reliance on personal experience of "social life itself." This view of experience makes two assumptions, both questionable: first, that publicly accessible writing does not connect directly with social life but that the memory of personal encounters does do so; and second, that inscription is always a representation (either true or false) of social life, but it can never constitute social life itself. Williams would almost certainly have disputed both these assumptions. It is therefore all the more surprising that he fails to make the point that since the nineteenth century, statistics has been not just a mode of representing a new kind of social life but also of constructing it.

In the newly constructed formations of the nineteenth century, administrative techniques had to be devised that would deal effectively with highly differentiated and continuously changing classes of population. The way in which such populations constituted a social problem (poverty, disease, education, racial imbalance, etc.) was identified, represented, and addressed in statistical terms.[16] Statistics was ideally suited to modern administration. More precisely, social surveys and probability theory have together become integral to modern life, and increasingly integral to life in societies that are becoming modernized. I will further explore the significance of statistics for modernization in the non-European world after a brief discussion of how the problem of representation was dealt with in the development of statistical thinking from roughly the last two decades of the nineteenth century through the first four of the twentieth.[17]

IV

The problem of representation in the history of statistical theory concerned the question of how one could grasp a complex and changing *whole* from knowledge of a *part,* and the answer to that question evolved out of changing political and conceptual practices in the nineteenth and twentieth centuries.

There were, in effect, two methods of generalization depending on whether the part was selected purposively or randomly. The first, associated successively with Le Play and his followers (1830–1900) and with Halbwachs (1900–1940), is similar to the kind of generalization that ethnographers offer on the basis of fieldwork experience. What is common to all these inquiries, otherwise so different, is that informants were deliberately chosen from among people known to the investigator, informants who were considered to be in a crucial sense at once trustworthy and representative. This required the classification of actors as typical on the basis of intuition and experience. Although ideas of probability were not entirely absent in the typification approach, they depended on the concept of the average, a concept that subsumed dispersion and variability in the typical figure who stood for the social whole.

These earlier studies were directed at particular sections of society who were the objects of reforming zeal: the working classes and the out-of-work in particular cities or trades—factory-hands, prostitutes, immigrants—that is to say, all those whose conditions of life were the source of moral and material danger to themselves and to others.

It was generally recognized that older stabilities were being radically undermined by political and economic developments, and that this was leading to serious social problems. But in order to understand and defend these older arrangements, so Le Play and his school argued, investigators would need to spend extended periods of time with their objects of study. For only through such intimate contact could the investigator hope to observe and understand social activities. Desrosieres notes: "That this observation should take account of the entire significance of actions which the investigator could not isolate and code in a priori terms, is found in other modes of knowledge-creation which developed subsequently, and which embody other ways of generalizing than that of representative sample: ethnological descriptions of non-Western societies based upon long and patient periods of fieldwork in the community by the investigator, psychoanalysis building a model of the structure of the unconscious on the basis of completely individual data, gathered in course of personal exchanges of very long duration" (1999, 223). Thus already in the nineteenth century we have in Le Play an emphasis on the importance not of the social survey but of participant observation as a precondition for representing significant social types. Trained as a minerologist before he became a social researcher and reformer, he conceived of the study of society as a kind of minerology, a science which depended on the collection and arrangement of specimens that represented a total system of classification.[18]

Although Halbwachs's study of working-class budgets is explicitly concerned with variations (indeed he is critical of Le Play for not taking these into account), the variations are, nevertheless, attributed to macrosocial causes, like those identified by Durkheim in *Suicide,* and thus subordinated to unvarying essences. I quote again from Desrosieres:

> The objective of [Halbwachs' study], however, is quite as much to identify the traits of a common "working class consciousness," whose relatively homogeneous character stems not from a divine essence as with Quetelet (Halbwachs was a materialist) but from common material conditions of existence, which a quasi-Darwinian adaptation leads to similar requirements both in practical life and in consciousness. It was because he was interested in this working-class consciousness that the problems of sampling did not present themselves in at all the same terms which they would do for those who, half a century later, would use such studies to promote national accounts. (1991, 226)

Incidentally, Kruskal and Mosteller point out that Lenin was already aware of the different implications of statistical representation in 1899. Thus in chapter 2 of *The Development of Capitalism in Russia* he criticized statisticians of the rural administrative districts for relying on averages in their representation of the agricultural population instead of analyzing the variability of economic circumstances that was so basic to the Marxist understanding of peasant class relations (Kruskal and Mosteller 1980, 174 n.4). But then Lenin's primary problem in that book was not the same as Halbwachs's. Lenin's concern with measuring the distribution of discontinuous variables issued from the Marxist concept of class as a contradictory, historical phenomenon.

It was ironically not the work of socialists like Maurice Halbwachs, who supported working-class movements, but the preoccupations of eugenicists like Francis Galton who advocated "race improvement" that enabled modern statistical theory to make a breakthrough.[19] This involved more than a mere awareness that averages could be misleading. Desrosieres describes this advance as follows: "By bringing attention to focus upon the variability of individual cases, with the notions of variance, of correlation and of regression, the English eugenists moved statistics from the ground of the study of wholes summarised by a single average (holism) to analysis of the distribution of individual values to be compared" (1991, 235).

The final phase in this development turned on a debate about the link between "random selection" and "what is known already." At first, even statisticians received the notion of the "representative sample" with skepticism, insisting that no sample could replace a complete survey. As one of them put it at the turn of the century, "No calculations when observations can be made" (Kruskal and Mosteller 1980, 175). But eventually this skepticism was overcome when the imprecise notion of "representative sample" gave place to the technique of stratified sampling according to a priori divisions of the (national) population. This did not happen until the idea of the representative sample having to be a microcosm of the total, national territory was abandoned.[20] The eventual realization, given developments in probability theory, that sampling by random selection was more reliable led to a conceptual break with territoriality. This did not mean, of course, that prior knowledge of a field of inquiry, a global knowledge of a situation or group, would be irrelevant to the statistician. It meant only that the solution to the problem of representativeness did not depend on complete and certain knowledge of the entire geographical area under investigation. It was precisely such uncertainty that probability theory was designed to deal with.

The modern concept of representativeness emerged in close connection with the construction of the welfare state (a process that began at the end of the nineteenth century) and the centralization of national statistics. Three developments occurring within and outside the domain of state practices were especially important in the history of statistical representations: social security legislation, markets for consumer goods, and market research and national election polls. All of them have produced social knowledge that is continuously and profoundly interventionist. They constitute social wholes that don't depend logically either on the intimate experience of a given region or on the assumption of typical social actors. They encourage and respond to individualized agents making individual choices in a variety of social situations. Ways of statistical calculation, representation, and intervention have become so pervasive that capitalist social economies and liberal democratic politics are inconceivable without them.

In a memorable passage in his history of probability, I. Hacking writes:

> Probability and statistics crowd in upon us. The statistics of our pleasures and our vices are relentlessly tabulated. Sports, sex, drink, drugs, travel, sleep, friends—nothing escapes. There are more explicit statements of probabilities presented on American prime time television than explicit acts of violence (I'm counting the ads). Our public fears are endlessly debated in terms of probabilities: chances of meltdowns, cancers, muggings, earthquakes, nuclear winters, AIDS, global greenhouses, what next? There is nothing to fear (it may seem) but the probabilities themselves. This obsession with the chances of danger, and with treatments for changing the odds, descends directly from the forgotten annals of nineteenth-century information and control. (1990, 4–5)

Statistical knowledge and statistical reasoning, Hacking reminds us, have become central to the way we conceptualize and respond to our modern hopes and fears. But they are central, also, to the grounds we now adduce for regarding some beliefs as more reasonable than others in a social world of uncertainty—grounds we inherit from classical probability theory's alliance with the Enlightenment.[21]

V

What is the relevance of what I have said so far for anthropology? I want to suggest, tentatively, that it is this: a mode of knowledge that grew out of counting large numbers of human beings living in variable conditions—bodies of knowledge that were continuously directed through economic and political practices at those variations—had to be marginal in a discipline that regarded itself primarily as interpretative rather than practical, that defined its object of investigation in terms of human subjects accessible to the fieldworker's personal experience, and that sought to represent what is locally typical.

There is now increasing awareness among many anthropologists of the limitations of fieldwork, of the need to pay greater attention to heterogeneities within wider spaces and over longer periods of time than personal observation allows. In a brief section entitled "Limitations of the Fieldwork Perspective" at the conclusion of his textbook on cultural anthropology, Roger Keesing notes that "The problem of sampling has become much more acute in larger-scale, more complex societies. Cultural diversity, large populations, social stratification, and rapid change have made fieldwork in large-scale modern societies, whether in the Third World or the West, a complicated business in which more concern with sampling, statistics, and methodological precision is needed" (Keesing 1981, 7).[22] This is an acute comment, but as I remarked earlier in my discussion of Raymond Williams, statistics is much more than a matter of representation; it is a tool of political intervention. And as a political tool it is infinitely more powerful than ethnographic representation—for good or for ill.

As a tool of social intervention statistical knowledge has been important not only to European societies. Especially from the latter part of the nineteenth century on, statistics became increasingly important in the European empires in Asia, the Middle East, and Africa. Its importance, however, was not reflected primarily in social anthropology as an academic discipline, but in colonial administration as a political discipline. Of course, academic ethnographers describing social change in particular localities of the non-Western world often employed statistics. But with some minor exceptions, colonial administrations did not depend on them. All administrators had their own resources for carrying out surveys, compiling tabulations, and keeping records. And of course, colonial administrators employed the notion of "native types" in their work. My point is that the practice of assembling and classifying figures periodically on births, deaths, diseases, literacy, crimes, occupations, natural resources, etc., was, from a governmental standpoint, not merely a mode of understanding and representing populations, but an instrument for regulating and transforming them.

This applies also, and even more strongly, to the "modernizing" nation-states that have succeeded European colonies. It is true that the statistics were (and are) often unreliable and based on questionable categories, that administration-inspired transformations were (are) often very uneven, producing unintended results, but that's not the point for the moment.[23] What matters is that the figures, and the categories in terms of which they were (are) collected, manipulated, and presented, belong to projects aimed at determining the values and practices—the souls and bodies—of entire populations. Central to these projects has been the liberal conception of modern society as an aggregate of individual agents choosing freely and yet, in aggregate, predictably (Metz 1987). The construction of modern society in this sense is also, of course, the construction of radically new conditions of experience.

Conventionally, anthropologists have dealt with societies that are not yet liberal in this sense, which makes typification a more plausible device for ethnography. It may be objected that statistical categories also typify, and that is certainly true. But they are more readily challengeable and alterable because they can be subjected to procedures of disaggregation. In that sense they do not depend on the personal experience of a knowing subject. Industrial working norms, to take one example, are based on statistical calculations of a typifying sort, but the norms are open to recalculation and negotiation in the familiar conflict between unions and employers. It is less easy to question the ethnographer's types or characters, partly because they are presented as indissoluble forms (to break up a character is to undermine its human integrity), and partly because they are guaranteed by the ethnographer's personal experience (she witnessed the character, the reader didn't).

Today each of the so called developing countries has its own tabulations, in which its relative successes and failures (from GNP and international debt, to health, family planning, and education, to its record on women's liberation and human rights) are measured, probabilized, and compared with the figures of other countries. Each nation-state compiles, manipulates, and acts upon its statistics and calculates the risks of its policies failing. So too do multinational corporations, the United Nations, and the World Bank. Within each nation-state and between them, almost all statistics are contestable; but in the domain of social power they have become indispensable. Groups opposing the policies of particular business enterprises, or of a local administration, or of a national government, or of international agents, contest the figures and the categories on which the figures are based, but in doing so they employ statistical arguments. In brief: moral and material progress presupposes the continuous use of comparative statistics. Put more strongly, the very concept of such progress is in great measure the product of statistical practices. The politics of progress differs precisely in this from the politics of reform: it is inconceivable without the concepts and practices of statistics. Progress—not mere reform—is the political aspiration that the non-European world has acquired from Europe.[24]

Statistics is a vital part of what I have elsewhere called "strong languages" (Asad 1986), discursive interventions by means of which the modes of life of non-European peoples have come to be radically transformed by Western power. Modern statistics is the strongest language of all. In saying this I do not refer to essentialized or biased Western representations of non-European peoples.[25] These have certainly been produced but this point is not part of my argument here. On the contrary, I argue that through statistics it is Western representations of modern (i.e., Western) society that are offered, adopted, adapted, and employed. What makes statistics a strong language is that statistical figures and statistical reasoning are employed in the attempt to reconstruct the moral and material conditions of target populations. The implications of this for the old problem of cultural relativism are worth noting. Statistics converts the question of incommensurable cultures into one of commensurable social arrangements without rendering them homogeneous; the ranking of every country differs and changes in complex ways even when several variables remain constant; flexible marketing caters to consumers seeking a variety of different (and incompatible) experiences. Note that I do not say statistical *thinking* solves the philosophical problem of incommensurability; I say that statistical *practices* can afford to ignore it. And they can afford to ignore it because they are part of the great process of conversion we know as "modernization."

In wielding social power through statistics, experience is valued not as a moment of awareness but as experimental practice, because it enables one to test the precise degree to which an objective has succeeded.

VI

The political success of statistics in the modern world is a fact of considerable anthropological significance. From this latter standpoint is something to be analyzed and explained as a cultural feature of modern social life. If I suggest that such an analysis be conducted, it doesn't follow that I think ethnographic fieldwork has no merit. Nor do I assume that there is any essential superiority between statistical or ethnographic methods. The only general assumption I make is that the rich historical tradition of anthropology is unduly narrowed if defined in terms of fieldwork.

Notes

1   For example, the compilation of vital statistics in the eighteenth century and "the avalanche of printed numbers" in the nineteenth were both crucial to developments in probability theory in different ways (see Hacking 1987; Datson 1987). In turn,

probabilistic sampling theory has come to be indispensable to social surveys (see section IV below).

2   Much later, anthropologists began to speak of "participant observation," a term that was popularized by American sociologists. In her interesting history of this concept, J. Platt writes:

> In the 1920s and 1930s, some of the key ideas now associated with 'participant observation' were associated with other methods and categories. . . . Although it is obvious that participant observation studies are quite likely to be in the 'case study' tradition in at least some of its senses, 'case study' can certainly not be translated as 'participant observation.' First, it is evidently a category not defined in terms of the manner in which its data are collected; second, insofar as data collection is mentioned, it is written or oral statements, often solicited, that are emphasized. When participation is mentioned, which it seldom is, it is primarily as a means to the elicitation of such statements. . . . Initially, at any rate, the mere idea of recording solicited data in the subject's own words was novel enough to seem a significant step in the direction of natural reality. . . . The idea that the further step of observing the behavior in its normal context should be taken was not raised [by sociologists]. The long march away from the library had only recently started, and perhaps merely living among people was seen as too like journalistic work from which the social scientists were anxious to distinguish themselves. (1983, 381)

For anthropologists, "living among people" could be articulated as a *method*, only when professional social scientists could be distinguished from such non-professionals as missionaries and administrators. According to Platt, E. C. Lindeman invented the term "participant observation," although he meant something very different from its usage today. For Lindeman, the "participant observer" was not the investigator himself but a member of the group being studied whom the investigator recruited as an informant (386).

3   Thus: "It is our capacity, largely developed in fieldwork, to take the perspective of the [small communities we study], that allows us to learn anything at all—even in our own culture—beyond what we already know. . . . Further, it is our location 'on the ground' that puts us in a position to see people not simply as passive reactors to and enactors of some 'system,' but as active agents in their own history" (Ortner 1984, 143).

4   Steiner was not thinking of statistical comparisons such as the monograph by Murdock.

5   J. Goody's materialist studies—notably *The Development of the Family and Marriage in Europe* (1983)—were influenced by this current although they do not belong to it. Incidentally, the recent inauguration of a periodical entitled *History and Anthropology* is an indication of a growing interest in analyses based on historical sources.

6   Compare Evans-Pritchard's account in *Social Anthropology* (1951) with the fuller scholarly one by J. Urry in *Ethnographic Research: A Guide to General Conduct* (1984).

7   In the section on method in the first chapter of *Argonauts of the Western Pacific* (1922), Malinowski employs the term *experience* in exactly this sense:

No one would dream of making an experimental contribution to physical or chemical science, without giving a detailed account of all the arrangements of the experiments. . . . In less exact sciences, as in biology or geology, this cannot be done as rigorously, but every student will do his best to bring home to the reader all the conditions in which the experiment or the observations were made. In Ethnography, where a candid account of such data is perhaps even more necessary, it has unfortunately in the past not always been supplied with sufficient generosity. . . . It would be easy to quote works of high repute, and with a scientific hallmark on them, in which wholesale generalizations are laid down before us, and we are not informed at all by what actual experiences the writers have reached their conclusion. (2–3)

8 P. Kaberry tells essentially the same story about the emergence of fieldwork, but with a somewhat different focus: "Until the end of the nineteenth century, most anthropologists wrote from the armchair and relied for their raw data on material recorded by missionaries, explorers, travelers, government officials, and settlers." Her attention is directed at the contrast between kinds of people who record the "raw data"— the professional anthropologist on the one hand, and non-professionals on the other— and not at the contrast between kinds of "raw material" (written accounts versus "social life itself"). But she shares with Evans-Pritchard the assumption that ideally the person who reworks the "raw data/material" should be the one who records/collects it (Kaberry 1957, 73).

9 S. F. Nadel drew a parallel between anthropology and psychiatry in the matter of interview techniques:

If it is true that the psychiatrist concentrates almost wholly upon problems concerning the personality of his patient, perhaps for him no interview can ever be a complete "failure": even the most negative reactions of the patient have their diagnostic significance. In social work generally [including social surveys] . . . the failure of an interview may obstruct the main source of information. It might be expected that in anthropology, with its pursuit of "objective facts," the failure of the interview would be equally serious. In fact, the success or failure of an interview, irrespective of the information which it produces or fails to produce, may itself be of diagnostic value to the student of culture. For the "objective reality" with which the anthropologist is dealing is a social reality, and the informant and his responses are themselves elements and factors in this social reality. (1939, 318)

10 The theme of Geertz's book is the way the individual character of a representative person and a representative civilization mirror each other in Islam (typified by Morocco and Indonesia).

11 "We are dealing not with two 'types' or 'forms' of domestic organization," Fortes wrote, "but with variants of a single 'form' arising out of quantitative differences in the relations between the parts that make up the structure. We can imagine a scale varying from perfect 'patrilocality' at one end to perfect 'avunculo-locality' at the other. . . . Individual households are scattered all along the scale; and over a stretch of time a particular household may change its position through the loss of some kinsfolk and the accession of others" (1949, 75). But because this interest in variability deals in averages it remains preoccupied with representing "types" as statistical "norms."

12 In *Political Systems of Highland Burma* (1954), Leach argued that because the Kachin Hills Area was not culturally homogeneous, he couldn't follow the "classical manner in ethnography" of choosing a locality "of any convenient size" for intensive study, and then writing "a book about the organization of the society considered as a whole" on that basis (60). Leach's procedure instead was to describe the Shan and Kachin categories common to the entire area, which help to generate a range of unstable political structures in a variety of ecological contexts and over a cycle of historical time. His overall conclusion was that "while conceptual models of society are necessarily models of equilibrium systems, *real* societies can never be in equilibrium" (4; emphasis mine).

13 In *Iconology* (1986), W. J. T. Mitchell argues persuasively against the belief that there is a radical difference between verbal and visual images. This argument seems to me especially relevant for examining critically the notion of the "ethnographic gaze." Because if "seeing" merges into "reading," the epistemological priority of fieldwork experience over textual engagement can be questioned. The anthropologist who collects his own material in the field has no more grounds for certainty than the anthropologist who reads texts composed by someone else.

14 " 'Writing up' is a transformation of data from the category 'what you know' into a new category: 'what you communicate.' The two are related: at least in an ideal world, what you know sets nearly all the limits of what you can write. And because you create both categories they may be linked also by your intentions from a very early stage" (Davis 1984, 295). The fact that data can be thought of as belonging to the category "what you know," and ceases to belong to that category (which "you create") when it is "written up," makes sense only because what the anthropologist knows is indissolubly linked to ethnographic experience.

15 Incidentally, when J. Scott contends, in her excellent article "The Evidence of Experience" that "the concepts of experience described by Williams [in *Keywords*] preclude inquiry into processes of subject-construction; and they avoid examining the relationships among discourse, cognition, and reality, the relevance of the position or situatedness of subjects to the knowledge they produce, and the effects of difference on knowledge" (1991, 783), she is of course criticizing not Williams but the concepts he has analyzed. The major limitation of Williams's article, in my view, is its almost exclusive concern with cognition. It has nothing to say about experience in the sense of a socially-developed, embodied capability, as in "an experienced mountaineer," "an experienced actor," "an experienced teacher"—in the Maussian sense of *habitus*. For anyone interested in the problem of subject-construction, the development of such capacities should be of major importance. When Scott insists that the denial of the discursive character of experience is merely an attempt to defend an unquestioned authority—"it is precisely the discursive character of experience that is at issue for some historians, because attributing experience to discourse seems somehow to deny its status as an unquestionable ground of explanation" (Scott 1991, 787). I think she moves too quickly in attributing obscurantist intentions to those she criticizes. The primary question I would suggest is whether the concept of discursive experience that is being employed prioritizes cognition at the expense of practice. In themselves, embodied practices are not a ground of explanation at all, they are

simply skills, abilities, virtues (in the Aristotelian sense) that are exercised with greater or lesser facility. It is only when they become objects of discourse that explanation—and criticism—can take place.

16 Even in early modern Europe, "political arithmetic," as it was then called, had a close connection with government, religious sectarianism, and commercial society. See the two articles by P. Buck (1977, 1982).

17 I am indebted in the account that follows to Desrosieres (1991), Hacking (1990), Kruskal and Mosteller (1980), and Lazarsfeld (1961).

18 Thus Le Play states, "In order to find the secrets of the governments which provide mankind with happiness based on peace, I have applied to the observation of human societies *rules analogous* to those which had directed my own mind in the *study of minerals and plants. I construct a scientific mechanism*" (cited in Lazarsfeld 1961, 314).

19 For a detailed discussion of the connection between projects of racial progress and statistical theory, see MacKenzie (1981).

20 But as Kruskal and Mosteller note, "Quota sampling in public opinion polling and marketing went on for years, and still continues, without much interaction with the work of academic or otherwise organized statistics" (1980, 191).

21 In the second half of the seventeenth century, the fledgling calculus of probabilities was first applied to the task of providing a mathematical basis for the rules of evidence then current in Roman and canon law. "In viewing their theory as the 'art of conjecture,'" writes L. Daston, "classical probabilists adopted the legal habit of thinking about probability epistemically, as a continuum of degrees of certainty. They also inherited a set of problems related to legal evidence—in particular, responsibility for establishing rational grounds for belief not only in the courtroom but in the world-at-large" (1987, 296). In the eighteenth century, the subjectivism of this notion of probability joined associationist psychology, and the two together helped to construct the Enlightenment conception of belief that was supported by reason. The classical probabilists held that their mathematical theory was simply "good sense reduced to a calculus," says Daston, but their "good sense" was simply the good sense of an Enlightenment elite. In our day, calculations of probabilities are regarded as crucial for arriving at rational decisions, although probability theory has developed considerably since then.

22 However, this awareness of the limitations of a tradition that represents the part as "a microcosm of the whole" (Keesing 1981, 6), seems to come up against a contrary tendency to regard the contemporary world as relatively homogeneous ("This stereotypic view, largely created by anthropologists, exaggerates the diversity of cultures" [7]). The resolution of this conflict clearly resides in a more precise specification of what is to be regarded as the same and what is to be regarded as different.

23 This has long been recognized. See Daniel and Alice Thorner for an impressive critique of the categories used in government statistics on the agricultural population of India (1962, chapters x–xv). In her splendid essay on a statistical report on urban workers in mid-nineteenth century Paris, Joan W. Scott demonstrates the political assumptions and concerns which motivated its classifications and inferences (1986).

M. J. Cullen argues that from its beginnings in the nineteenth century, quantitative social inquiry was inherently political (1975).

24 Incidentally, Foucault, who wrote insightfully about the modern concept and practice of government (which he called "governmentality") never theorized progress in that context.

25 Essentialized or biased representation in Western discourses of non-Western peoples is part of what critics have called "Orientalism"; "Orientalists" typically construct typifications.

References

Asad, Talal. 1986. "Concept of Cultural Translation in British Social Anthropology." In *Writing Culture: The Poetics and Politics of Ethnography*, edited by J. Clifford and George Marcus. Berkeley: University of California Press.

Atkinson, Paul. 1990. *The Ethnographic Imagination: Textual Constructions of Reality.* New York: Routledge.

Buck, P. 1977. "Seventeenth-Century Political Arithmetic: Civil Strife and Vital Statistics." *Isis* 68, no. 241.

—. 1982. "People Who Counted: Political Arithmetic in the Eighteenth Century." *Isis* 73, no. 266.

Comaroff, John L., and Jean Comaroff. 1992. *Ethnography and the Historical Imagination: Studies in the Ethnographic Imagination.* Boulder: Westview Press.

Condominas, G. 1973. "Ethics and Comfort: An Ethnographer's View of His Profession." *Annual Report, 1972.* Washington, D.C.: American Anthropological Association.

Cullen, M. J. 1975. *The Statistical Movement in Early Victorian Britain: The Foundations of Empirical Social Research.* New York: Barnes & Noble.

Daston, L. J. 1987. "The Domestication of Risk: Mathematical Probability and Insurance 1650–1830." In *The Probabilistic Revolution: Volume 1*, edited by L. Kruger, L. J. Daston and M. Heidelberger. Cambridge, Mass.: MIT Press.

—. 1987. "Rational Individuals Versus Laws of Society: From Probability to Statistics." In *The Probabilistic Revolution: Volume 1*, edited by L. Kruger, L. J. Daston and M. Heidelberger. Cambridge, Mass.: MIT Press.

Davis, John. 1984. "Data into Text." In *Ethnographic Research: A Guide to General Conduct*, edited by R. F. Ellen. London: Academic Press.

Desrosieres, A. 1991. "The Part in Relation to the Whole: How to Generalise? The Prehistory of Representative Sampling." In *The Social Survey in Historical Perspective, 1880–1940*, edited by K. Bales, M. Bulmer, and K. K. Sklar. Cambridge: Cambridge University Press.

Evans-Pritchard, E. E. 1951. *Social Anthropology.* London: Cohen and West.

Fortes, Meyer. 1949. "Time and Social Structure: An Ashanti Case Study." In *Social Structure*, edited by M. Fortes. Oxford: Clarendon Press.

Geertz, Clifford. 1968. *Islam Observed: Religious Development in Morocco and Indonesia.* New Haven, Conn.: Yale University Press.

—. 1973. *The Interpretation of Cultures: Selected Essays.* New York: Basic Books.

Goody, Jack. 1983. *The Development of the Family and Marriage in Europe.* Cambridge: Cambridge University Press.

Hacking, Ian. 1983. *Representing and Intervening: Introductory Topics in the Philosophy of Natural Science.* Cambridge, UK: Cambridge University Press.

—. 1987. "Was There a Probabilistic Revolution 1800–1930?" In *The Probabilistic Revolution: Volume I,* edited by L. Kruger, L. J. Daston and M. Heidelberger. Cambridge, Mass.: MIT Press.

—. 1990. *The Taming of Chance.* Cambridge, UK: Cambridge University Press.

Kaberry, Phyllis Mary. 1957. "Malinowski's Contribution to Field-work Methods and the Writing of Ethnography." In *Man and Culture: An Evaluation of the Work of Bronislaw Malinowski,* edited by R. Firth. London: Routledge & Kegan Paul.

Keesing, Roger M. 1981. *Cultural Anthropology: A Contemporary Perspective.* New York: Holt, Rinehart, and Winston.

Kruskal, W., and F. Mosteller. 1990. "Representative Sampling, IV: The History of the Concept in Statistics, 1895–1939." *International Statistical Review* 48.

Lazarsfeld, P. F. 1961. "Notes on the History of Quantification in Sociology: Trends, Sources and Problems." *Isis* 52, no. 168.

Leach, Edmund Ronald. 1954. *Political Systems of Highland Burma: A Study of Kachin Social Structure.* Cambridge, Mass.: Harvard University Press.

MacKenzie, Donald A. 1981. *Statistics in Britain, 1865–1930: The Social Construction of Scientific Knowledge.* Edinburgh: Edinburgh University Press.

Malinowski, Bronislaw. 1922. *Argonauts of the Western Pacific: An Account of Native Enterprise and Adventure in the Archipelagoes of Melanesian New Guinea.* London: G. Routledge.

—. 1935. *Coral Gardens and their Magic; A Study of the Methods of Tilling the Soil and of Agricultural Rites in the Trobriand Islands.* London: G. Allen & Unwin.

Metz, K. H. 1987. "Paupers and Numbers: the Statistical Argument for Social Reform in Britain During the Period of Industrialization." In *The Probabilistic Revolution: Volume 1,* edited by L. Kruger, L. J. Daston and M. Heidelberger. Cambridge, Mass.: MIT Press.

Mitchell, J. Clyde. 1967. "On Quantification in Social Anthropology." In *The Craft of Social Anthropology,* edited by A. L. Epstein. London: Tavistock.

Mitchell, W. J. Thomas. 1986. *Iconology: Image, Text, Ideology.* Chicago: University of Chicago Press.

Murdock, George Peter. 1949. *Social Structure.* New York: Macmillan.

Nadel, Siegfried Frederick. 1939. "The Interview Technique in Social Anthropology." In *Study of Society,* edited by F. C. Bartlett. London: Routledge & Kegan Paul.

Nadel, S. F. 1951. *The Foundations of Social Anthropology.* London: Cohen & West.

Ortner, Sherry. 1984. "Theory in Anthropology Since the Sixties." *Comparative Studies in Society and History* 26, no. 1: 126–166.

Platt, J. 1983. "The Development of the 'Participant Observation' Method in Sociology: Origin Myth and History." *Journal of the History of the Behavioral Sciences* 19: 381–386.

Richards, A. I. 1935. "The Village Census in the Study of Culture Contact." *Africa* 8: 35–49.

——. 1939. "The Development of Field Work Methods in Social Anthropology." In *The Study of Society: Methods and Problems*, edited by F. C. Bartlett. London: Routledge and Kegan Paul.

Richards, Audrey Isabel, and International African Institute. 1939. *Land, Labour and Diet in Northern Rhodesia: An Economic Study of the Bemba Tribe*. London: Oxford University Press.

Scott, Joan W. 1986. "Statistical Representations of Work: The Politics of the Chamber of Commerce's 'Statistique de l'Industrie a Paris, 1847–48'." In *Work in France: Representations, Meaning, Organization, and Practice*, edited by S. L. Kaplan and C. J. Koepp. Ithaca: Cornell University Press.

——. 1991. "The Evidence of Experience." *Critical Inquiry* 17, no. 4: 783–787.

Steiner, Franz. 1956. *Taboo*. New York: Philosophical Library.

Tylor, Edward Burnett. 1889. "On a Method of Investigating the Development of Institutions; Applied to Laws of Marriage and Descent." *Journal of the Royal Anthropological Institute* 18, no. 3: 145–272.

Urry, J. 1984. "A History of Field Methods." In *Ethnographic Research: A Guide to General Conduct*, edited by R. F. Ellen. London: Academic Press.

Williams, Raymond. 1982. *Politics and Letters*. London: New Left Books.

——. 1983. *Keywords: A Vocabulary of Culture and Society*. New York: Oxford University Press.

2 Colonial Anxieties

New Christians and New World Fears in Seventeenth-Century Peru

Irene Silverblatt

In 1639, Manuel Bautista Perez, along with ten others, was executed by order of the Spanish Inquisition's Lima office for secretly following Jewish beliefs.[1] In prison for over five years, Perez was under considerable pressure to confess to *Judaising:* Had he admitted to being a crypto-Jew and repented, his life probably would have been spared. Yet he refused. As a result of Perez's "obstinacy," so the Inquisitors declared, he was condemned to die.

Spanish colonialism brought the Inquisition to the viceroyalty of Peru in 1569,[2] and from the end of the sixteenth century until Peru declared independence from Spain in 1820, Spanish Inquisitors prosecuted men and women for clandestinely practicing Jewish rites. As Inquisition records from the first half of the seventeenth century and records of the lengthy trial against Manuel Bautista Perez indicate, the idea of the "Jew" grabbed colonial imaginations. "New Christians"[3] provoked terror and embodied social dangers; they were accused of various religious and legal transgressions, including engaging in conspiracies against Christianity and Christians.

The Spanish Inquisition was one structure of many involved in moral regulation. Nevertheless, it was responsible for the empire's rawest displays of cultural force. Through the great theater of power and religious ceremony—the *auto-de-fé*—and through the less visible influences of reputation and fear, the Peruvian Inquisition, like its counterparts throughout imperial Spain, clarified cultural blame for perceived threats to the colony's ethical, spiritual, and civic well-being. These threats included a range of heretical crimes committed by certain members of the colony's non-Indian population,[4] from blasphemy, witchcraft, fornication, and the solicitation of sexual favors by priests during confession, to the capital offense of covertly observing non-Catholic religions like Islam, Lutheranism, and Judaism.

Perhaps the bloodiest episode in Lima's Inquisitorial history was the auto-de-fé of 1639. Out of the seventy-two individuals who were penanced, eleven were accused of capital offenses—all charged with crimes in some way associated with Judaising. Among the condemned were men like Manuel Bautista Perez, rich and powerful merchants who refused to confess to heresies.[5] Inquisitors in Peru were asked by their superiors in Madrid to justify the broad sweep of arrests and the harshness of sentences.[6] They did so by appealing to the dangers crypto-Jews posed, not only to the ethical foundation of the colony, but to its very political security.

Accusations against Judaisers in the New World were similar to the charges levied against Jews and New Christians throughout Europe and the Iberian Peninsula.[7] The "Jewish problem" in seventeenth-century Peru had a centuries-long, continental pedigree, turning Jews into societal threats—the twisted rhetoric of Peru's conspiracy theories—framed a broad climate of suspicion that pervaded much of the Old World and the Spanish realm. Yet, the outrage and fear provoked by Peru's New Christians were also tied to the contradictions of the early modern, Hispanic, colonial world. They were an integral part of the turbulent cultural politics both generated by and shaping Spain's imperial state-making designs.[8]

The legacy of anti-Semitism in early modern Spain was distinguished by the activities of the Holy Office of the Inquisition, an institution that operated under the jurisdiction of the Crown and was the office's only structure of authority that functioned throughout the entire empire.[9] Established in 1483 with the specific charge to protect and defend Christianity, the Inquisition's initial task was to root out hidden Jews. The motivating fear was that Judaisers were making inroads into Spain's growing New Christian community and, through this process, corroding the religious foundation of Catholicism's most militant state.[10]

The impulse to create an institution as dramatic as the Inquisition to regulate religious belief was rooted in Spain's growing climate of hostility toward Jews and New Christians. The mid-fourteenth century was a turning point in both popular and official attitudes, as increasing numbers of Jewish districts suffered violence. By 1391, pogroms in many of the Peninsula's urban centers—Seville, Cordoba, Valencia, Barcelona—resulted in the destruction of Spain's principal Jewish quarters. Hundreds of Jews were murdered, and hundreds more were compelled to accept baptism. The large number of forced conversions marked the birth of a significant New Christian population in Spain; and, from the start, they were looked on with distrust and ambiguity as a "fifth column" inside the Church. Even though they no longer were practicing Jews,

New Christians continued to bear the weight of anti-Semitism—a phenomenon we see functioning vigorously in seventeenth century Peru.[11]

Accusations surrounding the Jewish menace were taken up and challenged in the mid-seventeenth century by Isaac Cardoso, a New Christian who spent most of his life on the Iberian Peninsula.[12] Born in Portugal and a much sought-after physician to Madrid's court society, Cardoso emigrated to Italy where he denounced Christianity, began living as a Jew, and penned an eloquent defense of the "Hebraic truth" in his apologia, *Las excelencias de los Hebreos*. Building his case around the refutation of ten *calumnias* (calumnies) of anti-Semitic belief, Cardoso's work pinpointed common, unfounded stereotypes and will serve as a starting point to examine these hateful ideologies.[13]

One "calumny" with terrible consequences for Jews and New Christians was that "[Jews] desecrate images, and are sacrilegious" (Cardoso, in Yerushalmi 1981).[14] Neither rituals nor sacred objects were safe, or so it was said: Jews on both sides of the Atlantic enthusiastically defiled statues of Jesus, the Virgin, and crucifixes; they also debased the sacraments, particularly Holy Communion, when the Eucharist, the embodiment of Christ, was consecrated (447–51).[15] Cardoso profiled several episodes in which New Christians were wrongly executed for abusing holy objects and described an incident in Lisbon, "when the host was stolen from the church called 'La Engracia.' The crime was attributed to a New Christian named Solis, without any proof, only because he was of the Hebrew Nation." Two years after Solis's execution, the thief was discovered. However, Cardoso goes on to say, "But at the time so great was the emotion and outcry against the Hebrew Nation, that all were in the gravest peril" (454). Such episodes also took place in the seventeenth-century Andes: The most notorious, occurring in Quito, had repercussions for New Christians living hundreds of miles away.[16] Not incidentally, among the many charges levied against Manuel Bautista Perez and other conspirators were that they mocked Christianity, disparaged the miracles of saints, and believed holy icons to be exemplars of Christian idolatry, as they cynically bought magnificent sacred objects to make their devotion visible and prove their faith in Christ.[17]

Cardoso's tenth "calumny against the Hebrew nation" was the claim that Jews coveted Christian blood—the infamous charge of "blood libel" or "ritual murder."[18] Historically, this accusation prompted violent responses often devastating to Jews or, after the Expulsion, to New Christians. Cardoso refuted this slander with the contemporary (1670) tragedy of Raphael Levi. Levi was accused of slaughtering a Christian boy in Metz for blood to enact a Jewish ceremony. Even after evidence was found linking the boy's death to forest animals, Levi was still found guilty and condemned to death by fire (459).[19]

Perhaps the most infamous case of blood libel in Iberia was the alleged ritual murder of "the holy child [*el nino inocente*] of La Guardia" in Toledo. According to legend, a mixed group of Jews and New Christians, needing the requisite blood for a potion to annihilate all Christians, conspired to crucify an infant and remove his heart. Six Jews and six New Christians were convicted of murder, and all were executed in 1491. One year later the Act of Expulsion, forcing Jews to either convert to Christianity or leave Spain, became law. According to popular and official wisdom, the case of the holy child was proof that the presence of Jews imperiled the religious integrity of Spain's New Christians, and justified the banishment of Jews from the realm. It also reinforced the prejudiced belief of many—and another of Isaac Cardoso's calumnias—that Jews actively sought to convert gentiles, an additional weapon in their arsenal to undermine Christianity (360). As we will see, this concern took on added meaning in seventeenth-century Peru when the label *New Christians*, or novices to the faith, could also refer to colonized *indios* and enslaved *negros*.

Rumors that Jews engaged in sacrilegious activities, seen as transparent assaults on Christ and Christianity, went hand in glove with accusations questioning the fealty of Jews to the nation-state, or, in the words of Isaac Cardoso's sixth calumny, "loyalty to the Princes." Jews would always side with Muslims against a common Christian enemy, according to the centuries-old axiom in medieval Spain. In his defense of the "Hebrew Nation," Cardoso took on one of the most popularized examples of Jewish treachery: Jews were said to have opened the gates of Toledo, a Christian city, to the conquering Moors in 714. For support, Cardoso turned to the work of the distinguished Jesuit historian Juan de Mariano, who argued forcefully that Christians, not Jews, were responsible for Toledo's surrender (444–45).[20]

Another stereotype familiar in Spain (and elsewhere) was that Jews used their facility in the world of commerce to the disadvantage and ruin of Christians. Popular hostilities against Jewish communities were often articulated in these terms: Jews—usurers and tax farmers, stealing money and other resources from the faithful—were bleeding Christians dry (Baroja vol. 1: 1986, 73–90). (No matter that only a minority of Spain's Jewish population ever had access to significant wealth [Kamen 1998, 11–14]). After the Expulsion, the taint of finance remained on those who were of Jewish descent. On the Peninsula, it was not uncommon for accused Judaisers to face the additional charge of usury (Kamen 1998, 255). Although this pattern of charges is not found in Peru, Lima's Inquisitors often considered statements about someone's money-making talents to indicate a Judaising bent.[21] Moreover, there was a strong belief that New

Christians used their monopoly over trade to the express detriment of Old Christians.

The threat of a Jewish conspiracy to destroy Christianity and its followers through vigorous attempts at conversion (particularly of vulnerable New Christians), avid expropriation of Christian resources, and treason against Church and state pervaded Spanish culture and stoked anti-Semitic fires.[22] Historians have argued that deeply rooted anti-Semitic beliefs could be called upon during periods of social conflict and political instability.[23] The Jew became a target of blame. This climate gave rise to the Act of Expulsion, the same climate in which the Holy Office of the Inquisition was born and nurtured (Baroja vol. 1: 1986, 125–64; Gitlitz, 1996, 18–27; Kamen 1998, 20–21).

By the end of the sixteenth century, the attributes Castilians attached to the categories of *Jew* and *New Christian* were absorbed by the Portuguese as well. It has been estimated that after the Act of Expulsion, at least fifty thousand Jews—half of all those who left Spain—resettled in neighboring Portugal, swelling the percentage of Jews living there to one-fifth of the country's inhabitants (Gitlitz 1996, 75).[24] In 1497, these emigrants again had to face the order to convert or be expelled. Most converted en masse, giving Portugal a coherent block of New Christians, many of whom retained their belief in Judaism and secretly practiced its rites.[25]

One hundred years later, prompted now by the Portuguese Inquisition's increasingly vicious attacks against Judaisers, waves of New Christians left their homes and emigrated back to Spain. This "return" migration had a significant impact on New Christian-Spanish relations on the continent, as well as in the viceroyalty of Peru. First, a substantial number of these emigrants to Spain—and eventually to the colonies—were involved in global trade, creating a notably Portuguese presence in commerce and finance.[26] Second, the mass exodus to Spain revived the Spanish Tribunal's concerns about a Jewish peril and prompted a renewed wave of inquisitorial activity. Many of those who emigrated to Peru had at least one relative who had been condemned on the Peninsula, and as such expressed their beliefs (and hopes) that the New World tribunals would be ineffective.[27] Finally, the flight to Spain fed a burgeoning Iberian stereotype, found both on the continent and in the New World, that all Portuguese, like all New Christians, were Jews (Gitlitz 1996, 51–53; Kamen 1998, 287–90).

Being known as Portuguese as well as New Christians and Jews, the migrants to the Americas could not escape being judged against the backdrop of Spain's foreign affairs—in particular, Castile's often ambiguous relationship with Portugal and Holland, both on the continent and in South America. Tensions with these two countries coalesced in the decades-long contest over territory in northeast Brazil, to which Portugal and Holland were both party. A Portuguese colony since the fifteenth century, Brazil came under the jurisdiction of the Spanish monarchy in 1580, when Felipe II assumed the Portuguese crown. The Spanish and Portuguese union was a complicated affair, and many Portuguese, aghast at what they believed to be Felipe II's usurpation of the throne, deeply resented being subordinated to a Spanish sovereign. Tensions between Castile and Portugal ran high: Many Castilians questioned the loyalty of Portuguese subjects and were disturbed by the growing involvement of Portuguese merchants in imperial commerce. Many Portuguese, likening life under Spanish rule to a kind of bondage, deplored attempts made by the Crown to impose a Hispanic model of monopoly trade on more liberal, Portuguese traditions (Elliot 1990, 249–84, 337–49; Gitlitz 1996, 43–46; Lockhart and Schwartz 1983, 221–27, 251). Further amplifying frictions was the fact that the majority of New Christians arrested (and executed) by the Lima Inquisition were either born in Portugal or had parents who were Portuguese natives. Their ancestry made them doubly suspect: As Portuguese, they were mistrusted for their fidelity to Lisbon, and as New Christians, they were mistrusted for being hidden Jews. These doubts were only compounded by the Dutch victory over Spain and Portugal in northeast Brazil.

The Dutch were Spain's principal enemies in European battles for control over South America, and during the first half of the seventeenth century, Dutch forces invaded port towns like Pernambuco, established footholds on South American soil, and generally wreaked havoc with Spanish trade (Altolaguirre 1930, 13, 194–297; Suardo 1936, 259–61). It was a Castilian commonplace that Portuguese New Christians were secret allies of the Dutch, and Spaniards blamed seditious Portuguese for Castile's initial loss of Bahia in 1624 (recaptured in 1625), as well as for their defeat in Pernambuco six years later.[28] It is not surprising that Spanish officials harbored gnawing—if not truly justified[29]— qualms about New Christian loyalties. New Christians and crypto-Jews could escape Spain's intolerance by settling in Holland (Kamen 1998, 42–43, 64–65, 290, 293–94, 297–98). To Spain's chagrin, once the Dutch settled northeast Brazil (1630–1654), the Jewish population—consisting of Dutch immigrants and former colonial New Christians—ballooned in size and openly observed the Jewish heresy (Gitlitz 1996, 61–62).

Peru's Inquisitors were well aware of the possible dangers presented by a Dutch colony where Judaism could be freely practiced so close to its borders. They feared that a vibrant Jewish colony in Brazil could renovate crypto-Jewish practices, facilitate Dutch political objectives, and perhaps even encourage New Christians arriving at Brazil's ports to migrate to the viceroyalty of Peru (Lockhart and Schwartz 1983, 250).[30]

Resentment of New Christians was never far from center stage. A letter sent in 1634 to the Inquisition's principal office in Madrid, for example, presented a litany of treasons familiar to Spanish as well as to Peruvian ears. Merchants—also indistinguishable from New Christians, Portuguese, and Jews—were no more than spies, the letter went. New Christians were taking advantage of their vast trading networks in Holland, Lisbon, Brazil, and Spain as they plotted to destroy the Spanish empire and the Christian world (Adler 1909, 45–51). The memo's author, a ship's captain, supported his case with "evidence" that a Dutch/Portuguese Jew, Antonio Vaez Henriques, also known as Mosen Coen, orchestrated the enemy's capture of Pernambuco (48). Additionally, a Jewish Dutch/Portuguese ship's commander named Diego Peixotto (with the same alias, Mosen Coen), "induced the [Dutch West Indies] Company to force the crew . . . who are *negros* . . . to come to them to learn their language" (49).

The captain's anxieties were echoed in the rhetoric surrounding Peru's New Christians during the 1620s and 1630s. As in Spain, commercial avarice and disloyalty to State and Church were building blocks of anti-Semitic discourse in Peru; unlike in Spain, however, there was also a pointed concern about Jewish/New Christian abilities to manipulate language. No doubt the "Jewish problem" in early seventeenth-century Peru had longstanding roots in Iberian history and prejudice; however, equally striking is the fact that its definition was shaped by the geopolitics of a New World empire. Here, being a Jew (or a New Christian or Portuguese) marked a new kind of conspiracy born in the Americas—a pact with Spain's enemies to undermine Iberian sovereignty over its New World possessions. Enemies could be foreign competitors over colonial territory, or perhaps even more treacherously, they could be "insiders," residing within the boundaries of imperial rule. New Christians were accused of cultivating subversive ties with the enemies within—indios and negros—as well as with Spain's foreign adversaries, like the Dutch.

The colony's take on the Jewish menace, then, elaborated a familiar but divergent set of charges: New Christians had usurped trade and merchandising to the detriment of Castilians; New Christians, with international ties, were not loyal to the Spanish empire; New Christians—merchants and traitors—aligned themselves with potentially subversive groups within the Colony (namely, indios and negros); and finally, New Christians were able to plot treachery with slaves and indios because of their remarkable ability to conspire in secret languages.

Conflicting sentiments, ideologies, and policy regarding New Christians vied for dominance in Peru in 1620s and 1630s. The wealthiest New Christian merchants were en route to becoming colonial aristocrats, championed in the highest places of ecclesiastical and secular government. At the same time, however, Lima's Inquisitors were stepping up their campaign against Judaisers, making New Christians the primary target. Stories began to spread of the growing number of crypto-Jews living in the viceroyalty (Kohut 1903, 166).[31] Warnings sent to the Lima office in 1636 alerted Inquisitors that many Jews, "most of them enjoying the rights of citizenship and living securely with their fellowmen," had settled in Chile alone (166). Now the Inquisitors were searching to find a "cure for this plague which, so dispersed and spread out, has been thriving in many parts [of the viceroyalty of Peru]."[32]

Fears concerning New Christian activity in the Peruvian economy began to mushroom, as Portuguese were reproached for monopolizing most, if not all, sectors of mercantile activity. An official report written from the Lima office to headquarters in Madrid laid out some of the Inquisitors' concerns:

> Since about six or eight years ago, they say many Portuguese have found a footing in the Kingdom of Peru. . . . [They] had early made themselves masters of the situation, commanding almost exclusively all the commerce of the kingdom, the thoroughfare called the "Street of Merchants" belonging to them alone. . . . They owned all the dry-good stores, all the stalls where they sold their wares out of chests and boxes . . . and more besides, were all literally theirs. Thus they monopolized the retail trade and traffic; so that from gold brocade to sackcloth, and from diamond to cumin seed, and from the lowest Black slave from Guinea to the most precious pearl passes through their hands. (Medina 1956: vol. 2, 45–46)

In the words of another, "A Castilian of pure stock has not a ghost of a show against these Portuguese . . ." (Kohut 1903, 166–67). And testimonies recorded during Inquisition trials are full of accusations that the viceroyalty's New Christians/Portuguese were plotting to take over the marketplace.[33]

Juan de Manozca, who came as an Inquisitor to Peru from Cartagena, fanned the growing undercurrent of suspicion. In Cartagena he was instrumental in bringing trials against slave women for practicing "witchcraft," and against Portuguese merchants for practicing Judaism. The Inquisitor turned to these targets again while in Peru. An aristocrat and metropolitan, Manozca was aghast at what he perceived to be the disarray of colonial life. The culprits were "witches"—non-native women who dangerously incorporated native customs into their conjuring repertoire—and crypto-Jews, who transgressed a range of traditional Hispanic categories of social and cultural order.[34]

Under Manozca's watch some of Peru's premier merchants were arrested and executed. Some, like Manuel Bautista Perez, figured among the colony's wealthiest subjects. Highly regarded by Lima's elite, they joined the ranks of New World "entrepreneur-aristocrats."[35] These men wore the accoutrements of their social standing, dressing in velvet and sporting swords; befitting their status as colonial "grandees," they cultivated a retinue of clients and servants. Lima's merchant-aristocrats, also intellectuals, housed great libraries and sponsored gatherings where pressing concerns of economics, political life, national history, and astronomy were discussed. Most were active participants in Lima society and prominent members of Catholic lay organizations. Not surprisingly, they cemented their status by establishing close ties to Lima's highest officials (Reparaz 1976, 36–38).[36] After the arrest of Perez and other principal merchants precipitated a collapse in trade and credit, the Supreme Council called Manozca to account for his actions. He did so by arguing that the threat New Christians posed to religious orthodoxy had extended into the political arena. The colony's survival was in jeopardy. Manozca had uncovered a plot brewing in the very jail cells of the Inquisition: Judaisers were stockpiling gunpowder earmarked for a second Dutch invasion of Peru's major port city, Callao.[37]

Anxieties that New Christians were promoting a Dutch invasion of the Pacific Coast were compounded by fears that New Christians were conspiring with slaves and indios. Viceregal authorities in general were concerned about the loyalties of African and native Peruvians. Spaniards recognized that they themselves were unpopular as the colony's privileged elite; they also recognized that they were as vastly outnumbered. One viceroy, in a written assessment of his term in office, expressed great distrust of the "negros, *mulatos, mestizos,* indios and *diversos colores* [people of various colors] . . . who were so numerous in comparison with the meager number of espanoles [in Peru]" (Altolaguirre 1930, 179). Another, in his 1628 account to the King and Council of the Indies, wrote of the need to keep vigilant and monitor the behavior of indios and negros. In his judgment, the threat to colonial order presented by the former paralleled the danger occasioned by the latter: "There are over twenty-two thousand negros living in Lima and its surroundings, and if they were ever to see espanoles losing in [battles with the enemy] there is little to assure us of them, because generally they love liberty . . . and for similar reasons one has to be suspicious of indios, so that everywhere, in these occasions, danger grows" (Altolaguirre 1930, 43).

Fears that New Christians were plotting religious sabotage served to intensify Spanish suspicions. As far back as 1602, a royal decree sent to the king's representative in Buenos Aires warned of the corrupting influence "created by the presence of many foreigners, and particularly Portuguese who have entered the country . . . with slaving ships . . . [,] New Christians and people with only little certainty in our faith, Judaisers. [Vigilance must be maintained] so that no error and evil sect is sown among the indios who are barely certain and instructed in our faith and vulnerable to any novelty" (Lewin 1950, 40). Solorzano, writing several decades later, echoed this apprehension. In his masterwork, a compilation of the laws of the Indies, he, too, warned that the Portuguese might undermine the faith of Peru's "simple people," new to Catholicism (Solorzano 1647, 262). Heresy marked the beginning of the slippery slope to treason.

Heresy and treason were as easily conflated as cultural ideas of what it meant to be Portuguese, New Christian, and Jew. The history of the Expulsion, of the Spanish and Portuguese Inquisitions, and of the migration of New Christians from Portugal to Spain lay behind this confusion of religion and nationality, of heresy and treason. However, the conflictive history of Spain and Portugal gave this semantic mix-up a deeper cast. As noted, most Portuguese resented being under the rule of a Spanish monarch, and Castilians, aware of their neighbors' profound discontent, had cause to be anxious about Portuguese loyalty. History has shown that Spanish distrust was well placed: Portugal fought for and won its independence in 1640. By assessing the Portuguese as potential traitors and garbling their identity with those of the New Christian and the Jew, Spaniards magnified the aura of suspicion surrounding any Portuguese. Inquisitors from the metropole were party to and sustained this cultural entanglement.

The purported links between indios, negros, and New Christians exacerbated these apprehensions, as prejudices about New Christians mirrored assumptions about indios and negros. Imperial stereotyping only heightened concerns about treachery: Spanish prejudice—demeaning indios and negros as either *gente simple* (simpleminded) and easily led astray, or vicious and barbarous and on the verge of rebellion—made both groups innately susceptible to Judaisers' corrupting influence (Altolaguirre 1930, 9; Cobo 1983, 21–22, 31–32; Lewin 1958, 40).[38]

European theories about the origins of humanity debated the common ancestry of Jews and Indians; for those who believed that native peoples were descended from the lost tribes, Jews and indios became natural allies. Since their first encounters, Europeans pondered the Semitic derivation of the New World's native peoples. Distinguished clerics, philosophers, and jurists engaged both sides of the dispute (Cobo 1983, 48; de Espinosa 1942, 18–21, 24). One of the more curious ties between "Israelites" and Indians was brought to the world's attention by Menasseh Ben Israel in his book *The Hope of Israel* (1987). The core of this treatise is an account presented to Menasseh, the chief rabbi of Amsterdam, by a Portuguese/New Christian merchant working deep in the interior of the Andes. Antonio Montezinos spoke to the rabbi about a group of Indians who told of an encounter they had had with a strange, unusual tribe. The tribe was, without doubt to Montezinos or Menasseh Ben Israel, one of the lost tribes of Israel, and Rabbi Menasseh Ben Israel made much of the connection, lobbying Oliver Cromwell to allow Jews to return to England.[39] Millenarian thinking swept England in the mid-seventeenth century, and one of the supposed precursors to the Messiah's advent was the discovery of Jews—the lost tribes—living dispersed throughout the world. The fact that *The Hope of Israel* had an extraordinary reception is evidence of the depth of European sentiment about an ancestral tie between both groups.[40]

Closer to home, Fray Buenaventura de Salinas and Antonio Vasquez de Espinosa, two well-known chronicler-priests who spent considerable time in Peru, held the opinion that Jews and indios were of the same stock. Writing in the first half of the seventeenth century, Vasquez de Espinosa was convinced that this shared ancestry helped account for their similarity in character and physique, as well as in religious practices and beliefs: "Indians are similar in every respect to the Hebrews from whom they derive . . . in physique and temperament and in other characteristics, such as their customs, rites, ceremonies, superstitions, and idolatries (de Espinosa 1942, 24). In 1653, Buenaventura de Salinas also pointed to their likeness of temperament as evidence of common descent: "cowardly, ungrateful, lazy, superstitious, crafty liars" (1957, 11).

Spanish ideologies also joined Jews and Indians via a shared, magical talent. Both popular and official wisdom surmised that Jews and indios could conjure wealth, and, just as mysteriously, make it disappear, especially if Old Christians were involved. According to Spanish lore, Peru's indios, outraged about their treatment by Iberian colonizers, conspired to prevent *espanoles* from sharing in the enormous underground wealth that was part of the Inca legacy. Awaiting the Incas' return, indios kept the whereabouts of these fabulous mines hidden, and "no amount of pleading, threats or punishment would make them reveal [these secrets] to Spaniards" (Solorzano 1647, 291). The same legal scholar who wrote about the ability of Indians to keep wealth from colonizers described a similar Jewish gift: The Jews/Portuguese would rather "swallow" their fortunes than surrender them to Spaniards. Ricardo Palma, recording Peruvian oral traditions in 1863, found that this bit of popular wisdom still survived two centuries after the Inquisition's principal campaigns against crypto-Jews had ceased (1910, 259).

Spaniards also coupled Jews and indios when they assessed their long-standing mission to evangelize the faith. Ever since the Expulsion, and with increased intensity in the early seventeenth century, Inquisitors labored to purify the Iberian Peninsula from Jewish contaminants; similarly, in the seventeenth century, some clerics were convinced of the need to rekindle drives to extirpate the native idolatries that they believed were destroying Peru. Missionaries sent to indigenous communities perceived their efforts in light of Spain's tumultuous religious past, understanding early Church strategies to convert "pagan" gentiles—particularly later attempts to convert Moors and Jews—as rehearsals for ventures in the Americas. When *doctrineros* like Joseph Arriaga assessed their mission in Peru, they were sobered by the difficulties of previous evangelizing campaigns in the Iberian Peninsula. If the task of rooting out the hidden evil of Judaism in a country as pious as Spain was monumental and ongoing, then what would the New World have in store for keepers of the faith? In his 1621 manual for priests on indigenous religion and how to expunge it, *The Extirpation of Idolatry in Peru*, Arriaga wrote: "For it has scarcely been possible to extirpate so evil a seed [Judaising] even in so clean a land [Spain], where the Gospel has been so continuously . . . and thoroughly preached and where the Most Righteous Tribunal of the Holy Office has been so diligently and solicitously vigilant" (1968, 9). The "disease of the Indians,"—their reluctance to denounce native religions for Catholicism—was not "so deeply rooted a cancer" as that of Moors and Jews, Arriaga assured his readers (6). Nevertheless, the disease of the Indians rampant in Peru, amplified concurrent anxieties over the New Christian presence.[41]

New Christians were said to communicate their heresies to one another and express their hatred of Christianity, as well as to turn "simple peoples" from the faith, in the thriving mercantile spaces of colonial life. As already noted, Spaniards feared the abilities of New Christians to seduce barely Christianized souls. Merchandising, a New Christian trait, presumably gave the heretics the opportunity to carry out their work. In testimony after testimony, witnesses pointed to the hubs, routes, and outposts of colonial mercantilism as the places where treachery ruled: the slave markets of Portobello (Panama), the entrepôts of Angola, Guinea, and Cartagena (Colombia), peddling routes stretching from Lima deep into Indian territories, Calle Mercader (Lima's bustling market street), and the warehouses in Lima's Saint Lazaro parish, where slaves were quartered. Commerce gave Judaiser traders, as agents of the big Lima merchants, the ability to spread their networks into the far reaches of the viceroyalty, where Spanish control over native peoples was most vulnerable.[42] Mercantile centers became places where New Christians could magically communicate political and religious subversions. Here indios, negros, and New Christians could engage in illicit conversations; moreover, they could do so secretly, for all were conversant in languages unintelligible to Old Christian ears.

One member of Lima's New Christian community, Thome Cuaresma, was renowned for his linguistic mastery. Said to be equally at ease among Judaisers and negros—he was the principal physician for both communities—Cuaresma was acclaimed for curing skills that were rooted in his ability to "speak their languages." His talents extended to a special gift, supposedly shared by many who were prosecuted in the auto-de-fé of 1639:

> They could communicate with each other [in the Laws of Moses] by means of this language and they would speak it, even though they were [standing] in front of Old Christians, without the [Old Christians] being able to understand that they were speaking about the Law of Moses.[43] [It was] a secret language, [spoken] right in front of Old Christians who just heard normal words, not that out-of-the-ordinary language, [and with] duplicity and scheming, so that the prisoner and the rest of his ancestry and kinship could converse conspiracies and heresies.[44]

Thus according to Inquisition sources, the ability of New Christians to speak special languages, including the languages of slaves, gave them dangerous powers in colonial Peru. These powers even reached into the bowels of the Inquisition. Since slaves performed most of the Inquisition's custodial duties, they were in a position to aid prisoners illegally. Cognizant of the problem, Inquisitors locked up all their slaves before the 1639 auto-de-fé was scheduled to take place. In spite of precautions, New Christian linguistic genius prevailed, and Inquisitors were unable to prevent communication between slaves and prisoners. As Fernando de Montesinos commented, "even though they only employed *negros bozales* [wild, born in Africa] recently captured and transported to Peru . . . the Portuguese could understand them . . . since they brought them from Guinea, knew their languages, and this has helped [New Christians] to communicate with each other" (Lewin 1950, 160–61). Not only did Spanish conspiracy theories presume rather fantastic linguistic infiltrations, but they also made customs of indigenous or African origin into heretical Judaic rituals. The long transcript of Manuel Bautista Perez's trial exposed a rather extraordinary development: Perez, head of an international trading enterprise whose agents traversed the world from Madrid and Seville, to Guinea and Angola, to the interior of the Andes (Reparaz 1976, 82–84), stood accused of practicing exotic Jewish rituals, with roots in Africa and the Andes. His major accomplice was his *compadre*, Diego de Ovalle. According to one testimony, when Diego de Ovalle asked Manuel Bautista Perez for some tobacco,

> [Manuel Bautista] would say, taking it with his fingers and pressing it to his nostrils, "Señor compadre, this tobacco is very good" and he would scatter it [on the ground] or blow on it.[45] Then, at other times, he [Diego de Ovalle] would say to [Manuel Bautista], "Isn't there some *colilla* to drink with water? (a root or fruit from Guinea which is brought from Cartagena and by drinking water after putting it in the mouth, it becomes sweet), and [Manuel Bautista] would order [his servants] to bring it.[46]

As if to reinforce the Jewish derivation of taking tobacco and drinking colilla (or *cola*), this witness added, "Ovalle and Manuel Bautista would speak to each other in a language only understood among themselves, talking about the Law of Moses."[47]

Later, when the Inquisitors compiled formal charges against Perez, they condensed these testimonies into the following accusation: "to continue with [accusations] that ritual offerings (*sacrificios*) were made in the prisoner's house, the prisoner was asked for tobacco and . . . he scattered it and blew on it, a gesture appropriate for libation and ritual offering, as is associated with many places in . . . the Old Testament."[48] The accusation continues:

> And other times, with the same intent, when the prisoner was with a certain person, in the presence of others . . . he was asked for cola . . . and drinking it, this certain person spoke with the prisoner . . . in the extraordinary (*trasordinario*) language. . . . All of the aforesaid was by way of treating . . . the Law of Moses with this dissimulation and scheming so that the prisoner and the rest of his caste and kinsmen could speak of it [the Law of Moses] in these languages without being understood by others, even if there were Old Christians present.[49]

Perez emphatically denied these allegations. He strongly objected to charges that he made ritual offerings to the God of the Old Testament, let alone with cultural artifacts from South America and Africa. Regarding the use of cola, Perez had the following to say to the Chief Inquisitor: First he reminded Manozca, who had come to Peru after heading the Inquisition in Cartagena, that "he should have heard of [cola] because it was so commonly used in Cartagena . . . and everyone there used it."[50] Regarding the use of tobacco, he explained that "whenever they came by tobacco, he pretended that he wanted to have some and he would take the tobacco pouch (*tabaquero*) and shake it and he would perform those customary artifices (*inbenciones*) that those who use tobacco do."[51] Manuel Bautista Perez might have made a pretense of taking tobacco, but in fact he did not use it. Perez thought consuming tobacco was a silly custom, he told the Tribunal, and didn't miss the opportunity to make fun of those who partook. Then Perez repeated his contention that drinking cola was quite a normal and accepted thing to do in the colonies. So, if anyone were to "ask for some sweet water in his house it would be possible to even toast to one's health, without anything else being implied."[52]

Far from having an Old World origin and, therefore, far from being a possible component of traditional Jewish ceremony, tobacco was first cultivated in South America. The accounts of tobacco's role in "ritual offerings"— blowing on it or scattering it—describe Andean tradition much more accurately than Hebraic.[53] Andeans believed tobacco had sacred and curative properties, and *sayri*, the Quechua word for tobacco, was a name associated with Inca royalty (Cobo 1983, 436–37; de Ayala 1980, 441–45). Nonetheless, the presumption that Jews and Indians shared ritual practices was not novel to Manozca's court. As we have seen, Antonio Vasquez de Espinosa, a cleric with no ties to the Inquisition, believed that the common origin of Jews and Indians explained the similarity of their "rites" and "ceremonies."[54]

Neither did drinking cola resonate with Judaic ritual. A popular African plant and beverage, cola was brought to the New World with the slave trade. No doubt it was, as Manuel Bautista Perez claimed, well known in Cartagena, one of the Spanish empire's principal slave depots. And, no doubt, Manozca was well aware of its origins.

Transforming drinking cola and sniffing tobacco into heretical Jewish practices seemed as fanciful to Manuel Bautista Perez as it does to us. However the intellectual and emotional climate of the colonial Spanish community, where currents of anti-Semitism merged with fears of indios and negros, most likely rendered this ideological distortion into a believable rhetoric. At the very least, the infusion of heretical Judaising with Andean and African traits fell within perceived boundaries of cultural possibility or truthfulness.[55]

That goods associated with processes at the heart of Spain's colonial endeavor—the conquest of indios and the expansion of the African slave trade— were conflated with the practices of Judaism is striking. Global commerce and cheap labor anchored Spain's colonial enterprise, and New Christians/Portuguese/Jews and indios/negros were key figures in this equation. At least according to stereotype, Portuguese/Jews/New Christians dominated international trade; indios and negros embodied the colony's sources of cheap labor. Both groups were needed for the success of Spain's global endeavors, and both were distrusted. New Christian merchants, slaves, and colonized Indian vassals were outside of the traditional institutions that had structured life in the Iberian peninsula before colonialism began to change the rules. In different cultural and economic ways, each signaled the novel social relations of the emerging modern world. This version of cultural finger-pointing hints at the tensions that animated the evolving modern/colonial economy, relations of political dominion, and the cultural order on which they both rested.

For many Spaniards, Peru was a land of opportunities unattainable in Europe; the New World, distant from metropolitan vigilance, held out a promise to loosen or turn a blind eye to some of the constraints hobbling social mobility in the Peninsula (*Descripción* 1950, 74). In the colonies, where merchandising and commerce promoted wealth, the wealthiest individuals forged a colonial "aristocracy." Manuel Bautista Perez, for example, took on all the behaviors and conventions of a prosperous nobleman: He was a member of Lima's most prestigious religious brotherhood; he was generous, hosting feasts and soliciting alms; he dressed in the finery of aristocrats; he was a much sought after patron of the arts. Reciprocally, as befit one of such noble demeanor, Lima society treated Manuel Bautista Perez like a patrician (Reparaz 1976, 36–38).[56] Luis de Lima, a merchant born in Portugal and executed with Manuel Bautista Perez, expressed the hopes and expectations placed in colonial Peru by would-be aristocrats: "The land of Peru was for the Portuguese the promised one, finding there riches, honor and esteem" (Lewin 1950, 183).

In Peru, transformations of social position went beyond the status that money could buy. New Christian men and women told tales of rebirth in the New World—baptized anew, as some would have it. Many called themselves Old Christians (and for good reason, once the Inquisition began to target New Christians).[57] Some, particularly those with family members who had been penanced by Inquisition tribunals in Spain and Portugal, changed their names. And some of these, to match their newfound colonial status, even claimed descent from Spain's most aristocratic lineages. Juan de Acosta, for example, whose father avowed descent from the Spanish nobility, claimed that "he is taken to be a noble man and his fathers and grandfathers clean of any stain of Moorish or Jewish blood."[58]

Manuel Bautista Perez was inscribed by societal contradictions pitting appeals to lineage and traditional hierarchy against appeals to worthiness and an emerging modern/colonial order built on mercantile wealth. This renowned, prosperous, and powerful merchant surely believed that aristocratic status was his due. Peru facilitated his pretensions as it facilitated the restructuring of his genealogy: Manuel Bautista Perez was no longer a New Christian—almost. He talked about trying to live in such a way that his Portuguese/New Christian background would become a ghost: he was visibly devout, distanced himself from Portuguese who had recently arrived in Lima, and spoke and wrote in Castilian and "never Portuguese," including the illegal messages sent from his cell to inmates and family.[59] In his own words he said that "he . . . never let it be known, either to persons from his household or outside it, that he was a New Christian . . . because he always tried to be taken for an Old Christian."[60] Although Manuel Bautista believed in the legitimacy of a social hierarchy that enslaved negros and coerced Indian labor, he also believed in the right of good Christian subjects, regardless of ancestry, to be justly recognized for their contributions to empire and Church. It was in this regard that he challenged Spain's racial definition of Jewishness and its accompanying structures of social hierarchy governed by purity of blood laws and an aristocratic ethos.

Inquisitors like Juan de Manozca, however, who presided over the 1639 auto, detested the ability of New Christians to sidestep the traditional, aristocratic hierarchy of Iberian society. For them, the Colony's openness—the permeability of its social boundaries—represented a severe threat to civic and moral order. And the New Christian/Portuguese presence in colonial Peru only swelled anxieties over other vulnerable points in the Colony's racialized and gendered structures of governance.[61]

The novel social relations made possible by conditions of colonial existence—conditions pulling New Christians, negros, and indios together in a variety of ways—only heightened the perceived dangers of all New World heresies. For some traditionalists, a trinity of obstinate New Christians/Portuguese, recalcitrant indios, and petulant negros was attacking Spain's divine mission to rule over a righteous and militant Catholic colony. Inquisitors in Lima saw themselves (or presented themselves) as the defenders of this sacred imperial trust and argued that their religious work not only impeded the spiritual damage that hidden Jews could cause in Peru, but, as Manozca argued, the political damage as well.

During the 1630s, Peru's Inquisitors promoted a racialized ethos of culture, while intertwining stereotypes of New Christians, indios and negros as part of an etiology of fear and blame. Other etiologies offered different visions of the colonial condition. The indigenous Peruvian chronicler Felipe Guaman Poma de Ayala suggested a distinctive perspective on New Christians and colonial justice in his thousand-page chronicle of protest to the Crown. A devout Catholic, yet highly critical of Spain's so-called Christian legacy in Peru, Guaman Poma argued that Indians, even pagan Indians, acted more like Christians than did Spaniards (1980, 339, 822, 863). Pursuing the play of ironies in social categories and social justice, Guaman Poma, in a rhetorical dialogue with the Crown, asked the King to consider the fact that "the Spanish nation was [at one time] Jewish" (882). So, then, who, in Guaman Poma's eyes, were the colony's New Christians? "Los indios y negros" (533).

Notes

This paper has benefitted from several hearings. In its roughest form it was presented at the 1995 meetings of the Institute of Early American History and Culture in Ann Arbor, followed by a presentation at the John Carter Brown Library 1997 conference, Jews and the Expansion of Europe: 1450–1800. I owe special thanks to Fred Jaher for his advice and insight, and for arranging for me to give a lecture at the University of Illinois, under the auspices of the Sheldon and Anita Drobney program for the study of Jewish culture and society of which Michael Shapiro is the gracious director. As always, I have benefitted from Ann Wightman's thoughtful and astute commentary. Thanks also to my colleague Claudia Koonz for her careful and thorough reading of a draft. I also want to express my appreciation to Don Donham, for inviting me to the Historical Anthropology Seminar sponsored by the Anthropology Department of Emory University, to Brian Keith Axel for organizing a volume built around presentations made to the Seminar, and to my fellow seminarians at Emory who asked wonderful questions—especially those I am still struggling to answer. And finally a word of special appreciation to the Guggenheim Foundation, whose 1994 Fellowship allowed me to conduct the research on which this article is based.

1   The classic study of the Inquisition in the viceroyalty of Peru is Jose Toribio Medina's two-volume *Historia del Tribunal de la Inquisicion de Lima* (1956). For a summary of the auto-de-fé where Manuel Bautista Perez was executed, see vol. 2, 45–146. More recent studies of the Inquisition in Peru include Delgado and Aparicio (1989), Ramos (1989, 1991), and especially, Hampe-Martinez (1996) for a current and comprehensive bibliography.

   Analyses centered on Peru's New Christian population include Lewin (1950), Quiroz (1986), and Reparaz (1976). Lewin describes the Inquisitorial processes against New Christians with a focus on anti-Semitism; Reparaz presents information from various sources about the Portuguese in Peru; and Quiroz relates the indictment of New Christians to the Inquisitors' need to acquire funds to support their operation.

2   Over the last two decades, scholarship on the Spanish Inquisition has grown enormously. Examples of recent, extensive overviews include Kamen (1985, 1998), Contreras (1997), and Villanueva (1984). Studies of the Inquisition in the English language were first developed by Henry Charles Lea, who wrote *A History of the Inquisition of Spain* (1906–7). These studies were renewed with the publication of Cecil Roth's *The Spanish Inquisition* (1932). Jose Toribio Medina, the great Chilean historian, pioneered works on the Inquisition in the Americas and Philippines, including the monumental *Historia del Tribunal de la Inquisicion de Lima* (1956). One of the important contemporary studies of the Inquisition in Spanish America is by Solange Alberro, *Inquisicion y sociedad en Mexico 1571–1700* (1988).

Scholarship on the Inquisition's relationship with Jews and New Christians has also blossomed. Monographs include Adler (1908), Roth (1932), Beinart (1981), Baroja (1972, 1986), Tejada (1988), Selke (1986), Ortiz (1993), and the controversial works by Benzion Netanyaju (1995, 1997). Seymore B. Liebman has published several important works on the viceroyalty of New Spain, including *The Jews in New Spain: Faith, Flame, and the Inquisition* (1970). David M. Gitlitz's *Secrecy and Deceit: The Religion of the Crypto Jews* (1996) is a grand synthesis of the history and traditions of hidden Jews in Spain and the New World, drawn primarily from Inquisition records.

3 *Conversos* or "New Christians" (as opposed to Old Christians) were Jews or Muslims who converted to Catholicism, or their descendants. In this paper primary reference is to the descendants of Jews. After 1492, following the Act of Expulsion, it was illegal for Jews to reside anywhere in the Spanish realm.

4 The moral behavior and customs of indigenous peoples were monitored by Church bishops. The Inquisition's jurisdiction did not extend to the colony's native populations. See Medina (1956).

5 The first published account of the 1639 auto-de-fé was written by the cleric Fernando de Montesinos. He was asked by the Tribunal to write a summary of the auto-de-fé, published that year as *Auto de Fé celebrado en Lima el 23 de enero de 1639*. Jose Toribio Medina published most of it in his history of the Lima Inquisition, *Historia del Tribunal* (1956), vol. 2 (106–62). Montesinos' *Auto de Fé* was also reprinted as an appendix in Lewin (1950). Both authors rely heavily on Montesinos' work to describe this event.

6 Regarding the concerns expressed by the Supreme Council in Madrid, see Medina. Kamen argued that in comparison to other European inquisitions, the Spanish Inquisition infrequently demanded capital punishment for heretical acts. See Kamen (198–203). However, Kamen also emphasized that crimes entailing the secret worship of non-Catholic religions were, by far, the most commonly punished by execution (203–4). Scholars of the European witch-craze have also noted the relative restraint of the Spanish Inquisition: see Henningsen (1980) and Levack (1987).

7 Spanish anti-Semitism is discussed in greater detail in the following pages. Spanish anti-Semitic ideologies, however, frequently engaged and were shared by belief systems found throughout Europe. There is extensive literature on European anti-Semitism during the medieval and early modern periods. For an excellent summary of the research on this subject in the early modern period, see Jaher (1996, 1–81). Also see Oberman (1984), Cohen (1982, 1991), and Katz (1993), which includes a current bibliography compiled by Bernard Dov Cooperman.

8 During the last twenty years, students of the processes of nation-state building, influenced by Antonio Gramsci, have been exploring the dynamics of class relations, state formation, and cultural practices. Although these studies have, for the most part, investigated the roads to nation-state building and capitalist development, I believe Gramscian insights are germane to the early colonial state as it drove the making of our modern world. The literature on the cultural politics at the core of state-making has grown enormously and I will cite here only a few of those works that have influenced my analysis: Corrigan and Sayer (1985), Thompson (1978, 133–65), Williams (1978, 75–144), and Hall (1997), Jean and John Comaroff have used

Gramsci along with Corrigan and Sayer in their important discussions of the cultural dimensions of the English colonial state in South Africa. See their *Ethnography and the Historical Imagination* (1992) and *Of Revelation and Revolution: Christianity, Colonialism, and Consciousness in South Africa*, 2 vols. (1991–1998). For a challenge to the assumption that modernity began with the Enlightenment, see these authors who argue that the modern world has its origins in the colonization of the New World: Dussell (1993, 65–75; 1998) and Quijano (1992, 437–47).

9 See Kamen (1988, 50) for the implications of the fact that the Inquisition was the only institution of Spanish government that traversed the entire realm.

10 As early as 1478, the Inquisition was established in Castile and tribunals were set up as autonomous courts in different Spanish cities. However, in 1483, a papal bull initiated the process that united the Inquisitions of the Crown under a single jurisdiction. See Kamen (1985, 18–43) and Gitlitz (1996, 18–25).

11 For more detailed discussions of this period see Kamen, *The Spanish Inquisition* (1985, 1–65), Gitlitz (1996, 3–34), and Baroja, vol. 1 (1986, 125–64).

12 Cardoso is the subject of an extraordinary biography by Josef Hayim Yerushalmi, *From Spanish Court to Italian Ghetto: Isaac Cardoso: A Study in Seventeenth Century Marranism and Jewish Apologetics* (1981).

13 Cardoso made each *calumnia* the focus of a book chapter: I. They adore false gods; II. They exude a bad odor; III. Jews have tails and Jewish men menstruate; IV. They pray three times daily against the gentiles; V. They persuade gentiles to accept Judaism; VI. They are unfaithful to the Princes; VII. They are wicked and cruel; VIII. They corrupt the Sacred Scriptures; IX. They desecrate images and are sacrilegious; X. They kill Christian children in order to use their blood in their rites. In Yerushalmi (1981, 360).

14 Regarding the calumny that Jews desecrated Christian images and ritual, see Yerushalmi (1981, 360, 447–54).

15 Also see Baroja, vol. 1 (1986, 181–92). Diego Lopez de Fonseca refers to the barbarity of Lisbon's Inquisitors, who cut off the hands and then burned alive someone who was falsely accused of stealing the Eucharist. See the Archivo Historico de la Nacion in Madrid, Seccion Inquisicion, hereafter AHN, Inq, Libro 1031, f.91v.

16 In 1649 a procession was held in Lima to avenge the alleged desecration of the Eucharist by Jews in Quito. This act was of such importance that a soldier, Josephe de Mugaburu, recorded it in his diary. See Mugaburu (1975, 25).

17 Some of the many examples found in Lima Inquisition testimony include Manuel Henriquez, AHN, Inq, Legajo 1647, no.11, f.95v; Manuel Bautista Perez, AHN, Inq, Legajo 1647, no.13, f.29v–30v; Felippa Lopez, AHN, Inq, Libro 1029, f.41–41v; Joan de Vicente, AHN, Inq, Legajo 1647, no.3, f.54; Francisco Nunez de Olivera, AHN, Inq, Libro 1029, f.46v, f.48v; Francisco Rodriguez, AHN, Inq, Libro 1029, f.36v; Manuel Rodriguez, AHN, Inq, Libro 1029, f.68; Antonio Leal, AHN, Inq, Libro 1030, f.127; Jean de Acevedo, AHN, Inq, Libro 1031, f.86v.

18 For accusations of blood libel in Spain, including the case of "el nino inocente de La Guarda," see Baroja (1986, 181–92), Kamen (1998, 22, 68), and Gitlitz (1996, 5, 23–24, 161, 190). Among other attributes, Christian blood was said to heal the monthly menstruation of Jewish men (Yerushalmi 1981, 130). For studies of ritual murder

accusations in Europe, see Roth (1935) and Hsia (1988). For an overall compendium with historical and anthropological slants, see Dundes (1991).

19 In addition, Levi was accused of magic, "saying that to this end he pronounced certain Hebrew words."

20 Providing an example more contemporary than eighth-century Toledo, Cardoso argued that Jews showed their commitment to the "Princes" when, in fourteenth-century Burgos (Spain), they refused to support Henry of Trastamara's insurgency against Pedro the Cruel, or when they defended Prague from Gustavus Adolphus during the Thirty Years' War.

21 For example, Jorge de Paz, AHN, Libro 1030, f.68v; Francisco de Vita Barahona, AHN, Cartas, Rollo 7, f.111–17; Manuel Henrriquez, AHN, Inq, Legajo 1647, no.11, f.61–61v,62,62v,64–64v; Manuel Bautista Perez, AHN, Inq, Legajo 1647, no.13, f.53.

22 Charges of Jewish treachery against Church and State were as deeply rooted in Spanish literature as they were in popular culture. The eminent Spanish playwright of the seventeenth century, Lope de Vega, dramatized ritual murder in *El nino inocente de la guardia*, and portrayed the treason of Jews in *El Brazil restituido*.

23 Academic interests in anti-Semitism and the history of Jews in Spain have been flourishing in tandem with work on the Inquisition. The growing bibliography is already substantial. I am unable to do it full justice here. In addition to the studies cited above on the Inquisition, one book stands out as a comprehensive and path-breaking account: Julio Caro Baroja's *Los Judios* (1986, especially vol. 1, 23–288). For Baroja's account of the role of economic and political tensions, see vol. 1 (87–90, 125–26, 133–48), and vol. 3 (17–32, 49–58). Also see Kamen (1998, 9–12).

24 Estimates range from fifty thousand to one hundred-twenty thousand, with the lower end seeming most likely. See Kamen (1998, 287) for the number of Jews living in Portugal.

25 Scholars have stressed the significance of this early history of Portuguese Jews converted as a block to Christianity for New Christian communities. See Baroja (vol. 1: 1986, 207–26); Kamen (1998, 287–90); Lockhart and Schwartz (1983, 225–26); and Yerushalmi (1981, 1–51).

26 The commercial interests of New Christians and Jews, along with their international ties, have been well noted. Among the many analyses, see Jonathan I. Israel's several pathbreaking accounts in *Empires and Entrepôts: the Dutch, the Spanish Monarchy and the Jews, 1585–1713* (1990) and *European Jewry in the Age of Mercantilism, 1550–1750* (1989). Of the sixty-two men and women who were penanced for Judaising in the 1639 auto-da-fé, forty-four had occupations associated with commerce or trade. For interesting cases against merchants brought before the Lima Inquisition, see Francisco Nunez de Olivera, AHN, Inq, Libro 1029, f.45v–49v; Antonio Fernandez, AHN, Inq, Libro 1029, f.57–59; Balthasar de Lucena, AHN, Inq, Libro 1029, f.61–65; Duarte Nunez de Zea, AHN, Inq, Libro 1029, f.65–67v; Bernabe Lopez Serrano, AHN, Inq, Libro 1030, f.280–280v; Alvaro Mendez, AHN, Inq, Libro 1030, f.367–69; Raphael Perez de Freitas, AHN, Inq, Libro 1030, f.418–19v; Luis de Valencia, AHN, Inq, Legajo 1647, no.12; Andres Nunez Xuarez, AHN, Inq, Libro 1029, f.53v–55v; Duarte Mendez, AHN, Inq, Libro 1028, f.339–44; Manuel Anriquez, AHN, Inq, Libro 1028, f.364–69; Diego Lopez de Fonseca, AHN, Inq, Libro 1031 f.89–95; Juan de

Acevedo, AHN, Inq, Libro 1031, f.77–87; Manuel Albarez, f.83; Rodrigo Baez Pereyra f.84; Juan Rodriguez de Silva, AHN, Inq, Libro 1031, f.99; Antonio de la Vega, AHN, Inq, Libro 1031, f.104; Bartolome de Silva, AHN, Inq, Libro 1031, f.136v; Matias Delgado, AHN, Inq, Libro 1031, f.138v-39; Gonzalo de Valcazar, AHN, Inq, Libro 1031, f.141; Sebastian Duarte, AHN, Inq, Libro 1031, f.186–95v; Luis de Valencia, AHN, Inq, Legajo 1647, no. 12; Manuel Henrriquez, AHN, Inq, Legajo 1647, no. 11; Manuel Bautista Perez, AHN, Inq, Legajo 1647, no. 13.

27   Examples from those testifying before the Lima Inquisition include Pedro de Contreras, AHN, Inq, Libro 1028, f.404, 407v; Duarte Mendez, Libro 1028, f.339v-40v; Diego Lopez de Fonseca, AHN, Inq, Libro 1031, f.95; Manuel Bautista Perez, AHN, Inq, Legajo 1647, no.13, f.17, f.29v, f.105v-6v, f.248, f.279v, f.342v; Manuel Despinosa f.145; Manuel Henrriquez, AHN, Inq, Legajo 1647, no.11, f.59, f.66v, f.90v, f.92–92v, f.106, 119v; Antonio de Acuna, f.90v; Manuel Anriquez, AHN, Inq, Libro 1028, f.365; Mencia de Luna, AHN, Inq, Legajo 1647, no.10, f.18–18v.

28   The Spanish victory over the Dutch in Bahia was commemorated by Lope de Vega in his play, *El Brazil Restituido.*

29   Although it is difficult to determine allegiances with great accuracy, evidence suggests that Brazil's New Christian population held divided loyalties: While some, principally crypto-Jews, might have sided with Holland, many, perhaps even the majority, fought to keep Brazil under Iberian control. See the excellent study by Anita Novinsky, *Crisaos Novos na Bahia* (1972). In a 1997 conference hosted by the John Carter Brown Library, "Jews and the Expansion of Europe: 1450–1800," Novinsky reiterated her belief that a significant proportion of New Christians remained loyal to Spain.

    In a similar vein, a commonplace of the time (as well as today) held that Portuguese Jews had controlling interests in the Dutch West Indies Company. After a careful examination of Company records, Jonathan Israel concluded that Jews never dominated the Dutch West Indies Company, even though some invested in it (1990, 356 n.2).

30   See also AHN, Inq, Cartas, Rollo 9, f.51, letter from Inquisitors Juan de Manozca, Andres Gaytan, Antonio de Castro y del Castillo to Muy P. Senor, 18 May 1636.

31   Jonathan Israel estimates that one quarter of the Spanish population in Buenos Aires and almost ten percent in Cartagena were Portuguese (1990, 277).

32   AHN, Inq, Cartas, Rollo 9, f.7, letter from Don Leon de Alcayaga Lartaun to Muy Poderoso S., 15 May 1636.

33   For examples see Jorge de Paz, AHN, Inq, Libro 1030, f.67B; Antonio Leal, AHN, Inq, Libro 1030, f.124, Lib.1030; Diego Lopez, AHN, Inq, Libro 1031, f.89B; Antonio de la Vega, AHN, Inq, Libro 1031, f.104.

34   For Manozca's zeal to persecute witches see Medina (1956: vol. 2, 18, 37) and Silverblatt (2000).

35   This is Steve Stern's felicitous phrase. New Christians could not formally become "aristocrats," since they were denied noble standing. But that did not stop many from trying to achieve nobility through marriage or a special grant, or simply by just acting as if they were aristocrats.

36   See also AHN, Inq, Libro 1047, no.13, f.309v; AHN, Inq, Libro 1047, no.13, f.309v.

37   AHN, Inq, Lib.1031, Carta a Madrid.

38   Note the similarities with stereotypes about women's susceptibility to diabolic influences. See Silverblatt (1987, 159–96).

39   Jews were expelled from England and France roughly two hundred years before the Spanish expulsion. See Kamen (1998, 10).

40   Menasseh Ben Israel and Montesinos were ambiguous about the "tribe's" lineage; in fact a careful reading of *The Hope of Israel* suggests that neither believed the tribesmen to have any genealogical relationship to Andean Indians. Menasseh Ben Israel's life and work have been the subject of recent scholarship. See Kaplan, Mechoulan, and Popkin, eds., *Menasseh Ben Israel and His World* (1989) for the most comprehensive collection of articles analyzing Menasseh Ben Israel and his times.

41   This argument about how fears of Judaising and native religious subversions reverberated and augmented one another is also made in light of witchcraft persecutions in Silverblatt (forthcoming).

42   Some examples from testimonies made by accused Judaisers and the witnesses against them: Antonio de Espinoso was taught Judaism in Guinea (see AHN, Inq, Libro 1031, f.104); Luis de Valencia was taught in San Lazaro (see AHN, Inq, Legajo 1647, no.12, f.23,38v), and communicated his faith throughout Europe, Africa, and the Americas (see AHN, Inq, Legajo 1647, no.12, f.98v); Manuel Bautista Perez preached Judaism in slave quarters in San Lazaro and was accompanied by Jorge de Silva, Diego de Ovalle, Sebastian Duarte, and Juan Rodriguez Duarte (see AHN, Inq, Legajo 1647, no.13, f.93–95v); Sebastian Duarte first learned the practices of Judaism in Guinea and conspired with his brother-in-law, Manuel Bautista Perez, and colleagues like Rodrigo Baez Pereyra, in marketing centers along the streets of Lima where merchandise was bought and sold, in the offices of other merchants, in slave houses, and in San Lazaro, where slaves were quartered (see AHN, Inq, Libro 1031, f.192–95v; AHN, Inq, Legajo 1647, no.13, f.153–58); Tome Cuaresma spoke of Judaism when he was in the "slave house" attending to the sick (see AHN, Inq, Legajo 1647, no.13). Manuel Henrriquez communicated his "heresies" with Rodrigo Fernandez in Cusco, Juan de Acevedo in Cartagena, and Juan and Tomas de Lima in his store. He was accused by the prosecutor of having Judaized in many places in Portugal, Madrid, Valladolid, Murcia, Seville, and in New World slaving centers like Cartagena and Panama, as well as Andean towns like Guancabelica and Cusco, and Lima (see AHN, Inq, Legajo 1647, no.11, f.51–51v, f.66v, f.67v, f.74v, f.81v–82). Don Simon Osorio was said to have learned the ritual calendar in France (see AHN, Inq, Legajo 1647, no.11, f.62); Luis de Vega learned in Antwerp (see AHN, Inq, Legajo 1647, no.13, f.116v–19); while walking toward the market stalls in Lima's main plaza, Manuel Bautista Perez told Antonio Gomez de Acosta he was Jewish and claimed he had begun to practice Judaism in the Indies (see AHN, Inq, Legajo 1647, no.13, f.169–70v). See also Lewin (1950, 40). For complex trading relations between Spaniards and indigenous representatives of native communities see Guaman (1980, 1000).

43   AHN, Inq, Legajo 1647, no.013, f.53v.

44   AHN, Inq, Legajo 1647, no.13, f.266.

45   AHN, Inq, Legajo 1647, no.13, f.53.

46   AHN, Inq, Legajo 1647, no.13, f.53–53v. The parenthetical definition is part of the original recorded testimony.

47 AHN, Inq, Legajo 1647, no.13, f.53v.
48 AHN, Inq, Legajo 1647, no.13, f.266.
49 AHN, Inq, Legajo 1647, no.13, f.266.
50 AHN, Inq, Legajo 1647, no.13, f.278v. See note 23.
51 AHN, Inq, Legajo 1647, no.13, f.278v–79.
52 AHN, Inq, Legajo 1647, no.13, f.278v–79.
53 See de Murua (1987, 436–37) for similar descriptions of the use of coca.
54 See n. 40.
55 Contrary to popular assumptions about the Spanish Inquisition, Inquisitors were not at will to make up testimony. Inquisitorial procedures were constrained by rules governing the legitimacy of evidence and all judgments were subject to review by superiors.
56 See also AHN, Inq, Legajo 1647, no.13, ff.2–37v and passim.
57 AHN, Inq, Legajo 1647, no.13, f.27v.
58 AHN, Inq, Legajo 1647, no.13, f.37–37v.
59 AHN, Inq, Legajo 1647, no.13, f.248–249v,260,315v. The phrase "never Portuguese" is found in f.315v.
60 AHN, Inq, Legajo 1647, no.13, f.342v.
61 See Silverblatt (forthcoming) for official concerns regarding the disorder of gender and racial structures, and Spalding (1974) for governmental apprehension about the ability of indios and mestizos to pass as espanoles.

References

Adler, Elkan Nathan. 1908. *Auto-de-Fé and Jew.* London: H. Frowde.

Alberro, Solange. 1988. *Inquisicion y sociedad en Mexico 1571–1700.* Mexico City: Fondo de Cultura Económica.

Arriaga, Father Pablo Jose de. 1968. *The Extirpation of Idolatry in Peru.* Translated by L. C. Keating. Lexington: University of Kentucky Press.

Ayala, Guaman Poma de. 1980. *El Primer nueva coronica y buen gobierno.* 3 vols. Edited by J. V. Murra and R. Adorno. Mexico City: Siglo Veintiuno.

Baroja, Julio Caro. 1972. *Inquisicion, brujeria y criptojudaismo.* Barcelona: Ediciones Ariel.

—. 1986. *Los Judios en la Espana moderna y contemporanea.* 3 vols. Madrid: Ediciones Arión.

Beinart, Haim. 1981. *Conversos on trial: The Inquisition in Ciudad Real.* Translated by Y. Guiladi. Jerusalem: Magnes Press, Hebrew University.

Cobo, Father Bernabe. [1653] 1983. *History of the Inca Empire.* Austin: University of Texas Press.

Cohen, Jeremy. 1982. *The Friars and the Jews: The Evolution of Medieval Anti-Judaism.* Ithaca: Cornell University Press.

Cohen, Jeremy, ed. 1991. *Essential Papers on Judaism and Christianity in Conflict from Late Antiquity to the Reformation.* New York: New York University Press.

Comaroff, Jean, and John L. Comaroff. 1991. *Of Revelation and Revolution: Christianity,*

Colonialism, and Consciousness in South Africa, 2 vols. Chicago: University of Chicago Press.

Comaroff, John L., and Jean Comaroff. 1992. *Ethnography and the Historical Imagination: Studies in the Ethnographic Imagination.* Boulder: Westview Press.

Contreras, Jaime. 1997. *Historia de la Inquisicion Espanola (1478–1834): herejias, delitos y representacion.* Madrid: Arco Libros.

Cordoba, Fray Buenaventura de Salinas y. 1957. *Memorial de las historias del nuevo mundo Piru.* Lima: Universidad Nacional Mayor de San Marcos.

Corrigan, Philip, and Derek Sayer. 1985. *The Great Arch.* Oxford: Blackwell.

Delgado, Paulino Castaneda, and Pilar Hernandez Aparicio. 1989. *La Inquisicion de Lima.* Madrid: Deimos.

Descripción del Virreinato del Perú: Crónica inédita de convienzos del siglo XVII. 1958. Rosario: Universidad Nacional del Litoral.

de Espinoza, Antonio Vazquez. 1942. *Compendium and Description of the West Indies.* Translated by Charles Upson Clark. Washington, D.C.: Smithsonian Institution.

Dundes, Alan, ed. 1991. *The Blood Libel Legend: A Casebook in Anti-Semitic Folklore.* Madison: University of Wisconsin Press.

Dussell, Enrique. 1993. "Eurocentrism and Modernity." *Boundary 2:* 65–75.

——. 1998. "Beyond Eurocentrism." In *The Cultures of Globalization,* edited by Fredric Jameson and Masao Miyoshi. Durham, N.C.: Duke University Press.

Elliott, J. H. [1963] 1990. *Imperial Spain.* New York: Penguin Books.

Gitlitz, David M. 1996. *Secrecy and Deceit: The Religion of the Crypto Jews.* Philadelphia: Jewish Publication Society.

Hall, Stuart. 1997. "Old and New Identities, Old and New Ethnicities." In *Culture, Globalization, and the World System: Contemporary Conditions for the Representation of Identity,* edited by Anthony D. King. Minneapolis: University of Minnesota Press.

Hampe-Martinez, Teodoro. 1996. "Recent Works on the Inquisition and Peruvian Colonial Society, 1570–1820." *Latin American Research Review* 31, no. 2: 43–63.

Henningsen, Gustav. 1980. *The Witches' Advocate: Basque Witchcraft and the Spanish Inquisition, 1609–1614.* Reno, Nev.: University of Nevada Press.

Hsia, R. Po-chia. 1988. *The Myth of Ritual Murder: Jews and Magic in Reformation Germany.* New Haven: Yale University Press.

Israel, Jonathan I. 1989. *European Jewry in the Age of Mercantilism, 1550–1750.* Oxford: Clarendon.

Israel, Jonathan I. 1990. *Empires and Entrepôts: The Dutch, the Spanish Monarchy and the Jews, 1585–1713.* London: Hambledon Press.

Israel, Menasseh Ben. [1652] 1987. *The Hope of Israel.* Translated by Moses Wall and Richenda George. Edited by Henry Méchoulan and Gerard Nahon. Oxford: Oxford University Press.

Jaher, Frederic Cople. 1996. *A Scapegoat in the New Wilderness.* Cambridge: Harvard University Press.

Kamen, Henry. 1985. *Inquisition and Society in Spain in the Sixteenth and Seventeenth Centuries.* Bloomington: Indiana University Press.

——. 1998. *The Spanish Inquisition: A Historical Revision.* New Haven: Yale University Press.

Kaplan, Yosef, Henry Méchoulan, and Richard Popkin, eds. 1989. *Menasseh Ben Israel and his World*. Leiden: E. J. Brill.

Katz, Jacob. 1993. *Tradition and Crisis: Jewish Society at the End of the Middle Ages*. Translated by Bernard Dov Cooperman. New York: E. J. Brill.

Kohut, George Alexander. 1903. "The Trial of Francisco Maldonado de Silva." *American Jewish Historical Society* 11.

Lea, Henry Charles. 1906–7. *A History of the Inquisition of Spain*. New York: Macmillan Company.

Levack, Brian. 1987. *The Witch-Hunt in Early Modern Europe*. London: Longman.

Lewin, Boleslao. 1950. *El Santo Oficio en América y el más grande proceso inquisitorial en el Perú*. Buenos Aires: Sociedad Hebraica Argentina.

Liebman, Seymore B. 1970. *The Jews in New Spain: Faith, Flame, and the Inquisition*. Coral Gables, Fla.: University of Miami Press.

Lockhart, James, and Stuart B. Schwartz. 1983. *Early Latin America: A History of Colonial Spanish America and Brazil*. Cambridge, UK: Cambridge University Press.

Medina, Jose Toribio. 1956. *Historia del Tribunal de la Inquisicion de Lima*, 2 vols. Santiago: Fondo Histórico y Bibliográfio J. T. Medina.

Mugaburu, Josephe, and Francisco Mugaburu. 1975. *Chronicle of Colonial Lima: The Diary of Josephe and Francisco Mugaburu*. Edited by R. Miller. Norman: University of Oklahoma Press.

Murua, Martin de. 1987. *Historia general del Peru*. Madrid: Historia.

Netanyahu, Benzion. 1995. *The Origins of the Inquisition in Fifteenth Century Spain*. New York: Random House.

——. 1997. *Toward the Inquisition: Essays on Jewish and Converso History in Late Medieval Spain*. Ithaca: Cornell University Press.

Novinsky, Anita. 1972. *Crisaos novos na Bahia*. Sao Paolo: Editóra Perspectiva.

Oberman, Heiko Augustinus. 1984. *The Roots of Anti-Semitism in the Age of Renaissance and Reformation*. Translated by J. I. Porter. Philadelphia: Fortress Press.

Ortiz, Antonio Dominguez. 1993. *Los Judeoconversos en la Espana moderna*. Madrid: Editorial MAPFRE.

Palma, Ricardo. 1910. *Apendice a Mis Ultimas Tradiciones Peruanas*. Barcelona: Tipografia Maucci.

Quijano, Anibal. 1992. "Colonialidad y modernidad-racionalidad." In *Los Conquistados: 1492 y la poblacion indigena de las Americas*, edited by Heraclio Bonilla. Bogota: Tercer Mundo Editores.

Quiroz, Alfonso. 1986. "La expropiacion inquisitorial de cristianos nuevos portugueses en Los Reyes, Cartagena y Mexico (1635–1649)." *Historica* 10.

Ramos, Gabriela. 1989. "La fortuna del inquisidor: Inquisicion y poder en el Peru (1594–1611)." *Cuadernos para la historia de la evangelizacion en America Latina*.

——. 1991. "La privatizacion del poder: Inquisicion y sociedad colonial en el Peru." In *Violencia y poder en los Andes*, edited by H. Urbano. Cusco, Peru: Centro de Estudios Regionales Andinos Bartolomé de Casas.

Reparaz, Gonzalo de. 1976. *Os Portugueses no Vice-Reinado do Peru: Seculos XVI e XVII*. Lisbon: Instituto de Alta Cultura.

Roth, Cecil. 1932. *The Spanish Inquisition.* London: R. Hale.

—. 1932. *A History of the Marranos.* Philadelphia: Jewish Publication Society of America.

Roth, Cecil, ed. 1935. *The Ritual Murder Libel and the Jew: The Report by Cardinal Lorenzo Gorganelli.* London: The Woburn Press.

Selke, Angela S. 1986. *The Conversos of Majorca: Life and Death in a Crypto-Jewish Community in XVII Century Spain.* Translated by H. J. Maxwell. Jerusalem: Magnes Press, Hebrew University.

Silverblatt, Irene. 1987. *Moon, Sun, and Witches: Gender Ideologies and Class in Inca and Colonial Peru.* Princeton: Princeton University Press.

—. Forthcoming. "The Inca's Witches: Gender and the Cultural Work of Colonization in Seventeenth Century Peru." In *Possible Pasts,* edited by Robert St. George. Ithaca: Cornell University Press.

Spalding, Karen. 1974. *De Indio a campesino.* Lima: Instituto de Estudios Peruanos.

Tejada, Luis Coronas. 1988. *Conversos and Inquisition in Jaen.* Jerusalem: Magnes Press, Hebrew University.

Thompson, E. P. 1978. "Eighteenth-Century English Society: Class Structure without Class?" *Social History* 3, no. 1:133–65.

Villanueva, Joaquin Perez, and Bartolome Escandell Bonet, eds. 1984. *Historia de La Inquisition en Espana y America.* Madrid: Biblioteca de Autores Cristianos: Centro de Estudios Inquisitoriales.

Williams, Raymond. 1978. *Marxism and Literature.* Oxford: Oxford University Press.

Yerushalmi, Yosef Hayim. 1981. *From Spanish Court to Italian Ghetto. Isaac Cardoso: A Study in Seventeenth Century Marranism and Jewish Apologetics.* Seattle: University of Washington Press.

The Kabyle Myth: Colonization and the Production of Ethnicity

Paul A. Silverstein

From 1830 to Algerian independence in 1962, military ethnographers and linguists collaborated with the colonial state in detailing a particular Berber tribal identity independent of the larger Arab polity in Algeria. Various origins were postulated, ranging from Arabian to Nordic via Numidian. During the anticolonial movement and in the years since independence, conflicting interest groups in Algeria have appropriated these definitions alternately to justify policies of Arabization and to underwrite Kabyle separatist endeavors. In parallel fashion, the French state has utilized such ethnographic theories and techniques regarding its Algerian colonial and postcolonial populations to support schemes of national integration based in the simultaneous positing of an essential Gallic/Frank identity and a universal citizenship where the practice of private, commensurate difference is constituted as a human right. This essay is a historical anthropological exploration of various constructions of Berber ethnic difference in Algeria and France. Beginning with colonial debates over the origins of Kabyle tribes, I interrogate the relationship between colonial, national, and regional integration projects and the myth of a spatially- and temporally-prior originality. In the end, I argue that producing national and transnational formations has always entailed ethnicization and racialization, rather than the erasure of other, potentially conflicting sets of socially constructed difference.

Nationalism-in-Reverse

Before addressing these issues, it is first necessary to situate the debates in their theoretical context. A number of recent works have been devoted to the role of ethnic groups in nationalist movements and contemporary nation-states

(Gellner 1983; Hobsbawm 1990; Smith 1986). Using a constructivist approach, they have driven home the notion that the nation is an invented entity, a recently formulated imagined community of compatriots separated by great distances, unaware of each other's physical existence, united through the common practice of modern, daily rituals (see Anderson 1991). My concerns with this literature are threefold.[1] First, there has been a tendency to reduce the relationship between nationalism and colonialism to one of derivation and modularity —a discourse originating in Western and Central Europe and flowing unilaterally to the colonies, where it is appropriated to a greater or lesser extent by Western-educated elites. Second, the authors' insistence on the imagined or invented nature of nations has largely occurred in contrast to ethnic groups (or *ethnies* in Anthony D. Smith's terminology [1986]) which they impute with a primordial authenticity. Third, in underlining the historical construction of European nations, the literature has paradoxically contributed, in the words of Michael Herzfeld, to the "hardening" of stereotypes through which essentialized conceptions of European national characters, and the relation of these characters to infranational differences resident within them, have been popularly reproduced (1984).

First of all, theories of nationalism within the fields of history and political science have consistently focused on the modern nation-state as the final product of a powerful set of discourses and practices which, emerging on the eve of the 1789 French Revolution, quickly spread in a variety of derivative or modular forms across the world until today becoming the singular, hegemonic form of sovereignty in geopolitics. With varying degrees of rigor, Eric Hobsbawm (1990), Benedict Anderson (1991), and John Breuilly (1985) each invoke this univocal interpretation. Hobsbawm clearly regards the nation-state as a form emerging in an industrializing Europe, though he wonders briefly whether its subsequent spread to the peripheries has in fact altered its original, metropolitan constitution (1990, 150–151). Anderson agrees implicitly, linking nationalism to the conjunction of linguistic standardization and capitalist technologies of production and distribution in Europe, though he actually traces its pre-nationalist roots to the peregrinations of American creolized elites. However, it is Breuilly who represents the best example of this tendency.

Breuilly holds a mainly state-centered understanding of colonial nationalism. All nationalisms, he claims, represent "an attempt to gain state power," and in colonial nationalisms the specific goal is to promulgate "an alternative political community to that offered by the colonial state" (1985, 137). Only by posing itself in such terms could a liberation movement gain legitimacy in a contemporary international spectrum predicated on the congruency (or at least hyphenation) of nations and states. "Nationalism provided a legitimate alternative to Empire. . . . However, in order to pose this alternative credibly nationalism usually needed to claim that it could form a successor state" (1985, 191). These European models had been appropriated by the Western-educated indigenous elite who had been the main beneficiaries of the "collaborator system" ironically established to maintain colonial power. As such, Breuilly views anticolonial nationalism as primarily a derived discourse of state power.

My second concern with the constructivist approach of theorists like Ernest Gellner and Hobsbawm, is the contention that *ethnies* constitute the a priori building blocks for national formations. They have claimed that industrializing Europe necessitated new forms of national social organization (in terms of common linguistic and cultural understandings) in order to foster the required internal market structure. For Gellner, this was to be accomplished primarily through the education system: "Modernization requires a new kind of mass education, which is standardized, public, secular, academy supervised and diploma conferring, because of industry's need for both generic and specialist training, of literacy and numeracy, and especially for a mobile workforce and population" (cited in Smith 1984, 455). Indeed, for Gellner, it is the monopoly of education rather than the monopoly of violence which underwrites national unity (1983, 34). Likewise, for Hobsbawm, the prime locus was in language policy: a modern, national society depended on the "homogenization and standardization of its inhabitants, essentially by means of a written 'national language' " (1990, 93). In either case, the elaborations of nations required the elimination of prior ethnic, linguistic, and regional attachments. "Nations as a natural, God-given way of classifying man, as an inherent political destiny, are a myth; nationalism, which sometimes takes pre-existing cultures and turns them into nations, sometimes invents them, and often obliterates pre-existing cultures: *that* is reality" (Gellner 1983, 48–49; emphasis mine). In this way, for these writers nations do not arise in the politicization of ethnies, but in their destruction and reworking. Primordial ties (of ethnicity, religion, territory, etc.), if anything, stand in the way of nationalist movements, and thus tribalism becomes anathema to modernity.

It is on this issue that the literature on nationalism dovetails with historical models of the Middle East based on the ethnic mosaic. This relatively new scholarship sought in part to reject an earlier Orientalist discourse which posited a singular Asiatic subject (generally translated as Arabo-Islamic civilization) and projected it, as Edward Said has pointed out (1978), across a homogenous spatial and temporal region. Instead, Carleton Coon and his theoretical disciples have reread the Middle East as a site for the interaction of multiple entities constituted by particular religious, regional, or ethnic affiliations (1958). Operating alternately through a diremptive division of labor or a protracted antagonism, these divisions were understood to be unproblematically existing, if problematically coexisting. Jews and Moslems, Sunnis and Shi'ites, Arabs and Berbers came to represent the transhistorical essences which mediate and even determine the specific historical structures (nationalist projects, socialist endeavors, Islamic movements) that mark the region.[2] For instance, in the introduction, entitled "The Middle Eastern Mosaic," to his recent work on minorities in the Middle East, Mordechai Nisan opposes "lower levels of community solidarity rooted in tribal, ethnic, or clannish ties" to higher, more general bases of social organization such as Caliphate Islam or, during the modern period, "shared civil sentiment" (1991, 6). Moreover, like Gellner and Hobsbawm, he describes the persistence of ethnic solidarities in modern times, the so-called "problem of polyethnic countries," as an "illness" which can become "terminal in its consequences" (1991, 8).

My final concern is that these theories of nationalism have underscored a binary opposition which contrasts France to Germany along the dichotomy of civilization (*civilisation*) and culture (*Kultur*). With reference to the eighteenth-century political philosophical debates occurring during the original outlining moment of the two nation-states, scholars like Breuilly (1985) and Rogers Brubaker (1992) have insisted that Germany followed the Romantic leanings of Johann Herder, Frederick Schlegel, and G. W. F. Hegel, among others, who viewed the world as naturally (perhaps genetically) divided into particularist groups (*Volks*); whereas France, following the liberal universalism of Jean-Jacques Rousseau and Denis Diderot, based its own national project on the uniting of primordial individuals into an enlightened society based on rights and duties. They have utilized these originary ideological moments to explain contemporary nationality and citizenship laws (viewed as the gatekeepers of national identity), particularly Germany's juridical emphasis on *ius sanguinis* ("right of blood") and France's legalized *ius solis* ("right of soil"). Moreover, in allying national projects with these ideological poles, they have tended to recapitulate the *doxa* of governmental discourse, namely that French national integration requires the active subsuming, if not erasure, of ethnic and religious differences into transcendent individual subject-citizens (see Brubaker 1992, Habermas 1993). Ethnicity, accordingly, cannot legitimately exist in France.

In the end, then, I would argue that constructivist theorists of nation-states are participating in a "nationalism-in-reverse."[3] For, whereas anticolonial nationalists were bent on erasing previously ascribed ethnic differences, on showing that such divisions were colonial constructs which obscured the true unity and authenticity of the nation, recent scholars have sought to deconstruct such nations and point out the true identity of the smaller ethnic groups. Thus, Hobsbawm makes a stark distinction between the "invented" nation of Algeria and the "genuine" nations of Berbers and Arabs (1990, 179), just as he does between traditions (1983). Likewise, constructivist scholars have reversed nationalists' positions regarding the originality of their nations by demonstrating their derivative character. Finally, whereas elites have justified their own nationalist endeavors by situating their aspirations within a geopolitical unity of nation-states, certain contemporary scholars of nationalism have undermined this unity by insisting on the essential differences of national projects, by outlining the inherent disunity of the nation-state system.

However, when examined both historically and ethnographically, the above reverse-nationalist arguments of modularity, primordiality, and differentialized state-national character prove misleading. In the first place, they ignore what Handler and Daniel Segal have termed the "colonial genealogies of nationalism" (Segal and Handler 1992, 2; see also Handler and Segal 1993; Segal 1991). They fail to account for a number of practices and techniques, from ethnological monographs to cadastral surveys, utilized by the French state throughout the colonial period to categorize and relativize cultural differences both at home and abroad. As this essay will demonstrate, the military assimilation of Algeria into France was accompanied by the reification of ethnic difference through the elaboration of the spatial and temporal origins of the colony's populations. Secondly, in elaborating these ethnic divides, military scholars contributed to the redefinition of the French nation within its imperial and European context. The Algerian colony, as a site of innovation and experimentation, provided the tools for the French state to monopolize its authority at home and slough off its undesirable masses. Thirdly, while inveighing against Anglo-American versions of protectoratism and later multiculturalism, the French state during the colonial and postcolonial periods actually underwrote the production of new ethnicities within and among its colonial and postcolonial populations. In the process, it established certain parameters outlining the "right to difference" in France, parameters which effectively categorized particular cultural features as commensurable or not with the French nation-state during its various periods. Today, fears over tribalism—coded as the rise of Islam in France—remain tempered by overt declarations of culture as an essential human right. To view this process as one of the univocal erasure of sub-national sociocultural differences, then, amounts to a mere scholarly appropriation of the French state's own ideology, their own myth of origin as it were. This ambivalence over the avowal and disavowal of ethnicity remains at the heart of France's social imaginary, from its imperial heyday to the eve of European integration.

Colonialism and National Integration

From the very beginning, assumptions of primordiality and modularity shared by theorists and critics of nationalism gloss over the historicity of ethnic categories and, likewise, the role of nationalist discourses in their constitution. In the first place, one must refocus on the colonial period as a determining moment in the production of both national and ethnic social formations. The conquest of Algeria played a significant role in the consolidation of France's national integrity, allowing the country to slough off its less desirable urban masses, experiment with the norms and forms of modernity (urbanization, secular education, etc.), and provide a rotating reserve army of laborers vital for the country's industrialization and later postwar reconstruction (Rabinow 1989; Talha 1989; Wright 1991). In this respect, one must go beyond Benedict Anderson's emphasis on creole pioneers on nationalism (1991) and link the development of European nationalist sentiment to the colonial process itself. Through various colonial discourses which associated the Indian populace with children (among which Marx's "On Imperialism in India" [1978] must be numbered), Britain was able to impute to itself "magical feelings" of being "an advanced culture where human reason and civilized norms had the greatest influence, and a polity farthest on the road to revolutionary self-actualization" (Nandy 1983, 35). In the case of France, this was exactly the *mission civilisatrice*, a self-aggrandizing ideological form which simultaneously justified colonial expansion and a pro-assimilationist national self-understanding. Such sentiments of superiority fed into a nationalism already underwritten by a "false sense of homogeneity" instilled in part through the mechanics of colonization. "Colonialism blurred the lines of social divisions by opening up alternate channels of social mobility in the colonies and by underwriting nationalist sentiments through colonial wars of expansion or through wars with other ambitious European powers seeking a share of colonial glory" (Nandy 1983, 33).

This interplay between metropole and colony in the entrenchment of a state-national regime of sovereignty and the putative elimination of social tensions arising from extant heterogeneous class and cultural loyalties is greatly illustrated in the military conquest of Algeria. Most histories of French colonialism, written by both French and Algerian authors, date the period of conquest as commencing with the July 1830 attack on Algiers by Charles X's fleet. This attack, understood by most contemporary observers as a punitive expedition for insults made by the Ottoman governor (*dey*) of Algiers to the French consul during an 1827 state visit (Andrieu 1894; Demontezon 1851),[4] actually inscribed itself in a series of conflicts among the French, European, and Ottoman states. Commercial relations between Algiers and Paris had stagnated since two shipments of wheat, delivered in 1798 by two Jewish-Algerian merchants, were confiscated by French port authorities without payment. Afterward, the dey refused the authorization of future shipments until the several million francs owed were paid in full (Moliner-Violle 1877). Further, throughout this period, French merchant vessels in the Mediterranean were repeatedly attacked by pirate ships emanating from the Barbary coast of North Africa and largely under the control of the dey of Algiers.[5] In the words of one observer, the 1830 attack on Algiers had as its secret goal the elimination of this piracy (Société de l'Afrique 1836).

Moreover, the attack was situated historically within the imperial competition of European powers, occurring within recent memory of Napoleon's loss of his outpost in Egypt to the British (1801). Many of those participating in the expeditionary force to Algiers were veterans of the Egyptian campaigns. Military plans were largely developed on the basis of the French army's experience in Egypt—from health precautions to institutions designed to govern the natives (the *bureaux arabes*) once conquest had been achieved (Lorcin 1995, 19). Since this earlier defeat, France had consistently set its sights on a reconquest of the Mediterranean, in part to facilitate the burgeoning trade with the East Indies (whose shipping lines were threatened by the British on the one hand and the Barbary pirates controlled by the Dey of Algiers on the other), in part to restore the Napoleonic Empire and the national prestige which had accompanied it (Cobban 1961, 41–42). Indeed, the popular media of the time would link the new African colony to the Belgian and German territories west of the Rhine river which had been annexed by France by 1799 and subsequently amputated by the 1815 Treaty of Vienna after the defeat of Napoleon on the Continent. It was even rumored in a 19 May 1833 issue of the Marseilles newspaper *Sémaphore* that Great Britain had offered to reconstitute these former provinces if French forces agreed to leave Algeria (cited in Guiral 1955). Whether this rumor actually held any validity proves less relevant than the facticity of its reception, that the colonization of Algiers served in part to reanimate the imagination of "national glory" (Guilhaume 1992, 61–62).

The issue of national unity was of particular concern at the time of the expedition to Algeria given the high degree of political turmoil with Charles X's government.[6] In a series of political blunders, Charles had managed to offend both the liberal and conservative political factions of the time, as he simultaneously reinstated clerical control of the educational system (a feature of the ancien régime to which the bourgeois, professional classes were particularly opposed) and minimized the indemnity paid to returned aristocratic émigrés who had fled France during the 1789 Revolution. Already in 1827, the Chamber of Deputies was evenly split between supporters and opposers of the monarch. In that year, the Minister of War wrote to Charles that an invasion of Algiers would be a "useful distraction from political trouble at home" which would allow the government "to go to the country at the next election with the keys of Algiers in its hand" (Ageron 1991, 5). This note, coinciding with the dey's insult of the French consul, convinced the king to begin a naval blockage of the port of Algiers. However, the blockade did not achieve the desired results, and by March 1830 the opposition had gained enough strength to pass a vote of no confidence against the government. The king responded in June by dissolving the chamber and calling for new elections the following month. He immediately ordered General Bourmont to attack Algiers, as—according to school textbooks used in France throughout the next century—he "counted on a military success to obtain favorable election results" (Auge and Petit 1906). While the elections would produce a chamber even more opposed to the government (274 seats against 143) than before, Charles and Prime Minister Polignac nevertheless felt that the quick, three-week success of the military expedition would enable them to reinforce their political control. On July 25, they issued the Four Ordinances which dissolved the newly-elected parliament, censored the press, rescinded the voting privileges from the professional classes by raising the minimum income for suffrage, and called for new elections on this basis. Unfortunately, Charles had overestimated the posterity achieved by the Algiers success, and within a week rioters had taken control of the Parisian streets and his regime had been toppled (Cobban 1961, 89–90).

While the final political result of Charles's actions was a dismal failure, the precedent of employing external colonization as an internal political strategy had nonetheless been set. If the 1830 conquest largely responded to the imperative of forging a national consensus around a decaying Bourbon Monarchy, of recovering a lost imperial prestige, the 1871 military expedition to Kabylia followed a similar logic of national integration for the nascent Third Republic formed in the wake of the fall of Louis Napoleon's Second Empire during the 1870 Franco-Prussian war.[7] Already in March 1870, the colonists in Algeria pushed through a new constitution to reestablish a civilian regime closely tied to the metropole that had been eliminated by Louis-Napoleon's military, "Arab Kingdom" (*Royaume Arabe*) government. In October 1870, the Crémieux Decree (named for the Jewish Minister of Justice, Isaac Crémieux) furthered these assimilation efforts by granting full French citizenship to Algerian Jews. The decree revised the Senatus-Consulte (Imperial Act) of 14 July 1865 which had created a secondary, subject (*sujet*) category for Algerian Jews and Muslims allowing them to enjoy most civilian and military rights but excluding them from political enfranchisement (and hence military duties) unless they abandoned their religious personal status (*statut personnel*) and accepted the French civil code concerning marriage and property. Given this requirement, during the period 1865–1870, only 142 Jews naturalized themselves (Ageron 1991, 39). The Crémieux decree was a response to this paucity given the particular need for conscripts to protect metropolitan France from an advancing Prussian army within its sights on the German-speaking French territories of Alsace and Lorraine (Bodley 1926, 39).

Following the defeat, the European powers allowed the colonial expansion in Algeria to continue apace in order to divert French attention from the lost territories of Alsace and Lorraine (Cobban 1965, 91). Indeed, such expansion greatly served the interests of the nascent Third Republic to defuse the urban social tensions which would poignantly surface in the 1871 Paris Commune. Laws enacted by the new civilian government in Algeria eliminated the influence which Muslim Algerian leaders had maintained under Louis Napoleon's "Arab Kingdom" policies, suspending the Senatus-Consulte of 22 April 1863 protecting tribal landholdings (*arch*), expanding the territory under French administration, eliminating the General Consuls (*conseils généraux*) legislative bodies on which Muslim subjects had representation, and reinstating a special "Arab tax" (*impôt arabe*) on Muslim non-citizens. Reacting largely to these new measures, a number of tribes in Kabylia (amounting to an estimated 200,000 armed fighters under the leadership of the Sufi *Rahmaniyya* brotherhood) rose up in February 1871 against the colonial government in a bitter insurrection which would last for nearly a year. Finally, by February 1872, the French colonial army had crushed the uprising with absolute vehemence, imposing an impossible indemnity of thirty-five million francs and confiscating 446,000 hectares of land in Greater Kabylia alone. In particular, the military government redistributed over 100,000 acres of this expropriated land as an emigration incentive to 1,183 Alsatian families who had fled to Paris before the invading Prussian armies and had joined the burgeoning, unemployed urban swell which had contributed to the Paris Commune revolts several months earlier (Julien 1963, 65; Talha 1989, 31). Meanwhile, the Kabyle leaders and their families joined the Communards in exile to New Caledonia, one of France's newly acquired Pacific colonies, while thousands of others were forced into a situation of migrant labor, bringing them to Tunisia, Algiers, and eventually France in search of work.

Having now consolidated its rule in both Paris and Kabylia, the Third Republic began to utilize the colony as a proving ground for national integration policies and, in doing so, further assimilate it into the metropole. In 1880, the Third Republic accommodated the loss of Alsace-Lorraine by legislatively assimilating the Algerian colony as three administrative departments, thus expanding France's effective territory fourfold.[8] From 1881 to 1882, the French prime minister Jules Ferry drafted a series of laws which put all local Algerian public services under the direct control of the respective French ministries (Collot 1987, 10–11). These measures actually predated the 1884 legislation on municipalities—allowing for the free election of local mayors as representatives of the state—which would have the same practical effects for peripheral regions within the metropole. Kabylia was particularly targeted in this incorporation. Mountain villages destroyed by French army troops during the 1856 and 1871 campaigns had their villagers relocated to model government villages built according to a logic of European social organization and surveillance (Bourdieu and Sayad 1964; Mitchell 1988, 44–48).[9] In 1874 autonomous legal jurisdiction in the remaining Kabyle villages (regulated by local, oral laws or *qanoun*) was abolished and regional courts were established. Economically speaking, the government sought to subsume village markets into the greater economy and, through the recruitment of local farmworkers into colonial plantations or industrial concerns abroad, introduce money (in the form of remittances) as the uniform standard of value (Sayad 1977).

In this sense, the colonial endeavor dovetailed with the production of a uniform spatial and temporal structure, in the realms of politics (*départements*), economics (capital), and culture (standard French), at the root of national construction. The famous "civilizing mission" (mission civilisatrice) perhaps had less to do with ideals of a universal human progress from savagery to civilization than it did with an imperative to secularize, enframe, or dis-enchant the territory and chronology of the natives encountered, and to integrate these spaces and times into a centralized, national structure (Mitchell 1988, 48–62, 64–69, 154–160).[10] Schools were viewed as the most important instrument or armament in this process ("La politique" 1924), with military leaders like the Maréchal Lyautey painting themselves as first and foremost teachers (*instituteurs*) and calling for an army of soldier-instructors (*soldats-instituteurs*) (Le Glay 1921, 13; see also Mitchell 1988, 69–94).[11] Alongside a number of village parochial schools established by army chaplains and members of the *Pères*

Blancs Jesuit order, Minister Ferry created in 1881 eight schools in Kabylia according to the secular, national education standards he had proposed two years earlier as Minister of Education and would apply more generally two years later throughout Algeria and France (Lorcin 1995, 190). Using the latest cartographic techniques, maps were drawn in greater and greater detail of the regions of Algeria and were incorporated into maps of the French Hexagon hung on Algerian schoolroom walls. The academic year followed the same rhythms and breaks as schools in Paris, without regard to the agrarian cycles or Islamic festivities. Secular textbooks imported from Paris declared that the students' history began with "our ancestors, the Gauls" (Citron 1994). In the end, both the military government and its civilian successor made a concerted effort to integrate the colony into the metropole spatially and temporally. Moreover, as I have shown, the colonies, rather than simply peripheral regions to which national standards were exported, reciprocally functioned as an integral element in the consolidation of a republican national regime. The central importance of this integrity definitively manifested itself eighty years later, in the national upheavals accompanying the wars of decolonization. Such a loss provoked not only the fall of one constitutional government in France, but also a fundamental transformation of French national identity from an Imperial to a European power.

Arabophobia

The constitution of the French nation-state in the late nineteenth century did not, however, merely involve the integration of peripheral populations through the simple erasure of autonomous regions constituted by ethnic or linguistic differences (the Berbers in the colonies; Occitans, Bretons, Basques in the metropole). Rather, these measures often involved the contradictory reification of these categories of difference themselves. Despite the claims made by politicians and theorists alike, the Arab/Berber split in Algeria, neither side having been eradicated nor merely persisting as a primordial survival, has in fact been continually recreated from colonial times through the present struggles. Techniques of enumeration and categorization (mapping, cadastral surveys, etc.) employed to consolidate rule and centralize authority throughout the Empire actually produced hierarchical schemas along which various populations were slotted. Building on the philosophical models posed by mid-century social evolutionists like Herbert Spencer and racial theorists like Arthur de Gobineau which had gained a central place in important Parisian research institutions (the Ecole Polytechnique, in particular), military geographers, linguists, and ethnologists catalogued and racialized traits, language forms, sociopolitical traditions, and religious rites they observed among the conquered peoples along a continuum of progress from savagery to civilization (Lorcin 1995; Said 1993). While the colonial mission civilisatrice sought to transform such "natural," incompatible differences into the mere folkloric appendages of a modern society, the continual use of such hierarchical schemas for governing purposes (for alliances, divide-and-conquer tactics, etc.) resulted in the unforeseen generalization and reification of sub-national categories of race, religion, and ethnicity as essential means of group identification.

Tocqueville and Algeria. The intimate connection between ethnological knowledge production and colonial conquest derives in no small part from the interventions of Alexis de Tocqueville. Having visited the new colony of Algeria in May–June 1841 and again in October–December 1846, Tocqueville became an ardent supporter of the colonial project, publishing a series of pointed letters and longer academic works, and serving on a number of colonial commissions while a member of the French Chamber of Deputies between 1842 and 1849 (Richter 1963; Todorov 1991). While initially defending France's right of war (*droit de la guerre*) to ravage (*ravager*) the country in order to defeat Abd el-Kader's revolt, Tocqueville later excoriated the French military for "having made Muslim society much more miserable, disorderly, ignorant, and barbarous than it was before meeting [the French]" (1841, 78; 1847, 170). He argued that military domination based on the conquest and enslavement of the populace must eventually give way to a civilian colonization based on the reproduction of centralized, republican political models of France, both for practical as well as ethical reasons (1841, 64, 114–19; 1847, 179).

In order to achieve this new society, however, a more detailed knowledge of the country's indigenous inhabitants was required. Tocqueville lauded the army for its "intelligence" and "brilliant courage," for its "patient and tranquil energy" which subjugated Algeria's population and opened up new avenues to understanding them: "Victory has allowed us to penetrate (*pénétrer*) their techniques, their ideas, their beliefs, and has finally delivered the secret to governing them.... Today we can say that the indigenous society is no longer veiled for us (*n'a plus pour nous de voile*)" (1847, 152). This sexualized link between colonial knowledge and power in the "penetration" and "unveiling" of Algerian society through its women would be continually reenacted throughout the colonial period: in the Orientalist paintings of Eugène Delacroix of voluptuous private scenes of "Algerois Women in Their Apartment"; in the profusion of colonial postcards of veiled, semi-veiled, and even bare breasted Algerian women (Alloula 1986; Borgé and Viasnoff 1995); and even in the anticolonial critiques of Frantz Fanon's revolutionary "Algeria Unveiled" essay (1965) and Assia Djebar's postcolonial literary dramatization-*cum*-eruption of Delacroix's harem scene (1980). Not merely a sexual act, the ethnological unveiling of indigenous society as described and prescribed by Tocqueville consisted of a rape, a ravaging of the native's culture as well as his land: "We can only study the barbaric peoples with guns in hand" (1847, 152). As such, it would not only be revealed, it would be taken away. "We know the history of the different tribes almost as well as they; we *possess* the exact biographies of all the influential families" (1847, 153; emphasis mine). And once taken, it could be replaced. Not only through the establishment of native intermediaries and Arab Offices (*bureaux arabes*), could the Algerian people be "put under surveillance" and their "actions controlled," but, according to Tocqueville, they could also be made to integrate the "French maxims" of "individual property and industry" (1847, 166–72). The civilizing mission conceived by Tocqueville, then, amounts largely to cultural rape.

However, as Tocqueville reminded his French parliamentary interlocutors, this civilizing project, while not as impossible as others had claimed, nonetheless needed to overcome several obstacles. The first of these concerned the nomadic character of Algerian tribes, their lack of spatial fixity, and hence their resistance to surveillance and civilization. Analyzing Abd el-Kader's revolt, Tocqueville underlined the leader's maintenance of the existing social structure: "He knows very well that the nomadic life of tribes is his surest defense against us. His subjects will become ours the day they fasten themselves to the soil" (1841, 80). In this respect, Tocqueville recommended "re-anchoring the tribes in their territories" rather than "transporting them elsewhere" and thus underwriting their anterior nomadic tendencies (1847, 174–75). Secondly, the natives' religiosity, and moreover their "fanaticism," posed an obstacle to their potential assimilation. In particular, Tocqueville noted the role of "fanatical beggars, belonging to secret associations, a type of irregular and ignorant clergy" in the recent armed resistance and insurrections organized along the lines of a *djihad* (or "holy war"—"*guerre sainte*") (1847, 173). Rather than being completely savage, Islam represented a "backwards and imperfect civilization," or rather a "half-civilization" caught in a "feudal" or "aristocratic" past (1841, 72–74; 1847, 169). The French needed to overcome this evolutionary *blocus* and bring Africa into the historical path of "the movement of the civilized world" (1841, 61).

However, in Tocqueville's analysis, not all of Algeria's indigenous populations (or "races") were alike in presenting these obstacles. If the colonial relations with the Arabs centered on those political and religious questions just posed, relations with the Kabyles (or "Cabyles" in Tocqueville's transcription) needed to be pursued in terms of "civil and commercial equity" (1837, 47). Tocqueville maintained that, as opposed to the Arabs, the Kabyles appeared anchored in their mountainous refuges, fixed to the material possessions and profits which came from working the land. If Arab tribes claimed territory according to the loose arrangements of communal *arch*, maintained through historical ties and agreements, Kabyle families retained holdings as individualized *melk*, closely resembling European systems of private property (Tocqueville 1837, 46; MacMaster 1993, 26). Further, unlike Arabs, Kabyles seemed to Tocqueville "less faithful" religiously and unwilling to suppress individual liberties in the interest of the group or community: "For the Cabyles, the individual is almost everything, society almost nothing." Even in the midst of the armed religious insurrection, Kabyle villagers continued to "frequent our markets and come rent us their services" (1837, 46). Given these cultural resemblances and "frequent, peaceful relations," Tocqueville concluded that however impenetrable their territory may be, the Kabyles would likely assimilate to French "mores and ideas" due to the "almost invincible attraction that brings savages towards civilized men" (1837, 47). In the end, the Kabyle becomes, in Tocqueville's account, the ideal target of the French cultural, if not territorial, rape: "[While] the Cabyle's country may be closed to us, the Cabyle's soul is open and it is not impossible for us to penetrate it" (1837, 46).

The Arab Obstacle: Nomadism and Islamism. Through these writings, Tocqueville succeeded in outlining the major avenues for the production of what would become known as the "Kabyle Myth."[12] Throughout the colonial period in Algeria (1830–1962), ethnological and military reports from Algeria outlined the ethnic boundary between Arabophone and Berberophone populations and used such a division to justify economic and social policy.[13] Following Tocqueville's injunction to "know thine enemy," the French Ministry of War initiated in 1837 a vast "Scientific Exploration" enterprise under the direction of the State-Major Colonel Bory de Saint-Vincent and manned by a "scientific commission" consisting of a group of trained and amateur historians, sociologists, and linguists in the employ of the colonial army (G. Mercier 1954). While the commission in its official capacity was short-lived (1840–42), its members would eventually publish thirty-nine independent works based on the research completed under its aegis, many of which—including Antoine Carette's *Etudes sur la Kabylie proprement dite* (1848) and later Louis Hannoteau and Aristide Letourneux's *La Kabylie et les coutumes kabyles* (1871)—would become the key ethnographic texts underlying the Kabyle Myth. Moreover, the scientific commission's immediate findings would provide the necessary reconnaissance information for the later full-scale invasion of Kabylia (1850–57—in spite of Tocqueville's objections), just as its final published works—specifically Hannoteau and Letourneux's study of Kabyle legal codes (*qanoun*)—would later facilitate the establishment of a centralized administration there (Favret 1968, 19; Lorcin 1995, 41–52). Colonization and military manuals incorporated "basic facts on the Algerian mentality" (irrationality, impulsiveness, fatalism, thievery, vindictiveness, susceptibility), and suggested corresponding actions which one should take: "Do not admit him into your house"; "Use simple words that he can understand"; "know to flatter him on occasion" ("Guide" 1881, 17–23; *El Moudjahid* 1959, 132–55). Through these arrangements, then, Tocqueville's discursive link between colonial knowledge and power came to fruition.

In particular, Tocqueville's identification of nomadism and fanaticism as the prime characteristics of Arab society and obstacles to the colonial mission civilisatrice would find itself replicated over the next hundred years in various guises as part of the "foundational myths" of the French colonial presence in Algeria (Guilhaume 1992). As I have discussed elsewhere, the sedentary/nomad dichotomy provided a frame for the reinterpretation of world history in terms of a primordial battle between "man-in-motion" and "man-at-rest," discursive poles which have largely underwritten the category of migration (Silverstein 1998; see also Hubac 1948). In the case of Algeria, this historical opposition was encapsulated in the colonial scholarship in geographic tropes, as one elementary school textbook recounted, an "incessant battle between the natural forces of the Mediterranean and those of the Sahara, the conflict between sedentaries and nomads, between men of the sea and men of the desert" (Fontaine 1957, 22). In the words of Emile Masqueray, the preeminent scholar of Kabyle segmentary organization, whose work would have a profound influence on Emile Durkheim, "One must always have this opposition [between sedentary and nomad] in mind when explaining contemporary Algeria" (1886, 16).

While, in point of fact, the Algerian Sahara was occupied throughout the colonial period by both Arabophones and Berberophones, it was the former who were consistently linked to the nomadic lifestyle. On the one hand, their nomadic wanderings posed a security threat to the colonial forces who had difficulty keeping track of potential sources of resistance. Military leaders like General Bugeaud addressed this problem through policies of forcible sedentarization and the creation of model villages. On the other hand, the Arabs' continual spatial movement implied the cultural and political characteristics of instability and disorganization, qualities understood as inherently opposed to modern civilization (Guilhaume 1992, 88; Lorcin 1995, 37–40). Indeed, colonial scholars understood the tribal organization of the Arabs as representing, according to development models being developed by Herbert Spencer and Lewis Henry Morgan, an earlier order of social evolution: The Arab "is an essential nomad who, besides, has not passed the stage (*stade*) of the clan in his evolution" (Gautier 1931, 19). Moreover, as a premodern nomadic pastoralist, the Arab had failed to modify the land itself, to plant crops and produce his livelihood. His lack of agri-*culture* was thus tied to his barbarism, his lack of culture.

> The Arab is the most incapable of farmers: he is only good at wasting and destroying the natural richness of the Tell, earth *par excellence* . . . and this is an inseparable result of the patriarchal regime of barbarism in which he delights . . . What did we find when our soldiers arrived to punish the pirates? Invading scrub brush and palm trees, and all the earth once again needing to be cleared [for planting]; and if today there exist real cultivated fields, it is to the colonizer whom Algeria owes thanks. (Pomel 1871, 18)

By reinforcing the image of a precolonial desert land, French colonists created the myth that it was *deserted*. In working the land, in making it fruitful and productive, they could justify their occupation of it (Guilhaume 1992, 232–36). As such, within the primordial war of sedentaries against nomads, colonization became the only and the only legitimate means of reopening the country to evolution, progress, and history in general.

The second obstacle to colonial assimilation outlined by Tocqueville and appropriated by military scholars concerned the reduction of Arab civilization to Islam, and the perceived incompatibility of the latter with French (Christian) modernity. Such a concern belied fears of Islam as a unifying political force during nineteenth-century anticolonial revolts (Abd el-Kader, Kabyle insurrection), a fear that was revived during the twentieth century by the nascent Arab nationalist movements in Tunisia and Egypt—as articulated in the writings of Mohammed Abdou and Jamal ed-Din al-Afghani (Lucas and Vatin 1975, 34). In colonial discourse, Islam served as the prime trope for explaining two opposed characteristics of the observed Arab personality: on the one hand, their bellicose, hostile natures, attributable to their religious fanaticism; and, on the other hand, their inveterate laziness, resulting from their reverent fatalism. Islam (or "Mahometism," as it was derogated), in this respect, provided the necessary complement to the Arabs' premodern nomadism: "Mahometism appears specially adapted to societies whose social evolution arrested in the phase of barbarous patriarchy . . . a theocratic status of which absolutism is the pivot and fatalism the measure" (Pomel 1871, 5–6). French observers argued that the Arabs' absolutism placed him in a "permanent state of war with the infidel, a duty of eternal war which cannot be suspended" (Servier 1923, 345–46). "Holy war is the aim of all the wishes, all the efforts of the Arab" ("Les Arabes" 1873, 49). Islam served as the main explanation for the horrors of war (beheadings, tortures, mutilations) witnessed by the French expeditionary forces during their conquest of Algeria, horrors attributable to the "vindictive and cruel character" of Arabs "who know no other law than that of the strongest" (Hamelin 1833, 7). Studies conducted by military ethnographers paid particular attention to those Algerian religious organizations, like the faith-healers (*marabouts*) and Sufi brotherhoods (*khouan*), which wielded mystical authority and were capable of organizing believers into potential violence (see De Neveu 1846; Rinn 1889). In the second place, scholars parallelly focused on a contradictory aspect of Islam— fatalism, the absolute reliance on Allah to determine one's future. They viewed it as the root cause of a long series of vices, "laziness, dissimulation, dishonesty, suspicion, unpredictability, love of voluptuousness, luxury and feasting" (Van Vollenhoven 1903, 169), decrying the Muslim Arab as a professional "sun-drinker" (*buveur de soleil*) (Docteur X. 1891, 55). This reverent laziness was understood to reciprocally weaken the Muslim's intellect, impeding all social progress toward modernity. "Intellectually, the Muslim is . . . a paralytic. His brain, subjugated for centuries to the stark discipline of Islam, is closed to everything not predicted, pronounced, specified by religious law. He is therefore systematically hostile to any novelty, to any modification, to any innovation. . . . Such a conception [of fatalism] prohibits all progress, and, in fact, immobility is the essential character of any Muslim society (Servier 1923, 346–47).

Moreover, French administrators perceived this essential religiosity of Arabs, their "unique creation" (Bertrand 1923, x), as an inherent stumbling block to their administrative or legal assimilation into the French nation. "In the Mahometian civilization, religion and law are too intimately confused for the juridical condition of Muslims to be identical to that of Frenchmen or Europeans" (Larcher 1903, 16). The Imperial Act of 14 July 1865 and later the 1870 Crémieux Decree had followed a similar logic in denying Muslim Algerians (and not Jewish Algerians) French citizenship unless they renounced their religious "personal status." When, in 1891, the Third Republic considered eliminating this last impediment and naturalizing all Algerians, a violent debate broke out within the Parliament. Senator M. Sabatier, addressing the Senate on 27 June 1891, opposed the reform on the grounds that it would implicitly condone "Coranic" civil and familial practices, from feudal land tenure to polygamy, which "escape French laws, not to mention French morality" (cited in Borgé and Viasnoff 1995, 18).

What was at issue, then, was not the individual's right of accession to French citizenship, but rather the feared legitimation of a religious body (the Muslim community as directed by the *khouan*) that through its fanaticism and fatalism would respectively undermine French state security and Christian morality. Beyond a "constant system of surveillance," the best way to reduce the authority of religious leaders who "exploit the ignorance of the people" was through the instruction of Muslim children in French language and ideas. "Instruction destroys prejudices, prevents the unreflected adoption of others' ideas . . . it will eliminate the multitude of absurd beliefs which the Arab people accept because they do not have the means to dispute them" (De Neveu 1846, 13).[14] Such a transformation, it was believed, would take "many generations" (Charvet 1892, 86).

In this respect, the civilizing mission went hand in hand with an educating mission and a Christianizing mission. Such a connection was explicitly made by Charles de Foucauld, explorer and colonial missionary in the Moroccan and Algerian Sahara who spent fifty years proselytizing and educating the Twaregs. "We, French, have two duties in Africa. The first is the administration and civilization of our northwest African empire. . . . In civilizing it, we lift its inhabitants morally and intellectually. . . . The second [duty] is the evangelization of our colonies" (Bazin n.d., 408).[15] In this respect, soldier-colonizers viewed themselves as doctors, bringing a sick Algeria back to spiritual, intellectual, and economic health: "When one encounters a sick person on the road, one brings him to the hospital and heals him without asking his opinion. . . . The human duty is to help every individual, to lend him aid and assistance. . . . Barbaric peoples are invalids; civilized peoples are doctors" (Servier 1913, 203). Through this association, the French forces morally justified their violent conquest, their rape of the Algerians' land and culture. As will be further detailed below, such a justification assumed an "intemporal myth" by which Arab-*cum*-Muslim civilisation was equated with a barbarous and oppressive past which the French forces had an ethical duty to eliminate in order to raise Algeria (and its impoverished people) to the present of modernity and the future of civilized nation-states (Guilhaume 1992, 196–98). What administrators and colonists continually feared in this temporal civilizing process was a resurgence of this Islamic past, a recalcifying of the primordial bonds which constituted Algeria's precolonial unity, a reawakening of the mythical *moul as-sa'a*, the divine Master of the Hour, the Exterminating Angel (see Tessier 1865, 304–6).

In the primordial battle between sedentaries and nomads, Christians and Muslims, the Mediterranean and the Sahara, the French administration sought an ally to aid them in their colonial venture (labor the fields, etc.) and to justify their civilizing mission. Following Tocqueville's lead, they specified a number of ethnic, racial, and religious divisions within Algeria's indigenous population: Turks, Moors (city-dwellers of Andalousian origin), Kougoulis (miscegenated Turks and Arabs), Bedouins (Arab desert nomads), Arabs, Jews, and Berbers (among which the Kabyles were numbered).[16] The Kabyles, initially due to generalized linguistic and physiognomic differences, were particularly highlighted within the colonial scholarship. Located in close proximity to Algiers, colonists developed close contacts with Kabyle villagers seeking work in the city or on the surrounding colonial plantations. Moreover, because of the seemingly isolated character of Kabyle mountain villages, Kabylia attracted military ethnologists and archaeologists as a site of pristine Algerian culture. Within a few short decades, a network of research centers, archives, and journals in both the Maghreb and France devoted to the scientific study of Berber language and culture was created in order to contrast the Berbers to their Arab neighbors.

The Kabyle Myth: The Space of Culture. First, these researchers sought to map out the exact contours of the Berber presence within the colony, spatially designating ethno-linguistic homelands within four particular regions within Algeria—the Aurès mountains (Chaouia), the Djurdjura range (Kabyles), the Lybian border (Mzabs), and the Sahara (Touareg). Along with laying out the boundaries of present-day Algeria, French administrators also subdivided Kabylia into "Greater Kabylia" and "Lesser Kabylia" along the Soummam river valley. "The French [created] the term 'Kabylia,' just as they had created the term 'Algeria'; they even multiplied it into Kabylias" (Morizot 1985, 18–19). In a sense, by establishing such a homeland and dividing it from Arab lands (despite its proximity to the capital of Algiers), the French sought to further reify the Kabyles as an entity that was mutually exclusive from and directly opposed to the Arabs. Thus, as in Benedict Anderson's "Map, Museum, and Census" 1991 addendum to *Imagined Communities*, the groundwork for ethnic, as well as national, divisions was laid out in and through the enumerating and classifying techniques of colonialism.

Second, the studies attributed a cultural particularity to the Berbers' spatial identity. This identity was largely defined in terms of the oppositions— between sedentary and nomad, Christianity and Islam—outlined above. If the

Arabs nomadically wandered the land, using it but not adding to it, conversely, the Kabyles were understood as the prototypical sedentaries, holed up in their mountain refuges, faithfully tilling the soil. "[The Kabyle] own land whenever possible. They hold in high respect all property and although there are often no markings, each property owner always knows the exact limits of what belongs to him" (Wysner 1945, 136). Scholars described the Berbers as frugal by nature, endowed with a "commercial instinct" which clearly demarcated them from the frivolous Arabs and brought them closer to the European colonizers (Demontès 1922, 9). These "puritan businessmen" (Chevrillon 1927, 84), as Daumas remarked in contrast to the Arabs who "hate work . . . work a great amount in every season; laziness is shameful in their eyes" (1855, 178; Daumas and Fabar 1847: I, 21). Unlike the immobile, changeable but lazy Arab, the Kabyles were seen as "patient, energetic, sober, intelligent, hard-working, strongly attached to their land" (Garrot 1910, 1046). Finally, in contrast to the Arabs, they "know the value of money . . . [and] contrary to the Muslim law, loan it out with interest, very great interest" (Daumas and Fabar 1847: I, 38).

If the Kabyles appealed to the French in their sedentary economic practices, they did so as well in their religiosity. Less fanatically attached to Islam, the Kabyles "have accepted the Koran but they have not embraced it" (Daumas and Fabar 1847: I, 77). From their worship of saints and reliance on faith healers to their failure to observe daily prayers, Ramadan fastings, and prohibitions on alcohol and pork, "the Kabyle people are far from the religious ideas of the Arab people" (Daumas and Fabar 1847: II, 55). Moreover, their lack of religiosity was symbolized by women. "Their religious notions are rather obtuse. Their women do not veil themselves at all" (Hamelin 1833, 15). According to the myth, the Kabyles held their women in high respect; Kabyle women were masters of the household and "have a greater liberty than Arab women; they count more in society" (Daumas and Fabar 1847: I, 40).[17] The divorced or repudiated woman, instead of being made a slave in her father's house, enjoys all of her liberties (Daumas and Fabar 1847: I, 34; Pomel 1871, 56–57). Moreover, the Kabyles, colonial scholars emphasized, did not practice the polygamy that their religion allowed them, "contenting themselves generally to a single wife" (Garrot 1910, 1047). In the end, then, the Kabyles seemed to approach French Christian morals in their practices, proving that their "Islamization" had always been superstructural: "Beneath the Muslim peel, one finds a Christian seed. We recognize now that the Kabyle people, partly autochtonous, partly German in origin, previously entirely Christian, did not completely transform itself with its new religion. . . . [The Kabyle] re-dressed himself in a *burnous*, but he kept underneath his anterior social form, and it is not only with his facial tattoos that he displays before us, unbeknownst to him, the symbol of the Cross" (Daumas and Fabar 1847: I, 77).

In parallel fashion, the Kabyle's political structure, not determined by Islamic absolutism, belied a proximity to French qualities of "Liberty, Equality, Fraternity." Colonial scholars characterized the Berbers as honorable warriors, fiercely defending their mountain refuges against all invaders (Phoenicians, Romans, Arabs, French).[18] Whereas the Arab accepted the tutelage of Islamic caliphs, the "fiercely independent" Berber, according to the reports, abhorred the very idea of central authority and was prepared to defend his absolute liberty to the death (Guernier 1950, 171–72). Their natural "anarchy" was seen to represent an underlying democracy, symbolized by the village council (or *tajmaât*) and its elected officials. "In this republic, the dominating spirit is that of republican equality" (Guernier 1950, 172; see also Masqueray 1886; Rambaud 1895; Trumelet 1863). Rather than assimilating the *shari'a* (Qu'ranic law) into civil life, the assembly rendered judgment on the basis of customary law (qanoun) (see Hannoteau and Letourneux 1871; Pomel 1871). These laws not only regulated individual contracts and feuds, but also determined the bases for social solidarity, defining the individual's duties to the community in terms of collective labor (*tiwizi*) and taxes. As such, "[The Kabyle's] political and social constitution is equally well different from that of the Arab people, and it must have been vigorously anchored in the mores and needs of the race for it to resist against the dissolving action of Islamism whose political regime presents an absolute contrast. In effect, instead of a despotic patriarchy which annihilates individual liberty, we find a democratic organization which is its antipode" (Pomel 1871, 56). In the end, Kabylia represented for these scholars a "savage Switzerland" composed of federations of independent tribes/cantons (Daumas and Fabar 1847: I, 419).

In this way, colonial scholars drew on economic, religious, and political comparisons to argue that the Kabyles were the exact cultural opposites of the Arabs. Rather than a single people united by a single religion, the Algerian natives were deemed to constitute in fact two peoples divided by a primordial hate. "Everywhere these two peoples live in contact, and everywhere an untraversable gulf separates them; they only agree on one point: the Kabyle detests the Arab and the Arab detests the Kabyle. Such a vivacious antipathy can only be attributed to a traditional resentment, perpetuated from age to age between a conquering and a vanquished race" (Daumas and Fabar 1847: I, 75; see also Tlemcani 1986). The same primordial struggle between the French colonizer and the Arab, between Christian and Muslim civilizations, between the Mediterranean sedentary and the Saharan nomad, was then mapped directly onto the Kabyle/Arab ethnic dichotomy.

As such, the Kabyles were constituted as the natural ally of the French colonizers, and were hence singled out as the privileged targets of the mission civilisatrice.[19] "If the utopia of assimilation is realizable between the European and the native . . . it is therefore the Kabyle race which will be solely capable of it" (Pomel 1871, 60). With Islam constituting for the Kabyles a "superficial varnish, a simple stamp," their transformation into colonial subjects would be comparatively unencumbered. "This feeble religious, and uniquely religious, imprint frees other domains and opens up for us a much greater field and possibilities for action and education than on the plain" ("La politique" 1924, 216). Moreover, with their sedentary history of working the land, their thrifty, proto-capitalist spirit, and their willingness to migrate in search of work, it was believed that, with a little training, the Kabyles "will easily assimilate to our ideas, to our labor methods" (Demontès 1930, 360). Indeed, the Kabyles' very lack of social and economic evolution was considered a boon for their colonial development under the tutelage of French educators. "The young Kabyles will very quickly become good laborers (bons ouvriers), even quicker than Europeans, for their primitive natures are the most receptive; they have a great vacuum to fill; they absorb knowledge almost without effort, unconsciously, as a dry sponge absorbs water. It is a virgin land where fecundity arrives almost spontaneously. They assimilate languages, arts, formulas with a marvelous promptness" (Rambaud 1892, 324). In this respect, as we have seen above, the French military observers viewed their colonization as a civilizing and educating enterprise toward the Algerian natives they encountered. With their soldiers serving, following Lyautey's directives, as actual and metaphorical doctors and educators, colonial observers began to see the French people as a whole in a paternalistic relation with the Algerian natives in general, and the Kabyles in particular, with the concomitant moral obligations implied in that relationship. "In Kabylia . . . the educator-people must share with its student the overabundance of goods derived from their association" (Daumas and Fabar 1847: I, 414). The Kabyle Myth thus served simultaneously to underwrite a double rape of Algeria's resources and cultures, underwriting both the practical mission of conquest and colonization and the ethical mission of civilization.

The Historical Record: Times and Others. Third, scholars plotted the spatial and cultural alliances and oppositions elaborated in the Kabyle Myth over time. Drawing on linguistic, archaeological, and physiological comparisons, a series of conflicting hypotheses concerning the ancient origin of Berber tribes were developed and argued in the colonial journals like the *Revue Africaine*, *Revue du Monde Musulman*, and the *Revue des Deux Mondes*. Some contributors, following the fourteenth-century observations of Ibn Khaldun, attributed a Semitic origin to Berber tribes as descendants of the Canaanites chased out of the Holy Land by the early Israelites (Mercier 1871; Odinot 1924; Tauxier 1862–1863). These military ethnologists regarded the observed sedentary position of the Berber tribes as a recent innovation, viewing them as naturally nomadic. "They still have the blood in their veins of the movement that motivated the migrations of their ancestors" (Odinot 1924, 140). Indeed, the entire history of North Africa could be read, according to one theory, as a succession of invasions by migrant peoples, as a perpetual movement from Orient to Occident stretching up until the sixteenth century (Tauxier 1862, 444). While Berber-speaking populations during the colonial period differentiated themselves from their Arabophone neighbors, there remained a cultural and linguistic Semitic kinship traceable across time and space. "If one observes the everyday life of the Berbers, one will see that their fibbery, their duplicity, their love for lies are comparable to the most puerile defects of their Arab brothers and their cousins, the Jews" (Odinot 1924, 148). In this respect, for these scholars, there remained for both Berbers and Arabs an unsurpassable gulf to European civilization, a gulf measurable in terms of a distant temporal and spatial origin evidenced by currently observable cultural traits.

Against these theories of cultural distance, other colonial observers insisted on the hybrid character of Berber tribes, as simultaneously belonging to the Orient and Occident. Whether as sedentaries or nomads, as relatively recent arrivals or virtual autochtones, the Berbers, according to such theorists, had integrated cultural features from Asia, Africa, and Europe (Mercier 1871; Rinn 1889). Linguistically, the Berber dialects were classified as Hamito-Semitic, with an estimated one-third of their vocabulary deriving from Arabic, and the rest from East African (Hamitic) tongues. Physically, Berber-speaking populations exhibited somatic features identifiable with a variety of geographic regions, from the dark skin of Africa to the high cheekbones of Asia to the green eyes of northern Europe. Moreover, according to these scholars, each successive invasion of the North African region—by Romans, Carthagenians, Arabs—had laid a sediment of cultural heritage absorbed and preserved in the social memory and everyday practice of the contemporary Berber peoples (Rinn 1889, 189). In this respect, the Berbers were identified, in their cultural, linguistic, and physiognomic hybridity, as the exemplars and vessels of a particular North

African history and identity, one in which Europeans and Arabs had played only a marginal role.

Parallel to this particularistic reading of North African history a Eurocentric one developed, one which insisted that the Berbers belonged directly to one or more European race (Brémond 1942; Guernier 1950; Maunier 1922). Drawing on a range of archaeological and physical anthropological evidence, these scholars traced the Berbers to ancient European tribal migrations from across the Mediterranean. While the archaeologist Louis Féraud (1863) first provided physical evidence for a Celtic presence in North Africa (in terms of stela monuments discovered near Constantine) in 1863, a Vandal origin of the North African Berbers had been hypothesized as early as 1792, nearly forty years prior to the foundation of the French colony (Ferrié and Boëtsch 1992, 190). This research reciprocally articulated with a debate occurring concurrently in France throughout the nineteenth century over the identity of the original, dominant race in Europe—whether the blond, doliocephalic Aryans or the brachycephalic Celts (see Martin 1881).

Indeed, the attribution of kinship with indigenous European peoples, whether Basques and Catalans, or Gaels and Celts, was more generally accompanied by heuristic attempts to understand the Arab/Berber divide via comparisons with other ethnic and linguistic divisions extant in Europe. Antoine Carette attempted to relate the ethnic divisions in Algeria to the medieval French regional/linguistic opposition between the northern *langue d'oil* and the southern *langue d'oc* (Carette 1848, 60–70).[20] While Carette associated Kabyle culture with the spirit of the northern langue d'oil, subsequent ethnological studies took exception, concluding the contrary (see Busset et al. 1929). Lucien Bertholon embodied this ethnogenetic controversy in his own writings, alternately identifying these blond-haired "native European Berbers" (*Berbères de souche européenne*) with Celts, Ligurians, Danubians, and Aegeans (1898). In spite of these particularities, however, many scholars would end up agreeing that "Barbary is a European Country." In the work of which the last quote was the subtitle, General Edouard Brémond concluded definitively: "There is absolutely no doubt that the [Berber] populations of North Africa were originally Mediterranean or Nordic European and have not since been modified" (1942, 114). Indeed, the Berbers' presumably republican political organization was understood to have derived with the French political system from classical antiquity (see Guernier 1950, 172; Masqueray 1886; Maunier 1922, 106). Brémond likewise identified the Berbers as having maintained many traditions (from clothing to architecture to funerary rites) at the origin of those extant in modern

Provence or Auvergne. In the end, Eugène Guernier opined, "The Berbers are part of the rational West in formal opposition to the Arabs, who are above all of the imaginative Orient" (1950, 173).

However, if the Berbers shared a racial and cultural kinship with the conquering French, their development, due to the anti-modern nature of Islam, had stagnated several centuries prior. Louis Milliot described the Berbers' socioeconomic institutions as "rude and primitive," resembling those of medieval France of the tenth century (1932, 129; see also Trumelet 1863, viii). Likewise, Carette, as we have seen, pinpointed linguistic divisions to compare nineteenth-century Algeria to France of the Middle Ages (Carette 1848, 60–70; see also Lorcin 1995, 43–45). Brémond concluded his study similarly: "If the Maghreb received nothing from Arabia, little from the Sudan, and almost everything from the Mediterranean, it has also many traits in common with our Middle Ages, traits which we have since forgotten" (1942, 362). As such, the Berbers, for colonial scholars, rather than primitive savages in need of salvation, represented an earlier period of Europe's own past, a past which could be resurrected and then modernized once the bark of Arab and Islamic civilization had been stripped away.

As such, the colonial debates over the origins of the colony's natives established a set of ethnic categories and oppositions which equated observable cultural phenomena with a variety of distant pasts. Such conflicting comparisons mark the structural ambivalence of a colonial project with both scientific and military goals, operating under a joint imperative to map out and classify ethnological differences and simultaneously assimilate such difference into the knowable and practicable. In assimilating Berber and Arab tribes to a uniform Semitic origin, colonial scholars portrayed colonialism as an inherent spatial conflict between East and West, between Islam and Christianity. Contrastingly, the association of Berbers with Europe's past underwrote assimilationist strategies of the colonial project, with the Berbers singled out as the privileged targets of the mission civilisatrice: In either case, the Berbers' cultural antiquity represented a threat to the spatio-temporal unity of the Empire, a threat of time that must be overcome lest it lead to sectarian tribalism (see Axel 1996). The ambivalent approaches to such difference—its isolation or assimilation—depended on whether the Berbers' relation to Islam, a religion approached as incommensurate with French norms, was constituted as basal or merely superstructural.

Conclusion: National Difference

I have sought to demonstrate the ambivalence of the French nation-state's management of ethnic difference, how it has simultaneously avowed and disavowed—produced and erased—sub-national categories of identity. In so doing, I have attempted to undermine assumptions of primordiality rampant within constructivist approaches to the nation-state and its discontents (those I have referred to as "nationalists-in-reverse"). Interestingly, as I have elaborated elsewhere (Silverstein 1996, 1997, 1998), cultural activists often use these same assumptions of primordiality to justify their own claims of originality and signal the oppression which they have experienced at the hands of nation-states.

Within the contemporary Berber movement in Algeria and France, various engaged intellectuals have made a concerted effort to portray Berberity as the true, originary identity of Algeria, the Maghreb, and the southern Mediterranean as a whole. They have returned to the writings of early Roman geographers (Sallustus, Procopius) and underlined colonial linguistic theories to demonstrate that Berber language and culture predated the arrival of Arabs in North Africa in the seventh century (Islamic armies) and the eleventh century (Benu Hillal). The efforts of the Algerian revolutionary parties from the 1920s to 1960s to unify the colony's indigenous populace under the then powerful anticolonial motifs of Arab nationalism and Islam, in the eyes of stalwart Berber activists amounted to the denial of the Algerian people of their essential Berber identity— the true identity of all Algerians, whether or not a given Algerian speaks a Berber dialect or recognizes him or herself as having Berber roots (Silverstein 1996). The current disunity of Algeria, embodied most poignantly in the current civil war that has claimed upwards of 100,000 lives over the last nine years, is seen in this regards as resulting largely from an identity crisis which has left the Algerian people utterly disoriented in an increasingly globalizing world, willing to grasp at the first strong organizing principle to arise—in this case, Islamic fundamentalism. A return to Algeria's fundamental identity, Berberity, thus is proposed as the needed solution. As such, these multiple appropriations and distancings, this continued ambivalence over the espousal and denial of cultural difference within the postcolonial period, point to the perduring character of coloniality within postcoloniality.

Notes

This essay, in its various incarnations over the past five years, has benefited enormously from generous comments and suggestions by a number of colleagues and teachers, particularly Andrew Apter, Brian Axel, Jean Comaroff, Jocelyne Dakhlia, James W. Fernandez, Lisa Hajjar, Zachary Lockman, Ussama Makdisi, Bill Sewell, Seteney Shami, and Ari Zolberg. I am additionally grateful to the staff of the Fonds Ninard collection of the Institut du Monde Arabe for their archival support during my research stay in Paris, 1995–1996.

1　For a thorough critique of the Eurocentric and primordializing tendencies within the social-scientific literature on nationalism, see Segal and Handler (1992, 4–8); Handler (1985).

2　Aziz Al-Azmeh has decried this logic as a "metaphysical discourse on identity" in which "infra-historical forces, such as primary communal, religious, or regional forms of social organization, are taken for the markers of suprahistorical continuity" (1993, 19). See also Chatterjee 1995 for a similar critique.

3　Richard Handler has similarly explored the "interpenetration of nationalist and social-scientific discourse," pointing out the "close congruence between actors' ideologies and observers' theories" in the case of Quebec (1988, 8).

4　The *dey* Hussein was reported to have yelled "Leave! Roman (*roumi*), son of a dog. Leave! Leave!" and to have slapped the consul across the face with his flyswatter (Garrot 1910, 648).

5　In addition to taxation, the Ottoman regency in Algiers depended on the profits of its corsairs (or *taïfa al-raïs*) as one of its major sources of income.

6　After the defeat of Napoleon in 1814, the Bourbon line was restored to the monarchy in the personage of Louis XVIII, brother of the late king Louis XVI, beheaded during the 1789 Revolution. Shortly after his installment, Louis enacted a constitutional charter which maintained the abolition of feudal privilege, underwrote the Napoleonic legal code, and established a bicameral parliamentary government. Charles X succeeded Louis after the latter's death in 1824.

7　Louis Napoleon, the nephew of Napoleon Bonaparte, came to power after the 1848 revolution, which topped the July Monarchy of Louis-Philippe, which had replaced the Bourbon Monarchy of Charles X. Viewed as the restorer of the first Napoleon's imperial legacy, he was elected President of the Second Republic under universal suffrage. Three years later, he dissolved the Legislative Assembly and declared himself Napoleon III, Emperor of France.

8　Algeria enjoyed a similar administrative status during the short-lived Second Republic (1848–1851).

9　Patrilineal compounds (*adrums*) were replaced with linear row houses absent the symbolic categories embodied in the Kabyle *axxam* (see Bourdieu 1977).

10　The "disenchantment" entailed in the consolidation of colonial rule should not be seen as necessarily antagonistic to the exoticizing (and eroticizing) character of French Orientalist discourse (see Alloula 1986; Bullard 2000; Said 1993). Indeed, one might argue that the former contributed to the latter, that attempts to homogenize spatio-temporal formations shifted fantasies of Algerian otherness to groups peripheral to the initial political-economic penetration—notably, women and nomads.

11　"Teachers have been invited to consider themselves as the agents and collaborators of the commandants and to inspire themselves from their advice. After the military conquest, the French language and idea have become the new weapons (*armes*) with which to enter into the fray (*mener le bon combat*)" ("La politique berbère du Protectorat." 1924, 252).

12　The appellation "Kabyle Myth" was first formulated by Charles-Robert Ageron in his seminal 1960 article, "La France, a-t-elle un politique kabyle?" ("Does France have a

Kabyle policy?"). He identified the myth of Kabyle superiority as operating primarily during the period 1840–1870, though with antecedents going back to 1826 (before the French occupation) and corollary attitudes continuing into the twentieth century. What changed, according to the author, was the assumption of the assimilability of the Kabyles (Ageron 1961; see also Guillaume 1992, 236–41; Lucas and Vatin 1975, 45). In the conclusion of this essay, I suggest that the Arab/Berber dichotomy has perdured well into contemporary discourses over national integration in both Algeria and France.

13 Often amounting to apologies or rationalizations for the colonial venture, these studies had as one of their primary goals to create a standard grammar and transliteration system for the various Berber dialects (see Carette 1848; Rinn 1889).

14 School textbooks, however, tended to reinforce ethnic stereotypes in their attempts to counter Arab "vices." One primary reader in use in Muslim colonies prior to independence relates the story of a colonial tax collector and an Arab market vendor. Having failed to pay his taxes, the Arab gives a false name when questioned by the tax inspector. When he is finally caught again, he must pay an even greater fine. The story ends with the moral: "Never aggravate your mistakes with lies" (Soualah and Salomon 1939, 122).

15 A similar connection between the civilizing, educating, and proselytizing projects was likewise made by those critics of the mission civilisatrice who believed colonial practices to be mis-prioritized. "The will to *civilize* (one should say *Europeanize*) some by religion, others by civil or even military administration, by schools or by the courts . . . seems to me the result of the same illusion, the same subjective error, brought about by the same prejudice of our civilization reputed superior by a literary auto-suggestion which leads our Latin spirits to view all life through educational systems. . . . Missionaries and colonizers, religious and secular, have lost sight of the practical side, the reality of life, the primordial material needs, and finally economic development which nature herself has put in primary position: *Primo vivere, deinde philosophari*" (Marchal 1901, 363–65; emphasis mine).

16 Throughout the essay, I follow colonial discourse and use the terms "Berber" and "Kabyle" nearly interchangeably, although technically "Berber" (or "Amazigh") is the collective name referring to all groups speaking a dialect of Berber (or Tamazight), including the Kabyles, Chaouia, Mzabites, and Touareg of Algeria, and the Chleu, Riffian, and Atlas peoples of Morocco. The word, "Berber," itself comes from the same Greek root as "barbarian," though its Arabic usage is generally attributed to a derogatory miscomprehension of Berber dialects as meaningless mumblings, as sounding like "brbr." More recently, the Berber Cultural Movements in Algeria and Morocco have emphasized "Amazigh" (pl. "Imazighen"), meaning "free men," as the more correct, emic appellation.

17 Ethnographic evidence was mobilized to claim that Berber culture was originally matriarchal and that the Islamic invasions only deposed a thin layer of patriarchialism on its surface.

18 Unlike Arabs, Kabyle fighters displayed intelligence, courage and honesty—rarely stealing and never cutting the heads off their enemy (Daumas and Fabar 1847: I, 35; Pomel 1871, 59).

19 Similar arguments of necessary protection underlined French policy in other parts of the Mediterranean, particularly in their 1860s establishment of a mandate state in Syria and Lebanon to protect the Christian Maronites from their "natural enemies," the Sunni and Druze Muslims.

20 "Oil" and "oc" represent alternate words for "yes" in the pre-French Latinate languages. "Oil" has become the "oui" of modern French, while the *langue d'oc* remains the close ancestor of contemporary Occitan dialects in the south of France.

References

Ageron, Charles-Robert. 1960. "La France a-t-elle un politique kabyle." *Revue historique* 223: 311–352.

—. 1991. *Modern Algeria: A History from 1830 to the Present.* Trenton, N.J.: Africa World Press.

Al-Azneh, Aziz. 1993. *Islam and Modernities.* London: Verso.

Alloula, Malek. 1986. The Colonial Harem. Translated by Myrna Godzich and Wlad Godzich. Minneapolis: University of Minnesota Press.

Anderson, Benedict. [1983] 1991. *Imagined Communities.* London: Verso.

Andrieu, H. 1894. *Petite histoire de l'Algérie. A l'usage des écoles primaires.* Miliana: A. Legendre.

Les Arabes et la colonisation en Algérie. 1873. Paris: Pougin.

Auge, C., and M. Petit. [1894] 1906. *Histoire de France.* Paris: Larousse.

Axel, Brian. 1995. "Time and Threat: Questioning the Production of the 'Diaspora' as an Object of Study," *History and Anthropology* 9, no. 2: 1–29.

Bazin, René. n.d. *Charles de Foucauld explorateur du Maroc, ermite au Sahara.* Paris: Plon.

Bennabi, Malek. 1948. *Les conditions de la renaissance. Problèmes d'une civilisation.* Algiers: Mosquée des Etudiants de l'Université d'Alger.

Benyahia, Mohamed Sadek. 1970. "Les mutations psycholoqiques dans la révolution algérienne." *Révolution africaine* 316: 26.

Bertholon, Lucien. 1898. "Notice sur l'origine des berbères de souche européenne." *Congrès de l'Association Française de l'avancement des sciences* 1: 533–541.

—. 1913. "Sociologie comparée des Achéens d'Homère et des Kabyle contemporains." In *Recherches anthropologiques dans la berbérie orientale, Tripolitaine, Tunisie, Algérie,* Vol. 1, edited by Lucien Bertholon and E. Chantre. Lyon: A. Rey.

Bertrand, Louis. 1921. *Les villes d'or. Algérie et Tunisie romaines.* Paris: Fayard.

Bodley, R. V. C. 1926. *Algeria From Within.* London: Hutchinson & Co.

Borgé, Jacques, and Nicolas Viasnoff. 1995. *Archives de l'Algérie.* Milan: Editions Michèle Trinckvel.

Bourdieu, Pierre. 1977. *Outline of a Theory of Practice.* Cambridge: Cambridge University Press.

Bourdieu, Pierre, and Abdelmalek Sayad. 1964. *Le Déracinement.* Paris: Editions de Minuit.

Brémond, Général Edouard. 1942. *Berbères et Arabes. La Berbérie est un pays européen.* Paris: Payot.

Breuilly, John. 1985. *Nationalism and the State.* Chicago: University of Chicago Press.

Brubaker, Rogers. 1992. *Citizenship and Nationhood in France and Germany.* Cambridge: Harvard University Press.

Bullard, Alice. 2000. *Exile to Paradise: Savagery and Civilization in Paris and the South Pacific.* Stanford: Stanford University Press.

Busset, Maurice et al. 1929. *Maroc et l'Auvergne.* Paris: Imprimerie Nationale.

Camps, Gabrielle. 1984. *L'Encyclopédie berbère.* Vol. 1. Aix-en-Provence: Edisud.

Capot-Rey, R. 1943. "La migration des Saïd Atba," *Revue Africaine* 388–389: 170–186.

Carette, Antoine. 1848. *Etudes sur la Kabilie proprement dite.* Paris: Imprimerie Nationale.

Charvet, C. 1892. *Notes sur l'Algérie par un Algérien.* Paris: Hennequin.

Chatterjee, Partha. 1986. *Nationalist Thought and the Colonial World.* Minneapolis: University of Minnesota Press.

—. 1995. *The Nation and Its Fragments.* Princeton: Princeton University Press.

Chevrillon, André. 1927. *Les Puritains du désert.* Paris: Plon.

Citron, Suzanne. 1994. "Imaginaire de la Nation française, xénophobie, et racisme." In *L'immigration américaine. Exemple ou contre-exemple pour la France,* edited by Sylvio Ullmo. Paris: Harmattan. 55–63.

Cobban, Alfred. 1961. *A History of Modern France, Volume 2: 1799–1871.* New York: Penguin Books.

—. 1965. *A History of Modern France, Volume 3: 1871–1962.* New York: Penguin Books.

Collot, Claude. 1987. *Les institutions de l'Algérie durant la période coloniale (1830–1962).* Paris: Editions du CNRS.

Colonisation de la régence d'Alger. 1836. Paris: Société d'Afrique.

Colonna, Fanny. 1983. "Présentation." In *Formation des cités chez les populations sédentaires de l'Algérie,* edited by Emile Masqueray. Aix-en-Provence: Edisud.

Comaroff, Jean, and John Comaroff. 1997. *Of Revelation and Revolution, Volume 2.* Chicago: University of Chicago Press.

Coon, Carleton. 1958. *Caravan: The Story of the Middle East.* New York: Henry Holt.

Dallet, J. M. 1982. *Dictionnaire Kabyle-Français.* Paris: Société d'Études Linguistiques et Anthropologiques de France.

Daumas, General Eugène. 1855. *Moeurs et coutumes d'Algérie.* Paris: Hachette.

Daumas, Eugène, and M. Fabar. 1847. *La Grande Kabylie. Etudes historiques.* 2 vols. Paris: Hachette.

Demontès, Victor. 1906. *Le Peuple algérien. Essais de démographie algérienne.* Algiers: Gouvernement Général d'Algérie, Direction de l'Agriculture, du Commerce, et de la Colonisation.

—. 1922–1930. *L'Algérie économique.* 3 vols. Algiers: Gouvernement Général d'Algérie, Direction de l'Agriculture, du Commerce, et de la Colonisation.

Demontezon, M.A. 1851. *La vérité sur l'Algérie.* Algiers: Dubos Frères.

De Neveu, Edouard. 1846. *Les Khouan. Ordres religieux chez les musulmans d'Algérie.* Paris: Guyot.

Desparmet, Jean. 1934. "L'histoire des Arabes et des Oulémas algériens." *L'Afrique française* (May): 274–281.

Di Lucio, C., H. Sarlin and P. Iton. 1938. *Géographie de l'Algérie.* Paris: Delalain.

Djebar, Assia. 1980. *Femmes d'Alger dans leur appartement.* Paris: Des Femmes.

Docteur X. 1891. *Simples réflexions d'un colon algérien.* Paris: Hennequin.

Doutté, Edmond, and Emile-Félix Gautier. 1913. *Enquête sur la dispersion de la langue berbère en Algérie.* Algiers: Jourdan.

El Moudjahid. 1959. "Extraits de *Formation civique et morale du contigent,* ouvrage édité par le Ministère Français de la Défense Nationale, 5ᵉ bureau" (15 January): 132–133.

Favret, Jeanne. 1968. "Relations de dépendance et manipulation de la violence en Kabylie." *L'Homme* 8 no. 4: 1–25.

Féraud, Louis. 1863. "Monuments dits celtiques dans la province de Constantine." *Bulletin de la société de l'archéologie de Constantine.* 214–234.

Ferrié, Jean-Noël, and Gilles Boëtsch. 1992. "Du Berbère aux yeux clairs à la race eurafricaine: La Méditerranée des anthropologues physiques." In *Le Maghreb, L'Europe et la France,* edited by Kacem Basfao and Jean-Robert Henry. Paris: Editions du CNRS. 191–207.

Fontaine, André. 1957. *L'Algérie, terre de contrastes et de conflits. Etude de géographie physique, humaine et économique à l'usage des classes du second degré et des cours élémentaires.* Oran: Fouque.

Garrot, Henri. 1910. *Histoire générale de l'Algérie.* Bastion Nord: Voutes.

Gautier, Emile-Félix. 1922. *Structure de l'Algérie.* Paris: Société d'Editions Géographiques et Scientifiques.

——. 1931. "Le Cadre géographique de l'histoire de l'Algérie." In *Histoire et Historiens de l'Algérie.* Paris: Alcan.

Gellner, Ernest. 1983. *Nations and Nationalism.* Ithaca: Cornell University Press.

——. 1972. "Introduction." In *Arabs and Berbers: From Tribe to Nation in North Africa,* edited by Ernest Gellner and Charles Micaud. Lexington, Mass.: Lexington Books.

Guernier, Eugène. 1950. *La Berbérie, L'Islam, et la France.* Paris: Editions de l'Union Française.

——. 1952. *L'Apport de l'Afrique à la pensée humaine.* Paris: Payot.

Guide de l'émigrant par un colon. 1881. Paris: Agence Territoriale Algérienne.

Guilhaume, Jean-François. 1992. *Les mythes fondateurs de l'Algérie française.* Paris: Harmattan.

Guiral, Pierre. 1955. "L'opinion marseillaise et les débuts de l'entreprise algérienne." *Revue Historique* 214 (July–September): 9–34.

Habermas, Juergen. 1992. "Citizenship and National Identity: Some Reflections on the Future of Europe." *Praxis-International* 12, no. 1: 1–19.

Hamelin, M. 1833. *Notice sur Alger.* Paris: Dentu.

Handler, Richard. 1985. "On Dialogue and Destructive Analysis. Problems in Narrating Nationalism and Ethnicity." *Journal of Anthropological Research* 41: 171–82.

——. 1988. *Nationalism and the Politics of Culture in Quebec.* Madison: University of Wisconsin Press.

Handler, Richard, and Daniel Segal. 1993. "Introduction: Nations, Colonies and Metropoles." *Social Analysis* 33: 3–8.

Hannoteau, Louis, and Aristide Letourneux. 1871. *La Kabylie et les coutumes kabyles.* Paris: Imprimerie Nationale.

Herder, Johann Gottfried. [1792] 1968. *Reflections on the Philosophy of the History of Mankind.* Chicago: University of Chicago Press.

Herzfeld, Michael. 1984. "The Horns of the Mediterranean Dilemma." *American Ethnologist* 11, no. 3: 439–54.

Hobsbawm, E. J. 1990. *Nations and Nationalism Since 1780: Programme, Myth, Reality.* Cambridge: Cambridge University Press.

Hobsbawm, E. J., and Terence Ranger. 1983. "Introduction." In *The Invention of Tradition.* Cambridge: Cambridge University Press.

Hubac, Pierre. 1948. *Les nomades.* Paris: La Renaissance du Livre.

Julien, Charles-André. 1963. "L'insurrection de Kabylie (1870–1871)." In *Preuves* (December): 60–66.

Kaddache, Mahfoud. 1973. "L'Utilisation du fait berbère comme facteur politique dans l'Algérie coloniale." *Proceedings of the First Congress of Mediterranean Studies of Arabo-Berber Influence.* Algiers: SNED.

Lacheraf, Mostefa. 1953. "*La Colline oubliée* ou les consciences anachroniques." *Le Jeune Musulman* (13 February).

Lapène, Edouard. 1839. *Vingt-six mois à Bougie.* Paris: Anselin.

Larcher, Emile. 1903. *Traité élémentaire de législation algérienne.* Vol. 1. Paris: Rousseau.

Le Glay, Général. 1921. "L'école française et la question berbère." *Bulletin de l'Enseignement Publique au Maroc* 33: 1–15.

Lorcin, Patricia M.E. 1995. *Imperial Identities. Stereotyping, Prejudice and Race in Colonial Algeria.* New York: I.B. Tauris.

Lucas, Philippe, and Jean-Claude Vatin. 1975. *L'Algérie des anthropologues.* Paris: François Maspero.

MacMaster, Neil. 1993. "Patterns of Emigration, 1905–1954: 'Kabyles' and 'Arabs.' In *French and Algerian Identities from Colonial Times to the Present,* edited by Alec Hargreaves and Michael J. Hefferman. Lewistown, N.Y.: Edwin Mellen.

Malte-Brun, Conrad. 1812. *Précis de géographie universelle et description de toutes les parties du monde sur un plan nouveau d'après les grands divisions du globe.* Paris: Editions Buisson.

Marchal, C. 1901. "Intervention." In *Congrès international de sociologie coloniale, 6-11 août 1900.* Paris: Rousseau.

Martin, Henri. 1881. "Discussion sur la communication de P. Topinard 'Les types indigènes de l'Algérie'," *Bulletin de la société d'anthropologie de Paris* 4:461–62.

Marx, Karl. [1853] 1978. "On Imperialism in India." In *The Marx-Engels Reader,* edited by Robert C. Tucker. New York: W. W. Norton. 653–664.

Masqueray, Emile. 1886. *Formation des cités chez les populations sédentaires de l'Algérie.* Paris: Ernst Leroux.

Maunier, René. 1922. "Leçon d'ouverture d'un cours de sociologie algérienne." *Hespéris* 11: 93–107.

Mercier, Ernst. 1871. "Ethnographie de l'Afrique septentrionale. Notes sur l'origine du peuple berbère." *Revue Africaine* 40: 420–33.

Mercier, Gustave. 1954. "L'exploration scientifique de l'Algérie." In *La Découverte de l'Algérie. Initiation à l'Algérie.* Paris: Maisonneuve.

Milliot, Louis, 1932. *Les Institutions kabyles.* Paris: Librairie Orientaliste Paul Geuthner.

Mitchell, Timothy. 1988. *Colonising Egypt.* Cambridge: Cambridge University Press.

Moliner-Violle, M. 1877. *Précis de géographie historique de l'Algérie.* Algiers: Adolphe Jourdan.

Montagne, Robert. 1947. *La civilisation du désert.* Paris: Hachette.

Morizot, Jean. 1985. *Les Kabyles: propos d'un témoin.* Paris: CHEAM.

Nandy, Ashis. 1983. *The Intimate Enemy: Loss and Recovery of Self Under Colonialism.* Delhi: Oxford.

Nisan, Mordechai. 1991. *Minorities in the Middle East.* Jefferson, N.C.: McFarland.

Odinot, Paul. 1924. "Les Berbères." *La Géographie* 41, no. 2: 137–49.

Peyronny, M. 1836. *Considerations politiques sur la colonie d'Alger.* Paris: Dentu.

"La politique berbère du Protectorat." 1924. *Algérie française, Renseignements coloniaux* (July): 214–255.

Pomel, Auguste. 1871. *Des races indigènes de l'Algérie et du rôle que leur reservent leurs aptitudes.* Oran: Veuve Dagorn.

Rabinow, Paul. 1989. *French Modern: Norms and Forms of the Social Environment.* Cambridge, Mass.: MIT Press.

Rambaud, Alfred. 1892. "L'éducation française des Musulmans d'Algérie." *La revue bleue.* (10 September): 321–28.

—. 1895. "L'Algérie devant les chambres." *La revue bleue* (16 February): 210–15.

Reclus, Elisée. 1876. *Nouvelle géographie universelle. La terre et les hommes.* Paris: Hachette.

Richter, Melvin. 1963. "Tocqueville on Algeria." *Review of Politics* 25: 37x–38x.

Rinn, Louis. 1884. *Marabouts et Khouan. Etude sur l'islam en Algérie.* Algiers: Jourdan.

—. 1889. *Les origines berbères. Etude linuistique et ethnologique.* Algiers: Jourdan.

Sahli, Mohammed C. 1953. "La colline du reniement." *Le Jeune Musulman.* (2 January).

Said, Edward. 1978. *Orientalism.* London: Routledge & Keegan Paul.

—. 1993. *Culture and Imperialism.* New York: Vintage.

Sayad, Abdelmalek. 1997. "Les Trois 'Ages' de l'emigration Algerienne en France." *Actes de la Recherche en Sciences Sociales.* 15 (June): 59–79.

Segal, Daniel. 1991. " 'The European': Allegories of Racial Purity." *Anthropology Today* 7, no. 5: 7–9.

Segal, Daniel, and Richard Handler. 1992. "How European is Nationalism?" *Social Analysis* 32: 1–15.

Sergent, Edmond. 1956. *La médecine française en Algérie.* Algiers: Institut Pasteur d'Algérie.

Servier, André. 1913. *Le Péril de l'avenir. Le nationalisme musulman en Egypte, en Tunisie, en Algérie.* Constantine: Boet.

—. 1923. *L'Islam et la Psychologie du musulman.* Paris: Challamel.

Silverstein, Paul. 1996. "Realizing Myth: Berbers in France and Algeria." *Middle East Report* 26, no. 3: 11–15.

—. 1997. "French Alterity: Articulating Intra-National Difference in the New Europe." *Hungarian Social Sciences Quarterly Special Issue:* 13–35.

—. 1998. *Trans-Politics: Islam, Berberity, and the French Nation-State.* Ph.D. diss., University of Chicago.

Smith, Anthony D. 1984. "Ethnic Persistence and National Transformation." *British Journal of Sociology.* 35, no. 3, 452 61.

—. 1986. *The Ethnic Origins of Nations.* Oxford: Basil Blackwell.

Société de l'Afrique. 1836. *Colonisation de la régence d'Alger.* Paris: Société de l'Afrique.

Soualah, Mohammed, and Louis Salomon. 1939. *Le Premier Livre de lecture et de langage à l'usage des écoles indigènes en pays musulmans.* 11th Edition. Algiers: Carbonel.

Talha, Larbi. 1989. Le salariat immigré devant la crise. Paris: Editions du CNRS.

Tauxier, H. 1862 1863. "Etudes sur les migrations des tribus berbères avant l'islamisme." *Revue Africaine* 18: 35–37.

Tessier, Octave. 1865. *Napoleon III en Algérie.* Paris: Chalamel.

Tlemcani, Rachid. 1986. *State and Revolution in Algeria.* Boulder: Westview Press.

Tocqueville, Alexis de. [1991] 1837. "Lettre sur l'Algérie." In *De la colonie en Algérie.* Brussels: Editions Complexe: 37–56.

—. [1991] 1841. "Travail sur l'Algérie." In *De la colonie en Algérie.* Brussels: Editions Complexe: 57–150.

—. [1991] 1847. "Rapport sur l'Algérie." In *De la colonie en Algérie.* Brussels: Editions Complexe. 151–179.

Todorov, Tzvetan. 1991. "Tocqueville et la doctrine coloniale." In *De la colonie en Algérie.* Brussels: Editions Complexe. 9–36.

Trumelet, C. 1863. *Les Français dans le désert. Journal d'une expédition aux limites du S'ah'râ algérien.* Paris: Garnier Frères.

Van Vollenhoven, Joost. 1903. *Essai sur le fellah algérien.* Paris: Rousseau.

Vivien, De Saint Martin. 1863. *Le nord de l'Afrique dans l'antiquité grecque et romaine.* Paris: Imprimerie Impérial.

Wright, Gwendolyn. 1991. *The Politics of Design in French Colonial Urbanism.* Chicago: University of Chicago Press.

Wysner, Glora M. 1945. *The Kabyle People.* New York: privately printed.

Developing Historical Negatives: Race and the (Modernist) Visions of a Colonial State

Ann Laura Stoler

We don't want to create imitation Europeans, we just need perfected natives.
—from the General State Archives in the Hague

The above statement captures both the arrogance of Dutch colonial authorities and a delusional confidence in their projects. Who made up the "we" went easily unstated, just as the possibility of social engineering was implicitly assumed. But what is unclear in this 1874 government report on impoverished Europeans in the Netherland Indies (and what to do about them) is the targeted population. At issue was a segment of nineteenth-century Indies society that official vernacular labeled "the so-called *inlandsche kinderen*," an ambiguous composite of those later known as "European paupers" but that most often included the "mixed-blood" ("Indo") poor. Neither "native" nor necessarily "children" (as a literal translation would suggest), the inlandsche kinderen were most commonly descendants of European men and native women whose economic destitution poised them as a potential threat: under adverse conditions viewed as "blanken-haters" ("white-haters"), under proper tutelage embraced as staunch supporters of Dutch rule.

At one level, this essay examines how colonial officials thought about and envisioned a response to what they saw as the disturbing increase in the late nineteenth century of a category of persons that uneasily straddled the Indies's colonial divide. But the sheer volume of documents, the unexpected profusion of proposals fashioned to deal with those who made up only a sliver of colonial society, turned my focus elsewhere; not away from the racial disorder of things, so much as into the nature of the archive that disquiet produced. For what is both obvious and striking about these documents on the inlandsche kinderen is that they are, in large part, not about events. On the contrary, this is an archive filled with rich ethnographic moments stored in the non-eventful: in drafts of proposals, in unrealized plans, in short-lived experiments, and in failed projects.

It is from this non-eventful quality of the archive that I take my cue. Rather than beginning from the notion that the colonial facts of the matter might be found in the concrete and discrete events that made up social reform (which policies were carried out and which not), here I take a different tack. I treat those unrealized and improbable plans and accretions of official knowledge as a diagnostic, both of deep anxieties about a Dutch national past and of an Indies colonial future, of a colonial utopia obliquely expressed.[1]

My contention is that these colonial utopias were not so much paradigms of conquest as blueprints of distress. They chart what Fredric Jameson might refer to as "the horizons" of administrative anxiety, the disjuncture between what was possible to think and impossible to implement in a colonial context and on Indies ground.[2] Some proposals had their referents in Europe, others in the Indies, still others in colonial contexts more far afield. Viewed as an ensemble, they map out an unexpected sociology of imperial breadth, of the production of transnational equivalencies and of an emergent colonial politics of comparison. Not least, they bear witness to how evidence of the casual linkages between race, class, and impoverishment was made credible, cross-referenced and stored.

This essay thus broaches an analytic and methodological quandary: what historical weight to assign to a set of improbable visionary designs that were, for the most part, never implemented? How to treat the history of the possible but unrealized, of what could be construed as non-events? What can we learn about colonial cultures and the states they sustained from what might have been, from what never happened, from exploring the counterfactual?[3] This is not a history of ideas, of mentalities or of representations, for it takes as its subject the uneven, shadow presence of what was imagined as the possible, the tension between what was realizable and fantasy, between plausible plans and implausible worlds. At issue here is not the relationship between text and context, but rather the changing force fields in which these models were produced. The analytic shift, in short, is from the high gloss print to the darkroom negative, from figure and event—that which is more often in historic relief—to field and ground.

As such, this essay is also about the colonial order of things as seen through its archival productions. What insights about the colonial might be gained from attending not only to colonialism's archival content but also to its particular and sometimes peculiar form? What can we learn from its densities and distributions, by thinking of archiving as a process rather than archives as things—by looking at archives as epistemological sites rather than as sources and at colonial archives as cross-sections of contested knowledge, and therefore, most importantly, as technologies of rule in themselves?

The archives on which I draw here are those of the Dutch colonial civil service from the 1830s through the early part of the twentieth century. If the inlandsche kinderen were underrepresented—indeed largely invisible—in state statistics, they were overly present in descriptive accounts. Although absent from contemporary Dutch colonial historiography, in documents of the Indies administration they are everywhere: in reports on public education and health, in discussions on the colony's economy, political unrest, and child welfare. This "present-absence" is not so much a contradiction as a marker of the phenomenon itself; of a racial and class category that expanded and contracted with changes in reformist strategies and colonial politics.

Romances of the Modern in the Colonial Archives

There are three models of reform that interest me here. One I call an "industrial romance" that imagined the making of an industrial labor force out of an unskilled, illiterate, poor, white/mixed-blood class. In this vision, this labor force would become the new "subordinate technical personnel" for a modernizing colonial state, a labor aristocracy armed with a moderate amount of European practical training and an abundance of local knowledge.[4] To be schooled as land surveyors, telegraph operators, post office workers, or skilled mechanics for heavy machinery, they would operate both the communication network and productive forces of an expanding, high tech capitalist colony.

Part of, and in tension with, this first vision was a second model that I call the "artisanal romance." This vision conjured the making of a class of European foremen, craftsmen and artisans who would both fulfill a demand for such labor and make up a solid *middelstand*—a dependable lower-middle class. This *ambachtstand* (artisanal class) and the jobs they would perform were imagined in impressive detail in the archives. They would be trained as piano tuners, clockmakers, tailors, cobblers, and truck farmers servicing the consumption needs and the cultural distinctions of a European enclave with an (as yet unrealized) expanded, comfortable middle class. The list is telling for it reflects longings for acquisitions and services that few Dutch inhabitants in the Indies could hope to have and few would ever have the means to afford.

The third model was ostensibly the most nostalgic of all. This was a "rural romance" that envisioned a placated mixed-blood population, living off a modest but respectable agrarian base, a landed yeomanry on a scale that was no longer possible in the Netherlands itself. The vision focused on children reared in agricultural colonies who would be trained for such future work and instilled with a firm attachment to the Indies soil. Here, future generations would serve as political middlemen, culturally and linguistically adept in the Indies—choice cultural brokers between native and European society but firmly committed to Dutch rule.

Such disparate and competing notions marshaled different sorts of comparative colonial knowledge, local familiarity, and scientific expertise. Not least they registered different interpretations of a usable past, divergent assessments of present risks, and conflicting visions of the future. Each refigures the appropriate sociological terrain for comparison; some speak in a language of racial attributes, others in one of class. Each posits a different assessment of the relationship between political disposition and inner character. Each too represents a different cropping of relevant knowledge, a different framing, and different ground.

These were utopian romances in more than one sense. Most obviously they were imaginative narratives, stories that had to capture their readers and were designed to persuade. Some were only schematic. Many more, however, were detailed and finely penned anecdotal ethnographies of a moving nature.[5] What characterizes all of them is a marked attention to affective states: to what habits of the heart might accompany a trade, to the character qualities of craftsmen, to the management of sentiment as well as the management of labor. They read as utopian because so many were unpractical and so often out of place.[6]

These alternatives obviously suggest different conceptions of where the inlandsche kinderen would best fit on the colonial landscape. But they also carve out a very different landscape of what future turn it might take. Some commentators had visions that resonated with Dutch experiments in social welfare planning. Others drew their blueprints from revamped models of modernity tried out in other contexts and in other parts of the colonial world. In turning to Australia, the Caribbean, and India, authorities reviewed experiments that were known to have gone dangerously awry or to have met with success. Here was an exemplary moment, neither the first nor the last, in which colonial projects were being weighed and evaluated in an international field, across colonies and across national borders.[7] The frequency and urgency with which British, French, and Spanish experiments were invoked or rejected as viable comparisons signal an expansion of the breadth of the colonial archive to include new comparative knowledge of colonizing missions, of mistakes they could learn from, statistics they would now need, pedagogic failures they could redress. As far-flung colonial contexts were brought into comparison, so too were metropolitan and colonial ones, reminders of the fact that nineteenth-century social reform and its concomitant solutions to pauperism, poverty, and recalcitrant workers were being played out on a broad imperial field.

The Making of a Colonial Category

The notion that this unmarked imperial "we" could, if it so desired, craft "imitation Europeans" (*naggemaakte Europeanen*), or, as presumptuously, that this was what the inlandsche kinderen were, begged certain questions. If many inlandsche kinderen were legally classified as European, then how could they be "imitations," "defective" versions of what they already were?[8] That it would be preferable to make them into "perfected natives"—for which the Indies administration professed to pine—was also odd. For a founding premise of most reform was that they should never ally with, feel affiliation for, or take their cultural cues from the native (*inlander*) population. How then could the inlandsche kinderen become perfected variations of those they were assiduously warned to avoid?

At the heart of these proposals and their alternate solutions were a set of different answers to similar questions. Could and should the inlandsche kinderen be shaped into Dutch middle-class tradesmen (a middenstand) or into an enlightened working class? Could a European middenstand be created in the colonies on the basis of skilled manual labor? Could manual labor (*handenarbeid*) ever be honorable for those who saw them themselves as white? Could one be truly Dutch in the colonies and poor white at the same time, or were these mutually exclusive categories? Was the very notion of poor white a disquieting colonial oxymoron?

Some planners addressed the dilemma of a colonial economy in need of technological expertise but feared the political consequences and financial burden of providing such education to the expanding population of quasi-Europeans, much less to the native population. Others raised concern over what kind of colonial community the Indies would become—whether an Australian settler model was a feasible option, whether "mixed-bloods" should partake as full-fledged members or as second-class citizens confined to its service sector.

Some participants in these debates saw the lessons to be learned from earlier labor policy in the Indies and took their illustrations from that context. Others, perhaps less familiar with local conditions, sought illustrations and answers farther afield. Some of the terms in which issues were raised signaled concerns about industrialization in the Netherlands, the fate of its craft industry, and worries that Dutch artisans might not survive the competition of Europe's new technologies. Other aspects of the debates were triggered by new negotiations in the mid-nineteenth century Netherlands between church and state over private charity and public assistance—the issue of whether care for the poor was a responsibility of private citizens or the new parliamentary state. A Dutch *burgerlijk* class, which had long prided itself on its charitable, philanthropic stance to the less fortunate, was rethinking its obligations toward the indigent members of a modernizing society. In both cases, the debates underscored not the hegemonic self-assuredness of a ruling class but one wrestling with a range of anxieties over the terms of its status and what would assure its place in an expanding colonial economy and an increasingly powerful administrative apparatus.

These protracted debates on the inlandsche kinderen in the Dutch colonial archives were never conversations among state officials alone. On the contrary, they enlisted a wide range of experts that went beyond civil servants, excolonial officials, and metropolitan advisors. "Expert witness" came from those in the fields of education and health care, industry and military establishments. School headmasters, religious leaders, directors of orphanages, naval factory supervisors, small businessmen, and civil servants were called upon to express their opinions, produce qualified knowledge, and demonstrate their expertise. Given the range, it is not surprising that their conclusions were different. What is striking is how differently they assessed the inherent capabilities of the inlandsche kinderen and what could be expected of them. All accepted the category of the "so-called inlandsche kinderen." Although official texts rarely expressed uncertainty about what population made up that category, few agreed on who they were.

By some accounts, the inlandsche kinderen were pauperized whites, subaltern soldiers, widows whose pensions were far too small, fair-skinned children conceived in the army barracks whose comportment, speech, and habits were locally learned and singularly Javanese. Some describe a population inhabiting the seams of colonial society, who lived in the back alleys of urban Batavia, in the shabby village compounds on the outskirts of Semarang, Batavia, and Soerabaya. Some were included because of their absence from the municipal civil registers, others because of where or how they lived. Officials alarmed at the numbers squatting in vacant lots and unoccupied houses of Dutch residents proposed tightening the vagrancy laws for those who seemed to possess neither job, education, nor home. In short these reports describe a population absent from official registers and standard histories:[9] European vagrants, homeless adults who begged in the courtyards of the manicured Dutch neighborhoods, barefoot, blonde-haired children whose light complexions belied tawdry beginnings and hasty marriages.

But this was only part of the picture. The term inlandsche kinderen sometimes included those approaching the lower-middle class, middenstand, as well as the obviously impoverished: children of mixed parentage schooled in state-run schools, children given up by their well-born Dutch fathers, or the offspring of soldiers (soldatenkinderen) of commoner European origin. Conflicting perceptions of who comprised the inlandsche kinderen were not taxonomic trivia. Different rehabilitative visions of what they could become were contingent on different understandings of who they were.

Their numbers thus were always difficult to assess. Were there only a score of white children on the streets of Batavia whose numbers were inflated to dramatize the severity of the poor white problem or were there distressed Europeans in the tens of thousands? As early as the 1850s, proposals to train forty—at the most eighty—youths in a craft school in Soerabaya were mocked outright by those dismissive of a plan that would reach so few. In the 1860s, local officials criticized government initiatives, contending that there were "not hundreds, but thousands of such children whose inclination to become an artisan class (ambachtstand) needed awakening.[10] Others scoffed at such a panic, estimating only a handful of dysfunctional youths could easily be absorbed into the native milieu. But an 1872 commission on destitute descendants of Europeans reported a "staggering increase of pauperism," tens and thousands of "embittered" paupers, scattered throughout the European urban enclaves, housed on their borders, squatting in abandoned homes.[11] Writing to the Governor-General in 1881, the Indies Director of Education warned that while European pauperism was hardly new, news of it was ever "louder" in government circles and the press; and such impoverishment was "ever more felt and ever more increasing from year to year."[12] Others painted a more sinister canvas still: an uncountable underclass of light-skinned inhabitants spanning generations, cultural chameleons alternately seen as misplaced natives, degenerate Dutchmen, fictive, defective, and fake Europeans.

Fashioning European Artisans in an Indies World

Of all the reformist visions that captured the imagination of Dutch colonial authorities in the nineteenth-century Indies, none generated more debate, elicited more opinions and produced more archived papers than that which centered on the creation of an artisan and craft-based training school—an *ambachtschool*—for "the impoverished descendants of Europeans" in west Java's large port city of Soerabaya. Soerabaya was not an unexpected choice; it had long been home to a large shipbuilding complex and a large population of Europeans.

One way to recount the story of this artisanal romance would be to trace the events that led to its succession of openings and closings over a period of some fifty years. In 1853, the school was first opened under private initiative and faltered three years later with insufficient government backing and little financial support. In 1857, a government commission proposed that the school be reopened, and it was in 1861 as a state-run institution. Within months its name was changed to an *industrieschool* but it too was closed in less than a decade with dwindling enrollments. By the early 1880s, the ambachtschool was deemed a fiasco, out of sync both with the labor demands of the Indies and with the employment aspirations of those who had invested their sons' futures in it.

One might also look to the number of students that passed through its doors. When the school opened in late 1853 there were forty-one male youths, rising to eighty-one two years later, dwindling back to fifty-one when it closed. Under the state's aegis, numbers were smaller still. Although more than seventy students had been enrolled between 1862 and 1864, fifty quickly dropped out and only twenty finished the course. In any one year, there were no more than thirteen students. By its closing in 1872, there were none. The continuing education school (*herhalingschool*) proposed in the 1880s to replace the earlier craft school seemed to have had no enrollment at all.

By most historical standards, Soerabaya's ambachtschool was insignificant and without success. But the school's openings and closings were, as I have suggested, a window onto much more. Debates about the feasibility and advisability of training poor Indos and impoverished Europeans were at once specific and global, concrete and abstract. Experts offered not only rich ethnographic detail and on-site knowledge but also defenses of competing standards of political rationality. Nor were the lengthy discussions about the school always tethered to the realization of the projects. As one harsh critic, van Hoevell, noted in 1858, debates in the Dutch parliament about the school's merits went on oblivious to the fact that the school itself had already been closed.[13] The following section turns to some of these debates, which were triggered by the prospect of such a school existing and succeeding after all.

A Colonial Oxymoron: European Status and Manual Labor

"Should [inlandsche kinderen] be made into a self-supporting middle class or into a working class that is skilled and distinguished from the natives?"[14] As it turned out, this question was a moot one as the Director of

Soerbaya's Marine workshop was quick to point out. In a letter to the Governor-General, he mocked the fantasy that the inlandsche kinderen could become the "core of future trade and industry" much less an "independent burgerlijk class," noting their "advanced age," their "illegitimate unions," their "abuse [of] hard drink" and their tendency to "languish with neither vitality nor the will to work."[15] How could they be made into useful citizens if a middle-class existence was ruled out? What kind of work could they perform to make them a respectable working class?

Solutions rested on definitions of character, disposition, and race. Some argued that the ambachtschool should train only Indies-born European orphans. Others argued that at least as many European-born "pure-blood" children were living off church charities and their need for skilled training was just as great. Those policy makers who held in the early 1860s that the inlandsche kinderen should be supplied with theoretical rather than practical training were adamantly opposed by others who argued that "theoretical knowledge" was "excessive"—that it "went too far."[16]

Central to the debate was whether those of European descent could be instilled with a desire to work if that work was manual labor. The stakes were, in part, over culture and identity—over the place of a work ethic in self-representations of what it meant to be Dutch. While many concurred that true Dutchmen had a desire and commitment to work, few agreed over whether those classified as European should have to do work that entailed manual labor. On the other hand, access to theoretical knowledge was rejected by those who feared it would prompt a desire for political entitlements that the Inlandsche kinderen should not possess.

These were not issues under discussion in the Indies context alone. The increasing presence of "vagabond Hollanders" and poor whites in South Africa were preoccupations of the British state as early as the mid-nineteenth century (Bundy 1984, 101–128; see also *Die Armblanke . . .* 1932). In India, proposals made in the early 1800s to recruit impoverished Scottish farmers imbued with "Saxon energy" to populate and protect Britain's prize possession were defeated in parliament and never carried out (Arnold 1983, 133–158). "Redlegs" in Barbados, British convicts in Australia, and French *petits blancs* farmers in Algeria offered ample evidence of European adaptation to physical labor in tropical climates.

But acclimatization was not what these debates were about. From the 1830s to the 1930s those inside and outside the scientific community repeatedly were called upon to assess whether Europeans could survive in the tropics, faced with the health risks of manual labor and the political consequences of allowing whites in the colonies to work with their hands.[17] The debate was transnational and trans-colonial, enlisting doctors, geographers, administrators, and those with local expertise. At issue was not physiology but the politics of race.

The question, as it related to the inlandsche kinderen was not whether Europeans in the tropics could do such work, but whether those of partial European descent were fundamentally disinclined to physical labor at all. Some versions of common knowledge had it that they sought only clerical and civil service jobs and refused any work resembling that performed by natives. Some saw their disdain for manual labor as a product of false vanity, haughtiness, and pretentious claims to European descent. In this view, refusal to do manual labor was *not* because they were European, but precisely because they were not, because of fictive European affinities among those who were inherently indolent and had partial native origins.

Some explanations of this disinclination to work focused on the racial attributes of mixed-bloods, other explanations on the class culture of subaltern Europeans, a disinclination "shared among the inlandsche kinderen, and *mestizen* in general, and more specifically by those of the lower and needy class."[18] In both cases it was indolence and insolence that were to be checked among those whose motives for their aversion may have been different but whose alternative prospects and stance toward such work looked from afar very much the same.

Discussion of the work ethic among the Indo and European poor seems to dominate these debates, but for some this was merely a distraction and not what these debates were really about. Van Hoevell, an outspoken Dutch critic of the Indies administration, contended that the government had sabotaged the first ambachtschool in Soerabaya from the start. By his account the school was closed not because it was a failure but because it had the potential to be a resounding success. He described a flourishing experiment in 1853, enthusiastically supported by Governor-General Duymaer van Twist, gaining more private donors each year, energetic students, and confidence in the project among the families whose sons were enrolled.

According to van Hoevell, all the school needed was some sort of acknowledgment from the Indies administration that they would honor the school's diploma and hire students who had earned its degree. But when former Minister of Colonies Pahud replaced van Twist as Governor-General, he did just the opposite: one of his first official decrees in 1856 was to limit state subsidies to the school. Not surprisingly private donors, following Pahud's lead, withdrew their support; students and their parents who had believed in the headmaster's insistence that artisanal work could be honorable for Europeans dropped out; others, disillusioned, did not even bother to enroll.

As van Hoevell noted, support for school was withdrawn not because it was not working (the European press in Java was full of praise for the experiment), but precisely because it was. Much of the administrative debate about the future fate of inlandsche kinderen centered on the political danger of a subaltern class whose resentment was born out of their poverty, but van Hoevell thought the Dutch administration's fear lay elsewhere: that access to education and skills would produce a sense of independence and self-worth, that a mixed-blood middelstand might become a reality—a politically vocal, Indo-European lower-middle class.

Educating Hearts and Minds

Van Hoevell's assessment went unattended by authorities although his analysis was prescient and probably correct. But new blueprints and a new commission investigating a government-backed industrieschool were in the making even before the first private initiative for the school had failed. In 1854 the Minister of Colonies wrote to the Governor-General in support of the establishment of an industrial or technical school where the descendants of Europeans could be trained to become land surveyors, tailors, shoemakers, carpenters, and wagonmakers. Students would be drawn from the local orphanage and do on-job training in the navy ateliers in Soerabaja. Training was to consist of formal classes and apprenticeship with skilled European craftsmen.[19]

This focus on inclinations and disinclinations to labor turned colonial officials repeatedly in one direction: to the formative, familial environments in which children lived, to the notions of nation, family, and work that they would acquire in their early years. Long exchanges over the age range for the craft and technical schools were only nominally about the physical stamina such work required. More importantly they addressed the age at which these institutions could "awaken the inclination to become an artisanal class (ambachtstand)."[20] Convinced that a "desire to work" (werklust) was missing among the inlandsche kinderen, it was sentiment that had to be kindled and redirected, not opportunity that needed to be changed.

One of those whose advice was sought by the commission was Heer de Bruin, a civil engineer long residing in Soerabaya, who thought such a school was doomed to fail. He noted that a training program organized around apprenticeship with skilled European supervisors was unrealistic because of the large number of Javanese workers needing "constant supervision" and already in the supervisors' charge.[21] There was no time for training and insufficient people; as importantly, close contact with those Javanese workers already employed in the workshops would do little to improve the morality of the Indo youths.

But de Bruin knew that a competent workforce was not all that the ambacht proposal was about. Noting that the Minister of the Colonies wanted "more than a simple manual labor force," he proposed what he called "the Spanish model" whose aim would be both to train an unskilled mixed-blood population and "improve the race." In his rendering of the Spanish model a number of orphans below the age of twelve are sent to the motherland with the girls brought up in cloisters and the young men taught a skill of their choice. Upon returning to the colony, the girls married Spanish workers from the craft industries and the young men wed Spanish girls.

Despite the sketchy nature of de Bruin's Spanish fantasy, the Governor-General was smitten with the plan. Reporting it to the Minister of Colonies he praised two points: that it would reduce the dangers of a displaced and discontent mixed-blood population and, as in the Spanish colonies, that it would "improve the race of European descendants." Adapted to the Indies, he envisioned sending annually hundreds of orphan children to be raised in the Netherland's municipal orphanages. The attraction of the plan was not the acquisition of specific labor skills, but what would be gained and learned by encouraging mixed marriages. According to de Bruin, the boys would marry Dutch girls and return to the Indies with a skill; and the girls would have domestic training for their future roles as wives and mothers. "The boys, married to Dutch women, would considerably improve the race, more Dutch ideas would exist and the language of the inlandsche kinderen would be purified, while the Dutch mothers would have an influence on developing the moral sensibilities and the desire to work of their children."[22] This "Spanish model" was never seriously pursued, blocked by a new Minister of Colonies who opposed the plan. Indies youth schooled in Holland, he argued, would be far behind their Dutch age mates and be mocked by them. He instead proposed that they remain in the Indies to "improve the race." But the notion that these children needed the habitus of Holland as well as its skills had other implications. For it demanded rethinking whether the costs of rearing and later schooling would be shouldered by individuals or by the state.

Arguing firmly against van den Bosch's oft-quoted statement from 1831 that it was the state's responsibility to care for the abandoned children of European descent, the Governor-General stated his position in no uncertain terms: it is the "responsibility of parents to bring up their children. I see no grounds on which this duty should be assumed by the state."[23] Dismissing evidence of an increasing number of abandoned youths of European descent, he held that the increase in European residents had brought with it more legal marriages and fewer orphans. His stronger objection, however, was that such an institution would make it easier for the "public to be too neglectful [of their offspring] and thus too eager to place their children there." There were already *armenschool* (schools for the poor) for destitute Europeans to attend. He would only concede to state support on a minimal scale for an institution that would provide for forty, at most eighty, orphaned youths.

One member of the Indies Advisory Council stood by the Governor-General, urging increased state investments in secondary education for the middenstand, not increased public charity. He noted that many Indies Europeans were impoverished because of "rash marriages" (*onberaden huwelijken*), and that as many of the "colored" (*kleurlingen*) were in economic distress. But other members of the advisory council stood firmly by van den Bosch's 1831 argument. The Council held that the "autocratic" structure of colonial authority and the absence of independent municipal bodies made it incumbent upon the state to make some form of poverty relief its responsibility—not on van den Bosch's moral grounds, but on the more pressing political argument that their neglect was a danger to Dutch rule.[24]

A disinclination to work among the poor may have only partially explained why Soerabaja's second attempt to establish an ambachtschool failed to thrive. The city's Resident, van Deventer, placed the blame for low school enrollments and high attrition elsewhere. The school was simply not providing training to those "lower classes and illegitimately born" needing public assistance, for whom it was ostensibly designed. Instead, it was gearing itself to the sons of the European *middenstand*—to Indies-born families who were enrolling their sons to avoid costly schooling in Holland, a requirement for civil servant posts that many could not afford. Student enrollments were low in 1862 when the school reopened, he argued, because there were not enough children from these middenstand families to fill the school. Little effort was ever made to recruit the inlandsche kinderen from the local European orphanages.[25]

Some middle-class families initially sought enrollment for their sons as an alternative to the civil service. But, as van Deventer recalled it, within a few years of the school's opening rumors had spread that after completing the three year course, opportunities were limited to menial jobs as tailors and shoemakers. Worse still, those few graduates who had gained employment complained that so much instruction had not served them well. Others fared worse, earning jobs as the "upper class of manual laborers" (*boven klasse der handwerksleiden*). In short, the school was successfully producing skilled manual workers, but the students "lacked both the desire and suitability" for such jobs. The school's annual report in 1867 concluded that without "the sort of private industry of Birmingham and Manchester," it was "natural" that many youths upon completing the course looked upon such labor with distaste. It was the middelstand who had become disillusioned with the school's limited prospects, not the orphaned children for whom the school was ostensibly designed.[26]

The decision to change the name from "ambachtschool" to "industrie-school" only ten months after it opened—an appeal to well-off (*gegoede*) families who previously had been unwilling to put their children in a school for manual labor—had its intended effect. It ensured that only children of the European middenstand would enroll. However, these youths from the "small Indies *burgerstand*," were also unfit for the schools. In van Deventer's view, they were so "morally and intellectually undeveloped" that the possibility of acquiring scientific knowledge was "virtually killed off" in their early years.[27] The school's annual reports repeatedly referred to the "neglected upbringing" of the youths and their complete "unsuitability for any education," to their "undeveloped reasoning skills . . . due to their exclusive use of the most narrow-minded and confining language of Malay." The fault lay with the parents, and more specifically with their native mothers, who were unwilling to entertain and ignorant of the "first and weightiest of principles: that upbringing and education must begin at birth." The school could obviously succeed with children of the lower-middle class who were already partially educated, but what, van Deventer asked, was the point if the destitute it was supposed to uplift were excluded from it?[28]

In van Deventer's estimation, the school's approach to training the inlandsche kinderen as "skilled workers and factory supervisors" was proceeding in the wrong way. Their accumulation of scientific knowledge was "useless" and "too comprehensive." His solution was to limit the school's scope to those students who would remain in the Indies, and invest state funds elsewhere. He proposed sending five "suitable and capable" students annually to the Netherlands for seven years of training and apprenticeship. But even this plan he admitted might be unrealistic because of their "aversion" to artisanal work and uncertain job prospects when they returned. In the end, he recommended that the ambachtschool be replaced with a "general training college" (*kweekschool*) where pupils could acquire preparatory skills for specific jobs as office workers, telegraphists, shipping agents, and archivists.

Van Deventer's appraisal was more articulate than most and more detailed than many but his basic premises were widely shared. The notion that children should be sent to the Netherlands, not just to learn a craft or trade, but to change their social environment and "their thoughts about the world," was based on a common contention: that the colony's economic and political viability were contingent on educating the hearts and minds of those who were a danger to it, and on managing their aspirations in the Indies world. As he put it, youths sent to the Netherlands "must not [conceive of themselves as] *heeren* (bosses/masters), they must not be burdened with more skills than they need . . . but only practical know-how for the tasks to which they are geared."

Van Deventer's focus on skills, sentiments and aspirations were shared but not his conclusions. Heer de Waal, then the Director of Education, objected to both its vision and scope. "How," he asked, "could we possibly uplift an entire class of people and not just a few individuals without building an institution on a colossal scale?"[29] He was equally concerned that students with free time would easily evade the school's control. He saw no assurance that upon completing the training van Deventer proposed—for inspectors, telegraphists and box-office clerks—students would even find jobs. Who and what, he asked, would the ambachtschool serve? Were the inlandsche kinderen really going to be able to work? He thought not. And if so, was the state going to support them or just send them back to their villages of origin?[30]

De Waal's warning was simple. As he put it, there was "no need for *ambachtslieden* in the major cities, since even skilled European-born and trained ambachtsman in the Indie's smaller towns could not find sufficient work. To make the inlandsche kinderen into ambachtslieden would too end in failure." Reminding the city's officials again that the purpose of the school had been to "uplift the inlandsche kinderen out of their destitute conditions," he urged that it be tied to the needs of the Soerabaja orphanage and remain so.[31]

De Waal's objections to sending them to the Netherlands were stronger still: If ten were sent a year, that would mean support in the form of housing, clothing, and food for forty students in four years. The financial costs were huge; the plan was absurd. De Waal instead proposed to make the Soerabaja ambachtschool into an industrial school, to set up continuing educational schools (*herhalingscholen*) attached to the public elementary schools in Java's three major urban centers, and to allocate a portion of the Indies budget for poverty relief and nurseries (*bewaarscholen*) for needy inlandsche kinderen in the same three cities of Java.

Whether the inlandsche kinderen were to be provided with theoretical knowledge and advanced education or merely practical know-how divided those who adhered to the artisanal romance from those who did not. The unresolved question remained the same: Could the inlandsche kinderen be incorporated into the Dutch fold without granting them other politically and economically costly entitlements?

Tracing the Industrial Romance: Lessons from Elsewhere

The inlandsche kinderen were not only targets of reform but objects of utopian visions about the colonial modern. Some imagined that they would man a new modernized technology but stay subordinate to that system. Others sought to provide them with carefully circumscribed practical training but not the theoretical knowledge that might afford them unrealistic aspirations and "illusions about the future."[32] In short, the inlandsche kinderen were to provide the amenities and comforts of a European bourgeois lifestyle for a growing colonial community that they themselves, reared in austere institutional environments, would never want to attain, or expect to enjoy or afford.

Some proposals sought to gear its prospective students to jobs in modern private industry, while others wanted to limit their training as "ambachtsman or machinists, not as engineers."[33] Tailoring and shoemaking, which had "already become predominately sweated trades by around 1850" in the Netherlands, were precisely the crafts that the Indies administration sought to promote for the inlandsche kinderen in the same period (van Lente 1990, 101).

Not surprisingly, early debates over the technical and skilled training of the inlandsche kinderen looked to the Netherlands, but not always for a model on which to draw. Dutch metropolitan and Indies colonial visions sometimes collided and sometimes merged. To some commentators, nineteenth-century Dutch society was the dominant figure against the backdrop of Java. For others, concerns about the rate of industrial developments in the Netherlands were less relevant than the Indies' emergent industrial needs.

The height of the artisanal vision, strongest during the 1850s and 1860s and in sharp decline by the 1880s, may have reflected the fluorescence of craft industries in the Netherlands more than the feasibility and desirability of their promotion in the Indies context itself. How the Dutch middelstand would adapt their craft industry to increasingly competitive production in industrializing Europe was partially echoed in the Indies as well. But some developments may have gone in the other direction. Whether these blueprints for artisanal schools in the Indies prefigured those in the Netherlands is not clear. What we do know is that discussions around the need for artisanal training among a European underclass in the Indies began in the 1830s, coinciding with similar discussions in the Netherlands and far before such schools were first set up in the metropole on a large scale (Brugmans 1929, 174). As early as 1835, an establishment for the *"ambachtelijke"* (skilled, craft-based) training of Indies-born children of European descent took as its aim the "creation of a industrious burgerstand [middle class], at the time, totally absent" (cited in Brugmans 1938, 87; see also Lente

1990, 99–119). Craft guilds had long been abolished in the Netherlands, but craft schools had not yet replaced them. A French writer could still observe in 1851 that industrial training in the Netherlands was the least developed of all the Western European states. With the growth of modern industry throughout Europe in the mid-nineteenth century came a new demand in the 1860s for vocational schools in the Netherlands. But whether they were designed to train artisans in traditional crafts, or more ambitiously to retool them for modern industry is not easy to tell.[34]

Some argued that the schools had another purpose all together: namely, to deter working class youths from participation in the growing trade union movement (Brugmans 1938, 86; van Lente 1990). Here too assessments of indolence and insolence converged. Not infrequently, supporters and critics of the ambacht initiative noted a similar working-class "preference for leisure" and lack of *werklust* in the Netherlands itself (Mokyr 1976, 215). Doubts as to whether the Netherlands' laboring class was up to the technical challenge of industrialization made the common pairing of "native" and "indolence" less exclusive since it was a term some associated as easily with the Dutch working class (Mokyr 1976, 194).[35]

Among those whose advice was sought early on in the ambacht initiative was the director of Soerabaja's naval factory—who argued that the real problem lay not with the inlandsche kinderen at all. They held that natives of European descent with whom they had worked were neither lazy nor incompetent but "industrious and well-behaved," well-prepared to learn skills but lacking opportunity and stimulation that would push them in that direction. In their estimation this was a population not wanting in comparison to European recruits, but with proper training preferable to them. As they put it, the inlandsche kinderen already had "knowledge of the language, population, customs and climate while the European would need an acclimatization period. [He] would feel attached to the enterprise established in the interest of his fatherland. Not belonging to the favored class of Indies society, his expectations and sense of entitlement will not be high."[36] It was this population, they argued, who could provide what the colony needed: namely, a ready supply for the maritime industry of subordinate technical personnel.[37] But the poor population of European descendants was increasing too fast for one or two industrial schools to accommodate. In their estimation, a modernizing colonial needed to train more than the inlandsche kinderen to envision industrial training on a much broader scale.[38]

The more serious problem they thought was with those coming from Holland who were already wasted when they arrived. Dissipated in hard drink and past their prime, they lacked "vitality" (*levenskracht*) and zest for work and would contribute nothing to the Indies' moral environment. The idea of creating an independent *burgerklasse* from this population was absurd. Their argument anticipated a theme that Soerabaja's Resident van Deventer was to bring up a decade later—namely that the creation of a "subordinate but technologically skilled personnel" would benefit not just the needy but also "the entire growing class of the population of European descent" who would not be content to remain office scribes and factory hands but who sought "work that they could judiciously and independently carry out." Throughout the second half of the nineteenth century, it was self-worth in labor and political independence that were seen to go dangerously hand in hand.

The industrial vision did not remain a romance for long. By 1874, it was considered a total fiasco. The commission on needy Europeans began each of its reports by observing that the "cultivation of ambachten will no longer be our exclusive priority." Instead, attention was turned to the "upbringing of the child" (*opvoeding van het kind*), to nurseries, to good elementary education and opportunities in agriculture. The commission noted that the Soerabaja *ambachtschool*'s state subsidy had gone from 30,000 *gulden* in 1861 to 5,000, then 1,000, and finally 300 gulden by 1872 when it closed.[39] One instructor on leave in Holland who learned about the school's "temporary" closing wrote to the Minister of Colonies that the school's problems stemmed from a basic assumption: that its students had a "practical know-how" when they had no practical knowledge at all.[40]

The 1874 pauperism commission rejected the ambacht initiative outright, but this was not the end of efforts to make it work. In 1882, it was reopened as an "evening school" (*burgeravondschool*) with new direction. Again the Director of Education posed the question of thirty years earlier—whether the "so-called inlandsche kinderen can be made into a true artisan class"—and answered an emphatic "no,"[41] noting that "laziness, unwillingness, and indifference" among the "indolent indische youth" was evident throughout the 1860s and was still the case. But he was convinced that indolence was not the real problem since he knew scores of Indo youths lacking in neither energy nor will. It was "haughtiness" (*hooghartigheid*) and "false pride" that were at the root of the problem and would remain so "as long as our society has the peculiar character it does": "The *inlandse kind* [sic] above all else, were fearful and apprehensive of being confused with natives and would not choose to be part of a European ambachtstand. . . . [They] are ashamed of their workclothes, and of the company they keep in their workplaces."[42] Of the 123 orphans sent to the

Soerabaja ambachtschool, only twenty-eight made use of their specialized training (nine machinists, eleven overseers, three workers in the military atelier, four smiths, one technical engineer). Forty others became office clerks and scribes, seventeen joined the military, ten disappeared. The Director of Education concluded that they had little desire to become *handwerkleden* and that efforts to form a "*handwerksklasse* among the inlandsche kinderen. . . . were a total failure." This was not least of all because they could not possibly compete with the sort of fine-tuned apprenticeship that Javanese and Chinese workers were able to attain in their free time, preparing them for jobs they willingly performed for a small wage. The Indo-European manual laborer, he concluded, was "on very dangerous terrain."

In short, one could not create an entire artisan class: there was a lack of desire, too much competition, and no room for such a class of Indo-European *handarbeiden.* In the 1880s the analysis was similar but the conclusions were not the same. One alternative proposal, that an ambachtschool should be reorganized "only for Europeans and Indo-Europeans" had some support. Thus van Schouwenburg, Director of the *hooger burgerschool* in Semarang, wrote in 1881: "Nothing can be more beneficial to Indies society than that it go about forming a class of industrious citizens (*burgers*) who, by honest and honorable *handenarbeid* will provide for their own needs and those of the public and as such will be the connecting link now broken between the foreign ruling and native ruled race."[43] The Director of Education dismissed van Schouwenberg's optimism, noting that the Soerabaja *burgeravondschool* had not come close to accomplishing such a goal. It was neither a craft nor an industrial school. He criticized the new proposal on the grounds that there were simply "no children from the Indies' better classes who wanted to learn a craft or have such a job." He urged that the school orient itself to training bosses and foremen, not to providing technical skills.

A report on the school in 1883 extracted these conclusions: (1) that the Indies badly needed technicians and whether it trained inlandsche kinderen for those jobs or others, it certainly needed some population to do them; (2) that education of the inlandsche kinderen be limited to practical, not theoretical, knowledge since costs were too high; (3) that the European students should not be turned into common workers (*werklieden*) but into persons suitable as managers, supervising the work of others; and (4) that they should provide the Indo and European youths with practical training but no more, giving them the opportunity to enter government service at the lower ranks where exams were not required. Some of these plans were fleshed out unevenly and with different degrees of success. The school that replaced Soerabaja's ambachtschool counted 265 students by 1901. European youths were no longer recruited for manual jobs, and theoretical training of inlandsche kinderen was abolished across the board.[44]

Retrospectively, the ambachtschool in Soerabaja presents itself as a conception and practice that was unrealistic, utopian, and doomed to be a fiasco from the start. And my attention to the noneventful here suggests that it was so. Its failure is presented as one deriving from a disjuncture between vision and reality, and from a population stymied by its own attitudes toward manual labor: false vanity, haughtiness, arrogance, a refusal to sit at a carpenter's bench over a desk. But as we have also seen, not everyone agreed. Van Hoevell's assessment a half century earlier had been on the mark. The Ambachtschool was not a fiasco; it was made into one and pointedly sabotaged by the state.

What is striking in these conflicting and confused arguments is how much they changed. Over a seventy-year period, appraisals varied widely as to whether an ambachstand could really be created out of orphaned youths, *Ambacht* schools, heralded in the 1860s as the solution to pauperism among European descendants, were seen as badly misguided twenty years later. By the 1880s, both the artisanal and industrial romances had largely collapsed, only to be resuscitated and transformed twenty years later. But by then, the size of the poor European and Indo population was vast. The attention of the 1901–1902 Pauperism Commission, like that of the Indo-European population itself, had turned elsewhere.

Tracing the Rural Romance

The rural romance that took off in the 1870s was directly responsive to the failures of the ambacht efforts but also to what the Indies administration called a "terrifying increase of European pauperism" threatening society with "a disastrous cancer." The Indies Advisory Council expressed alarm "that Europeans and their descendants . . . were living in wretched conditions" in virtually all the Indies' cities, in Batavia, Soerabaja, and Semarang, "probably the worst of all."[45] Villages on the outskirts of cities were reportedly filling up "with a class that does not properly belong there"—with people out of work and out of place.[46] The fact that the rural option outlined a much more limited set of financial responsibilities for the state conferred on it broad administrative appeal.

The small-scale proposals made for industrial schools in the 1860s now seemed totally out of line with the numbers at risk. By the time of the 1874 pauperism commission, there was widespread official agreement that the in-landsche kinderen were neither "inclined nor suitable for handenarbeid." Each of the commission's subsection reports began with a statement that the ambacht-school plan was a failure, thus explaining the commission's new focus on nurs-eries, agricultural institutes for orphans, and children's agricultural colonies.

As early as 1854, the Indies Advisory Council had already recommended that an Indies-based ambachtschool should be established on the famous Met-tray model, first developed in the Netherlands and then copied in England, Bel-gium, and France. Mettray was an agrarian colony designed for the re-education of delinquent children and young vagrants through agricultural work (Dekker 1998, 130–47). In the Indies its emphasis would be similar but slightly dif-ferently framed: "To develop religious sensibilities in the hearts of the youth through continuous surveillance of their behavior, allowing them to resist their tendencies to indolence and to develop their skills and character . . . [Only then would they form an] esteemed and cultivated middenstand who would make up a solid element and support European colonisation."[47]

Thus the agricultural initiative was a response to the failed industrial vision in other ways. For one, the children would be captured young, not at ten to twelve years as with craft training, but rather at the more "kneadable" age of three to four years. Second, the agricultural colonies would promote modest aspirations, simple clothing, and a simple lifestyle: The girls must have nothing more than a blouse (kebaja) and a sarong but, as with the boys, they would have a special outfit to wear on holidays. The aim must have been more to make perfected natives than to make imitation Europeans.

This initiative addressed the third shortcoming of the ambacht course; namely the haughtiness and insolence that was seen to stand in the inlandsche kinderen's way. The agricultural colonies were designed to curb frustrations by curbing desires, by carving out a habitus for European descendants that by defi-nition meant that they could not really be considered European. Children were to be schooled in those tasks that would allow them to become boerenstand (farmers). But more importantly, they were to be schooled to embrace the hon-est values that such a rural, family-based lifestyle required. To that end, the children's agricultural colonies were to assign mothers and fathers to the or-phaned children who would provide the discipline and affection they purport-edly lacked. Widows, otherwise unable to provide for their own children, would be enlisted as supervisors with their children maintained at the colony's cost.[48] Finally, such rural institutions would remove the children from natives (and Europeans), unlike the ambachtschool's apprenticeship programs where native and Indo were placed in close contact. The children would produce their own food, learn about agriculture, and "be separated from all natives, even servants."

The Indies Council enthusiastically endorsed the plan. By the Council's assessment, the proposal would provide the inlandsche kinderen with the opportunity to earn a living in agriculture: "Both the less fortunate as well as others—some for a wage—could be formed into 'competent farmers.'" Upon coming of age, the state would provide them with a parcel of land and a cash advance. The council insisted that such agricultural institutions would work along with state institutions to train the young for crafts, factories, and industry. Public and private charities would continue their relief efforts.

The rural romance may have been compelling on paper but in practice many thought it was not. Agricultural children's colonies, applauded as ideal sites to nurture independence and self-sufficiency, were seen by their critics as something else. The Director of Education bluntly described why he was so opposed:

> These plans force a question: are we speaking of a school of correction or of a penal colony, a depot for delinquents? People want to place young people of both sexes on an uninhabited and deserted island that has no housing; at the same time the land will be brought into cultivation by this brigade of chained youths! What a joyless life for which these youths will be prepared. Not seeing any other human beings but their comrades and guards, they must live in the small confines of the garden in which the institution is established; bound to a forced labor which is entirely against their inclinations. What an existence! What is the difference between such an establishment and a penal colony?[49]

He derided the illusion that children would develop a taste for agriculture and take pride and pleasure in their new fatherland: "But no, this is not what will happen. They would use their freedom to return to their native places. There they would be without any help in strange surroundings. The young women would service the Chinese and Europeans, the boys would end up in jail." In short, the inlandsche kinderen would return to the destitute conditions from which they came. The proposal that children's colonies (*kindercolonie*) should be established on "wasteland" outside of Java struck him as misguided. He proposed instead that the children be raised on Java, agreeing with van Delden that they should be "isolated but certainly not cut off from European surroundings. The choice of place is very important if the goal is the improvement of a race and if we want to include as many children as possible." Responding to van Delden's plan to gather 750 children in such a rural orphanage, the Director feared that education, order, and discipline would suffer. How could they possibly educate such large numbers in practical agriculture without a hugely expanded personnel? Moreover, even if that were conceivable, it would do nothing for the "hundreds of children who remain badly cared for and without supervision in the villages and who belonged in the school." But he was more concerned that if children could still enjoy good food, education (*onderwijs*), and upbringing (*opvoeding*) with the small numbers presently in the orphanages, larger numbers would make that impossible. If those children now housed in smaller orphanages were brought to a central institution, their conditions would only worsen.

Unlike van Deventer who applauded the Dutch model agricultural colony of Mettraij, the Director of Education criticized it on the grounds that such large institutions would not work in the Indies; nor was there proof that they had ever worked in Europe. He pointed out that Mettray had produced more soldiers than farmers and that the largest orphanages were a breeding ground for "prisoners and whores." The most successful system in Europe was the adoption of orphan children, something that was not viable in the Indies where there were not enough suitable families to support the effort. He concluded that private initiatives were the only answer since the state could not provide subsidies on such a scale.

Other European institutions of confinement were pulled up as models, but almost as quickly turned down. The proposal of the 1874 pauperism commission to set up workhouses (*werkhuizen*) for Indo-Europeans on Java, like those in the towns and smaller cities of Europe, enjoyed favor for a short time. But once again the Director of Education accused the commission of being totally out of touch with reality: it knew nothing of the nature of the European workhouses, much less what their charges had become. In general, the work provisioning programs in Europe had a poor record of success. If in Europe, the impoverished European looked upon the workhouses as a last resort, in the Indies "such institutions would more humiliating still," and the perception would be worse. Instead, he urged a model that he thought would avoid humiliation for those it targeted: the creation of agricultural, not craft, schools on a Froebel scheme for nursery school-age children that would "train them in agriculture, animal raising, butter and cheese production, and in the making and tending of orchards."[50]

This rural romance, like its ambacht counterpart, had its European template. The notion of setting urban orphan children in agricultural settlements was a vision that accorded with the belief that children needed to be removed from urban environments and placed in more natural or rural settings. The "kinder-garten" movement of the mid-19th century and the orphan trains that farmed urban youths out to the rural western region of the United States later in the century were derived from a similar vision, if not the same plan. The rural romance took its inspiration from less obvious sources as well, like the self-sufficient agrarian colonies of the nineteenth-century socialist utopian movements. While these socialist communities would replace the need for property, marriage, and religion in the Indies, these were the very values that rural colonies were designed to nurture and maintain: to encourage marriage and to imbue religious dedication, sexual morality, and a commitment to private property that would serve youths well as independent farmers in a new settler society.

These rural romances cut across metropole and colony in other, similar ways. Both took the agrarian model as a preferable solution to pauperism than relief programs that would more seriously burden the state. But the self-sufficient ethic that underwrote these rural nostalgias often resembled what they were supposed to replace. William Cobbet criticized these utopias as "parallellograms of paupers," not desirable projects for the future. Lewis Mumford described Robert Owen's "project for a model industrial town" as one that had "more of the flavor of a poor colony than that of a productive human society" (Mumford 1922, 123). Similar criticisms were directed at the Indies' kinder-colonies; they too were viewed as punitive pauper colonies more than once.

Where utopian and colonial visionaries differed was in how they conceived of the moral and cultural training of the young, where it should occur, under whose aegis, and at what age. In the Indies, children's agricultural colonies, industrial schools, nurseries, and various sorts of apprenticeship programs were envisioned as sites for learning self-discipline and constraining expectations, and as places where the spartan conditions of labor and living would serve those ends.

These projects too had little success. Nor is it clear they were ever intended to be realized. Here too it was lamented that the Indies mixed-blood population had little inclination for manual labor, and that few would be content "behind a plough." But the notion of recovering an agrarian space in Indies society for those uncomfortably positioned within it—unlike the vision of a craftsmen class—was not only prompted by preindustrial nostalgia and industrializing anxieties. It was a romance that was to be embraced by a wider swath of European society; indeed, land to the Indo-European tiller became a major platform at the turn of the century for a growing Indies European population increasingly discontent with the European-born monopoly on economic resources, social status, and political rights.[51]

transpar'ency, n. picture . . . shown up by light behind negative (photog.) Image on glass with reversed lights and shadows from which positive pictures are drawn—*Oxford English Dictionary*

Debates on the inlandsche kinderen called on a predictable array of metaphors and on a biopolitical discourse of racialized enemies within—of degenerate class renegades threatening the body politic, the moral well-being of its children, and the safety of its citizens. The fantasy that the Indo and European poor could be more than mere copyists and "writing machines," and perform more than a rote task, was for some of the colonial elite more disquieting than the dangers of their continued impoverishment.

But architects of colonial policy enjoyed little consensus among themselves. Civic leaders and public administrators, businessmen, school teachers, and social reformers locked heads repeatedly in their fantasies about the fate of the inlandsche kinderen and why they were as impoverished as they were. Between the 1840s and early 1900s they were the object of varied strategies seeking to confine their movements and seal their fate as modest but respectable loyalists, as those whose political claims would be tethered to the continued denial of native rights, whose investments in a racial hierarchy would remain strong, but whose sense of entitlement would be limited to legal European equivalency, not equal social or political status. As such, the Indies administration embraced reformist gestures but withdrew financial support, declaring plans defunct before they were even tried. They devised and dissembled projects that might allow those with "native blood" to man a modernizing state but not to assert control over new channels of communication, information, and technology. Demands for a skilled labor force in a modernizing economy butted up against fears that an educated labor force would press for more than the state was willing to provide.

Accusations of "indolence" and "insolence" coded who was unworthy of entitlements. Containing one and braking the other produced a gridlock on reform but not on the discourse of race. Racial taxonomies and debates about capability flourished in this reformist period in which little happened, in which few projects were implemented, and few reforms were passed. The craft, industrial, and rural romances rose and fell as reams of classified inquiries swelled the state archives, justifying why little, despite the state's best efforts, could be safely carried out.

These were colonial negatives in more than one sense: they were cropped and re-cropped and redeveloped. They are absent from colonial histories because they were more often discarded in process and never *occurred*. As blue-prints of distress they underscore what was deemed to have gone awry in the Netherlands, what was wrong with Dutch colonial society, what might be excised from that picture, and what could not be touched up. What such an archive produced was not reform, but a new compendium of expert knowledge. It conferred on the problem of "mixed-bloods" and "poor whites" that of an erudite and specialized colonial field. Not least, the archive underscored that the debates and politics surrounding emergent welfare states in the second half of the nineteenth century were being played out with new kinds of comparison in a broad imperial field.

Notes

This chapter is from my forthcoming *Along the Archival Grain: Colonial Cultures and their Affective States*, to be published by Princeton University Press.

1   See Stern (1992, 6) in which the conquistadors' "contending paradigms or utopias" are used to describe the colonizing project in sixteenth-century Latin America.

2   On Jameson's notion of political and semantic horizons of possibility see *The Political Unconscious* (1981, 74–93).

3   I thank James Johnson, a political scientist at the University of Rochester, for pointing out the convergence between Geoffrey Hawthorn's *Plausible Worlds: Possibility and Understanding in History and the Social Sciences* (1991) and an earlier version of this essay presented as a Lewis Henry Morgan lecture in 1996.

4   AR, Verbaal 9 July 1860, no. 13. Letter of 24 November 1858. Konsideratien en advies van de Direckteuren van het marine establissement en de fabriek voor de marine te Soerabaja. All archival references are to the General State Archives in the Hague (designated as AR) unless otherwise noted.

5   See the Concise Oxford Dictionary (1964, 1084).

6   See the etymological entry for "utopia" as derived from "nowhere": f.Gk *ou* not + *topos* place] (*Oxford*, 1434).

7   On the rise of international fora in which colonial knowledges were produced and shared, see my introduction with Frederick Cooper to *Tensions of Empire: Colonial Cultures in a Bourgeois World* (1997).

8   When this 1874 statement reappeared in the 1901 Report on European Pauperism, the terms did not remain the same: *naggemaakte Europeanen* was replaced by *gemankeerde Europeanen*, underscoring how much an "imitation" was indeed a "defective" product. See *Het Pauperisme onder de Europeanen in Nederlandsch-Indie. Deerde Gedeelte. Kleine Landbouw.*

The phrase was reworked yet again some years later. In 1916 a report on education recommended segregated schools for the inlandsche kinderen (separating them from Europeans and from the Javanese) in the following way: "If people want the native (den Inlander) in general to share in Western civilization, then one should guard against fostering imitation-Europeans [imitatie-Europeans], hybrids with no inner strength, useless in the Netherlands as in the East-Indies itself. . . . What the Indies needs is not a generation of imitation-Europeans, but of developed natives who along with a broad knowledge of the old Indies civilization and culture has learned as much as possible from Western culture, who would appreciate its benefits without losing contact with their own people". Praeadvies omtrent punten van den agenda van het Koloniaal Onderwijs-Congres, den Haag, 28–30 August 1916. Source: Vollenhove Instituut, Leiden.

9   See, for example, two recent studies of urban colonial society in Soerabaya and Se-marang in which the "Indo" and impoverished Europeans are not mentioned: Cobban (1988, 266–291) and Frederick (1983, 354–371).

10   AR, KV 9 July 1860. Governor-General's summary report to the Minister of Colonies concerning "Inrichting van een ambachtschool te Soerbaja."

11   AR, KV 24 March 1874.

12   AR, KV, MR 904/x, 14 April 1876. Letter of the Director of Education to the Governor-General, 18 Sept 1881.

13   See Van Hoevell's scathing criticism of government policy toward the school in his article "De Ambachtschool te Soerabaja" (1858: I, 129–49) in the *Tijdschrijft voor de Nederlandsche-Indie*, a publication for which he was editor and principal writer.

14   AR, KV 24 November 1858. Considerations and advice of the directors of the naval establishment and naval factory in Soerabaja.

15   AR, KV 9 July 1860, no. 13; 24 November 1858.

16   AR, KV 9 July 1860. Summary Report from the Governor-General to the Minister of Colonies. Also see *Die Armblanke-Vraagstuk in Suid-Afrika. Verslag van die Carnegie-Kommissie* (1932).

17   As the debate was framed, there was no reference to the fact that European men had ever worked in the Indies doing manual labor. But a longer view of Indies history suggests that this was not the case. In the late seventeenth century and eighteenth century, Batavia had a specially designated *ambachtskwartier* (artisans' quarter) pop-ulated by slaves, freemen, and nearly 400 Europeans working as, among other things, carpenters, shoemakers, smithies, glassmakers, cabinetmakers, and woodcutters. I know of no accounts that document what happened to European artisans when Daendals, the Governor-General during the brief British interregnum, abolished the artisan quarter in 1809. See *Oud Batavia* (1922, 356–360).

18   AR, Verbaal 9 July 1860. Report from the Governor-General to the Minister of Colo-nies.

19   AR, KV 22 July 1854, no. 7. Letter from Minister of Colonies to the Governor-General.

20   AR, KV 9 July 1860, no. 13. Letter of Director of the Naval establishment and the Directory of the naval factory in Soerabaja, 24 November 1858.

21   AR, 28 February 1855; KV 9 July 1860, no. 13.

22   AR, Verbaal 9 July 1860.

23   AR, Verbaal 16 April 1854, no. 3. Letter from Governor-General to Raad van Indie, Bogor, 9 September 1854.

24   AR, Verbaal 16 April 1854. From the Raad van Indie to the Governor-General, 20 Oc-tober 1854.

25 AR, KV 18 August 1868. Letter from the Resident of Soerabaja, van Deventer, to the Director of Education, 31 October 1868.

26 AR, KV 18 August 1868. Ibid.

27 AR, KV 18 August 1868. Ibid.

28 AR, KV 18 August 1868. Quoted by van Deventer from the 1864 Annual Report of the Soerabaja ambachtschool.

29 AR, KV 13 March 1869. Letter from the Department of Education to the Governor-General.

30 AR, KV 13 March 1869. Ibid.

31 AR, KV 22 January 1868. Letter from the Director of Education to the Resident of Soerabaja.

32 AR, Verbaal 18 August 1868. Letter of 31 October 1868 from van Deventer to the Director of Education.

33 AR, KV 9 July 1860.

34 Van Lente notes that one of the early vocational schools in the Hague opted to strengthen the crafts while allowing them to be competitive with large-scale industry. Offering courses for electricians, gas fitters, and motor mechanics, it advocated a renewed appreciation of craft produced articles, not a modernization of them (van Lente 1990, 103–105).

35 Mokyr notes the fear "that a large number of unemployed, which were reported to be teeming in the Dutch cities, may have been to a large extent voluntary rather than involuntary unemployment" (1976, 194). He cites a late eighteenth-century Dutch periodical complaining that Dutch workers seemed to "prefer the austere living that they can make from alms to a richer existence they could enjoy if they had been willing to work" (194).

36 AR, KV 9 July 1860, no. 13; 24 November 1858.

37 AR, KV 9 July 1860; 24 November 1858, no. 13. Konsideratien en advies van den Direkteuren van het marine establissement en de fabriek voor de marine te Soerabaya.

38 Verbaal 9 July 1860. Letter from the Governor-General to the Minister of Colonies.

39 AR, MR 904, 18 September 1881. Letter to the Governor-General from the Director of Education. Of the 31 students at the school, by the end of 1862 only 14 were left. How many were from the orphanage and without tuition, and how many were not is not indicated. In the school's annual report the following year, the number of entering students was thirty-five but by the end of the year it had declined to twenty-three, attributed in part to students who left for other jobs, but more importantly to the youths' "ill-preparedness" to follow the course. By 1864, the prospects of the school looked even worse. Between 1862 and 1864, about seventy students had been provided with training, of which only twenty finished their studies. The remaining fifty had dropped out. By December 1864, only four students were prepared to sit for the exam in the graduating class. The 1865 report was the first to acknowledge the school's failure, noting that graduates were finding it extremely difficult to find suitable employment, principally because manual labor held so little attraction for them. With little knowledge of Dutch and no further education they had no chance of being promoted. Van Deventer opined that they needed real technical training in

electricity and magnetics, not lessons in a manual craft [AR, KV 18 August 1868. Letter from the Resident of Soerabaja to the Director of Education].

40 AR, Verbaal 21 January 1872, no. 5.
41 AR, Verbaal 29 July 1882, no. 8852. Letter from the Director of Education to the Governor-General, on the subject of the Burgeravond school.
42 AR, Verbaal 29 June 1882, no. 8852.
43 AR, Verbaal 21 September 1883, no. 49 (no. 3672). Afschrift 170. Letter of the Director of the Hooger Burgerschool in Semarang, 22 December 1881.
44 AR, KV 1902–1903: 186.
45 AR, 7 Maart 1873.
46 AR, MR 904. 1876 Report of the Director of Education.
47 AR, Verbaal 16 April 1854. Report from the Raad van Indie to the Governor-General, 20 October 1854.
48 AR, KV 28 Maart 1874.
49 AR, KV 24 Maart 1874, no. 47. "Notas voor de Inlandsche Kinderen," Heer van Delden.
50 MR 904. 1876 Report of the Minister of Education, 14 April 1874.
51 On the politics of an Indo-European movement that focused on a bid for land (and its unexpected political allies) see Drooglever (1980) and Stoler (1992, 545–48).

References

Arnold, David. 1983. "White Colonization and Labour in Nineteenth Century India." *The Journal of Imperial and Commonwealth History* 11, no. 2: 133–58.

Brugmans, I. J. 1929. *De Arbeidende Klasse in Nederland in de 19e Eeuw*. S-Gravenhage: Martinus Nijhoff.

Bundy, Colin. 1987. "Vagabond Hollanders and Runaway Englishmen: White Poverty in the Cape before Poor Whiteism." In *Putting a Plough to the Ground: Accumulation and Dispossession in Rural South Africa, 1850–1930*, edited by W. Beinart, P. Delius and S. Trapido. Johannesburg: Raven Press.

Cobban, Allan. 1988. "Kampungs and Conflict in Colonial Semarang." *Journal of Southeast Asian Studies* 19, no. 2 (September): 266–91.

Dekker, Jeroen. 1998. "Transforming the Nation and the Child: Philanthropy in the Netherlands, Belgium, France and England." In *Charity, Philanthropy and Reform: From the 1690s to 1850*, edited by Hugh Cunningham and Joanna Innes. New York: St. Martin's Press.

Die Armblanke-Vraagstuk in Suid-Afrika. Verslag van die Carnegie-Kommissie. 1932. Stellenbosch: Pro Ecclesia Drukkerij.

Drooglever, P. J. 1980. *De Vaderlandse Club*. Amsterdam: Franeker T. Wever.

Fowler, H. W., and F. G. Fowler, eds. 1964. *The Concise Oxford Dictionary*. London: Clarendon Press.

Frederick, William. 1983. "Hidden Change in Late Colonial Urban Society in Indonesia." *Journal of Southeast Asian Studies* 14, no. 2 (September): 354–71.

Hawthorn, Geoffrey. 1991. *Plausible Worlds: Possibility and Understanding in History and the Social Sciences*. Cambridge: Cambridge University Press.

Het Pauperisme onder de Europeanen in Nederlandsch-Indie. Deerde Gedeelte. Kleine Landbouw. 1981. Batavia: Landsdrukkerij.

Hoevell, Van. 1858. "De Ambachtschool te Soerabaja." *Tijdschrijft voor de Nederlandsche-Indie* 1: 129–49.

Jameson, Fredric. 1981. *The Political Unconscious: Narrative as Socially Symbolic Act.* Ithaca: Cornell University Press.

Landbouw, Kleine. 1901. *Het Pauperisme onder de Europeanen in Nederlandsch-Indie. Deerde Gedeelte.* Batavia: Landsdrukkerij.

Lente, Dirk van. 1990. "The Crafts in Industrial Society: Ideals and Policy in the Netherlands, 1890–1930." *Economic and Social History in the Netherlands* 2: 99–119.

Mokyr, Joel. 1976. *Industrialization in the Low-Countries, 1795–1850.* New Haven: Yale University Press.

Mumford, Lewis. 1922. *The Story of Utopias.* New York: Boni and Liveright.

Oud Batavia: Part I. 1922. Batavia: G Kolff.

Stern, Steve. 1992. "Paradigms of Conquest: History, Historiography, and Politics." *Journal of Latin American Studies* 24: 1–34.

Stoler, Ann Laura. 1992. "Sexual Affronts and Racial Frontiers." *Comparative Studies in Society and History* 34, no. 3: 545–548.

Stoler, Ann Laura. forthcoming. *Along the Archival Grain: Colonial Cultures and their Affective States.* Princeton: Princeton University Press.

Stoler, Ann Laura, and Frederick Cooper, eds. 1997. *Tensions of Empire: Colonial Cultures in a Bourgeois World.* Berkeley: University of California Press.

Winsemius, Johan. 1936. *Nieuwe-Guinee als kolonisatie-gebied voor Europeanen en van Indo-Europeanen.* Ph.D. Dissertation. Faculty of Medicine: University of Amsterdam.

3 Marginal Contexts

Culture on the Edges: Caribbean Creolization in Historical Context

Michel-Rolph Trouillot

Le lieu est incontournable. —Edouard Glissant

Creolization is a miracle begging for analysis. Because it first occurred against all odds, between the jaws of brute and absolute power, no explanation seems to do justice to the very wonder that it happened at all. Understandably, the study of Creole cultures and languages has always left room for the analyst's astonishment. Theories of creolization or of Creole societies, assessments of what it means to speak—or to be—Creole are, in turn, still very much affected by the ideological and political sensibilities of the observers (Bolland 1992; Calvet 1997; Chaudenson 1993; Le Brun 1996; Price 2001; Price and Price 1997).

It may not be possible or even meritorious to get rid of these sensibilities. Still, the knowledge of creolization can benefit from a more ethnographic approach that takes into account the concrete contexts within which new cultural ideals, practices, and patterns—none of which can be reduced to the other—developed in the Americas. The plantation society, the plural society, and the Creole society models—even Nigel Bolland's "dialectical" approach (Bolland 1992)—all seize on creolization as a totality, thus one level removed from the concrete circumstances faced by the individuals engaged in the process. All these models invoke history; some even use it at times. Yet the historical conditions of cultural production rarely become a fundamental and necessary part of the descriptions or analyses that these models generate. Calls for a more refined look at historical particulars (see, for example, Mintz 1971; Mintz and Price 1992) remain largely unheeded. Worse, current apologists of *créolité* (see, for example, Bernabé et al. 1989; Confiant in Watts 1998) pay even less attention to the historical record than did their predecessors in cultural nationalism, perhaps because the historiography of slavery is much weaker in French than in Dutch or, especially, English.

This chapter, which draws primarily from the experience of Afro-Caribbean peoples, tries to give due credit to the creativity that Africans and their descendants demonstrated right from the beginning of plantation slavery. However, praise for the creativity of Afro-Caribbeans may mask the struggles also inherent in creolization unless we take the analysis one step closer to changing historical contexts. From a wide range of changing historical circumstances, I abstract four contexts as key heuristic devices: a frontier context, a plantation context, an enclave context, and a modernist context. I then return to the plantation context to illustrate the many ways in which such a framework may improve our knowledge of creolization.

Although the historical situations treated here come from the Caribbean record, this treatment may be useful to historically oriented cultural anthropologists and linguists in general, inasmuch as it directly faces the issue of our management of the historical record. As ethnography became a defining moment of anthropological practice, we have learned to give a distinctive priority to the micro-level and the specific situations it reveals. That emphasis has not stopped us from making generalizations. In many ways, it has often helped us make better generalizations. When it comes to the past, however, we often move from the general to the particular as if our historical master tropes—colonialism, slavery, racism, and the domination they register, from the imposition of Christianity and enforced segregation to the spread of European languages and gender roles—could actually help paint concrete situations on the ground.

Yet useful as these master tropes may be in sketching the horizon of an era and the outer limits of a social formation, they cannot convey the lived realities of actual populations, past or present. Indeed, they are sometimes misleading. To be sure, we tend to rely on them in part because the historical record is weak at describing the people we usually study, when it does not silence most of their practices altogether. The tendency to overgeneralize is an understandable response to the silences that pertain to the production of sources, archives, narratives, and historical retrospective (Trouillot 1995). Yet these silences should not imply that we in turn silence whatever record is available or discard as epiphenomena the spatial and temporal limits of the sociohistorical process. In short, we need to historicize and contextualize as much as the empirical evidence allows. The meta-theoretical point of this paper, the need to historicize creolization, holds true for all of our master tropes. The four contexts outlined here suggest possibilities for pruning out of the meager (yet available) record heuristic devices that would move historical anthropologists closer to the actual situations with which we must deal.

The African American Miracle

From the family plots of the Jamaican hinterland, the Afro-religions of Brazil and Cuba, or the jazz music of Louisiana to the vitality of Haitian painting and music and the historical awareness of Suriname's maroons, the cultural practices that typify various African American populations appear to us as the product of a repeated miracle. For those of us who keep in mind the conditions of emergence and growth of ideals, patterns, and practices associated with African slaves and their descendants in the Americas, their very existence is a continuing puzzle. For they were born against all odds.

The Antilles alone suffice as exemplars of the repeated wonder.[1] Manifestations of Afro-Caribbean cultural life emerged unexpectedly, unforeseen developments of an agenda set in Europe, by Europe, and for Europe. Caribbean territories have experienced Western European influence longer than any other area outside of Europe itself. They are territories that Europe claimed to shape to fit its particular goals, territories through which Europeans moved as if they were empty lands. And indeed, they were emptied, in so far as the native population had been wiped out without even the dubious privilege of slow death on a reservation. Almost everything that we now associate with the Caribbean—from sugarcane, coffee, mangoes, donkeys, and coconuts, to the people themselves, whether African or Asian in origin—was brought there as part of the European conquest.

Cultural concerns did not figure among European priorities during most of the conquest. For more than a century, the search for gold and the rivalries it provoked obliterated most other issues. Then, from the seventeenth century on, European attention slowly turned to the production of agricultural commodities in the tropical areas of the mainland and in the Antilles. Cultural considerations entered into the design of plantation America, but only as prerequisites of political and economic domination, as corollaries of the plantation system. Thus, although the Afro-Caribbean world came to life on the plantation and in part because of the plantation, Afro-Caribbean cultural patterns and practices emerged against the expectations and wishes of plantation owners and their European patrons. They were not meant to exist.

Because they were not meant to exist, many observers came to believe that Caribbean culture did not exist, in spite of all evidence to the contrary. Up to the second part of the twentieth century, most observers and many speakers viewed the Creole languages of the Caribbean as burlesque versions of European tongues, "*français petit nègre*," "patois," "broken English," unworthy of serious attention from linguists and writers.

Interestingly, however, Afro-Caribbean ideals and practices never became exactly what European planners and owners might have expected. From the very beginnings of slavery, it was clear that the Africans and their descendants were shaping modes of behavior, patterns of thought and their expression. Caribbean languages provide good examples of this creativity. Africans brought to the Caribbean during the slave trade spoke a wide variety of African languages. Yet in many circumstances, they were also forced to draw from the vernacular(s) of their respective masters. That itself is not surprising. More interesting is the fact that, once taken over by the slaves and their descendants, European dialects did not remain the same. They acquired sounds, morphological and syntactical patterns unknown in Europe. More important, they were shaped to express the joys, pains, and reflections of hundreds of thousands of humans. In one word, they were creolized.[2]

From Creole Linguistics to Créolité

For a number of reasons, these Creole languages became the first products of the creolization process to attract the attention of scholars.[3] First, Creole languages were obvious. The features that demarcated them from European vernaculars could not be denied (Magens 1770). On the contrary, these features had to be acknowledged if only for the purpose of communication. Even when the linguistic status of Creoles was denigrated, such denigration also reinforced the acknowledgment that they were different. Second, a vibrant tradition in the observation of non-Western languages existed in Europe since at least the seventeenth century. Lastly, language was politically safe—or thought to be so. It was thought to be amenable to study without long encounters with a mass of natives. It was one of the few products of creolization least likely to engage the scholar in immediate political controversies about the people who had been creolized.

Controversies there were, however, especially on the matter of origins. Here also, wonderment played its role. Since the early nineteenth century, analysts felt the need to explain the puzzle of the emergence of Creole languages, to ponder the significance of their existence (Gilbert 1986). This obsession with origins, still central to Creole linguistics (Alleyne 1980; Arends 1995; Baker 1994; Muysken and Smith 1986; Wekker 1996), gave rise to two methodological tendencies.

First, since actual slave speech was for all practical purposes inaccessible, creolists tended to infer the past from the present. Current Caribbean speech or changing patterns in more recent non-Caribbean Creoles supposedly documented what must have happened in some undetermined pan-Caribbean past. Second, since the ultimate purpose of the exercise was, more often than not, to explain or dissipate the wonder of Creole emergence, creolists tended to apply one exclusive all-encompassing theory after another. Either all Creoles had evolved from a singular source, most probably a Portuguese pidgin (monogenesis theory); or all followed the same "West African" grammatical principles (substratum theory); or again the same genetically programmed elementary structures (bioprogram theory).

From an epistemological and methodological viewpoint, the striking similarity between these theories is their exclusiveness. Their adherents, past and present, right or wrong, tend to be virulently monocausal. In the words of Claire Lefebvre (1986, 282), creolists "[try] to explain everything the same way at the same time."[4] Fidelity to a unique explanation in turn tended to preclude detailed examination of changing historical contexts in spite of Sidney Mintz's crucial demonstration at the first major international conference on Creole languages in Mona, 1968, that the study of linguistic change had to take into account "the sociohistorical background" of creolization (Mintz 1971). Available documents were not used to their full potential. Known historical facts, periodization, empirical questions of space and time, demography and social norms, took secondary positions within predeveloped schemes. Even when Creole linguistics focused on the past, even when it emphasized the process of linguistic change, it generally ignored the sociohistorical process. History was always evoked, often used, yet rarely treated in its complexities.

Since the mid 1980s, in part in response to Derek Bickerton's bioprogram hypothesis (Bickerton 1984), in part because of the influence of non-Caribbean creolists (see, for example, Romaine 1988; Sankoff 1980; Siegel 1987), linguists have become increasingly aware of the historical complexities involved in Afro-Caribbean creolization. The amount of time separating two hallmark conferences (Hymes 1971; Muysken and Smith 1986) reveals a tremendous growth in historical sophistication between the late 1960s and the mid1980s. However, such ongoing sophistication (see Baker 1994; Cérol 1992; Chaudenson 1992; Gilbert 1986; Lefebvre 1986; Rickford 1986) has yet to inform fully the study of specific linguistic changes within particular historical contexts.

The linguistic stalemate is reinforced by the lack of exchange between linguists and non-linguists and by the weaknesses of cultural theories of creolization. First, students of sociocultural history have yet to provide answers to the linguists' sophisticated questions. Moreover, in recent years, grand pronouncements by some cultural and literary critics have increased the gap between many linguists' empirically oriented inquiries and sociocultural theories of creolization. For instance, the repeated announcement that the world is now in—or moving toward—a state of hybridity or creolization (see Bernabé, Chamoiseau, and Confiant 1989; Hannerz 1987, 1992) is too sweeping to stimulate a dialogue between the cultural theorists who make such statements and historical linguists interested into knowing who actually learned what from whom and when in particular Caribbean territories (see Cérol 1992; Rickford 1986, 1987). On the contrary, such sweeping statements reinforce, perhaps inadvertently, the proclivity to treat creolization as a totality, thereby reinforcing the worst tendencies of the sociocultural theorists.

Indeed, both the tendency to infer the past from the present and the predilection for all-encompassing explanations, which together characterize Creole linguistics, reappear in sociocultural studies of creolization with some noteworthy differences. First, the technical apparatus of Creole linguistics could not be transferred to studies of creolization outside of language. Whereas linguists generally agree on micro-methodologies and definitions (for example, what noun phrases are and how to break them down), social scientists and cultural theorists do not have this fundamental agreement on a technical apparatus. Thus, second, non-linguist students of creolization find themselves in the awkward situation of having fewer agreed-upon tools to do yet a larger job. Sociocultural life is an object of study admittedly more fluid and harder to delimit than language, which it encompasses. Without a common technical apparatus, the theoretical claims made by students of sociocultural creolization are even less controllable than those of the linguists. Or, to put it differently, the distance between these claims and the organization of the facts into a coherent object of study is greater than in linguistics. Faced with the wonder of creolization, the need to explain a cultural emergence that seems to defy their implicit assumptions about "culture," social scientists used strokes as broad as those of the linguists but on a greater range of topics. This range has actually increased with time. With methodological issues further relegated to the back burner, current studies of creolization return, as part of a cycle, to the wonder of origins with the added value of the ideologies of the day.

The increased relevance of ideology is understandable. First, social scientists are increasingly aware that creolization still goes on. Even though analysts are not much closer to an agreement in defining creolization as an object of study than they were, say, in the 1950s, they have both the increased feeling of being witness to the ongoing wonder and the conviction that it matters how they explain it. Second indeed, the ongoing denigration of many African American populations continues to incite praise for the "creoleness" that they are said to typify (Bernabé et al. 1989). Third, now that globalization and hybridity have become suspiciously fashionable—some would say too fashionable (Harvey 1995; Mintz 1996; Williams 1995)—the creolization process in the Afro-Americas appears, in retrospect, as an early state of grace only now accessible to the rest of humanity (Gilroy 1993; Hannerz 1992). The cultural idealism that now so happily masks increased inequalities worldwide further fuels the ahistorical tendencies of creolization studies. Indeed, if there is a difference between the *créolité* movement of the 1990s and predecessors such as Haitian *indigénisme* of the 1930s (Trouillot 1993) and the Jamaican Creole-society school of the 1950s and 1960s (Bolland 1992), it is the increased persistence to further divorce the wonder of creolization from the very history that made it possible (Price and Price 1997).[5] As social theory becomes more discourse oriented, the distance between data and claims in debates about creolization and *créolité* increases. Historical circumstances fall further into a hazy background of ideological preferences.

The Contexts of Creolization

Historical circumstances are what I would like to emphasize here in arguing that creolization cannot be understood outside of the various contexts within which it occurred.

Many factors shaped such contexts. First among these was the regimentation of the populations involved, notably their regimentation as labor force. The nature and degree of such regimentation necessarily skewed the daily expressions of cultural creativity. In the second half of the eighteenth century, the kind of materials needed, available, and used to produce culture were quite different for the member of a canefield gang in Barbados than for an enslaved coffee grower in Dominica or in Saint-Domingue. Regimentation, including labor regimentation, crystallized such differences. Differences in labor regimes, in turn, proceeded from the crops involved and also from the number of years a particular crop had been cultivated in a territory (Berlin and Morgan 1993; Higman 1984; Trouillot 1982, 1984). Regimentation, so construed, thus centers around labor but includes all the factors that limited daily activities of the laboring populations both before and after slavery.

Second, the frequency and nature of outside contact—in and out migrations, communications, the ease or difficulty of individual movement—also helped to define the context of creolization. Clearly, creolization must have proceeded differently in contexts marked by a constant influx of enslaved Africans than in situations where such influx was negligible. Third, the frequency and nature of contact among Africans, among Europeans, and between members of these two groups also helped to shape modes of cultural appropriation and adaptation. Fourth, creolization cannot be understood without some attention to its participants as conscious subjects of history. Edouard Glissant (1995) suggests that creolization implies some awareness of heterogeneity, the impossibility to deny mixed origins. But surely, that awareness includes both an implicit sense of cultural ideals—what Mintz (1971) calls "target cultures"—and an implicit attentiveness to facts of power on the ground, which Glissant himself tends to neglect (Trouillot 1997). Cultural ideals and power relations, including actors' understandings and interpretations of the stakes and forces available to reach their self-defined goals, fundamentally shape the context of creolization.

A short example may make the point. We can assume that to practice what is now known as Haitian vodoun is to engage knowingly or not in creolization. Yet even if we assume an unchanging content to vodoun—a dubious assumption indeed—we must concede that what it meant to serve the gods changed in space and in time. Imagine first the negotiations, trials, and tactics necessary for African-born slaves just to set a ritual in colonial Saint-Domingue: how to do it away from the masters' ears; whom to include and on what grounds; which gods to evoke or invoke. Imagine, then, the relative freedom of association and the related freedom of choice in the isolated mountains of independent Haiti, away from memories of both Europe and Africa before the growth of the Catholic clergy at the end of the nineteenth century. Imagine, in turn, the fears unleashed by the U.S. occupation of 1915–34 and renewed by the repressive anti-vodoun campaigns of the 1930s and 1940s. Today, the change is monumental: The holders of state power in Haiti officially recognize vodoun as religion. Even before that recognition, vodoun had become truly transnational. Some of its canonical rituals are routinely held in Cuba's Oriente or in Brooklyn, New York. Not all its practitioners are Haitian. Some are white North Americans. Yet the poverty of the Haitian countryside has also undermined vodoun at the base, limiting its ritual possibilities among the peasantry (Murray 1977). Throughout all this, nevertheless, vodoun has figured and continues to figure as a key manifestation of Haitian worldview, an emblem of successful creolization. There is no way to follow that thread of continuities and breaks without evaluating these changing contexts.

In short, we need a framework to approach the changing contexts of creolization. Using time, space and power relations as my main markers, I suggest four such contexts for the study of creolization: 1) a frontier context; 2) a plantation context; 3) an enclave context; 4) and a modernist context.

Each of these contexts emphasizes in turn one of the factors highlighted earlier. The regimentation of populations is the defining moment of the plantation context. The frequency and quality of contact within a particular area help to distinguish the frontier context just as modes of outside contact help to distinguish the enclave context. The awareness of heterogeneity and power are inherent in the context of modernity. Since all four factors are always relevant, it follows that these contexts are heuristic devices.[6]

At any rate, the contexts described here are not meant to duplicate real-life situations, but they may help us understand such situations by focusing attention on "the specific sorts of community settings within which groups became further differentiated or intermixed" (Mintz 1971, 481). They do not delineate fixed periods: Often they overlapped in historical time within the same territory. What I hope they do best is to sketch with broad strokes the strikingly different historical dynamics of creolization as a cultural process so as to bring forward the particulars of the populations involved.

The *frontier context* acknowledges the situation, privileged by Chaudenson (1992), where conditions of relative isolation, the loose labor regimen imposed on the slaves, and the demographic weight of the European population implied a fair amount of contact between African slaves and European colonists. That situation historically prevailed before the full development of the plantation in most Caribbean societies, but the frontier context also described most territories—especially the larger or more mountainous ones—long after the rise of the plantation economy. Further, the long duration of a frontier situation in the Spanish Caribbean may help to explain the markedly different base and outcome of the creolization process there, notably the absence of Creole languages.

By *plantation context*, I have in mind situations defined primarily by plantation slavery both during and immediately after the centuries of legal enslavement. Most enslaved Africans and their immediate descendants throughout the Americas engaged creolization within a plantation context until—and at times well into—the second half of the nineteenth century.

By *enclave context*, I mean situations marked by the relative autonomy and isolation of the populations under study. Early maroon societies from St. Vincent to Suriname, the Haitian peasantry from 1804 to the 1880s, and highland villagers in the Windward Islands up to the first decades of the twentieth century creolized mainly within such enclaves.

The *modernist context* became dominant only with the decline of the plantation. I do not mean by this that modernity itself came late to the Caribbean or is a post-plantation phenomenon. On the contrary, the Caribbean was in many ways as modern as Europe by the first quarter of the seventeenth century, especially because of the plantation (Trouillot 2000). Indeed, creolization itself is a modern phenomenon if only because it implies the awareness and even the expectation of cultural differences (Glissant 1995; Mintz 1996). Further, frequency and ease of contact with the outside world marked the daily routine of many urban slaves, especially in the port cities where news of other territories circulated to an extent we have yet to appreciate (Scott 1986).

My modernist context combines elements of both modernity and modernization. It implies a different kind of technical and institutional support to creolization. It implies also a sense of global history and the awareness of progress—or backwardness—which are part of modernity, and which spread quite unevenly among Caribbean populations from early conquest until the second third of the twentieth century. The degree to which the awareness of both "target cultures" and facts of power become explicit and voiced, and the degree to which organic intellectuals harness institutional and technical support for cultural practices help define a modernist context.[7]

These four contexts bring us closer to actual situations, yet we need to clarify them further by way of a number of changing parameters: The relative proportion of populations of diverse origins, including individuals of mixed descent (Mintz 1971); the impact of prior creolization, including the spread of institutions that solidified that creolization; and the extent of social differentiation are among such parameters. Their relevance will vary with the case under study, but the point is to use these four contexts as starting points and to refine them with the relevant particulars so as to get closer to actual situations.

Thus the scheme outlined here puts on hold most theories of creolization and Creole societies for trying to do too much, too fast. In that sense, I am not proposing an alternative model. Rather, I am suggesting that we have not thought enough about what went on in specific places and times to produce a model sensitive enough to time, place, and power. The plantation context illustrates the complexities we need to address.

The Plantation as Cultural Matrix

During the long centuries of the slave trade, Africa was no more static or culturally unified than Europe was at the time. We simply do not know enough of African variations and change. Ignorance and ethnocentrism may explain the general tendency to acknowledge differences among Europeans and ignore them when referring to Africans. Additionally, whereas European residents of particular territories usually came from similar, if not the same, milieus, enslaved Africans did not necessarily end up among tribal fellows. Further, the Middle Passage had removed the African-born slaves from their roots, without the possibility open to many Europeans of maintaining regular contact with their original milieu. Thus, although they kept their memories, they could not reproduce the societies whence they came.

Only since the 1980s have we begun to acknowledge the restrictions imposed by the trade and plantation slavery on African cultural transfers, but the achievement seems even more spectacular against this limiting background. As Sidney Mintz and Richard Price (1992, 10) argue in the ground-breaking essay that launched this new awareness, given the conditions of their passage, the enslaved "were not able to transfer the human complement of their traditional institutions to the New World. Members of tribal groups of differing status, yes; but different status systems, no. Priests and priestesses, yes; but priesthoods and temples, no. Princes and princesses, yes; but courts and monarchies, no."

Limitations applied as much to the collective as to individuals. Surely no African slave came to the Caribbean carrying a drum from the motherland. But the memory of African music lingered long enough to catch up with the memory of drum-making; and Afro-Caribbeans used their new environment to create drums and music that were close to those of Africa yet distinctively Caribbean. Likewise, their dances may have been influenced by the minuets and waltzes they learned to play sometimes for their European masters, but their own Sunday performances were not likely to be minuets and waltzes (though some musicologists may rightfully argue that these were also influenced by minuets and waltzes). In short, Africans and their descendants had to create, so to speak, a new cultural world, with elements gathered from the many African areas from which they came and the pool of ideals and practices of the Europeans who dominated them.

How was such a process of selective creation and cultural struggle—in a word, creolization—possible among the enslaved? How could Africans and African Americans forge entirely new values, ideals, and patterned practices out of the remnants of Old World types, both African and European? How did they come to dominate the process of cultural formation in societies such as those of the Caribbean where they were kept by daily terrorism at the bottom of the sociopolitical ladder?

Sidney Mintz and Richard Price (1992) suggest that the West African cultural heritage is to be found mainly in unconscious, underlying "grammatical" principles: cognitive orientations, attitudes, and expectations common to the diverse communities whence most of the enslaved came. They argue that these underlying principles ordered the process of creolization by making certain choices more appealing or more significant than other possible ones.

This argument needs to be refined in light of more sustained research on the institutional impact of African ethnicity on slave practices in specific territories. In other words, the underlying principles that Mintz and Price highlight had to work through posited tensions among Africans in order to produce meaningful practices, as well as their institutional support—and we need to know how and when that happened. More important, however a modus vivendi on cultural grammar was obtained among slaves, shared principles—old and new—had to survive the European exercise of power. How did they do so? When and how were they given space and time to breathe and to breed? How did they survive and reproduce themselves enough to generate new institutions?

Answers to these questions, tentative as they may be, require that we turn to the plantation. African American slavery was plantation slavery. The plantation was the institution around which the system was built; it provided the model after which were shaped the actual units on which slaves labored. But to phrase it this way is already to suggest that the word *plantation* covers in fact different types of realities that we may want to keep separate even if for heuristic purposes: the institution itself, in the restricted sense of a type of agricultural enterprise; the socioeconomic and political system built upon it (in this particular case, plantation slavery); and the actual units of production modeled after this ideal type.

As a form of labor organization, the plantation is an agricultural enterprise, distinguished by its massive use of coerced or semi-coerced labor, producing agricultural commodities for markets situated outside of the economy within which the plantation itself operates. One of the better treatments of the type comes from sociologist Edgar T. Thompson (1975). Thompson suggests that as a unit of production, the plantation is an economic institution, an agricultural unit operating with an industrial dynamic. It is also, in his view, a settlement institution, in the sense that it arranges peoples in a new territory, and a political institution, inasmuch as it operates as a small state with an authoritarian structure. Plantation owners claim a monopoly of violence and control over the life of the people who inhabit the plantation. The plantation is, finally, a cultural institution. It tends to generate a distinguishable way of life for owners and workers alike, but it also divides them along racial and ethnic lines. It is a race-making institution (Thompson 1975, 31–38, 115–17).

Needless to say, few if any actual populations ever exactly matched the prototype. Whether inferred or planned, social models are peculiar kinds of abstraction, the dual products of the typological exercise that projects them and the historical units through which they are actualized. In other words, *the* plantation, as such, never existed historically, not even in the Americas of slavery. Rather, thousands of plantations did that tried to conform to the ideal type, but always within the limitations imposed by specific circumstances. This is an obvious enough assertion, but it implies that in almost every instance there were varying limits to economic efficiency, to the organization of settlement, to planters' political power, or to the cultural apartheid premised in the organization of labor. The very actualization of the institution, whether or not premised on the planter's pursuit of the ideal type, allowed the slaves much more room to maneuver than implied by the type itself.

Latitude came also from elsewhere and, perhaps, in more important ways. Units of production never operate alone. As units of production serving distant markets within the strict order of slavery, the plantations of the Americas felt even more the pressures of the system. Indeed, we can conceptualize an inherent tension between plantation slavery as a system and the actual units of production. This is not to suggest that the units and the system belong to the same order of things, but the fact that the system is a construct does not make it any less real than actual estates. It had its requirements, its logic, but the very fact that this logic and these requirements were not of the same *kind* than the daily exigencies masters and overseers had to face within individual units of production created an inherent tension.

Reactions to marronage provide us with a good entry point in this world of tensions and broken lines. In principle, throughout the Americas, slaves were forbidden to leave the plantations without authorization, and infractions to this code were punished. On the ground, however, planters' attitudes varied according to the particulars of the case at hand: the time of the infraction, its mode of discovery, the climate of the colony, the individual slave involved, or indeed the personality of the owner or overseer. More important, beyond these variations, planters often acknowledged a difference between desertions intended to be final and temporary absences. The French even distinguished them by name, coining the former *grand marronage* as opposed to the more benign forms of *petit marronage*. Throughout the Americas, whereas system and practice tended to overlap in cases of the first kind, planters sometimes closed their eyes to instances of petit marronage if slaves ran away to visit relatives, to take part in certain rituals, or sometimes even to make a symbolic gesture of protest.

This indulgence did not necessarily come from kindness. Its deepest roots were systemic: Planters knew that the code was not always enforceable, that not all instances of unauthorized absence could be punished without encroaching on the working routine of their particular plantation. One suspects that slaves came to the same realization and took repeated risks at manipulating this systemic fissure, often to their detriment, but as often perhaps with the hoped-for results. Communication across plantations, for instance, must have depended on such "illegal" absences as much as on the "free" time officially allotted by the planters. And as slaves repeated such manipulations—on the one hand acknowledging the system, on the other circumventing its actualization in carefully chosen instances—they solidified the *détour*, the social time and space they controlled on the edges of the plantations.

Thus, even though grand marronage stands as a privileged example of African American resistance under slavery, maroon societies (Price 1979) are better depicted by what I call the enclave context. Petit marronage, in turn, stands as a more accurate model for the kind of behavior through which most slaves established the institutional continuity of Creole patterns within the plantation context. For a majority of enslaved Africans and African Americans, prior to the mid-nineteenth century, creolization did not happen away from the plantation system, but within it.[8]

This creation was possible because slaves found a fertile ground in the interstices of the system, in the latitude provided by the inherent contradictions between that system and specific plantations. Afro-Caribbean cultural practices developed within the plantation system, but on the margins of the units through which the ideal type was actualized. They were born within *the* plantation but on the edges of *particular* plantations. The tensions between the logic of the system and the daily life of actual estates provided a context full of minute opportunities for initiatives among the enslaved. We need to look closely at the mechanisms by which slaves seized upon these contradictions and repeatedly turned latent opportunities to their advantage, further stretching the time and space that they controlled. But even before further empirical research on the so-called slave sector illuminates these mechanisms, we can assess the opportunities. I will give one more example of an opportunity seized upon by the slaves, one quite different from planters' attitudes toward petit marronage, but which ultimately makes the same point.

In many Caribbean societies, slaves were allowed by their masters to grow their own food, and at times, to sell portions of what they harvested. This was a fundamental contradiction within the plantation system. The practice of allowing slaves to cultivate their own gardens whenever they were not working on plantation crops emerged because particular planters wanted to save money, given the high cost of imported food.[9] Planters were not in the business of feeding slaves. The name of the game was profit, and it was to enhance their profits that many planters passed on to the slaves the responsibility of feeding themselves. Indeed, the extent and viability of slave provision grounds depended on a series of factors operating within the unit of production and the impact of these factors on the planter's cost-accounting. Steep and broken terrain, less fertile land not used for the production of plantation staples, and the flexibility of the work regimen, all worked to reinforce the use of provision grounds within a unit. So did, within a territory where cash was largely unavailable, the availability and acclimation of imported plants and animals.

Eventually, however, these practices, which first emerged because they provided concrete advantages to particular owners, went against the logic of the plantation system itself. Provision grounds provided both time and space that was both within the order dictated by the plantation and yet detached from it. They provided a space quite distinct from the plantation fields sown with sugarcane, coffee, and cotton—space where one learned to cherish root crops, plantains, and bananas; space to raise and roast a pig, to run after a goat, or to barbecue a chicken; space to bury the loved ones who passed away, to worship the ancestors, and to invent new gods when the old ones were forgotten.

Time used on the provision grounds was also slave-controlled time to a large extent. It was time to "create culture" knowingly or unknowingly. It was time to develop new practices of labor cooperation, reminiscent of—yet different from—African models of work. Time to talk across the fences to a passing neighbor or to cross the fences themselves and fish in the adjacent rivers. Time to mark the work tempo with old songs, to learn rhythm while working, and to enjoy both the rhythm and the work. Time to create new songs when the old ones faded away. Time to take care of the needs of the family, to meet a mate, to teach children how to climb a tree. Time indeed to develop modes of thought and codes of behavior that were to survive plantation slavery itself.[10]

Such survival, in turn, depended on the consolidation of institutions. For instance, we know that in some colonies—Saint-Domingue, for instance— slaves sold part of their product at urban markets. We can assume that the practice of producing and, especially, producing for sale involved a number of individual and economic decisions. Slaves not only had to engage in a cost-benefit analysis, as any petty producer would, but in a cost-benefit analysis that took into account their ideals (what and when to cultivate; how to profit; what to buy with the profit, for whom, and why). Such a culturally informed cost-benefit analysis, in turn, necessarily implied the distribution and consolidation of roles within the household, the distribution and consolidation of statuses across households. In short, practices of that kind—and there were many more we need to think about—also influenced the institutions that would survive slavery.

How they did so remains open to serious concrete investigation. Such investigation can only benefit from analyses that try to integrate the four contexts suggested here. As enclaves and plantations slowly gave way to populations that experienced creolization mainly in a modernist context, how did cultural content and, especially, patterns of accommodation, resistance, and struggle change? For instance, how did the transformation of target cultures accommodate the perception of past practices? We can already assume that here again, historical particulars played their role. Contact between different populations within and across political boundaries, an influx of newcomers, the impact of prior creolization, political control, and social differentiation enter here again. But my main point is exactly that we need to rehistoricize creolization.

Haiti provides a telling argument for the historicization I propose. In the eyes of students of language and culture, it stands as the prototype of a Creole country, with more than seven million unilingual speakers of Haitian Creole. Yet when Haiti became independent in 1804, the vast majority of its population were African-born slaves for whom Creole was *not* a native language.[11] Historical linguists and anthropologists have passed over this well-known yet highly inconvenient fact exactly because it does not fit squarely theories that treat creolization as an ahistorical totality.[12]

Creolization is a process rather than a totality. To enable us to seize it in its movement, I have suggested the use of four contexts as heuristic devices, but keeping in mind that these contexts often overlapped in particular places and times. My longer exploration of the plantation context is meant as an illustration of the complexities we need to acknowledge at the very beginning. Ideally, the analysis would need to integrate the overlap of the four contexts in historically specific cases. The point remains that we need to look at creolization as a process, constantly influenced not only by prior history but also by the numerous factors that characterize(d) the times, the territories, and the peoples to which it bears witness.

Plantation Coda

The provision grounds of slavery, the reluctant tolerance toward petit marronage, and the unequal ranking and treatment of slaves constitute only conspicuous examples of tension among many to be found in the plantation context. The general lesson remains the same. Cultural practices markedly African American emerged at least in part because of the slaves' ability to use the contradictions inherent in the fundamentals of the system and the daily workings of specific plantations. Time and space matter enormously here—that is, social time and social space seized within the system and turned against it.

This ability to stretch margins and circumvent borderlines remains the most amazing aspect of African American cultural practices. It encapsulates their inherent resistance. African American cultures are cultures of combat in the strongest possible sense: They were born resisting. Otherwise, they would not have existed at all, for they were not meant to exist. But the resistance they encapsulate is not best seized by the epics that typify cultural nationalist treatments of creolization. The heroism of the creolization process is first and foremost the heroism of anonymous men, women, and—too often forgotten—children going about the business of daily life. And for more than three centuries, such daily life was conditioned primarily by the plantation.

African American cultural practices emerged on the edges of the plantations, blurring the logic of an imposed order and its daily manifestations of dominance. Filtering in the interstices of the system, they conquered each inch of cultural territory they now occupy. In that sense, the plantation was the primary cultural matrix for African American populations, but it was so against the expectations of the masters. It was an imposed context—a rigid one—an institution forced on the slaves, but one within which they managed their most formidable accomplishment: that of creating what has indeed become a New World.

Notes

This chapter began as a contribution to the colloquium "The Plantation System in the Americas," April 1989 Louisiana State University, Baton Rouge, 27–29. A much revised version appeared in *Plantation Society in the Americas* (Trouillot 1998). I thank Edouard Glissant who invited me to Baton Rouge, the participants who commented on the original paper, the National Science Foundation for supporting my fellowship at the Center for Advanced Study in the Behavioral Sciences (Stanford University) where the first revisions occurred, Marie Espelencia Baptiste and Niloofar Haeri who shared their views on creolization, A. James Arnold, and the anonymous reviewer for *Plantation Society* for their comments. Brian Axel, Michel DeGraff, Richard Price, and an additional anonymous review helped make this version a better one.

1   Even if we define *culture* in the restricted sense of artistic and intellectual production ultimately sanctioned by power (what some anthropologists call "high culture"), in relation to their size, the Caribbean islands have given birth to an impressive array of individuals who left their intellectual mark on the international scene. But the real achievement is that of the anonymous men and women who have woven, along

the centuries and in spite of slavery and other forms of domination, the cultural patterns on which rest the highly individualized performances of the intellectuals.

2 The extent of linguistic creolization varied. In some cases, creolization led to the rise of entirely new languages spoken by the entire population, like Haitian Creole, now the language of Haiti, or Lesser Antillean (also a French-based Creole and common to Martinique, Guadeloupe, and to a lesser extent, Dominica and St. Lucia). Saran emerged in Suriname, Papiamento, in Curacao. In many of the former British territories, we witness a different phenomenon. The linguistic spectrum presents itself more like a continuum with the more Creolized forms at one end and the forms closer to the European standard at the other.

3 Of course, sociohistorical studies of the Caribbean have dealt with creolization since colonial times (Lewis 1983), but the delineation of creolization and of its products as a specific object of scholarly research and the subsequent labeling of creolists as specialists of the field so defined first happened in linguistics. Ironically, Lefebvre's own relexification model does not fully escape the monocausal tradition or the selective linkages between facts and theory (see Calvet 1997, 232).

4 The créolité movement, which sprang from Martinique in the late 1980s, succeeded in renewing attention to the creolization process and in introducing Parisian literati to the spectacular literary production of the French Caribbean. Yet it is best seen as a sociopolitical reaction to the successful francization of Martinique since the island became an overseas department of France (with Guadeloupe and French Guiana), rather than a systematic reflection on the creolization process or even a literary movement per se. (See Arnold 1994; Price 2001; Price and Price 1997; and Watts 1998.)

5 In a similar vein, Robert Chaudenson (1992) suggests that creolists distinguish between two historical phases: a "habitation society" made of small units and demographically dominated by Europeans, and a "plantation society" proper that usually follows this first phase. Baker 1994 also proposes a three-event chronology as a modification of Chaudenson. These models are macro-sociological, even though they constitute major improvements on earlier schemes that paid less attention to history. Yet there is no reason to assume that a single phase or event characterized the contact situation or the entire character of any Creole society at any single moment in real time.

6 Late twentieth-century developments in linguistic ideology and speech practice in Haiti and the geographical and social expansion of both reggae music and Rastafarianism within and beyond Jamaica are two cases that may illustrate the point even briefly. The increased technical and institutional support for Haitian as a language—from its use in print and audiovisual media in Haiti and abroad to its official recognition as one of the two national languages—is part of a process of a modernization. (This modernization is now obvious, but keep in mind that Napoleon's army issued proclamations in Creole to the revolutionary slaves.) These recent technical and institutional changes intertwine with modernity, via the recognition of difference and the recognition of an identity that claims to be specifically Haitian. Similarly, reggae music and, by extension, Rastafarianism have benefited from the profound changes in both technology and communication that have affected the music indus-

try worldwide. But the opportunity that these changes offered had to be seized by artists, cultural nationalists, and local entrepreneurs quite aware of Jamaican modernity. In Jamaica as in Haiti, organic intellectuals have integrated the knowledge that the world is now their context, if not always their interlocutor.

7   Even the Haitian Revolution, which stands as the most significant act of resistance against slavery, does not actually fit the grand maronnage model. To start with, there is no evidence of a continuous maroon community in the northern part of Saint-Domingue where the revolution started. Rather, in part because the local topography prevented the establishment of permanent camps where fugitives could regroup, the slaves from that region could not escape the contradictions of the system through organized forms of grand maronnage (Trouillot 1977, 76–77). Indeed, our knowledge so far suggests that the original rebellion primarily involved slaves located on the plantations that were burned, even though some historians infer maroon participation. Further, there are indications that slave drivers and privileged slaves established the inter-plantation network of communication without which the widespread revolt that destroyed the northern plains and launched the revolution would have been impossible.

8   For more detailed treatments of the provision grounds in the Caribbean, see Mintz (1978, 1984); and Trouillot (1988, 69–75).

9   It is not at all surprising that when slavery ended, Caribbean slaves did the most to maintain access to their provision grounds. And almost everywhere after the end of slavery, planters unanimously condemned the former slaves' attachment to these provision grounds.

10 Population estimates in the Caribbean are not fully reliable. Yet most sources suggest that prevolutionary Haiti counted nearly six hundred thousand people at the start of the slave uprising of 1791. By 1804, the number of whites was down to five thousand; the number of blacks and mulattoes who were free before the revolution was down to twenty thousand and the number of slaves down to about three hundred seventy-five thousand, most of whom were born in Africa.

11 Contributing to this silencing is the additional inconvenience that a major fault line within the revolutionary forces was the opposition between the leadership, composed mainly of black Creoles, and the middle and lower ranks of the revolutionary army, composed mainly of Africans (Trouillot 1995).

12 For instance, although a society such as eighteenth-century Saint-Domingue between 1763 and 1789 was primarily a plantation society, one would need to examine the relative impact of port cities (where creolization had a strong modernist component); the impact of Le Maniel's maroon enclave (where creolization was obtained among Africans relatively isolated from the main population); and the impact of coffee areas (where a frontier context prevailed) (Debbasch 1979; Trouillot 1980). Similarly, while most rural areas in port-independent Haiti—the era during which both Haitian Creole and vodoun solidified—functioned as enclaves without European presence or African input, one cannot ignore the impact of port cities and that of prior creolization. In short, the research should eventually look at specific regions within a territory with an eye on continuities and ruptures in the historical process.

References

Alleyne, Mervyn C. 1980. *Comparative Afro-American.* Ann Arbor, Mich.: Karoma.

Arends, Jacques, ed. 1995. *The Early Stages of Creolisation.* Amsterdam: John Benjamins.

Arnold, A. James. 1994. "The Erotics of Colonialism in Contemporary French West Indian Literary Culture." *New West Indian Guide* 68, no. 1/2: 5–22.

Baker, Philip. 1994. "Creativity in Creole Genesis." In *Creolization and Language Change,* edited by Dany Adone and Ingo Plag. Tübingen, Sweden: Niemeyer.

Berlin, Ira, and Philip D. Morgan, eds. 1993. *Cultivation and Culture: Labor and the Shaping of Slave Life in the Americas.* Charlottesville: University Press of Virginia.

Bernabé, Jean, Patrick Chamoiseau, and Raphaël Confiant. 1989. *Éloge de la Créolité.* Paris: Gallimard.

Bickerton, Derek. 1984. "The Language Bioprogram Hypothesis." *Behavioral and Brain Sciences* 7: 173–221.

Bolland, Nigel. 1992. "Creolisation and Creole Societies." In *Intellectuals in the Twentieth-Century Caribbean,* edited by Alistair Hennessy. Basingstoke: MacMillan Caribbean.

Calvet, Louis-Jean. 1997. "Les faits et la théorie." In *Contacts de langues, contacts de culture, créolisation,* edited by Marie-Christine Hazaël-Massieuz and Didier de Robillard. Paris: L'Harmattan.

Cérol, Marie-Josée. 1992. "What History Tells Us about the Development of Creole in Guadeloupe." *New West Indian Guide* 66, no. 1/2: 61–76.

Chaudenson, Robert. 1992. *Des îles, des hommes, des langues. Essai sur la créolisation linguistique et culturelle.* Paris: L'Harmattan.

Chaudenson, Robert. 1993. "Research, Politics, and Ideology: The Case of the Comité International des Etudes Créoles." *International Journal of the Sociology of Language* 102: 15–25.

Debbasch, Yvan. 1979. "Le Maniel: Further Notes." In *Maroon Societies,* edited by R. Price.

Gilbert, Glenn. 1986. "The Language Bioprogram Hypothesis: Déjà Vu?" In *Substrata versus Universals in Creole Genesis: Papers from the Amsterdam Creole Workshop, April 1985.* Amsterdam/Philadelphia: John Benjamins.

Gilroy, Paul. 1993. *The Black Atlantic: Modernity and Double Consciousness.* Cambridge: Harvard University Press.

Glissant, Edouard. 1995. *Introduction á une poétique du Divers.* Montreal: Presses de l'Université de Montréal.

Hannerz, Ulf. 1987. "The World in Creolization." *Africa* 57: 546–59.

—. 1992. "The Global Ecumene as a Network of Networks." In *Conceptualizing Society,* edited by Adam Kuper. London: Routledge.

Harvey, David. 1995. "Globalization in Question." *Rethinking Marxism* 8, no. 4: 1–17.

Higman, B. W. 1984. *Slave Populations of the British Caribbean, 1807–1834.* Baltimore, Md.: Johns Hopkins University Press.

Hymes, Dell, ed. 1971. *Pidginization and Creolization of Languages.* Cambridge: Cambridge University Press.

Le Brun, Annie. 1996. *Statue cou coupé.* Paris: Jean-Michel Place.

Lefebvre, Claire. 1986. "Relexification in Creole Genesis Revisited: The Case of Haitian

Creole." In *Substrata versus Universals in Creole Genesis: Papers from the Amsterdam Creole Workshop, April 1985*. Amsterdam/Philadelphia: John Benjamins.

Lewis, Gordon. 1983. *Main Currents in Caribbean Thought*. Baltimore, Md.: Johns Hopkins University Press.

Magens, Joachim M. 1770. *Grammatica over det Creolske sprog, som bruges paa de trende danske eilande, St. Croix, St. Thomas og St. Jans I America. Sammenskrevet og opsat af en paa St. Thomas indföd mand*. Kopenhagen: Trykt udi det Kongelige Wayenshusets Bogtrykkerie, af Gerhard Giese Salikath.

Mintz, Sidney W. 1971. "The Socio-Historical Background to Pidginization and Creolization." In *Pidginization and Creolization of Languages*, edited by Dell Hymes. Cambridge: Cambridge University Press.

Mintz, Sidney W. 1978. "Was the Plantation Slave a Proletarian?" *Review* 2, no. 1: 81–98.

Mintz, Sidney W. 1996. "Enduring Substances, Trying Theories: The Caribbean Region as Oikoumenê." *Journal of the Royal Anthropological Institute* 2, no. 2: 289–311.

Mintz, Sidney W., and Richard Price. 1992. *An Anthropological Approach to the Afro-American Past. The Birth of an African-American Culture: An Anthropological Perspective*. Boston: Beacon Press.

Murray, Gerald F. "The Evolution of Haitian Peasant Land Tenure: A Case Study in Agrarian Adaptation to Population Growth." Ph.D. diss. Columbia University.

Muysken, Pieter, and Norval Smith. 1986. *Substrata versus Universals in Creole Genesis: Papers from the Amsterdam Creole Workshop, April 1985*. Amsterdam/Philadelphia: John Benjamins.

Price, Richard, ed. 1979. *Maroon Societies: Rebel Slave Communities in the Americas*. Baltimore, Md.: Johns Hopkins University Press.

—. 2002. "On the Miracle of Creolization." In *Afro-Atlantic Dialogues: Anthropology in the Diaspora*, edited by Kevin A. Yelvington. Santa Fe, N.M.: School of American Research Press.

Price, Richard, and Sally Price. 1997. "Shadowboxing in the Mangrove." *Cultural Anthropology* 12, no. 1: 3–36.

Rickford, John R. 1986. "Short Note." *Journal of Pidgin and Creole Languages* 1, no. 1: 159–63.

Rickford, John R. 1987. *Dimensions of a Creole Continuum: History, Texts, and Linguistic Analysis of Guyanese Creole*. Palo Alto, Calif.: Stanford University Press.

Romaine, Suzanne. 1988. *Pidgin and Creole Languages*. London: Longman.

Sankoff, Gillian. 1980. *The Social Life of Language*. Philadelphia: University of Pennsylvania Press.

Scott, Julius Sherrard, III. 1986. "A Common Wind: Currents of Afro-American Communication in the Era of the Haitian Revolution." Ph.D. diss. Duke University.

Siegel, Jeff. 1987. *Language Contact in a Plantation Environment. A Sociolinguistic History of Fiji*. London: Cambridge University Press.

Singler, John V. 1986. "Short Note." *Journal of Pidgin and Creole Languages* 1, no. 1: 141–45.

Thompson, Edgar T. 1975. *Plantation Societies, Race Relations, and the South: The Regimentation of Populations*. Durham, N.C.: Duke University Press.

Trouillot, Michel-Rolph. 1977. *Ti difé boulé sou istoua Ayiti.* New York: Koléksion Lakansièl.

—. 1982. "Motion in the System: Coffee, Color, and Slavery in Eighteenth-Century Saint-Domingue." *Review* 5, no. 3: 331–88.

—. 1984. "Labour and Emancipation in Dominica: Contribution to a Debate." *Caribbean Quarterly* 30, no. 3/4: 73–84.

—. 1988. *Peasants and Capital: Dominica in the World Economy.* Baltimore, Md.: Johns Hopkins University Press.

—. 1993. "Jeux de mots, jeux de classe: Les mouvances de l'Indigénisme." *Conjonction* 197 (Jan.–Mars): 29–44.

—. 1995. *Silencing the Past: Power and the Production of History.* Boston: Beacon Press.

—. 1997. Review of *Introduction á une poétique du divers,* by Edouard Glissant. *New West Indian Guide/Nieuwe West Indische Gids* 71, no. 1/2: 109–12.

—. 1998. "Culture on the Edges: Creolization in the Plantation Context." Special issue of *Plantation Society in the Americas,* "Who/What Is Creole?" 5, no. 1: 8–28.

—. 2000. "Alter-Native Modernities: Caribbean Lessons from the Savage Slot." Paper presented at the American Anthropological Association Meeting, San Francisco, Calif. (November).

Watts, Julia H. 1998. "An Interview with Raphaël Confiant." Special issue of *Plantation Society in the Americas,* "Who/What Is Creole?" 5, no. 1: 41–59.

Williams, Brackette F. 1995. Review of *The Black Atlantic,* by Paul Gilroy. *Social Identities* 1, no. 1: 175–92.

Race, Gender, and Historical Narrative in the Reconstruction of a Nation: Remembering and Forgetting the American Civil War

Bernard S. Cohn and Teri Silvio

Robert E. Lee's surrender at Appamatox did not end the American Civil War. This has been recognized for over a century both by those who ostensibly lost the war, American Southerners, and by those who ostensibly won, African Americans in particular. In the 1990s, not only are the cultural and economic issues over which the war was fought—for instance, the idea of a separate Southern culture, the relative powers of the nation and the states, the nature of racial difference, the meanings of slavery and emancipation—still very much alive in the U.S. popular imagination, but the ways in which that war was memorialized and historicized have themselves become the focus of legal, artistic, and academic debate. There have been court cases over the public display of the Confederate flag and other Confederate symbols. A decision in June 1995 by the city council of Richmond, Virginia, to erect a statue of African American tennis champion and civil rights activist Arthur Ashe on Monument Avenue beside equestrian statues of the Confederate army generals provoked a long and heated debate. And Ken Burns's documentary *The Civil War* which created a pastiche both of Civil War era artifacts—photographs, paintings, letters, and diaries—and a variety of historical analyses—"Great Man" history, popular social history, economic history, military history—was the most watched program in PBS history.

Since Benedict Anderson's *Imagined Communities*, much work on nationalism has focused on the print media, and how it creates, for readers, a sense of the nation as Anderson defines it, "an imagined political community . . . both inherently limited and sovereign" (1991, 15). The Confederate States of America (CSA) in both its creation and its dissolution challenged several of the characteristics which Anderson and others have seen as integral to modern nationhood. As a state founded on a slavery economy, the CSA imagined a community that was metaphorically fraternal and yet not—even theoretically—horizontal.

After the war, a sense of cultural, political, and economic separateness re-mained, despite the fact that the CSA was no longer co-extensive with a sov-ereign state, and no such sovereignty could be imagined. Charles Reagan Wilson writes that "the dream of a separate Southern identity did not die in 1865. A Southern political nation was not to be, and the people of Dixie came to accept that; but the dream of a cohesive Southern people with a separate cultural identity replaced the original longing. The cultural dream replaced the political dream" (1980, 1).

The means by which both North and South memorialized their dead heroes after the war challenged the sort of coherent sense of imagined commu-nity that we associate with the nation-state. Or, more accurately, most forms of memorial, including building monuments, celebrating Memorial Day, and col-lecting relics, had widely differing intentions and effects, both for different groups of people and over time. While some types of memorial created the sense of a community of anonymous but linked individuals traveling through "empty homogenous time" which Anderson sees as the hallmark of modern national-ism, others were ritual events or public, physical experiences designed to create a "collective effervescence" associated more with the "premodern" community. Monuments, battlegrounds, graves, photographs, medals, even pieces of rope—the survivors of the Civil War used all of these in attempts to fix the meaning of the war. This essay explores some of the ironies of the great hopes invested in such objects and sites, the paradoxes in the creation of collective memory and its decay. Monuments, museums, and mementos intended to keep the memories of war forever alive and forever sacred have been appropriated for political purposes far different from those envisioned by their creators. Or they have become taken-for-granted pieces of local scenery, their original purposes forgotten.

Neither of us are specialists in American history, and this essay is not intended to be a comprehensive study. In it, a few of the modes by which the Civil War was memorialized by both the victors and the vanquished are traced, focusing on activities that are public, communal, and physical: the building and dedication of monuments, burial practices, the collection of souvenirs, and the preservation of battle grounds, tracing both their genealogy in the post-Revolutionary War era and their fates in the twentieth century. These modes were frequently woven together in the actual practices of memorialization in both the North and South, and their replication provided a link between state and popular practices.

Memories of nationally significant events tend to be translated into a physical repertoire of remembrance at those points in time we will call "the edge of memory," when the generations who carry the living memory of great events (such as wars) begin to pass away. Many of the modes of enshrining national memory significant in the process of recreating the nation after the Civil War and that are still significant to American national identity today have their roots in the memorial practices developed after the Revolutionary War and the establishment of the American state. We will begin our story in 1825, fifty years after the start of the War for Independence, when the need to pass on the memory of the nation's founding events became an urgent concern of both the state and the public.

Lafayette and Bunker Hill

The first war memorial built in the United States was a large obelisk erected at Bunker Hill, outside of Boston, Massachusetts. This had been the site of a successful battle waged by the American continental army against the British forces in June 1775. The monument was erected to mark the fiftieth anniversary of the battle. The dedication of the monument was highly significant, as General Lafayette, who had fought in the Continental Army and was looked upon as the figurative "younger son" of George Washington, was in attendance. The American congress had, in anticipation of the fiftieth anniversary of the battle, invited Lafayette to return from France as the "Guest of the Nation." In 1824–1825, Lafayette was taken on a grand tour of all of what was then the United States, as well as territories which were not yet part of the country. The occasion of Lafayette's tour through large and small towns throughout America provided an opportunity to celebrate what was seen as the great expansion of the United States, its booming economy and growing population. The tour was the occasion for a remarkable outpouring of civic feeling. At every town, Lafayette was greeted with banquets, balls, and parades, and was presented with a variety of mementos.

Central to these festivities was an effort to maintain the memory of the American Revolution, and above all, the cult of George Washington. The aging generation which had fought the war saw the maintenance of its memory as central to the maintenance of the well-being of the union, in terms of a set of constituent civil institutions. The enshrinement of the memories of Washington and the American victory was framed in terms of the passing of memory from an older generation to the next. In this sense, Lafayette functioned as a living monument, bringing together the purpose of a monument with an actual set of memorial practices. Lafayette's visit was supposed to pass on sacred memories to succeeding generations through a mode framed in terms of kinship and genealogy: The repeated message to the younger generation who participated in the festivities was, "You have seen Lafayette, the 'younger son' of Washington, and you will tell your children that you saw him." The presence of Lafayette at the dedication ceremony added a direct link to the sacredness of the egalitarian principles of the nation via the personal connection with both Washington and the French Revolution.

It is significant that the Bunker Hill monument took the form of an obelisk, since the use of the obelisk to mark an historic event, to create an aura of immortality, can be traced back to the Roman Empire. The Romans were the first to appropriate Egyptian obelisks by relocating them to Rome. For Europeans, obelisks came to signify the transcendence of the present, to guarantee the maintenance of history. The Bunker Hill obelisk also provided a link to George Washington and his fellow revolutionaries as a reminder of the role of Freemasonry in the revolution.

In his speech to dedicate the Bunker Hill monument, Daniel Webster took the occasion to remember the events being celebrated and to extol the valor of those who fought and died at Bunker Hill. He also sought to imbue the site itself with sacredness, thus creating an obligation upon future generations to remember the sacrifice of the revolutionary heroes. The monument thus became the permanent guarantor of the sacredness of shared sacrifice and spilled blood.

Lafayette's tour engendered new popular practices of remembrance, as well as the more official practices created by state and civic institutions. The collection and production of memorabilia gave the idea of passing memory from one generation to the next a physical form, creating a repertoire of remembrance in a pre-photographic, pre-mass media age. These souvenirs took two forms, relics—objects used by Washington or Lafayette, locks of their hair, and so on— and souvenirs made for the occasion, from oil portraits to commemorative chairs, gloves, and toby jugs.

Benson Lossing

Thirty years after Lafayette's tour, when the passing of living memory of the revolution was imminent, Benson Lossing, a writer and journalist, set out to revisit the major scenes of the battles of the American Revolution. His method was to travel to the actual sites of major events and collect objects, such as artifacts used by important generals, as well as reminiscences of those who had taken part in the revolution. He eventually traveled through all thirteen original states, as well as parts of Canada, and produced a massive two-volume work, *The Pictorial Field-Book of the Revolution, or Illustrations, by Pen and Pencil, of the History, Biography, Scenery, Relics, and Traditions of the War for Inde-pendence.* Aware that he was working at the edge of memory, Lossing expressed his concern about the rapid disappearance of the physical traces of the war, particularly in the landscape itself. He graphically expressed his view:

> Half-hidden mounds of old redoubts; the ruined walls of some stronger fortification; dilapidated buildings, neglected and decaying, wherein pa-triots met for shelter or in council; and living men, who had borne the musket and knapsack day after day in that conflict, occasionally passed under the eye of my casual apprehension. For years a strong desire was felt to embalm those precious things of our cherished household, that they might be preserved for the admiration and reverence of remote posterity. . . . I knew that the invisible fingers of decay, the plow of agriculture, and the behests of Mammon, unrestrained in their operations by the prevailing spirit of our people, would soon sweep away every tangible vestige of the Revolution, and that it was time the limner was abroad. (Lossing, viii)

Lossing's *Field-Book* is crucial to understanding the development of the connections between narrative, landscape, and memory in the maintenance of a historical sense of the nation after the Civil War. Lossing's narrative can be seen as setting out a form of sacred topography that becomes enshrined in the form of a metonymic repertoire. For Lossing, preservation was far more important than monument building. His reaction to the sight of the Bunker Hill monument was one of extreme disappointment. The monument was grand, he admitted, but all traces of the ditches and mounds dug out by the Continental army, all "vestiges of the handiwork of those in whose honor and to whose memory this obelisk was raised," had been destroyed (Lossing, 558). The combination of Lossing's positivist assumptions about the possibility of identifying and pre-serving objects and terrains "as they really were" with his narrative structured around movement across a topography has carried forward into the practices of reconstructing national memory up to the present.

Lossing's work is particularly interesting in that he seeks to create a coherent and systematic narrative of the events for the reader. Lossing faced the problem that a strictly chronological narrative was impossible, given that the events of the Revolutionary War had taken place simultaneously in various parts of the American colonies. Lossing's solution was to create a narrative around his travels across the terrain of the war. Rather than providing a neatly bounded narrative, he created a guide to the sites he defined as being particu-larly significant. Lossing thus became a forerunner in providing a set of histo-riographic and cultural practices which Americans now take for granted. In

Lossing's book, we can see the predecessors of the ubiquitous historical markers found along American highways, the movement to preserve battlefields "as they were," the popular culture practice of collecting memorabilia, and the obsession of Civil War buffs with details, from the precise movements of troops during specific battles to the exact number of buttons on the left side of Stonewall Jackson's jacket.

Separate Memories

In the decades immediately following the Civil War, the North treated the South as a defeated enemy, placing civil restrictions on the citizens of the former Confederacy as well as leaving in place an army of occupation. The economy of the Southern states, which had been an agrarian one based on slave labor, was in ruins, not only from the usual ravages of war, but also to the complete restructuring of the economy necessitated by the emancipation of the slaves during the war. For the North, on the other hand, the war had been a spur to industrialization and the development of railroads.

Immediately after the war, first in the North and then increasingly in the former Confederacy, there was an extraordinary explosion of monument building. In literally every town and city in the United States, monuments were built to honor those who had died in the war. In the North, these monuments were meant to glory the sacrifice and prowess of victors. For the former Confederate states, the effort was to create a perpetual monument to the valor of the Southern soldiers and to affirm the righteousness of what became sentimentalized as the "Lost Cause." This battle of representations continued up until the turn of the twentieth century, when reconciliation became one of the central goals of memorialization of the war. The weapons in this battle of representations ranged from objects as small and mundane as buttons and pieces of rope to the two huge monuments carved in the sides of mountains by the artist Borglum, one a tribute to the heroes of the nation, including Lincoln, on Mount Rushmore, and its counterpart, an enormous frieze of Confederate generals on horseback carved into the face of Stone Mountain in Georgia.

The iconography of remembrance in the North burgeoned even as the war was still going on. Monuments were erected in almost every town, either in a major cemetery or in the town square. In the Southern states, economic conditions, as well as the presence of an occupying army, limited the range and elaborateness of sites of remembrance for Confederate soldiers. The first and most widely utilized image for Union war memorials was that of a soldier, usually standing at parade rest. Both Northern and Southern memorial associations often brought mass-produced statues from the same factories, and these statues became standard features of the American landscape. Both the Union and Confederate armies were made up of separately recruited units based on government entities of varying size, from counties to states. The overall result of the proliferation of soldiers' monuments was to create an iconography of artifacts with multiple referents—the same image could represent the soldiers of a given town or city, the state, or the nation itself.

Bones and Bronze: Memorializing the Little Dead

One central difference between the North and South, up until the beginning of the twentieth century, lay in the burial of dead soldiers and the significance which could be ascribed to cemeteries. The Civil War was the first time in U.S. history when the bones of the war dead took on public significance, and their placement became a matter of deep concern to the state. The profound influence of this state obsession with bones can still be seen in American foreign policy toward Vietnam and Korea.

The aftermath of the Battle of Gettysburg, which took place on 1–3 July 1863, and was in retrospect seen as the crucial battle of the Civil War in the eastern theater, represented a turning point in the relationship between the bodies of the war dead and the nation. Previous to the Battle of Gettysburg, little attention had been paid to the recovery and identification of the bodies of those who were killed. The dead were usually buried close to where they had fallen, and identification of the dead and notification of their families was an individual matter. The soldiers had to depend on their fellow combatants to notify their kin if they were killed or wounded. Before going into battle, soldiers usually tried to carry identifying objects or letters on their person so that if they were killed, people would know who to notify and where to send the body. The recovery and burial of bodies was haphazard and dependent upon the battlefield's proximity to a town with an undertaker. Local undertakers would, for a price, either bury bodies or embalm and encoffin them and ship them back to their families.

The Battle of Gettysburg lasted three days, and when the Confederate troops retreated, the bodies of hundreds of dead soldiers, both Union and Confederate, lay scattered over the area. Immediately after the battle, little effort was made to bury the dead. Only in subsequent weeks, when the health hazards became truly horrific, was a systematic effort made to identify and to bury the Union dead. The Confederate dead, even if they could be identified, were buried in unidentified mass graves. By the end of July, it was realized that there would have to be a systematic effort made to identify and bury individual Union soldiers. Although the Union Army was seen as an entity, each state recruited its own militias. The state of Pennsylvania took the lead in developing a systematic effort to identify and bury the Union dead and organized the other Union states to establish a Soldiers' National Cemetery at Gettysburg. This was the first effort by the state in the American Civil War to officially memorialize those who had died. The Pennsylvania legislature decided that a monument should be erected to the memory of the Federal troops who had fought at Gettysburg. Edward Everett, a famous orator, was invited to give an address over the bodies of the fallen, and President Lincoln was invited to dedicate the cemetery in autumn of 1863. The brief "Gettysburg Address" he gave on this occasion continues to be the most famous oratorical piece in American history. Over the next several years, the landscape of the fields on which the battle had taken place around the town of Gettysburg was transformed into a forest of marble, as each state militia erected monuments to its fallen.

Gettysburg was not the only national cemetery established during the war, and after the war, it was superseded by the National Cemetery at Arlington, Virginia. The way in which bones functioned as a conduit between religious and civic notions of the sacred is evident in the story of the origins of Arlington cemetery. One of the main theaters early in the war was the area in and around Washington, D.C. itself, and a considerable network of military fortifications had developed around the capital city, including hospitals. Arlington Cemetery had its origins early in the war, when it became necessary to establish burial grounds for the interment of soldiers who died in these hospitals of wounds, disease, and infection. The site was selected by Montgomery Meigs, the Quartermaster General of the Union Army. Meigs was born and brought up in Georgia, but he opted to stay in the Union Army when the Civil War broke out. He was particularly bitter about the men who had chosen to fight for the Confederacy, whom he perceived as traitors. When the need for a Union army cemetery arose, Meigs selected a portion of the estate of Arlington House, just across the Potomac River from the capitol, which had been the estate of Robert E. Lee's wife and Lee's home up until the start of the war. Over the course of the war, large numbers of Union soldiers were buried in common graves in what had been Lee's wife's rose garden. This was a purposeful decision. Meigs consciously sought to desecrate the property of Lee and his family, at the same time ensuring that the site would be forever Union land by sanctifying it with the bones of Union soldiers. When Arlington was made into a national cemetery, the site came to embody the victory of the Union. It gradually became a central part of the creation of Washington, D.C. as a sacred site for the nation. Arlington remains a site of extraordinary national significance, the hallowed ground where those who are seen as great figures within the national narrative—particularly those who died in defense of the United States—are buried.

Arlington's status as an American Valhalla has been maintained through exclusivity. Despite the fact that the bodies of Confederate soldiers were interred on the grounds, for several years after the war, the families of these soldiers were not allowed to decorate Confederate graves and were occasionally denied entry to the cemetery at all. Today, the U.S. government still controls who may be buried in Arlington, and thus, who may be considered an appropriate hero of the nation.

The work of memorialization of the war dead as national heroes was done by state legislators and later the federal government. At the local level of the town, this office was performed largely by women. In the former Confederacy, then, where the CSA no longer was a state, women played a particularly important role in the creation of a sacred mnemonic landscape. The connection between women and the sacredness of the Lost Cause is particularly evident in the efforts to create a counter-Valhalla for the South at Hollywood Cemetery in Richmond. In Richmond, the site of the most important cemeteries and monuments dedicated to the Confederate armies, nearly all of the organizing of memorial activities was done by committees of women. It was, in fact, the women of the Hollywood Memorial Association who first instituted Memorial Day, choosing 31 May 1866, "the fifth anniversary of the day Richmonders first heard the cannon fire of the Civil War" (Mitchell, 65), for a massive clean-up and decoration of the Confederate graves. Nearly all of Richmond participated. Such celebrations occurred throughout the South and maintained much of the form and function of Lafayette's visit, bringing together all of the generations of a city or town, with special emphasis placed on passing on memory to the children.

One of the first monuments to the Confederate dead was also erected at Hollywood Cemetery by the women's committee in 1868. This monument took the form of an Egyptian pyramid and was built of granite from the James River. Both the laying of the cornerstone and the placing of the capstone provided occasions for festive public rituals.

In this local–level process of memorialization, mementos played a part, as they had with the memorialization of the Revolutionary War. Among the items for sale at the three-day fund-raising bazaar held by the ladies of the Hollywood Memorial Association were "letters written by various Confederate generals, inkstands made from the bones of horses killed in battle during the war, and porcelain likenesses of Robert E. Lee" (Mitchell, 72). Similar articles, including photos of the great Confederate generals, were also placed inside the cornerstone of the monument itself.

Anniversary celebrations became one of the major modes of remembering the national narrative and impressing it into the minds of the young. Memorial Day celebrations were established in both North and South almost immediately after the end of the war. These anniversary celebrations were primarily directed toward children, and children's participation, not just observation, became a standard feature of Memorial Day activities. In this pre-radio, pre-television age, memorialization played a large part in such ceremonies. One practice that lasted up until the twentieth century was the annual recitation by school children of the Gettysburg Address and a variety of patriotic poems. Memorial Day celebrations became an increasingly important integrative ritual, as it provided a sort of rolling history, picking up each new war and wrapping it into a sort of snowball of heroism.

Lincoln and Lee: Cults of the Big Dead

The battle of representations between North and South was also carried out through the cults of dead leaders, particularly Abraham Lincoln in the North and Robert E. Lee in the South.

The death of Abraham Lincoln was a crucial event in America's national narrative. Lincoln died in Washington, D.C., and his family decided that he should be buried in Springfield, Illinois. The procession of the funeral train which carried Lincoln's body from the capital to Springfield served as an integrative rite. The funeral train retraced in reverse Lincoln's journey from a Springfield law practice to the Senate and the White House. This tour, like Lafayette's tour as the Guest of the Nation, was also an opportunity for the confirmation of the expansion of the United States.

The creation of monuments to Lincoln created a crucial link between the midwest, Illinois in particular, and the national capital. The architect of the Lincoln Memorial in Washington, D.C. consciously saw the monument as a means to align and integrate the other monuments into a sacred complex. The monument was placed to create an alignment in which the viewer's line of sight could trace the key moments in the national narrative, from the Capitol to the Washington Monument, to the Lincoln Memorial, and then across the Potomac to Arlington. A sacred zone was thus created in which each monument/moment is distinct, but where they collectively represent the nation itself.

In Richmond, Virginia, the former capital of the Confederate nation, a similar sacred zone, Monument Avenue, was created. In the founding moment of this site, several of the modes of memorialization previously discussed were brought together in an extraordinary sense of Durkheimian affirmation of solidarity. On 7 May 1890, the vast majority of the population of Richmond assembled at the Richmond railroad station to participate in the transportation of four large cartons containing the parts of a statue of Robert E. Lee that had been commissioned by the Ladies' Lee Monument Association. Throughout the battle of representations in the decades after the war, there was no more dramatic event than the arrival of this huge equestrian statue of Robert E. Lee, the general who represented the embodiment of all the virtues of the Lost Cause. It was seen as fitting that the first great equestrian statue to be erected in post-Civil War Richmond should be that of Lee.

During the period of Reconstruction, literally thousands of monuments were produced of varying size, type, and aesthetic quality on both sides. In this battle of representations, the South was at a great disadvantage due to its lack of industrialization: Statues had to be either Yankee-made or commissioned in Europe. Many Italian stonecutters thus became the beneficiaries of this battle, as they provided many of the monuments and much of the marble supplied to both North and South. The size of the statue prohibited casting the statue in Virginia, and such a sacred piece at that time could not, for emotional and cultural reasons, have been cast in the North. Instead, the Association commissioned Antonin Mercie, a French sculptor, and the finished statue was shipped from Paris to New York, and then by rail to Richmond.

The site selected for the statue was at the top of a hill overlooking the city, an area that was being dedicated to the memory of great Virginians. After its long journey from France, the statue arrived on the flats at the Richmond railroad station. The Monument Association then faced the difficult task of hauling the extremely large, heavy set of crates containing the statue up the hill. They decided that this difficulty could be transformed into the occasion for a memorable event. A date and time was announced for the population of the city to assemble at the rail yard, and ropes were attached to the four crates.

On the morning of May 7, thousands of men, women, and children, some in their best attire and all in a festive mood, assembled to assist in pulling the crates up the hill to the site of the pedestal for the monument. Together, in relay fashion, the citizens of Richmond hauled the crates in a procession. A portrait of Lee was attached to the front of the first crate to lead the way. When all four of the crates had been pulled to the top of the hill, an extraordinary sense of accomplishment and euphoria was evident, and those assembled began to cut pieces of the ropes to take as souvenirs of this extraordinary event (somewhat to the chagrin of the businessman who had supplied the rope). The Southern Historical Society Papers described the event under the wonderful heading, "Rope Appropriation":

> A sudden light seemed to dawn upon the pullers that some souvenir was the appropriate thing for such an occasion, and as the rope was about the only available stuff, the cutting was at once begun. . . . The ladies, as soon as they became owners of any of the precious strands, adorned their gowns with it by tying it through the button-hole, and the men either hid the hemp in their pockets, or followed the example of the fair sex. . . . About one-fourth of the ropes, which are the property of Mr. W. A. O. Cole, was rescued from the hands of the people, but the other three-fourths will be put away by its owners, and long after the pulling episode will have been forgotten the rope will be a reminder of the day just passed. Many of those who tugged at the rope, male and female, wore bits of rope on the breast on their return as badges of honor. (Southern Historical Society Papers, 258–59)

In effect, two things were being established by this civic event. First, it created a sacred center for the city. Second, it provided the participants with an experiential memory, one that could be maintained and passed down through the saving of the pieces of rope as family heirlooms. Again, women were the prime movers in creating this event, and again, the emphasis on children was clear. The Lee Monument Association was composed of women from the Hollywood Memorial Association, and it was reported of the crowd that assembled to haul the statue that "woman was probably in the majority—grand-mother, mother, maiden, children by the hand, infant in the arms—all with flushed cheeks and warm eyes" (Southern Historical Society Papers, 248).

Freezing Time, Preserving the Land

If such scenes as Lincoln's funeral train and the great Lee statue haul attest to the continuing influence of modes of remembrance established during the post-Revolution period in Lafayette's tour, the influence of Lossing's ideals of precise historical preservation was also evident in the post-Civil War era— sometimes in direct conflict with the process of monument-building. It should come as no surprise that during the Civil War, Lossing himself turned to the new, "unmediated" technology of representation, photography. His pictorial history of the Civil War was a collection of the photographs of Matthew Brady. However, the older technologies which Lossing had used and his technique of travel narration were not entirely superseded. The role of historian John Bachelder in memorializing the Battle of Gettysburg is a prime example.

John Bachelder, long before the end of the war, had set himself the task of historicizing it. He described his project quite self-consciously: "At the commencement of the war I determined to attach myself to the army and wait for the great battle which would naturally decide the contest; study its topography on the field, and learn its details from the actors themselves, and eventually prepare its written and illustrated history" (Bachelder, 35). He arrived at Gettysburg immediately after the battle and began to make an isometric drawing of the entire topography of the battle. He interviewed as many of the participants as he could find and took tours of the site with veterans, so that they could determine the exact placement and movements of each state's troops over the course of the three days of the battle. Thus, as early as 1863, there was the realization that central sites would be created that would provide a national historic geography.

Bachelder marketed his reconstructions in several forms: as narrative history, in the form of cycloramas, and as engravings which individuals could buy. Like Lossing's *Pictorial Field-Book*, the paintings Bachelder commissioned and designed placed the viewer in a traveling mode. Even the engravings were of such size that they required the spectator to walk in order to see the battle "as it actually happened," translating simultaneous events into a temporal sequence.

Concomitant with the creation of a forest of stone monuments at Gettysburg, Bachelder was instrumental in an effort to preserve the forests of trees, the actual landscape, exactly as it was during the battle. The tension between the three modes of memorialization—monument-building, landscape preservation, and commercialization—was thus carried through from the post-Revolution period into the twentieth century.

Reconciliation

Beginning in the 1870s and 80s, there began to be a sense in both the North and South that reconciliation was necessary, not just in terms of the reestablishment of civil liberties in the South, but also in terms of reintegrating American cultural identity. In the subsequent period of reconciliation, the Confederacy came out victorious, both in terms of the popular imagination and the restructuring of American society. The reintegration of the South into the Union required some profound acts of forgetting, in particular the abandonment of any policy to integrate the former slaves who had been emancipated during the war into the new nation. The political and economic issues of the Civil War became secondary to an imperial project that included not only expansion overseas (in the Spanish-American War) but the Americanization of the vast number of immigrants who came to the United States from Europe in the decades after the Civil War. The revalorization of Southern chivalry at the expense of American blacks, of which the film *Birth of a Nation* is a prime example, can also be seen in the integration of the South into the sites of national remembrance created through the media previously discussed—national and local cemeteries, soldiers' monuments, and Memorial Day celebrations.

As with the Revolutionary War, the approach of the end of living memory was a great spur to the building of monuments and the creation of rituals of remembrance. The central importance of the battle of Gettysburg in particular was kept alive through the regular celebrations of its anniversary. On the fiftieth anniversary of the battle, in July 1913, the federal government sponsored one of the largest of the national rituals of reconciliation. Transportation and facilities were provided for a grand reunion of all of the veterans of the Union and Confederate armies who could be identified and were physically able to attend. Like Lafayette, these veterans had already become monuments in and of themselves. Over fifty-five thousand veterans revisited the battlefield, and a series of events and personal encounters were arranged, including speeches and an event in which the veterans of both sides lined up to shake hands across a stone wall that had been the scene of a crucial campaign in the battle. These activities were both a last-ditch effort to reinscribe the memory of the Civil War and an enunciation of its end. The symbolic power of the reunion was the statement of an end to the distinction between Confederate and Union. The next year, a baroque monument to the Confederacy was erected at Arlington, symbolically reintegrating the Confederate soldiers into the national heroic narrative.

The invisibility of blacks in these modes of reconciliation is striking. Although Lincoln's Gettysburg address, delivered at the dedication of Gettysburg as a national soldiers' cemetery, had made the emancipation proclamation crucial to the ideals of the Union, at the fiftieth anniversary celebrations, there was no mention of the freeing of the slaves. On the contrary, speeches made reference to the "Anglo-Saxon valor" that united the veterans of North and South. To this day, the only African-Americans who are immortalized in stone dedicated to the memory of the Civil War are a loyal slave who bid his master farewell on the side of the Confederate monument at Arlington, and soldiers in an all-black regiment who are dwarfed by the figure of their white commander, to whom the monument is dedicated. Here the memorials reflect social policy, for this was also the period of the reinscription of blacks' second class status in the Jim Crow laws, the beginning of scientific racism, and the first legislation that limited immigration by race.

It is easy to see precisely what is at stake in the controversy over the placement of the statue of Arthur Ashe on Richmond's Monument Avenue. For, if the integration of Southern identity into the Union was predicated on sacrificing the integration of racial Others, then the integration of a black local hero into this Southern identity threatens not only that identity in itself, but also its status within the integrated nation.

Chicago

The process of reconciliation took on a different tone in the North than in the South, and the rest of this chapter will focus in particular on how this process occurred in the city of Chicago. Chicago is a city that was essentially made by the Civil War. It had a strategic location in relation to military geography of the war, as it had both land connections to the South by rail and by river via the Mississippi. The Civil War was fought in three major locations: In and around Washington, D.C., the area around Chattanooga, Tennessee, and Atlanta, Georgia. The transportation network based in Chicago spanned the full regional extent of the war, giving Chicago rapid access to all three major theaters. The city was also particularly important in the process of memorializing the Civil War: The Grand Army of the Republic, the Union veterans' association, was based there. The way in which Chicago transformed in the popular imagination from the quintessential Union city to the quintessential American city reflects the overall process of reconciliation and cultural integration as it occurred in the North.

In the 1890s, a sort of "normalization" of the war experience that would have been impossible in the South occurred in the popular culture of the North. One fine, if bizarre, example of this was the Libby Prison Museum, established by Charles Gunther on Chicago's near north side. Charles F. Gunther was born in Illinois and had worked as a purser on a Confederate riverboat during the Civil War. He was an entrepreneur and collector who had made his fortune in candy (he claimed to have invented the caramel chew). In 1889, Gunther purchased Libby Prison, which had been a p.o.w. camp for Union soldiers in Richmond. The Civil War was the first American war in which there were such camps, and the extraordinary bitterness engendered by the fratricidal war was manifested in the treatment of prisoners on both sides. Libby Prison had been particularly notorious for its overcrowding, lack of food and medical care, and a lack of sanitation that led to hundreds of deaths from disease. Gunther managed to ship the prison, brick by brick, to Chicago. Once there, he reconstructed the building, filled it with exhibits of Civil War memorabilia, and opened it to the public as a commercial museum. The museum exhibits focused on the horrific, including a blood-stained towel that had been placed under Lincoln's head after he was shot, and tree stumps filled with shot from Gettysburg, as well as the usual letters written by generals, uniforms, and so on. Gunther also added such exotica as shrunken heads from the Amazon and the "skin of the serpent that tempted Eve in the Garden of Eden." Gunther's museum presents a distinct contrast to the museum established by the Ladies of Richmond. Although similar objects could be found in both museums—generals' letters, uniforms, swords— in Richmond they were treated as objects of veneration. The setting of Gunther's museum, on the other hand, rendered the relics of the war objects of pure curiosity, needing no particular explication. Such a presentation would have been impossible in the South, and indeed, the Libby Prison Museum was opposed by Southerners living in Chicago at the time, who feared it would incite anti-Southern sentiment. It is telling that the site of Camp Douglas, the P.O.W. camp located in Chicago itself in which Confederate soldiers had been incarcerated, was not preserved or marked, let alone exhibited as a museum.

A new enemy, and a new war, are a time-honored solution to the problem of how to unite former enemies. In the case of the American Civil War, it was not even necessary to begin a new war; it sufficed to incorporate the Southern military into an ongoing one: the genocidal war against America's indigenous population, carried out continuously between the Revolutionary and Civil Wars. European nationalisms have generally created relations to past populations (Celts, for example) from whom they claim to have descended. With the movement of Europeans across the Atlantic, a different relationship was set up to the autochthonous peoples who had already created civilizations and who were part of a continental arena. The master trope for the understanding of American history has been based upon the idea of discovery. Of course, this idea is based upon an enormous conceit, as what we now think of as North America was already well-explored by indigenous populations by the time of European colonization. The European immigrants saw North America as wild, in need of settling. Almost immediately following the Civil War, soldiers from both the Union and Confederate armies (including many African-Americans) were recruited into the project of "winning the West" from the Indians. The chivalric code of the Confederacy proved particularly adept in colonizing the U.S. armed forces, and the ideology of the military is still dominated today by this code.

Up to the 1890s, this war had remained largely invisible in the American landscape. Around the twenty-fifth anniversary of the Civil War, when reconciliation of North and South became a major goal of both the state and veterans' organizations, the figure of the American Indian became increasingly visible in the American memorial landscape, especially in the midwest. The process of remembering this previously unmarked war played an important part in the forgetting of the divisions of the Civil War.

The Chicago World's Fair of 1893 provided an important forum for this shifting of focus from the Civil to the Indian Wars. One of the most enduring contributions to the master narrative of American history was written for the celebration of the four hundredth anniversary of the landing of Columbus. This was Frederick Jackson Turner's defining lecture on the nature of the American frontier, delivered at the World's Fair. Turner argued that much of American national character had been shaped by "the frontier experience." Turner observed that the U.S. census was a demographic artifact that could be used to trace the westward movement of the frontier and, based on it, declared that the frontier had disappeared with the spread of the European population through all of the territory between the coasts.

That same year, the first of the many statues of American Indians that now grace Chicago was unveiled. This was the statue of the so-called Dearborn Massacre, created by artist Carl Rohl-Smith for the Chicago Historical Society. It was originally placed at the spot where the incident had taken place. The statue represented a series of events that had taken place during the War of 1812, when a group of English soldiers and their Indian allies came from what is now Detroit and attacked the Europeans and "friendly" Indians in Chicago. The statue itself represents an incident in which a "friendly" Indian, Black Partridge, saved the life of the wife of one of the American officers stationed at Fort Dearborn; friezes on the pedestal represent other moments in the evacuation of the fort.

The Dearborn Massacre statue was followed by others commemorating the Indian Wars, including an imposing equestrian statue of Philip Sheridan, a Union general well noted for his aggressive personality. Sheridan was posted to the west after his harsh administration in Louisiana and Texas during the Reconstruction period proved too controversial, and he was among those most important in pursuing the massacre and displacement of Indians in the upper midwest. The Indian past of Chicago is represented in a number of statues placed prominently on Outer Lakeshore Drive along Lake Michigan. Most of these monuments are of Indians already seemingly slated for disappearance. One depicts an Indian holding aloft a peace pipe. Another shows Indians in a nuclear family unit, complete with mother, father, children, and family dog.

Today, Chicago's Indian past is largely forgotten. After the World's Fair, the Dearborn Massacre statue was moved to the foyer of the Chicago Historical Society, located at a major intersection in the city. When a group of American Indians protested against the representation of Indians as bloodthirsty savages, it was moved back to its original site on Prairie Avenue, just to the south of the city center, which had been the site of several mansions of the wealthiest families of Chicago. Now it stands, more or less abandoned, in the back garden of one of these mansions. Black Hawk, the major leader of the Indians in the midwest during the Indian Wars, is remembered primarily through the name of Chicago's hockey team.

Oak Woods Cemetery

The history of Oak Woods Cemetery provides an apt figure for our conclusion. The bodies of those who had been interred in the old Chicago City Cemetery were removed to Oak Woods Cemetery, located on Chicago's South Side, after the original City Cemetery land was transformed into a park dedicated to Abraham Lincoln during the latter part of the Civil War. A statue of Abraham Lincoln was also placed in Oak Woods. During the war, the bodies of the Confederate soldiers who had died at Camp Douglas were buried there. In 1896, a Confederate veterans' organization in Chicago decided to erect a monument to these Confederate fallen. The monument was dedicated in an elaborate ceremony in which both Confederate and Union veterans participated. Following the pattern we have noted in the South, women played an important role in this ritual. In one part of the ceremony, a number of women in white dresses stood on pedestals and recited dedications as former Confederate officers spiked the cannons which surround the monument.

With the great migration of African Americans from the rural South to northern cities, the South Side of Chicago became a primarily black neighborhood, one of the major centers of African American culture and politics in the twentieth century. The integration of African Americans into the U.S. military, which had begun with the Indian Wars, was solidified during the First World War. In 1928 the first monument to commemorate the sacrifices of an all-black regiment was erected in Chicago. This monument was located a block from the site of the former Camp Douglas, in the shadow of the towering pedestal of the tomb of Stephen Douglas, on whose estate the prison had been built. There is an irony to this location, given that Stephen Douglas is most noted for being the man who lost to Lincoln in his bid for the senate and an advocate of the southern states' rights to maintain slavery. Adding to this irony is the fact that both the neighborhood surrounding Douglas's tomb and the neighborhood surrounding Oak Woods Cemetery were by the 1950s solidly black middle class. Although Olympian runner Jesse Owens, a hero for both the African American community and the nation, was buried there, the black people who lived near the cemetery only gained the right to enter it after the civil rights movement of the 1950s and '60s. In recent years, the cemetery experienced a revival when Chicago's first African American mayor, Harold Washington, was buried there in 1987, and it now caters primarily to Chicago's black middle class. It is now those who were excluded in the process of post-Civil War reconciliation who are deciding whether that war's legacy will fade into the American landscape or be reappropriated through new forms of remembrance.

References

Anderson, Benedict. 1991. *Imagined Communities: Reflections on the Origin and Spread of Nationalism.* London: Verso.

Bachelder, John B. 1870. *Description of the Painting of the Repulse of Longstreet's Assault.* Painted by James Walker. New York: John B. Bachelder.

Fiftieth Anniversary of the Battle of Gettysburg. 1913. Report of the Pennsylvania Commission. Harrisburg, PA.

Lossing, Benson J. 1855. *The Pictorial Field-Book of the Revolution.* Vol. I. New York: Harper and Bros.

Mitchell, Mary H. 1985. *Hollywood Cemetery: The History of a Southern Shrine.* Richmond: Virginia State Library.

Patterson, John S. 1989. "From Battle Ground to Pleasure Ground: Gettysburg as a Historic Site." In *History Museums in the United States: A Critical Assessment,* edited by Warren Leon and Roy Rosenweig. Chicago: University of Illinois Press.

Peters, James Edward. 1986. *Arlington National Cemetery: Shrine to America's Heroes.* Kensington, Md.: Woodbine House.

Southern Historical Society Papers. "The Monument to General Robert E. Lee."

Underwood, John C. 1896. *Report of the Proceedings Incidental to the Erection and Dedication of the Confederate Monument.* Chicago: Wm. Johnston Co.

Wilson, Charles Reagan. 1980. *Baptized in Blood: The Religion of the Lost Cause, 1865–1920.* Athens: University of Georgia Press.

4 Archaeologies of the Fantastic

Fantastic Community

Brian Keith Axel

Since the 1950s, Bernard S. Cohn's explorations in historical anthropology have persistently illuminated disparate formations of power and knowledge that constitute both India as a spatio-temporal entity and "*the people* who are bearers of [that] entity" (Cohn 1957, 51; emphasis mine). Following Cohn's lead, I turn to the problem of the production of the people of India since Independence in 1947. My inquiry focuses on the trials and tribulations of national integration (*rashtriya ekta*), the convoluted intersections of cartography and "terrorism," and the stark ambivalence of the logic of citizenship. My basic argument may be stated simply, and intends to be a corrective to analyses which isolate the importance of space in nation-formation: the techniques and technologies that make up the "territorial sovereignty and integrity" of India rely on a production not just of differences—but *different temporalities* that may be incommensurable with, and may form a threat to, the basis of the nation-state. This essay, thus, takes up a debate about the production of space and the people of India that Cohn inaugurated during the 1950s.

In spring 1957, at an interdisciplinary conference at the University of Chicago, Cohn first introduced a critical formulation of space into South Asian studies by resisting the use of *region* as an analytic category commonly deployed in the area studies approach to "Indian civilization." For Cohn, what was more important were the historical processes "by which diverse elements are related to one another to form the civilization" (1957, 51). Considering the social scientific procedures and cartographic classifications that constituted and mapped definitive relations between categories of place and people in terms of race, language, and culture, Cohn argued that "we must get away from a static picture of regional cultures and attempts to set up co-ordinate categories. Different regions will have to be characterized in different ways and at different times in their history" (1957, 61).

Eight years later, Cohn chaired a panel for the 1965 Association for Asian Studies Conference on "Indian Regional Elites." The panel formed the basis for a series of informal conversations and correspondences (called by Robert Crane an "informal junta") about the problem of region. This dialogue led to the organization of an interdisciplinary conference at Duke University in 1966 and a subsequent publication in 1967, both titled "Regions and Regionalism in South Asian Studies."

By considering the ambivalence of "the platitude 'unity in diversity,'" Cohn's work began with a reflection on the tension between emphases on the "total entity" and emphases on "regional difference" evident in social scientific attempts to "make sense" out of modern Indian society (1967, 5). From this point, Cohn developed a critique of the establishment of the region as an object of study, by discussing how "regions, even the assumed enduring ones subsumed under the concept of 'historical regions,' are of a changing nature through time" (1967, 16). Of utmost importance were "the consequences of British rule and modernization on the nature and conceptualization of regions, regional culture, and regionalism" (1967, 16). Cohn elaborated this proposition through an extensive analysis of the imbrication of colonial domination with the practices of the survey of India, mapping, the printing press, education, and the social sciences. Based on this analysis, the crucial point Cohn introduced was the distinction between *region* and *regionalism*, a distinction that reflects back on the ambivalent articulations of the "total entity" and "difference." *Region* refers to the "means of classification of a wide variety of kinds of data," whereas *regionalism* refers to "conscious or unconscious development of symbols, behaviors, and movements which will mark off groups within some geographic boundary from others in other regions for political, economic, or cultural ends . . . regionalism [relates] to *a call to action*" (1967, 21; emphasis mine). In other words, region refers to the reified, objective character of a totality, and regionalism refers to the performative, subjective character of difference. In the end, Cohn explained this distinction in terms of a paradox of modern Indian history: "At the same time that British rule was establishing some of the preconditions of a national identity in the modern sense of the word, it also established the conditions for regionalism in the form that we have come to know it from the late nineteenth century" (1967, 26).

Cohn's presentation at the conference provoked a variety of responses. In particular, Burton Stein proposed serious disagreements with Cohn's paper that deserve consideration. According to Stein (1967), Cohn's formulations "should not have been permitted to survive the first session" (1967, 41). In addition to claiming that Cohn's definition of region was a "helpless gesture" which "says nothing," Stein articulated another definitional "caveat" about the term *subjective region:* "It is the *actual* distributions of some trait or trait complex with which most of us are concerned when we speak of regions, and since this is true, I am at a loss to understand the meaning of 'subjective region'" (1967, 41). Stein preferred the cartographer Schwartzberg's "purposive" definition of region which, for Stein, should have become the working hypothesis of the conference: "A region . . . is a perceived segment of the time-space continuum differentiated from others on the basis of one or more defining characteristics" (1967, 41).

The debate between Cohn and Stein has not lost significance for historical anthropology today, not least of all because of the perpetuation of the cartographic notion of "a perceived segment of the time-space continuum" among some scholars interested in postmodernity or postcoloniality. In recent decades, however, the concern has been with a crisis in perception of a time-space continuum. This concern stems from Fredric Jameson's series of articles (1984, 1988) that spell out the problem of postmodern experience in terms of an apparently new spatial totality, an "international space" or a "postmodern global space." The crisis instituted by this "absent totality"—a "coherent new type of space in its own right" (1984, 88)—is that there is "a gap between phenomenological perception and a reality that transcends all individual thinking" (1988, 353). Concurrently, in Jameson's terms, "the subject has lost its capacity to extend its pro-tensions and re-tensions across the temporal manifold, and to organize its past and future into coherent experience" (1984, 71). Calls for a reorientation in analysis of the perception of this time-space continuum have come from many disciplines, including David Harvey's (1989) formulation of "time-space compression," and Akhil Gupta and James Ferguson's popular call to rethink "difference through connection" by understanding how a community is formed "out of the interconnected space that always already existed" (1992, 8).

These conceptualizations, which suggest provocative ideas about the relation of space and difference, must be considered carefully, particularly in the way they substitute one kind of spatio-temporal totality (the nation-state) with another (global capital) which becomes the new generative force of perception. Specifically, they begin with a posited new spatial totality. The viability of this newness relies upon the presumption of what came before—prior spaces (i.e.,

Jameson's passage from "market to monopoly capital," Gupta and Ferguson's "colonialism [that] represents the displacement of one form of interconnection by another") and prior subjects (i.e., Jameson's "class" or Gupta and Ferguson's "cultures [which] have lost their moorings in definite places"). Ironically ignoring Lefebvre's insistence on subjecting to critique "space in its totality or global aspect," these scholars, in "fetishizing" absolute and abstract space, shift analysis from the "production of space" to "things in space" (Lefebvre 1993, 37).[1] Concurrently, from these teleological premises detailing a movement from prior to present entities, difference is transformed into distance that in postmodern space is annihilated, compressed, or unbound (Bhabha 1994).

Rather than outline a critique of these works, I would like to indicate the necessity of reconsidering such formulations and moving beyond them. First is the problem of recuperating cartography's principle of a spatial totality. The procedures of cartography have been based upon the fantasy of an original unity or totality (the earth) which is the starting point for the production of differences (i.e., territories).[2] From this basis, cartography posits a teleological movement: These differences have or will come to be arranged into new totalities (i.e., nation-states) that, furthermore, should constitute a community of totalities (e.g., the United Nations). The cartographic understanding of difference must be made clear. In cartography, difference is a matter of *distance* and more specifically, distance measured between equivalent units (points) that may be designated in terms of longitude and latitude. Formally, difference is a relation of part to part, units that, since manifesting equivalent aspects of the original totality (the earth), must be constituted as exchangeable. In short, the cartographic principle of space as a totality demonstrates the *productivity of measurement* as a process of subjectification, constituting relations of difference/distance as signifiers of an original, a priori, totality.

The cartographic principle of spatial totality and the transformation of difference into distance have historically been constituted in relation to the pedagogical procedures of nation-states—which leads to my second point. To demonstrate this, one need only reflect on the way the Indian nation-state constitutes the possibility (or plausibility) of articulating and "nationalizing" the "heterogeneity" of its population through the valorization of "unity in diversity"—and the various official slogans of *rashtriya ekta, qaumi ekta,* and national integration. Consider the representation displayed and exhibited in Delhi (and in most national newspapers) during the fiftieth anniversary of the United Nations in 1996: a map of India superimposed upon an Indian flag. The map, showing no internal boundaries, instead displays (in Hindi) the words:

EKTA
rajya-anek
dharam-anek
bhasha-anek
jati-anek
granth-anek
PHIR BHI HAM SAB
EK[3]

Not one—one, not one—one, not one—one, not one—one. Addressed to the people of India and to the international community of the UN, this reiterative utterance of ambivalence refers to a history of practices by which the Indian nation-state, despite the finality of the image of the People-as-One, has been compelled to repeatedly articulate and enforce sovereignty through the elaboration of an originary totality (*phir bhi ham sab ek* / still we are all one). Within this history, the problem of rashtriya ekta has been elaborated through metaphors that conceptualize differences as distances that may be connected. Thus, in 1984 as the "Sikh problem" in Punjab became more threatening to "national integration," Indira Gandhi stated: "[The object of national integration] is not for confrontation but to build bridges between communities, between races, between nations" (Bhattacharya 1985, 195).[4]

To return to the work of Bernard Cohn: The foundationalist idea of space and time as things that, in segments or wholes, preexist perception was exactly what Cohn was hesitant to concede. He was attempting to formulate an understanding, not just of subjectivity, but of the production of space and time, and more specifically, of how India has been constituted *as* a continuum of space and time that supposedly exists prior to both scholarly analysis and the "call to action" of regionalism. In this respect, Cohn's conceptualization of "objective" and "subjective" is crucial for it points not only to the frailty of any notion of a totality—India—but also to an ambivalence that marks the constitution of the people of India—an ambivalence by which the image of totality confronts and is confronted by the indeterminacy of the performative subject.

The Indian nation-state's productions of space are only in a very limited sense about the inscription of "geographical" or "physical" distinctions upon the nation's landscape. More precisely, as has already been noted, it is important to understand how these productions, while facilitating the designation and enforcement of certain territorial categories (boundaries, frontiers, interiority, exteriority), rely upon, and are imbricated with, the constitution of various forms of difference and temporality.

The Restricted Zone

The image of the people of India emerges as a specific historical process—and as a transformative process central to the repeated reconstitution of the Indian nation-state. This transformative process can be explored more closely from the margins, so to speak, of the nation's space.

Before the publication of the inaugural issue of the *International Journal of Punjab Studies* in January 1994, the editors of the journal, comprising the world's most distinguished scholars of Sikh studies, found themselves in an unforeseen conflict with certain representatives of the Indian nation-state. The journal was created to bring together scholarship, not just on Indian and Pakistani Punjabs, but also on a "third Punjab," defined as the "strong vibrant Punjabi diaspora that covers most of the developed world." The production of knowledge of these "three Punjabs," however, was apparently not the point of conflict with the Indian government. Rather, the problem was the journal's cover design: a map of an undivided Punjab. Sage Publications in New Delhi notified the journal's editors in England that they risked imprisonment for publishing and exporting such a map. The editors, wanting to hasten the publication, redesigned the cover, which now displays an abstract series of lines indicating a global projection of the earth.

Understanding the exact terms of the conflict between the *International Journal of Punjab Studies* and the Indian nation-state is important. Based on two constitutional acts directly concerned with the access of a national and international audience to forms of representations of India, the government of India has imposed specific requirements on the scale and contents of maps published in India. For the most part, these interdictions concern the cartographic representation of what the Survey of India calls the "Restricted Zone." The Restricted Zone refers to the entire periphery of the territory of India, including all of Jammu and Kashmir, all of the northeast states, all of the outlying islands, and most of Punjab.

The first prohibition on cartographic representation, drawing authority from the Official Secret Act (Act No. 19 of 1923) as amended by Act 24 of 1967, is extremely clear-cut.[5] In precise terms, the Indian government does not allow the publication of maps of the Restricted Zone on scales of 1:1 million and larger. Maps on acceptable scales cannot depict contours, trigonometric/spot heights, spherical lines/ticks or their values, mile/kilometer stone ticks, or "vital areas and defence installations." In other words, these guidelines forbid any "accurate" cartographic representation of the Restricted Zone. According to the Official Secret Act, any transgression of these guidelines is "likely to affect the sovereignty and integrity of India." Thus, "a person guilty of an offence under this section shall be punishable with imprisonment for a term which may extend to three years, or with fine, or with both."

The guidelines of the second prohibition, while being less explicit, cover a broader domain of possible transgressions. Section 2 of the Criminal Law Amendment Act (Act No. 23 of 1961) states: "Whoever by words either spoken or written, or by signs, or visible representation or otherwise, questions the territorial integrity or frontiers of India in a manner which is, or is likely to be prejudicial to the interests of the safety or security of India, shall be punishable with imprisonment for a term which may extend to three years, or with fine, or with both." The Survey of India clarifies the relation of this statement to cartography: the publication of any map "depicting *inaccurate* external boundaries and coast-lines of India tantamounts to questioning the territorial integrity of India."

It is not likely that the initial cover design of the *International Journal of Punjab Studies* depicted the Restricted Zone on a large scale or displayed specific forms of representation which would be of interest only to cartographers or military institutions. The more likely point of conflict was that the map, which combined East and West Punjab, showed neither international nor interstate boundaries of the present day. In this case, the journal's potential offense would have fallen under the jurisdiction of the Criminal Law Amendment Act: a problem of questioning the territorial integrity and frontiers of India by inaccurately depicting the Restricted Zone.

The interdiction that the *International Journal of Punjab Studies* nearly transgressed is not a small or isolated matter. Nor is the production of representations of Punjab. Despite the generalizing nature of Indian constitutional law, the opposition of the Indian government to the journal's cover cannot be separated from the significance of a cover displaying an image of Punjab and indications of a "third Punjab." Overdetermined by histories of displacement, violence, and discourses about separatism and terrorism (which have their beginnings well before 1947), Punjab, in being constituted as the Sikh Homeland, has become an index for the Sikh (see, for example, Axel 2001). Conversely, in the nationalist discourse, the Punjab/Sikh has become an ambivalent sign of difference—the simultaneous source of an indispensable contribution to the nation-state's totality and of a repeated threat.[6] Through the procedures of cartographic imagery, the *International Journal of Punjab Studies* points to the problem of questioning or affecting the sovereignty and territorial integrity of India. A more general problem about the production of difference is also opened. Why is the idea of a Sikh homeland a threat? Addressing this question will also help clarify the various forms of difference upon which turn the nation-state's desire ("unity in diversity") and fear ("fissiparious tendencies").

The Limit of Sovereignty

The story of the *International Journal of Punjab Studies* does not demonstrate merely how the juridico-political procedures of the Indian nation-state are preoccupied with certain minute details of producing and representing the space of the nation. The particular characteristic of the conflict also demonstrates the central importance of an *image* to the processes of recognition, identification, and articulation of the fantasy of sovereignty (Axel 1998, 2001; Berlant 1991; Bhabha 1994; Lefort 1986; Metz 1982; Mulvey 1989). Hence, forms of cartographic technology and representation have become sites for the convergence of a variety of legal and juridical discourses about the sovereignty and integrity of India. The conflict is also suggestive of a certain anxiety, indicating how "the demand for a holistic, representative vision of society could only be represented in a discourse that was *at the same time* obsessively fixed upon, and uncertain of, the boundaries of society" (Bhabha 1994, 144).

One way to understand this anxiety is to consider how the Restricted Zone has become a sign for the limit of Indian sovereignty and territorial integrity—a limit in the double sense of marking the territorial border of Indian interiority/exteriority as well as signifying the instability and indeterminacy of the margins of identity.

Punjab—in the 1990s not so much a state adjacent to a border but rather a "sensitive border state"[7]—has repeatedly been constituted as just such a limit. First of all, the Restricted Zone of Punjab may be understood as a site for the production of a territorial boundary susceptible to the "influx and infiltration" of "external forces" that, according to discourses on Indian national integration, "attempt to drive a wedge between communities in Punjab with a view to bringing about a similar cleavage all over the country."[8] In the terms of this discourse, in the 1980s and 1990s and previously, the external forces that intrude upon the territory of India have been of several kinds: for example, drug dealers, gun-runners, and spies trained or facilitated by Pakistan's Inter-Services Intelligence (ISI), an agency that, by helping external forces cross the border, is continually perpetuating "designs to foment communal trouble" within India.[9]

Punjab, though, is also susceptible to designs that may or may not necessitate such a border crossing but that have definitive effects for the constitution of the people of Punjab as a marginal people, a people living *within* a sensitive border. These designs come from what the *International Journal of Punjab Studies* calls the "third Punjab," wherein, according to LaBrack's popular formulation, the "Punjabi village remains the psychological 'homebase,' but increasingly 'home' is in England, Canada, or the United States" (1989, 289). The post-1984 activities, after the siege of the Golden Temple, of Khalistani militants from Canada or England, who are supposedly supported by the ISI and move through Pakistan into Punjab, are one of several extremely significant factors in this formulation (Axel 2001). Also of concern to the Indian nation-state are the "new patrons" living in the third Punjab who, through the medium of "remittances," have, most significantly since the mid-1970s, produced an "external economy" for Indian Punjab (Helweg 1979; Labrack 1989; Nayyar 1994). The effects of this "external economy" mark the landscape of the Restricted Zone in the form of new houses and telecommunications technologies (Helweg 1979; Labrack 1989) and also in the form of *gurdwaras* (Sikh temples)— including an exact-to-scale replica of the Golden Temple in Mastuana. What also marks the landscape of Punjab is the military presence of the state, counted in 1990 as one of the highest per capita police deployments in the world.[10] In March 1996, in preparation for the Lok Sabha elections, the Party's government "stepped up" this "surveillance" when more than two hundred companies of paramilitary forces, seventy thousand policemen, and fifteen thousand Home Guards were sent to Punjab "to ensure free, fair, and peaceful polling."[11]

This last example, of the "stepping up" of a military presence, suggests another way that the marginality of Punjab and the Sikh people have been susceptible to, or constituted by, certain designs—specifically, those of the government of India which, to use Appadurai's words, have been involved in creating "a vast network of formal and informal techniques for the nationalization of all space considered to be under its sovereign authority" (1996, 189). Within these techniques, though, the nation-state constitutes the Sikh people in terms of an image of "unity in diversity" just as the *indeterminacy* of the Sikh people intrudes on and disrupts the formations of power and knowledge productive of the sovereignty and integrity of the People-as-One. This formulation suggests another way to understand the restricted zone.

In March 1996, while troops were being transported into Punjab, Congress (India's leading governmental party at the time) introduced a program called "Spiritual Journeys with Indian Railways," which would provide a "much needed New Direct Express Train" connecting Amritsar, "famed city of the Golden Temple," with Nanded, Maharashtra, "home of the Hazur Sahib Gurdwara (where Guru Gobind Singh passed away)." This train, the "Sachkhand Express," was one of several new trains "launched . . . for the benefit of Pilgrims . . . for easy and direct access to your favourite Pilgrimage Spots and Dhams." As part of a much publicized campaign, Congress published a half-page advertisement in the *Hindu* that displayed a map of India, delimiting no interstate boundaries and flanked by pictures of then Prime Minister Narasimha Rao, S. B. Chavan, Suresh Kalmadi, and S. S. Ahluwalia. Within the map, labeled "not to scale," lines indicated railroad tracks between the different dhams, including one line directly between Amritsar and Nanded.

It is possible to provide an analysis of this campaign in terms of a question of cartographic representation. For example, one might point out how the cartographic imagery does not correlate to the "real" landscape. The representation displays a railroad line running directly between Amritsar (lying on the border of what would be Pakistan) and Nanded (in the center of India); but in actuality Amritsar does not lie on the border and Nanded is not precisely in the middle of India, nor does the railway go directly between the two but runs from Amritsar to New Delhi and then to Agra, Bhopal, and Purva.[12] Or, one might consider the Sachkhand Express in terms of an irony of displacement constituted in the conjunction of global capital and the nation-state: That is, the Express may signify a project to displace Sikhs from the Restricted Zone, denying them a "firm territorialized anchor," which in turn compels Sikhs to recreate a "culturally and ethnically" distinct place or imagined homeland (see, for example, Gupta and Ferguson 1992). Such a critique, however—judging the "inaccuracy" of representation or the "blurring" of "actual places and localities"—is no critique at all. It is a discursive repetition—amounting to an affirmation of or a quest for a posited original difference or real place—that cannot specify the productivity and ambivalence of the nation-state's objectifying procedures. The point here is that within the fantasy of the sovereignty and integrity of India, there is the ambivalent desire both for the production of Sikhs and Punjab as different and for a displacement or integration of that difference. It is important to specify this ambivalence because it is there, within that vicissitude, that the possibility for a disruption or the articulation of an incommensurability emerges.

Consider the ceremony in which the Sachkhand Express was "flagged off" in Amritsar.[13] There were actually two ceremonies, both performed on the train, just before 6:30 A.M. (the time of departure) on March 7. At the "official" function, held at the tail-end of the train and attended by Kalmadi and Ahluwalia, R. L. Bhatia (Minister of State for External Affairs) flagged off the train. At the other end of the train, attended by members of the Sikh Shiromani Gurdwara Prabandhak Committee (SGPC), Manjit Singh Calcutta (Secretary of the SGPC) garlanded the engine drivers.[14] This alternative flagging off exemplifies what de Certeau would call "poaching," a form of activity that, using the structures imposed on it, remains heterogeneous to those structures and sketches out "the guileful ruses of different interests and desires" (1984, 34).

But it is also possible to see how the challenge of the SGPC's ruse was immanent to the official flagging off function itself. Before the official flagging off, Kalmadi made a brief speech reported in the *Hindu:*

> Mr. Suresh Kalmadi said a long-pending demand of the Sikhs to link the two Takhts had been fulfilled. . . . To keep pace with the rapid industrial progress it had become necessary to improve the rail network in the country. Industry was no longer confined to certain pockets, but had spread to remote corners of India and as a result it had become all the more vital to improve the railway infrastructure. . . . During the last five years, 5000 km of rail lines had been converted from small and medium gauge to broad gauge. Earlier, only 300 km had been upgraded to broad gauge.

A certain dialogic is involved in Kalmadi's speech that needs to be clarified. The mention of gauge conversion refers to Project Unigauge, another Congress campaign also widely publicized during March 1996. This project was hailed as a sign of Indian modernity and integration: "Coupled with the Policy of Economic Liberalisation, Project Unigauge will usher in a new era of development and progress in hitherto less developed areas reducing regional imbalance in economic development." The slogan of Project Unigauge was: "One Country— One Gauge: Gauge Conversion contributes to National Integration."[15]

Note the ambivalence within Kalmadi's speech-act, moving from "long-pending demand of the Sikhs" and "rail network in the country" to "remote corners of India"—an enunciation making the Sikh citizen both the pedagogical object of the authoritative address of the nation and the subject whose practices (riding the train and being pilgrims) must signify the contemporaneity and progress of the people of India.[16] This ambivalence rests tenuously on the utterance "long-pending demand of the Sikhs." Note also the discursive production of the Sikh as a specific subject of difference—the demanding subject. In Kalmadi's acknowledgment of a Sikh demand, there is a separation of the Sikh, as a difference, from the putative singularity of the people of India. With that separation, a division immanent to the sovereignty of the nation is momentarily and dangerously identified. The identification of division is desired (for it constitutes the authority of the nation-state and the valorized "diversity"), yet there is the possibility that the demanding Sikh subject may not return with a gesture of *national* identification.

Reproducing Demand

Kalmadi's speech was not the first instance of discourse to interpellate the Sikh subject through the category of demand (see, for example, Axel 2001). Indeed, historically, the Sikh subject has been repeatedly produced around the category of demand, and specifically a demand articulated in antagonistic relation to the repeated production of the image of Indian rashtriya ekta. Conversely, at least since Jawaharlal Nehru's 1946 statement that "the brave Sikhs of Punjab are entitled to special consideration [and] I see nothing wrong in an area and a set up in the north wherein the Sikhs can also experience the glow of freedom" (Khushwant Singh, 291), the demand of the Sikh subject had been constituted as a form of performativity organized around the imaginary of a Sikh homeland (Axel 2001).[17]

The history of the production of the "Sikh demand" may be positioned within a more general history of national integration. As formulated between 1947 and 1956, national integration set a major precedent not only for productions of the Sikh subject, but also for productions of the limit of Indian sovereignty and the space of the Restricted Zone. During these years the category of national integration, defined primarily by the Patel Scheme, was constituted in terms of the emerging relationship between particular territorial units and the production of a total territorial unit, the Indian nation.

Specifically, the procedure of the Patel Scheme was first, to shape and merge the Indian States into viable administrative units, second, to position these units into what would become the constitutional structure, and third, to constitute for India "a place in the world polity" (Patel 1949, 51).[18] In 1947 with the "lapse of British suzerainty," 552 Indian states regained their position prior to suzerainty. Except for Hyderabad, Kashmir, Bahawalpur, Junagadh, and the northwestern frontier states, all states acceded to the Dominion of India by 15 August 1947. Under the Patel Scheme, between 1948 and 1950, 216 former Indian states merged into contiguous Indian provinces (forming Part B in the First Schedule of the Constitution).[19] Sixty-one states were converted into centrally administrative areas for administrative or strategic reasons (forming Part C in the First Schedule of the Constitution). Into new viable units known as the Union of States (also under Part B), 275 states merged. By 1956 with the Constitution (Seventh Amendment) Act and the States Reorganization Act, the number of states was reduced from twenty-seven to fourteen and the process of national integration was considered to be "culminated": With this Act, the Indian states lost their former identity, and since the Part A, B, and C states were constituted as equivalents and placed under a single category, India supposedly became one integral, uniform, and federal entity.[20]

The integration of India under the Patel Scheme followed guidelines that were to be embodied in the Indian Constitution in 1949. This is an important point that must be spelled out. Unlike the United States, India was not created by states "agreeing" to give up their sovereignty to the one sovereignty of the Indian nation—rather, the creation of an independent Indian nation generated the problem of creating a constituency of states. The Indian Constitution and its amendments stipulate that: 1) the Constitution does not offer any guarantee to the states against affecting their territorial integrity without their consent (i.e., the central government can redraw the map of its territory at any time by forming new states or by altering the boundaries of the states as they exist); 2) no state may change its own boundaries; 3) the central government may consider the pleas of an existing state or a group of people to change its boundaries or become a new state only under certain conditions of "consensus," and especially only in terms of a *secular demand*; 4) advocacy of secession will not have the protection of the freedom of expression.

Demand, as a form of performativity constituting the Sikh subject in relation to Indian sovereignty and integrity, has been indissolubly related to the histories of the Patel Scheme and the discourses of the Indian Constitution. It is important to specify that it has been the Shiromani Akali Dal, the frequently changing and fragmenting "Sikh" political part of Punjab, that has taken on the authority of articulating demand, deeming itself "the very embodiment of the hopes and aspirations of the Sikh nation (qaum) and as such . . . fully entitled to its representation" (Gopal Singh 1994, 137). In the history of practices organized by the various Akali groups, the character of demand and its negotiations with the Indian nation-state have changed according to different circumstances.

After the Radcliffe Award in 1947—which demarcated "the boundaries of the two parts of the Punjab on the basis of ascertaining the contiguous majority areas of Muslims and non-Muslims"[21]—between 1948 and 1966 the government of India officially redrew the map of Punjab three times because of or in spite of Akali "agitation." First, in 1948, a division was made between the Patiala and East Punjab States Union (PEPSU)—formed out of Patiala, Nabha, Jind, Faridkot, Kaparthala, Kalsia, Malerkotla, Nalagarh—and the state of Punjab (Gursharan Singh 1991). Second, on 1 November 1956, a new Punjab was formed by merging PEPSU with the rest of Punjab (Gursharan Singh 1991, 240). Third, on 1 November 1966, the Punjabi Suba was formed, comprised of Jullundur, Hoshiarpur,

Ludhiana, Ferozepur, Amritsar, Patiala, Bhatinda, Kapurthala, and parts of Gurdaspur, Ambala, and Sangrur. Chandigarh, declared a union territory, was made the shared capital of Punjab and the newly formed Haryana.[22] Thus, by 1966 the state of Punjab was reduced to a territorial area of small proportions, compared to the post-Partition territory that extended from Lahul and Spiti in the north to Palwal, south of Delhi.

During these years, up until 1966, the Akalis formulated the Sikh demand in terms of a desire for a Punjabi-speaking state, rather than a Sikh state, because the Constitution would only recognize a secular demand. As Sardar Hukam Singh stated at the presidential address of the Sikh National Convention in 1950: "The cry of establishing Khalistan [is unwise]. . . . The demand for a Punjabi-speaking state is quite a legitimate demand; it is covered by the national policy and the national constitution."[23] Nevertheless, Akali leaders, like Master Tara Singh, "made no secret of the fact that they had used the linguistic argument to gain a state in which the Sikhs would be in a majority and so be able to ensure the preservation of Sikh traditions and identity" (Khushwant Singh, 310). As such, the pertinence of claims to a Punjabi-speaking majority had less significance than the production of a sovereign authority (that of the Sikh qaum or nation) based upon a temporality (that of the inauguration of the Sikh Order of the Khalsa in 1699) that not only preexisted Independence but was also separate from the valorized teleological development of the Indian nation-state (see, for example, Axel 2001).

The orientation of the Sikh demand changed as the territory of Punjab changed, as different forms of protest emerged in other parts of India (i.e., Potti Sriramulu's "fast unto death" for the formation of Andhra Pradesh in 1952), and as the nation-state experienced international crises (i.e., the "Chinese Incursion" in 1962, the "22-Day-War" with Pakistan in 1965). For example, in the 1950s the Akalis encouraged the use of the slogan *azad Punjab*, which the central government had made illegal. This led to a confrontation in which the police entered the Golden Temple in May 1955, letting off tear gas and making arrests. In the 1960s the Akalis organized several *morchas*, non-violent protests volunteering imprisonment. Between 1960 and 1961, over fifty-seven thousand volunteers were arrested, and Fateh Singh went on a "fast unto death," which was halted on 9 January 1961, when the government released the prisoners and said they would look into their demands.

In 1966 after the formation of the Punjabi Suba, Sant Fateh Singh, one of the Akali leaders reflected: "The Punjabi Suba is our last demand" (Khushwant Singh, 308). This statement notwithstanding, with the production of Punjab as a territory on the margins, or a border state, there ensued a proliferation of Sikh demands. Initially these took on two trajectories. The first was articulated by the Akalis in the new Punjab and constituted in relation to the central government's failure to fulfill the conditions of the Punjabi Suba as formulated in 1966. Particularly, Chandigarh was to be the capital of Punjab, Punjabi-speaking areas contiguous to Punjab were to be brought into Punjab, and control of the waters of the Sutlej, Ravi, and Beas rivers was to be given to Punjab. The second was articulated by Jagjit Singh Chauhan in England and America and constituted in relation to Sikhs living around the world: In 1971, Chauhan published a half-page advertisement in the *New York Times* advocating a sovereign Sikh state, Khalistan, and attempted to put the "Sikh case" before the United Nations.

My aim here is not to detail the history of transformations of the Sikh as a demanding subject, or of the demands themselves, or of the production of a "third Punjab" that has reconstituted the significance of the Sikh subject in terms of a "world community" (see, for example, Axel 2001). Rather, the point is that demand has not only become a category of repetition (in relation to the repeated addresses of the nation-state), a form of performativity (that resists encompassment within the sovereignty and integrity of the Indian people), and a means for constructing authority in terms of a temporality incommensurable with the nation-state (that of the Sikh order of the Khalsa). Demand has also become a means of reproducing both the Sikh subject and the Indian nation-state in terms of a teleology of violence. The historical writings of Khushwant Singh exemplify this teleological formulation:

> The government's tardiness in resolving these basic issues gave the Akalis grounds to charge it of being anti-Sikh. They [the Akalis] assiduously cultivated a discrimination complex and kept adding to their list of demands. On its part, the central government, instead of conceding what was legitimately asked for, adopted delaying tactics thus forcing the Akalis to launch a succession of passive resistance movements which often escalated into violence. Alongside the peaceful *morchas* grew terrorism which the police countered by brutal repression, often killing innocent people in staged encounters and torturing suspects. Police methods proved counter-productive and brought more recruits to terrorist groups. (1991, 342)

Reinserting the Sikh subject into this teleological formulation is troublesome. In a way that inverts the significance of the demand in Kalmadi's address, the demand positioned within this teleology erases the indeterminacy of the Sikh subject. The category of demand is separated from both the productivity of the nation-state and the performative negotiation of incommensurable difference. In other words, agency is positioned within the category of demand, and demand becomes a coherent category of marginality and irreverence to sovereignty and integrity. Such a view not only legitimizes and gives reason to violence; it positions violence as an effect of difference rather than a constituent element in the production of difference.[24]

Fantasy and Difference

The question of difference can also be approached by reflecting on the relationships between national integration (rashtriya ekta), sovereignty, and citizenship. Since the culmination of national integration under the Patel Scheme in 1956, the desire of national integration has not ceased but rather proliferated. The repeated address of ekta has been organized and mediated by the procedures of the National Integration Committee (NIC), the "sentinel of the nation's unity."[25] The NIC was initially convened by the Congress Working Committee in 1958, after the 1957 Jabalpur riot, to address the emerging problem of "fissiparious tendencies in the body-politic of our country" (Aiyer 1961). The NIC has been reconstituted several times since 1958, and discourses on national integration have repeatedly identified the urgent problem of the "contemporary" social situation in India by reference to Nehru's words: "Let us the citizens of the Republic of India . . . bring about this synthesis, the integration of the Indian people . . . so that we might be welded into one, and made into one strong national unit, maintaining at the same time all our wonderful diversity" (Vyas: 245).

Since 1958, the category of national integration has been reconfigured in different ways, referring first to problems of education and raising national consciousness, then to problems of valorizing unity and diversity, and then in the 1980s and 1990s to problems of defense from the internal dangers of caste-ism, communalism, and separatism.[26] The continual applicability of Nehru's narrative to these diverse historical processes illuminates how, in the discursive production of "national unit," the nation is always emerging.

The juridical discourses of the Supreme Court constitute the repeated problem encountered in producing citizens as an unfortunate effect of forgetting: "We tend to forget that India is a one nation and we are all Indians first and Indians least [sic]" (Vyas 1993, 2). For Indira Gandhi, who often presided over the NIC between 1960 and 1984,[27] this ambivalence, which marked citizens as potential adversaries, emerged despite the fact that "there is a oneness among our people which has held us together."[28] That citizens may represent a threat to sovereignty and territorial integrity is, in Indira Gandhi's terms, the natural consequence of a slippage of "social cohesion" that needs to be continually and persistently maintained.

In 1983, Indira Gandhi, through the NIC, instituted a fifteen point program providing comprehensive instructions for the production of the "internal defence of India." In her formulation, the threat from within the nation is analogous to the threat from without:

> National integration is the internal defence of the country—the domestic and civilian counterpart of the work of the Defence Services do to safeguard the territorial integrity of the nation. . . . No country can ignore defence. It cannot assume that just because it is sovereign, its neighbors will not attack it. It has to be vigilant, ever careful not to lag behind technology. Similarly, we should not imagine that merely because we are free and have a Constitution, the social cohesion will remain on its own. It has to be guarded just as the nation's frontiers are guarded. But in one case we have the defence forces and in the other it has to be all the citizens.[29]

Thus, the citizens of India take on the double role, constituted as both the subjects and objects of civilian defense services, both the forces of "internal defence" and potential/actual violators who cannot maintain "social cohesion" on their own. Not being able to maintain social cohesion, though, the citizen risks being constituted either as a representative of forces deriving from a prior society, or a foreigner, or both.

What I am trying to point out here is not so much Foucault's distinction of a juridical system which defines subjects according to universal norms and egalitarian principles, yet veils the constitutive disciplinary mechanism (the "counter-law") that institutes "insuperable asymmetries" (Foucault 1979, 222–23). Nor am I indicating the "philosophical poverty and even incoherence" of the nation as an "imagined community" (Anderson 1991, 5). Rather, I would like to put my argument in terms of the *fantasy* of the nation-state.

Fantasy may be understood as a crucial aspect for the production of a peculiar and powerful *collective* subject, "the People of India," and in this chapter I use the term *fantasy* exclusively to refer to this domain—that is, to the historical formation of the nation-state.[30] Part of the discourse of the nation-state, as I have demonstrated in my discussion of national integration, constitutes the nation and the citizen as always emerging. The repetitive productions of the nation-state's emergence are inseparable from the reconstitution of what I am calling fantasy, which envisages the oneness of the people both as already constituted and as just ahead. The working of fantasy marks the nation-state's sovereignty with a certain ambivalence the moment it emerges as such, for it illuminates the fictive, though no less real, character of the nation-state's totality.

Not a "visual fallacy" or "involuntary delusion" implying the separation of an internal world of "imagination" and an external world of "reality" (Burgin 1986; Laplanche and Pontalis 1986; Rose 1996), fantasy, rather, indicates the ambivalent processes that form the basis for identifications with an image of a totality (the nation-state). Played out in terms of the production of certain pleasures, desires, prohibitions, displacements, spatial scenes, and disjunctive temporalities, fantasy is central not only to the production of a national affect, but also to the means by which simultaneously "national culture becomes local" and "local affiliations" are disrupted (Berlant 1991, 5, 49). In other words, national fantasy, at least in part, has much to do with the constitution of relations of identification that transform individuals and bodies into representations and representatives of an abstract entity. Following Lauren Berlant, we may see the fantasy of the nation-state as operating at the level of the "national symbolic," a register of language and the law concerned at once with generating a national history, transforming individuals into citizens, and "interpellating the citizen within a symbolic nationalist context" (Berlant 1991, 225). Fantasy, indeed, underscores the points at which the register of the symbolic meets the constitution of the images of the People-as-One and territorial integrity, the "origins" for the people and territory, and the laws regulating practices that must represent their proposed sovereignty.

In the history of productions of the Indian nation-state, there have been several "myths of origin," so to speak, not all of which conjoin with an image of the People-as-One.[31] What I am interested in now is the way the image of the People-as-One, conflated with a notion of the origin of the nation, has marked out an anterior temporality that forms the precedent for explanations of national territory, sovereignty, and integrity on the one hand, and for regulatory practices on the other. This, though, is not an instance of what Benedict Anderson has outlined. "The objective modernity of nations to the historian's eye," he argues, is opposed by "their subjective antiquity in the eyes of nationalists" (1991, 5). In contrast the Indian nation-state, in the social and material process of the objectification under discussion here, is constituted as essentially modern.

An important historical reference for this fantasy is in the Indian Supreme Court's 1955 proclamation, which dramatized the moment of emergence of the Indian nation-state as the *beginning* of a history:

Every vestige of sovereignty was abandoned by the dominion of India and by the States and surrendered to the peoples of the land who through their representatives in the Constituent Assembly hammered out for themselves a new Constitution in which all are citizens in a new order having but one tie and owing but one allegiance, devotion, loyalty, fidelity to the sovereign, democratic Republic that is India. At one stroke territorial allegiances were wiped out and the past was obliterated except where expressly preserved, at one moment in time the new order was born and its allegiances springing from the same source, all grounded on the same basis, the sovereign will of the people of India with no class, no caste, no race, no creed, no distinction, no reservation.[32]

In the same way that Louis Dumont describes "structure" as a "form of organization that does not change [but] is replaced by another" (1980, 219), or that Claude Lévi-Strauss explains that "languages can only have arisen all at once" (1987, 59), the fantasy of the new order of Indian sovereignty elaborates a rupture constituting identity "at one stroke," "at one moment in time."[33] This fantasy of a classless society with a singular, undifferentiated territory at its base constitutes the foundation of the nation-state's integrated totality not as something known through "experience," but as an image that "transcends both individual experience and what is imagined" (Laplanche and Pontalis 1986, 16).

According to Albert Dicey and his successors in constitutional law, a certain desire—the "desire for union"—is a prerequisite for the formation of a "federal" system (Basu 1995; Dicey 1924; Krishnamurti 1939; Sharma 1968).[34] Additionally, such a desire, embodied in the "opinion of the population of the territory" and "freely expressed by informed and democratic processes," is a definitive factor in the UN's charter which determines "whether a territory is or is not a territory whose people have not yet attained a full measure of self-government" (Sharma 1968, 202–3).[35] There is an important connection between this desire and the fantasy of the nation-state. Jean Laplanche and Jean-Bertrand Pontalis (1973, 1986) have explained that rather than being the object, fantasy is the setting for desire (Burgin 1986, 1992). In the Indian nation-state's fantasy of the People-as-One, the fulfillment of desire—the formation of the sovereign subject—necessitates an annihilation that the fantasy setting elaborates as a series of images collapsed into a simultaneity. Within this setting the moment of simultaneity, positing a teleological movement, conjoins desire and pleasure with a certain violence:[36] "At one moment in time" incommensurable territories, pasts, and social divisions are obliterated and a new order is put in its place characterized by new forms of valorized difference that are commensurable. In short, the moment of emergence of the nation-people portrays "the transformation of the individual from a member of a tribe or village or a caste or a creed or a language group to a citizen of India" (Vyas 1993, 83).

It is important to specify the quality of the new space of the nation-state that the fantasy constitutes. In dramatizing a rupture, a moment of separation that creates the land of the people, the fantasy of the nation-state thus produces not only the sovereign subject but also a prior subject of difference defined by a previous territorial allegiance, all of which the space of the nation-state must contain.[37] This is what I mean by *anteriority*. In other words, the fantasy that inaugurates a spatial separation between a putative interior and exterior necessitates a *temporal* production of a "before," without which the telos of the nation-state cannot progress. The history of cartography has an important relation to this fantasy procedure, producing time through space.[38]

Cartography is of central importance to the nation-state's fantasy, not least because it signifies a valorized past that within the fantasy has been expressly preserved by the nation-state: "The Survey of India is the *national survey and mapping organization* of our country . . . and is *the oldest scientific department* of the Government of India. It was *set up in 1767*" (Survey of India 1995). In other words, cartography represents a past prior to the emergence of the new order, that, unlike the subjects and territories of prior difference, has the sanction of a fantasy that produces and selectively abolishes a past. But apart from its position within the fantasy of the People-as-One, cartography has an important significance for the historical constitution and reiteration of that fantasy.

Cartography prior to 1947 may be understood as a product and vehicle of colonial domination that not only transformed land into territory but also constituted colonial sovereignty. Cartography sought to produce and visualize knowledge of India as a whole constituted by innumerable differences. Post-1947 cartography, as a technique of enumeration and visualization, has been reconstituted as an apparatus of the nation-state's power that is both "totalizing" and "individualizing" (Appadurai 1996; Cohn 1996). "Drawing up maps of zones and sub-zones of selected material traits which appear to have persisted over long historical periods,"[39] the Survey of India has been involved not only with the production of India's frontiers and boundaries discussed further below, but also with the constitution and visualization of the internal differentiation of India (i.e., "culture areas") in the most minute fashion—village settlement patterns, types of cottages, staple diet, kinds of fats and oils used, kinds of oil presses, types of plows, types of husking implements, men's dress, women's dress, foot gear, and bullock carts (Cohn 1966). Cartography, by generating and visualizing constitutive relations of people and places, has not merely made possible a certain scopic recognition of the formative moment of the "new order" of new territorial allegiance—the sight, both pleasurable and violent, of subjectification. Cartography has also constituted the anterior difference from which, in the fantasy of the People-as-One, the nation-state must emerge. In the national cartography, the production of particular places facilitates a displacement (or the abolition of places) dramatized in the fantasy of the territorial integrity of India, without which the new order of the nation cannot emerge. In this case, the words of de Certeau are particularly appropriate: "The places people live in are like the presences of diverse absences. What can be seen designates what is no longer there" (1984, 108).

Constituted in the interrelated production of cartography and fantasy, the ambivalence of the valorized unity in diversity of the people of India may be understood to turn upon a complex relation of diversity to difference, illuminating how difference cannot be singularized. Two forms of difference are at stake here. First of all, for unity in diversity, the subject of difference is the individual transformed into a citizen—this is a subject constituted at the time of the advent of the "new order" of the nation-state. In distinction, the emergence of the nation-state necessitates the production and valorization of the ontological integrity of a particular subject of difference *before* the imposition of the law of the nation: insofar as the desire for union is based on a prior disunion of difference, and insofar as the constitution of the sovereignty and integrity of the nation-state is signified by the absence of incommensurable difference established through annihilation and incorporation.[40] Difference thus has become both a valued sign of democracy and the basic premise legitimizing the use of violence within a given territory: Prior difference stands against the egalitarian desires of representational democracy, and thus the return of difference as incommensurable is always a potential threat that the nation-state must perpetually negotiate. Through these negotiations, the nation-state repeatedly inserts into the present the fantasy moment of origin.

The Questioning Subject

In light of these reflections on time, space, difference, and the marginality of the Sikh subject, the national fantasy of sovereignty and integrity can be reconsidered from another position, that of the cartographic production of the Indian totality. To do this, let me return to the problem of the Restricted Zone.

Recall the prohibitions articulated in the Official Secret Act and the Criminal Law Amendment Act: Anyone who publishes or circulates a map that is "likely to affect the sovereignty and integrity of India" or that "tantamounts to questioning the territorial integrity of India" shall be "punishable with imprisonment for a term which may extend to three years, or with fine, or with both." What is interesting here is that the juridico-political procedures of the Indian nation-state produce a specific kind of subject of difference—the questioning subject—characterized by a discursivity and addressivity that may be facilitated by and embodied in maps or visual representations in general. These juridico-political procedures also constitute a sovereign subject—the people of India—the extent and limit of which is circumscribed by the territorial integrity of India. Additionally, these procedures position the questioning subject in a specific antagonistic relation with the sovereignty and territorial integrity of India, a relation that maps mediate.

The anxiety of the Indian nation-state, formed around this antagonistic relation, may be described in functional terms. The questioning subject, in many ways like the demanding Sikh subject, signifies a lack of knowledge or respect for the sovereignty and integrity of India, thus taking on the quality of an outsider—the enemy of the People—whose appearance calls forth the imperative of the Indian nation-state to anxiously elaborate and enforce its sovereignty and integrity. In turn, the opposition of the questioning subject and the sovereign subject qualifies the space of the Indian nation-state as an interiority that serves as the base from which relations with a threatening exteriority can be managed. The Restricted Zone demands careful surveillance because, being contiguous with an international boundary, the periphery of the nation-state's territory may constitute a conjunction as well as a disjunction between interiority and exteriority. The Restricted Zone, in this sense, is like the older cartographic category of the "frontier zone," of which East has written: "In the frontier zone are usually concentrated a large part of the defensive forces and strongholds of the state, for the purpose of the frontier is to create a strong frame within which the state may exercise its functions and its citizens may live in security" (1965, 98). In this functional conceptualization, cartography thus serves to delimit and visualize (or conceal for purposes of defense) the division of a spatial totality into values of interiority and exteriority.

Let me take this formulation a few steps further to show how a functional reading belies an ambivalence in the form of the nation-state. The authority of the government of India, which determines what is "likely to affect the sovereignty and integrity of India" or what "tantamounts to questioning the territorial integrity of India," is based in part upon the power to produce and evaluate forms of knowledge as accurate or inaccurate. The enactment of this authority, though, is characterized by a certain vicissitude. On the one hand, it is illegal to produce and circulate a detailed map of the Restricted Zone (in other words, a map which is "accurate"); yet, on the other hand, it is illegal to produce and circulate a map of the Restricted Zone which is "inaccurate" in its depictions of the boundaries and frontiers of India.

These two mutually incompatible assertions have certain implications that need to be spelled out. First of all, if the rules were followed, it would be impossible for any institution other than the Survey of India (for the exclusive use by the government of India) to make a map of India. What makes the questioning subject a threat is not only that it expresses doubt or incomprehension regarding the territorial integrity of India, but also that it produces and circulates maps that display this particular lack. What makes the Survey of India a protectorate of sovereignty and integrity is that it does not make available any detailed or large-scale maps of the Restricted Zone. This suggests, though, that it is impossible for the people of India, who embody ultimate sovereignty, to know or represent precisely the constitution and limits of their (India's) sovereignty and integrity. Not having the ability to know or represent their own sovereignty or integrity, the people of India now appear to take on the qualities that define the alterity of the questioning subject. Unable to know what the sovereign subject must know, are the people of India not bound to question the integrity of India? And simultaneously, is the Indian nation-state thus not bound to regard the people of India with varying degrees of affection and hostility? This ambivalence, by which the part that stands in for the whole paradoxically reintroduces the figure of the other, is indicative of a split that interrupts any notion of spatial totality, exteriority, or interiority—not between state apparatus and society, or between (national) self and (external) other (or, for that matter, between the demanding Sikh and the nation), but within the sovereign subject.

This ambivalent process of social identification exemplifies an important point of mediation and discernment between the psychoanalytic subject of fantasy and the object of the nation-state's fantasy. According to Torok, in psychoanalytic theory, the "intrusion of fantasy causes the ego to give up its own self-government for a moment. . . . While remaining the seat of its actions, the ego momentarily refuses to be its author . . . the ego is as yet incapable of assuming responsibility for either the affect or the representation" (1994, 35). It is exactly this repeated yielding of the "individual" ego that forms the basis for, in the UN's terminology, the self-government or independence of the collective sovereignty of the people. In other words, constituted through historically specific and repeated productions of fantasy, it is the nation that claims (or disowns) responsibility and authorship for individual action, as well as affect and representation.

In other words, in psychoanalytic theory, fantasy is conceived of as a symptom that indicates the possible existence of the ego, an abstract structure. In terms of the nation-state, fantasy does not intrude upon the "self-government" of the nation, but constitutes the people as sovereign, the space of sovereignty, and the disjunctive temporality of authority and responsibility. In short, fantasy constitutes an ambivalent self-government of the nation. Within these terms, we see the limits of any notion of imagination, with its fixation on the individual, and offer instead an analytic of the nation as *fantastic* community.

The Nightmare of Diversity

I would like to conclude by returning to South Asian studies in spring 1957, this time not in the United States but France. It was then that, in the inaugural issue of the journal *Contributions to Indian Sociology,* Louis Dumont began to develop a critique that would reorient the direction of Indian studies. By reconstructing a "proper relation between [sociology] and Indology," Dumont asserted that "we learn in the first place never to forget that India is *one*" (1957, 7, 9). According to Dumont, although "the unity of India is a sort of common-place," it was nevertheless "essential that this unity be postulated from the outset" (1957, 9). The problem of diversity was central of importance: The postulate that "India is one" did not prevent the recognition of regional or social difference; rather, it was through diversity that the original position of the totality of India was verified. Thanks to the appropriation of the notion of totality into Indian sociology from Indology, Dumont claimed, "the sort of nightmare of perpetual diversity which haunts the naive observer is banished" (1957, 13).

Dumont went on to develop the basic formulation to banish diversity in *Homo Hierarchicus* (1980). In this monumental text the main argument is that caste is a religious hierarchy encompassing economic and political formations. More particularly, hierarchy is the essence of India, and caste is its expression. The idiom of expression, its mode of manifestation, is the ideology of religion. The structure of hierarchy is rooted in the forms of relations of the parts (particular castes) to the whole—not, as postulated in other forms of structuralism, in the specific relations of part to part (Radcliffe-Brown 1952). The forms of these relations and the basis of religious ideology are determined by a basic opposition of pure and impure. Ultimately, the system of (unchanging) identity, which encompasses the contradictions of politico-economic change, constitutes India as a whole.

I bring up Dumont because, despite being relegated to a seemingly minor position in South Asian studies in the United States today, his work set a definitive precedent that in many ways has organized much of the research on India.[41] Particularly, Dumont produces India as a spatial totality which is, on the one hand, natural and originary and, on the other, constitutive and ultimately determining of identity. Given these propositions, the point I would like to make is evident: In Dumont's theory, positing India as a spatial totality is a means of constituting an Indian time (of the ancient system of caste) that is repeated and embodied in each instance of diversity.

Henri Lefebvre has noted, "Not everything has been said—far from it—about the inscription of time in space" (1993, 130). We may reconsider Lefebvre from a critical position whereby the production of an apparently totalized space has become inseparable from a particular temporalization—in this case of points of anteriority. We may also begin to question whether or not proposals of the identity and wholeness of the sovereign subject, the citizen, or the People, can remain anywhere other than at the level of fantasy.

Notes

Research for this chapter was conducted at different times between 1995 and 2000 in India, England, and the United States. My thanks to the archivists of the Parliamentary Library and the Nehru Memorial Museum Library in New Delhi and of the British Library in London. Support for research and writing was provided by the National Science Foundation, Fulbright-Hays, the Mellon Foundation, and the Harvard Academy. My gratitude to Arjun Appadurai, Bernard S. Cohn, Jean Comaroff, Homi Bhabha, and Lauren Berlant who read several versions of this chapter at earlier stages.

1 This shift is ironic because Jameson, Harvey, and Gupta and Ferguson claim to be following Lefebvre's lead.

2 One might note Gupta and Ferguson's basic misconception of cartographic procedures: "The representation of the world as a collection of 'countries,' as in most world maps, sees it as an inherently fragmented space" (1992, 8).

3 *Ekta* (unity/identity/integration), *rajya* (state)-*anek* (not one/several), *dharam* (religion)-*anek*, *bhasha* (language)-*anek*, *jati* (caste)-*anek*, *granth* (holy book)-*anek*—*phir bhi ham sab ek* (even then/still we are all one).

4 Consider also Ziauddin Khan's formulation: "[National integration] involves a dismantling of social and emotional distances, and building bridges over regional, cultural, and religious differences" (1983, 4).

5 Quotes in the following passages come from two governmental documents: "Instruction for Publication of Maps by Central/State Government Departments/Offices and Private Publishers," Government of India (1987) and *Constitution Amendment in India*, Lok Sabha Secretariat, R. C. Bhardwaj, ed. (1994).

6 Consider, for example, the words of Indira Gandhi on 1 November 1966, after ten

years of conflict with Sikhs over the creation of a Punjab Suba: "Punjab takes new shape on 1 November as a predominantly Punjabi-speaking state. With the fulfillment of this aspiration, I trust the dynamic people of Punjab will apply themselves with renewed energy to the task of agricultural and industrial development. Their record since independence in building up a new economy has been a proud one" (Sharma, 161).

7 "Punjab Police Told to Step Up Surveillance." *Hindu* (16 March 1996).

8 Report of the National Integration Committee (NIC) (7 April 1986).

9 Ibid.

10 NIC (11 April 1990).

11 *Hindu* (22 March 1996).

12 The question of cartography is not a matter of judging degrees of failure or concealment in representing cultural diversity or of dismissing the way maps "capture the world in miniature" (Duncan and Ley 1993, 2).

13 "Train Linking Two Takhts Flagged Off on Return Trip," *Hindu* (8 March 1996); "Two Functions Held to Flag Off Train," *Times of India* (8 March 1996).

14 The SGPC is the organization that claims responsibility for administering and regulating Sikh religious practices and temples in India and around the world.

15 *Hindu*, half-page advertisement (3 March 1996).

16 Bhabha explains the distinction of the pedagogical and performative: "The people are the historical 'objects' of a nationalist pedagogy, giving the discourse an authority that is based on the pre-given or constituted historical origin *in the past*; the people are also the 'subjects' of a process of signification that must erase any prior or originary presence of the nation-people to demonstrate the prodigious, living principles of the people as contemporaneity: as that sign of the *present* through which national life is redeemed and iterated as a reproductive process" (1994, 145).

17 The demand for a Sikh homeland in relation to a proposed independent India can be understood in terms of a genealogy prior to 1946 (see, for example, Axel 2001). I would note also that Kalmadi's use of *demand* to refer to a desire for a train connecting Amritsar and Nanded is a familiar if bizarre equivocation of political rhetoric, but it is not entirely unfounded. In the "Revised List of 15 Demands Received from the Akali Dal by Government in October, 1981," demand number eight called for the renaming of the Flying Mail Train to the Harimandir Express (Khushwant Singh, 459).

18 The following is a summary from Basu (1995, 65–71), *Report on the Working of the Ministry of States* (March 1949), *Report on the States Reorganization Commission* (1955), and the *White Paper on Indian States* (1948). See also Patel (1949).

19 Part A in the First Schedule of the Constitution referred to the Indian provinces.

20 Such a celebratory moment may be considered premature considering Kashmir—not a minor example—and that because of the very tenets of the Constitution, the integration and reorganization of territories could possibly—and indeed has—continued without pause (for example, the subsequent formation of Arunachal Pradesh, Gujarat, Goa, Haryana, Himachal Pradesh, Manipur, Meghalaya, Mizoram, Nagaland, and Tripura).

21 K. Singh (1991, 473–483).

22　K. Singh (1991, 307); see also the documents on "The Reorganization of Punjab" in Sharma (1995).

23　Pamphlet, "Presidential Address of the Sikh National Convention Held at Jallian-wala Bagh, Amritsar, on 17 December 1950" (Daryaganj, Delhi: Ashoka Press).

24　Taussig's reflections on this problem are relevant: "There is something frightening, I think, merely in saying this conjunction of reason and violence exists, not only because it makes violence scary, as if imbued with the greatest legitimating force there can be, reason itself, and not only because it makes reason scary by indicating how it's snuggled deep into the armpit of terror, but because we so desperately need to cling to reason—as instituted—as the bulwark against the terrifying anomic and chaos pressing in on all sides" (1993, 222).

25　NIC (7 April 1986).

26　NIC proceedings (1960, 1967, 1981, 1984, 1986, 1990, 1993); Lok Sabha Debates (#2494, 7/8/85; #251, 5/11/86; #462, 25/11/91; #1401, 3/3/94); Rajya Sabha Debates (#320, 6/11/86; #2497, 29/8/90; #498, 4/9/91); LARRIS, Press Clipping section, National Integration (1993–1995).

27　NIC Report (1960).

28　NIC (11 April 1990).

29　Lok Sabha Debates (#2494, 7/8/85); NIC proceedings (12 January 1984).

30　This is an important distinction. In this historical case, I am arguing that there is something very specific about the formation of the nation-state and its regulatory procedures. Fantasy designates this difference (and provides the basis for a critique), a difference that is distinct from the way Khalistan is positioned within Sikh diasporic life. The diaspora, to put it crudely, is neither a new kind of nation-state nor a nation-state in nascent form.

31　For example, speaking as leader of the Jana Sangh Group in Parliament in 1961, A. B. Vajpayee (India's present-day prime minister) argued that the origin of the modern Indian nation-state derives from an immeasurable past that grants India a pre-given authority as an exclusive Hindu state: "India is an ancient nation. Its emancipation from the foreign yoke in 1947 marked just the commencement of a new chapter in its history" (National Integration, Note submitted by Sh. A. B. Vajpayee, leader of the Jana Sangh Group in Parliament at the National Integration Conference held at New Delhi, 28–30 September 1961). Ironically, it may be noted that Vajpayee, during his first short tenure as prime minister, went in May 1996 to the Golden Temple in Amritsar where he said: "It is time to forget the past and look forward" (Asian Age, 27 May 1996). In a recent unpublished piece, "A Different Modernity: Colonialism, Nationalism, and the Idea of India," Gyan Prakash argues cogently that, in creating an Indian nationalism prior to 1947, Gandhi and Nehru, their differences notwith-standing, maintained a similar understanding of the origins of the nation. This is an important point because the Gandhian/Nehruvian fantasy of India's origin, suc-cessively taken up by right-wing Hindu parties, could not be understood as the basis of the nation-state after 1947, particularly in constitutional law.

32　Virendra Singh v. State of U.P. (1955), SCR 415 in Vyas (1993, 435–36).

33　Considering my discussion of the Patel scheme, it may be important to note that another aspect that the fantasy of the nation reflects is a certain form of forgetting, not of difference, but of the negotiation of the nation-state as a spatial totality.

34 Whether or not India is federal, quasi-federal, or a unitary system has been a matter of much debate (see, for example, Basu 1995).

35 In Annex B (Internal Self-Government), see, for example, Section 1, Form of Government: Complete Freedom of the People of the Territory to Choose the Form of Government Which They Desire. Resolution 742 (VIII) of the General Assembly (27 November 1953) (Factors Indicative of the Attainment of Independence or of Other Separate Systems of Self-Government).

36 In 1993 Justice S. Mohan, Judge of the Supreme Court, reiterated this formulation of desire in terms of national integration, "which requires abolition of the hereditary social structure." He said: "The object is to create a sense of oneness as belonging to one nation, speaking one voice. Unity in diversity is the crying need of the home. . . . All communities must be drawn into the national mainstream. . . . This idea of one nation must penetrate into nook and corner. . . . A national character arises from the yearning of men to be united in a bondage of oneness" (*Hindustan Times*, 3 April 1993).

37 This is an important point at which to distinguish the fantasy of the People-as-One from the fantasy of origin as elaborated in psychoanalysis. As Laplanche and Pontalis summarize, "[The fantasy of origin] tries to cover the moment of *separation* between *before* and *after*, whilst still containing both" (1986, 24). In formal terms, the distinction is that the fantasy of the nation-state does not disavow separation or difference; what is disavowed is the ambivalence of the desire regarding difference (as something valorized and feared).

38 Note the distinction I am making from Jameson's argument regarding the domination of categories of space over time (1984, 64), or Harvey's argument that "progress entails . . . the ultimate 'annihilation of space through time'" (1989, 205).

39 Anthropological Survey, quoted in Cohn (1966, 19).

40 For analyses of the way "before the law" indicates an anteriority, the ontological integrity of the subject as temporally prior, see Butler (1990, 35–78) and Derrida (1987, 139–148).

41 And this, despite Appadurai's interventions (1986, 1988).

References

Official Documents from Parliamentary Archives, New Delhi, India

Larris, Press Clipping Section, *National Integration*.
Lok Sabha Debates (#2494, 7/8/85; #251, 5/11/86; #462, 25/11/91; #1401, 3/3/94).
National Convention on Unity and Democracy, 27–29 January 1968.
National Integration Committee, Verbatim Record of Proceedings, 12 January 1984.
National Integration Council: Verbatim Record of Proceedings, 7 April 1986.
National Integration Committee, Verbatim Record of Proceedings, 11 April 1990.
Proceedings of the Meeting on the Standing Committee of the National Integration Council Held on Friday, 22 October 1993.

National Integration, Note submitted by Sh. A.B. Vajpayee, Leader of the Jana Sangh Group in Parliament at the National Integration Conference held at New Delhi, on 28, 29, and 30 September 1961.

Rajya Sabha Debates (#320, 6/11/86, #2497, 29/8/90; #498, 4/9/91).

Report of the National Integration Committee, 1960.

Report of the National Integration Committee, 1967.

Survey of India: Instruction for Publication of Maps by Central/State Government Departments/Offices and Private Publishers.

Books and Journals

Abraham, Nicolas and Maria Torok. 1994. *The Shell and the Kernal.* Chicago: University of Chicago Press.

Aiyer, C. P., ed. 1961. *Disintegration and How to Avert It.* Bombay: Bharatiya Vidya Bhavan.

Appadurai, Arjun. 1986. "Theory in Anthropology: Center and Periphery." *Comparative Studies in Society and History* 28, no. 2: 356–61.

———. 1988. "Putting Hierarchy in Its Place." *Cultural Anthropology* 3, no. 1 (February): 37–50.

———. 1996. *Modernity at Large: Cultural Dimensions of Globalization.* Minneapolis: University of Minnesota Press.

Axel, Brian Keith. 1996a. "Time and Threat: Questioning the Production of the Diaspora as an Object of Study." In *History and Anthropology* 9, no. 2: 415–43.

———. 1996b. "Notes on Space, Cartography, and Gender." In *The Transmission of Sikh Heritage in the Diaspora,* edited by Pashaura Singh and N. Gerald Barrier. New Delhi: Manohar.

———. 1998. "Disembodiment and the Total Body: A Response to Enwezor on Contemporary on South African Representation." In *Third Text,* no. 43 (summer): 3–16.

———. 2001. *The Nation's Tortured Body: Violence, Representation, and the Formation of a Sikh "Diaspora."* Durham, NC: Duke University Press.

Arnold, David. 1988. "Touching the Body: Perspectives on the Indian Plague," in *Selected Subaltern Studies,* edited by Ranajit Guha and Gayatri Spivak. Oxford: Oxford University Press.

Basu, Durga Das. 1995. *Introduction to the Constitution of India.* Delhi: Prentice Hall.

Bhabha, Homi K. 1992. "Postcolonial Authority and Postmodern Guilt." In *Cultural Studies,* edited by Lawrence Grossberg, Cary Nelson, and Paula Treichler. New York: Routledge.

———. 1994. *The Location of Culture.* London: Routledge.

Bhattacharya, Vivek R. 1985. *Towards National Unity and Integration.* Delhi: Metropolitan.

Blunt, Alison, and Gillian Rose, eds. 1994. *Writing Women and Space: Colonial and Postcolonial Geographies.* New York: Guilford Press.

Breckenridge, Carol A., and Peter van der Veer. 1993. *Orientalism and the Postcolonial Predicament.* Philadelphia: University of Pennsylvania Press.

Burgin, Victor. 1986. "Diderot, Barthes, Vertigo." In *Formations of Fantasy,* edited by Victor Burgin, James Donald, and Cora Kaplan. New York: Routledge.

——. 1992. "Perverse Space." In *Sexuality and Space*, edited by Beatriz Colomina. Princeton, NJ: Princeton University School of Architecture.

Butler, Judith. 1990. *Gender Trouble: Feminism and the Subversion of Identity*. New York: Routledge.

Caveeshar, Sardul Singh. 1950. *Sikh Politics*. Delhi: Ashoka Press.

Cerney, J. W., and B. Wilson. 1976. "The Effect of Orientation on the Recognition of Simple Maps." *The Canadian Cartographer* 13, no. 2: 132–38.

Chakrabarty, Dipesh. 1983. "Conditions for Knowledge of Working-Class Conditions: Employers, Government, and the Jute Workers of Calcutta, 1890–1940." In *Selected Subaltern Studies*, edited by Ranajit Guha and Gayatri Spivak. Oxford: Oxford University Press.

Chatterjee, Partha. 1993. *The Nation and Its Fragments: Colonial and Postcolonial Histories*. Princeton, NJ: Princeton University Press.

Cohn, Bernard S. 1957. "India as a Racial, Linguistic, and Cultural Area." In *Introducing India in Liberal Education*, edited by Milton Singer. Chicago: University of Chicago Press.

——. 1967. "Regions Subjective and Objective: Their Relation to the Study of Modern Indian History and Society." In *Regions and Regionalism in South Asian Studies: An Exploratory Study*, edited by Robert Crane. Duke University: Monograph and Occasional Papers Series, no. 5.

——. 1977. "African Models and Indian Histories." In *Realm and Region in Traditional India*, edited by Richard Fox. Duke University: Monograph and Occasional Papers Series, no. 14.

——. 1987. *An Anthropologist Among the Historians and Other Essays*. Delhi: Oxford University Press.

——. 1996. *Colonialism and Its Forms of Knowledge: The British in India*. Princeton, NJ: Princeton University Press.

Colomina, Beatriz, ed. 1992. *Sexuality and Space*. Princeton, NJ: Princeton University School of Architecture.

Cormack, Leslie B. 1994. "The Fashioning of an Empire: Geography and the State in Elizabethan England." In *Geography and Empire*, edited by Neil Smith and Anne Godlewska. Oxford: Blackwell.

Crane, Robert. 1967. *Regions and Regionalism in South Asian Studies: An Exploratory Study*. Duke University: Monograph and Occasional Papers Series, no. 5.

Crow, Dennis, ed. 1996. *Geography and Identity*. Washington, D.C.: Maissoneuve Press.

Daniel, E. Valentine. 1984. *Fluid Signs: Being a Person the Tamil Way*. Berkeley: University of California Press.

de Certeau, Michel. 1984. *The Practice of Everyday Life*. Berkeley: University of California Press.

Deol, Gurdev Singh. 1992. "Political Philosophy of Guru Gobind Singh." *Spokesman* (13 January 1992).

Derrida, Jacques. 1987. "Devant la Loi." In *Kafka and the Contemporary Critical Performance*, edited by Alan Udoff. Bloomington: Indiana University Press.

Dicey, Albert Venn. 1924. *The Law of Constitution*. London: Macmillan.

Dirks, Nicholas B., ed. 1992. *Colonialism and Culture*. Ann Arbor: University of Michigan Press.

Dumont, Louis. 1957. "For a Sociology of India." *Contributions to Indian Sociology* 1 (April): 1–41.

——. 1964a. "Nationalism and Communalism." *Contributions to Indian Sociology* 7: 30–70.

——. 1964 b. "Note on Territory." *Contributions to Indian Sociology* 7: 71–76.

——. 1980. *Homo Hierarchicus: The Caste System and Its Implications*. Chicago: University of Chicago Press.

Duncan, James, and David Ley, eds. 1993. *Place/Culture/Representation*. London: Routledge.

Foucault, Michel. 1979. *Discipline and Punish: The Birth of the Prison*. New York: Vintage Books.

Fox, Richard. 1977. *Realm and Region in Traditional India*. Duke University: Monograph and Occasional Papers Series, no. 14.

Gordon, East W. 1965. *The Geography Behind History*. New York: Norton and Co.

Gregory, Derek. 1994. *Geographical Imaginations*. Cambridge: Blackwell.

Grewal, J. S. 1990. *The New Cambridge History of India: The Sikhs of the Punjab*. Cambridge: Cambridge University Press.

Guha, Ranajit. 1983. "The Prose of Counter-Insurgency." In *Selected Subaltern Studies*, edited by Ranajit Guha and Gayatri Chakravorty Spivak. New York: Oxford University Press.

Gupta, Akhil, and Ferguson, James. 1992. "Beyond 'Culture': Space, Identity, and the Politics of Difference." *Cultural Anthropology* 7, no. 1: 6–23.

Harley, J. B. 1988a. "Maps, Knowledge, and Power." In *Iconography and Landscape*. Cambridge: Cambridge University Press.

——. 1988b. "Silences and Secrecy: The Hidden Agenda of Cartography in Early Modern Europe." *Imago Mundi* 40: 57–76.

——. 1989. "Deconstructing the Map." *Cartographica* 26, no. 2: 1–20.

——. 1992a. "Art, Science, and power in Sixteenth-Century Dutch Cartography." *Cartographica* 29, no. 2: 10–19.

——. 1992b. "Rereading the Maps of the Columbian Encounter." *Annals of the Association of American Geographers* 82, no. 3: 522–35.

Harvey, David. 1989. *The Condition of Postmodernity*. Oxford: Blackwell.

Helgerson, Richard. 1992. *Forms of Nationhood: The Elizabethan Writing of England*. Chicago: University of Chicago Press.

Helweg, Arthur. 1979. *The Sikhs in England: The Development of a Migrant Community*. Delhi: Oxford University Press.

Hooson, David. 1994. *Geography and National Identity*. Oxford: Blackwell.

Inden, Ronald. 1990. *Imagining India*. Cambridge: Blackwell.

International Journal of Punjab Studies. 1994. vol. 1, no. 1.

Jameson, Fredric. 1984. "The Cultural Logic of Capital." *New Left Review* 146: 53–92.

——. 1988. "Cognitive Mapping." In *Marxism and the Interpretation of Culture*, edited by Cary Nelson and Lawrence Grossberg. Urbana: University of Illinois Press.

Kaur, Rajinder. 1992. *Sikh Identity and National Integration*. New Delhi: Intellectual Publishing House.

Keates, John S. 1973. *Cartographic Design and Production*. New York: Longman Scientific and Technical.

Khan, Ziauddin. 1983. *National Integration in India: Issues and Dimensions*. Delhi: Associated.

Krishnamurti, Y. G. 1939. *Indian States and the Federal Plan*. Bombay: Ratansey Parker and Co.

Kuper, Hilda. 1972. "The Language of Sites in the Politics of Space." *American Anthropologist* 74, no. 3: 411–25.

LaBrack, Bruce W. 1988. *The Sikhs of Northern California: 1904–1986*. New York: American Migration Series.

——. 1989. "The New Patrons." In *The Sikh Diaspora: Migration and Experience Beyond Punjab*, edited by Gerald Barrier and Verne Dusenberry. Columbia, Mo.: South Asia Books.

Laplanche, Jean and Jean-Bertrand Pontalis. 1973. Entry on "Phantasy (or Fantasy)." In *The Language of Psychoanalysis*. New York: Norton.

——. 1986. "Fantasy and the Origins of Sexuality." In *Formations of Fantasy*, edited by Victor Burgin. New York: Routledge.

Lefebvre, Henri. 1993. *The Production of Space*. Oxford: Blackwell.

Lefort, Claude. 1986. *The Political Forms of Modern Society: Bureaucracy, Democracy, Totalitarianism*. Cambridge: MIT Press.

Lelyveld, David. 1993. "The Fate of Hindustani: Colonial Knowledge and the Project of a National Language." In *Orientalism and the Postcolonial Predicament*, edited by Carol Breckenridge and Peter van der Veer. Philadelphia: University of Pennsylvania Press.

Liben, L. S., and R. Downs. 1989. "Understanding Maps as Symbols: The Development of Map Concepts in Children." In *Advances in Child Development and Behavior*, edited by John Reese. Vol. 22. San Diego: Academic Press.

Livingstone, David N. 1992. *The Geographical Tradition*. Oxford: Blackwell.

——. 1994. "Climate's Moral Economy: Science, Race, and Place in Post-Darwinian British and American Geography." In *Geography and Empire*, edited by Neil Smith and Anne Godlewska. Oxford: Blackwell.

Ludden, David. 1993. "Orientalist Empiricism: Transformations of Colonial Knowledge." In *Orientalism and the Postcolonial Predicament*, edited by Carol Breckenridge and Peter van der Veer. Philadelphia: University of Pennsylvania Press.

Metz, Christian. 1982. *The Imaginary Signifier: Psychoanalysis and the Cinema*. Bloomington: Indiana University Press.

Misra, R. P. 1969. *Fundamentals of Cartography*. Prasaranga, India: University of Mysore.

Monmonier, Mark S. 1982. *Computer-Assisted Cartography: Principles and Prospects*. Englewood Cliffs, NJ: Prentice-Hall.

——. 1993. *Mapping It Out: Expository Cartography for the Humanities and Social Sciences*. Chicago: University of Chicago Press.

Moyer, R. 1978. "Psychophysical Functions for Perceived and Remembered Size." *Science* 200: 330–32.

Muller, J. C., ed. 1991. *Advances in Cartography*. New York: Elsevier Applied Science.

Mulvey, Laura. 1989. "Visual Pleasure and Narrative Cinema." In *Visual and Other Pleasures*. Bloomington: Indiana University Press.

Nash, Catherine. 1994. "Remapping the Body/Land: New Cartographies of Identity, Gender, and Landscape in Ireland." In *Writing Women and Space: Colonial and Postcolonial Geographies*, edited by Alison Blunt and Gillian Rose. New York: Guilford Press.

Nayyar, Deepak. 1994. *Migration, Remittances, and Capital Flows: The Indian Experience*. Delhi: Oxford University Press.

Oberoi, Harjot S. 1987. "From Punjab to 'Khalistan': Territoriality and Metacommentary." *Pacific Affairs* 60, no. 1 (spring): 26–41.

—. 1994. *The Construction of Religious Boundaries: Culture, Identity, and Diversity in the Sikh Tradition*. Oxford: Oxford University Press.

Orlove, Benjamin. 1993a. "The Ethnography of Maps: The Cultural and Social Contexts of Cartographic Representation in Peru." *Cartographica*, Special Monograph 44, "Introducing Cultural and Social Cartography" (spring): 29–46.

—. 1993b. "Putting Race in Its Place: Order in Colonial and Postcolonial Peruvian Geography." *Social Research* 60, no. 2 (summer): 301–36.

Patel, Sardar. 1949. *On Indian Problems*. Government of India: Publications Division.

Prakash, Gyan. 1990. *Bounded Histories: Genealogies of Labor Servitude in Colonial India*. Cambridge: Cambridge University Press.

Radcliffe-Brown, A. R. 1952. *Structure and Function in Primitive Society*. New York: Free Press.

Raheja, Gloria G. 1988. *The Poison in the Gift*. Chicago: University of Chicago Press.

Richards, Thomas. 1992. "Archive and Utopia." *Representations* 37 (winter): 104–35.

Robinson, Arthur H. 1952. *The Look of Maps: An Examination of Cartographic Design*. Madison: University of Wisconsin Press.

Robinson, Arthur H., and Barbara B. Petchenik. 1976. *The Nature of Maps: Essays Toward Understanding Maps and Mapping*. Chicago: University of Chicago Press.

Robinson, Arthur H., and Randall D. Sale. 1953. *Elements of Cartography*. New York: Wiley.

Rocher, Rosane. 1993. "British Orientalism in the Eighteenth Century: The Dialectics of Knowledge and Government," in *Orientalism and the Postcolonial Predicament*, edited by Carol Breckenridge and Peter van der Veer. Philadelphia: University of Pennsylvania Press.

Rose, Gillian. 1997. "Spatialities of 'Community,' Power and Change: The Imagined Geographies of Community Arts Projects." *Cultural Studies* 11, no. 1: 1–16.

Rose, Jacqueline. 1996. *States of Fantasy*. Oxford: Clarendon Press.

Rundstrom, Robert A., ed. 1993. *Introducing Cultural and Social Cartography* (a Special Edition of *Cartographica*). Monograph 44. Toronto: University of Toronto Press.

Saggi, P. D. 1968. *We Shall Unite: A Plea for National Integration, Unity Builds the Nation, People Build Unity*. New Delhi: Indian Publications.

Schwartzberg, J. E. 1992. *Historical Atlas of South Asia*. London: Oxford University Press.

Sharma, P. K. 1995. *The Story of Punjab: Yesterday and Today*, vol. 2. Delhi: Deep and Deep.

Sharma, Sudesh. 1968. *Union Territory Administration in India.* Patiala: Chandi.

Shiryaev, E. E. 1977. *Computers and the Representation of Geographical Data.* New York: Wiley.

Singh, Gopal. 1994. *Politics of Sikh Homeland.* Delhi: Ajanta.

Singh, Gurmit, ed. 1989. *History of Sikh Struggles.* Volume 1 (1946–1966). Delhi: Atlantic.

Singh, Gursharan. 1991. *History of PEPSU: Patiala and East Punjab States Union (1948–1956).* Delhi: Konark.

Singh, Kirpal, ed. 1991. *Partition of Punjab—1947.* Delhi: National Bookshop.

Singh, Khushwant. 1991. *A History of the Sikhs.* Volume 2 (1839–1988). Delhi: Oxford University Press.

Soja, Edward W. 1989. *Postmodern Geographies: The Reassertion of Space in Critical Social Theory.* London: Verso.

Taussig, Michael. 1993. "Maleficium: State Fetishism." In *Fetishism as Cultural Discourse,* edited by Emily Apter and William Pietz. Ithaca, NY: Cornell University Press.

Taylor, Fraser. 1983. *Graphic Communication and Design in Contemporary Cartography.* New York: Wiley.

Vico, Giambattista. 1991. *The New Science of Giambattista Vico.* Ithaca, NY: Cornell University Press.

Vyas, Mohan K. 1993. *National Integration and the Law: Burning Issues and Challenges.* Delhi: Deep and Deep.

Wood, Dennis. 1992. *The Power of Maps.* New York: Guilford Press.

Yaeger, Patricia, ed. 1996. *The Geography of Identity.* Ann Arbor: University of Michigan Press.

Žižek, Slavoj, 1989. *The Sublime Object of Ideology.* London: Verso.

——. 1991. *For They Know Not What They Do.* London: Verso.

Occult Economies and the Violence of Abstraction: Notes from the South African Postcolony

John L. Comaroff and Jean Comaroff

New situations demand new magic.—E. E. Evans-Pritchard, *Witchcraft, Oracles and Magic among the Azande of the Anglo-Egyptian Sudan*[1]

Human beliefs, like all other natural growths, elude the barrier of system. —George Eliot, *Silas Marner*

I

Consider the following four fragments, four notes from postcolonial South Africa. Each is drawn from the contemporary archaeology of the fantastic in this new global age, this "Age of Futilitarianism" wherein postmodern pessimism runs up against the promises of late capitalism.

The first. In March 1996, in a far northeastern village, a baboon, taken to be a witch in disguise, was killed by "necklacing," the infamous manner in which collaborators were dealt with during the late apartheid years.[2] Baboons have long been thought of as potential witch familiars;[3] indeed, a state commission recently referred to them as "professors of witchcraft" (Ralushai et al. 1996, 22). The animal in question "was huge . . . and was carrying a plastic bag" ("South African Villagers" 1996)—this last object was presumably suspect, because it might be used to conceal body parts cut from human victims or, more mundanely, to transport ill-gotten goods. Said the woman who set off the alarm, "There was definitely witchcraft here. Just look at how long it took to catch alight and at how small its body is now that we have . . . killed it" ("South African Villagers" 1996).

The second. "Is it a duck? No, it's the Howick monster," wrote Ellis Mnyandu on June 10 of the same year.[4] Curious crowds visit the Howick Falls in KwaZulu- Natal to glimpse the mysterious twenty-five-foot creature. Absolom Dlamini has not actually caught sight of it yet, but he says there is "a fearsome spirit here which makes you feel like you are being dragged [in]. . . . [It] proves there is a monster down there." Bob Teeney, a white businessman (afficionados of the fantastic in this New Age form a rainbow coalition) claims to have seen and to have photographs, taken by a tourist, of mom, pop, and baby monsters. He argues that they belong to "an aquatic, snake-like dinosaur family known as Plesiosaur." These beasts, say scientists, have been extinct for six million years, give or take a million, and they never lived in fresh water to begin with. An anthropologist, also disappointingly matter-of-fact, assures us that there is no physical object there at all, that the story recuperates an old Zulu myth about a water serpent.[5] Science (and ethnographic authority) aside, people have flocked to the place. If nothing else, this has promoted local commerce, including the sale of likenesses. One sculptor, a crippled craftsman from Zaire, has become a convert. "First I believe in God and then the monsters," he says. "I am making more money than I used to. I call it monster-money" (Mnyandu 1996).

The third. Since 1994, notes Lumkile Mondi, there has been a rise of pyramid-saving schemes in the countryside—some of them founded by old anti-apartheid activists, now "development entrepreneurs," to deal with the destitution of rural blacks.[6] These schemes undertake to pay three times the initial stake, depending for their viability on more and more people signing on. But many investors were not taking their money at maturity, waiting rather to cash in huge sums later on.[7] Mondi says that the managers of one scheme found themselves with R46m, more than they could handle. So they asked a team of authorities—including Mondi himself—to intervene under the Bank Act. Mondi goes on to say that he had been manning a toll-free line to answer investors' questions and also to investigate the "fetishism [of] money and problems of accumulation in rural households." The callers had disconcerted him: he was accused of selling out to "the Boers" by abetting government efforts to control local economic initiatives, even threatened with necklacing. Apartheid, they told him, had made them desperately poor. And the postcolonial state had not helped them. For recompense, they believed, "God brought the scheme to them and changed their lives."[8] Similar schemes are also rampant in white South Africa at present, despite the regulatory efforts of the Business Practices Board and Internal Revenue.[9] One unsubtly titled pyramid scheme, "Rainbow," demands a R10,000 stake and is run in great secrecy by an anonymous cabal with a Liverpool address.

It is said to "conduct [meetings] with an almost religious fervour" and to threaten anyone who divulges the nature of its practices (Cameron 1997).

The fourth. Johannesburg, April 29, 1996. A thirty-eight year old man is arrested in a shopping mall after "trying to sell a pair of blue eyes." The *Star*, the city's largest circulation paper, says that this incident "might be linked to the murder of street children for . . . traditional medicines" ("S. African arrested"). Body parts, it adds, were regularly used in potions for fertility, for success in business, and for luck in love. Those of white children fetched the best prices; hearts and sex organs, too, were in great demand. This tale of an oculist in the economy of the occult was not unusual. The local press is full of such cases, and courts have been kept fairly busy trying those accused of disemboweling their victims, often babies and youths, and either retailing organs in the market in viscera or using them for their own ends (see Wright 1996).[10] Not only body parts, but whole persons too: witches are said to bring the dead back to life as zombies so that they might work for their necromantic masters. Thus, in KwaZulu-Natal, some eighteen months ago, the kin of eleven children killed in a bus crash, allegedly caused by magical intervention, refused to allow them to be buried because they believed that "witches [had] abducted them after bringing them back to life" ("South African Witches" 1996). The bodies in the mortuary, which they had identified earlier, were no longer those of the people they knew. An old woman, suspected of the evil, was dragged from her home and killed by schoolmates of the deceased, who were in turn, jailed.

These fragments may appear lurid, even salacious, from the cool distance of "Academia Americana." In their own context they are not that at all. Each of them, moreover, has parallels elsewhere; indeed, those parts of Europe and the United States beyond the ivory tower, the parts in which ordinary people live, produce their own fair share of the fantastic (Jean Comaroff 1994; Comaroff and Comaroff 1993; see also Geschiere n.d.). The Howick Monster recalls not only its Loch Ness prequel, which it is said to resemble. It also resonates with celluloid cosmologies of the Jurassic kind, making a mammoth montage of the Spielberg mindscape, the Scottish landscape, and Zulu mythology—all the while tapping into an increasingly pervasive obsession with the return of extinct creatures of superhuman potency (note here W. J. T. Mitchell's interesting thesis that the dinosaur is the new American totem). The Leviathan of Natal belongs to a planetary species whose existence confounds the virtual with the veritable, the cinematic with the scientific, gods with godzillas, the prophetic with the profitable.

Likewise, think of the pyramid schemes in South Africa, schemes that put "con" in economics. These recall the ten or so whose crash sparked the Albanian revolution early in 1997.[11] They also bring to mind other scams and stratagems, different yet similar, that flow from a promiscuous mix of scarcity and deregulation. Such schemes—a few legal, many illegal, some alegal—are springing up all over the place nowadays, especially in post-revolutionary societies.[12] Moreover, they are registered at addresses halfway across the world from the site of their local operation, escaping control at least for a time, by insinuating themselves into the slipstream of the global economy.[13] These schemes cover a wide gamut, from familiar forms of chain letters, through national lotteries and offshore (or on-reservation) gambling, to aggressively speculative investment in the stock markets of the world—now itself heavily invested in global funds, which has led to an upsurge of "pump and dump" swindles.[14] There has even arisen a Universal Church in South Africa whose altar piece proclaims the prospect of BMWs in return for prayer.[15] All of these things have a single common denominator: "the magical allure of making money from nothing."[16] Like attempts to weave gold from straw, an alchemy associated with an earlier transition in the economic history of Europe (Schneider 1989), they promise to deliver almost preternatural profits, to yield wealth sans perceptible production, value sans visible effort. In its all-conquering, millennial moment, it appears, capitalism has an effervescent new spirit—a kind of magical, neo-Protestant zeitgeist—arising at its core.[17] *Vide*, the Foundation for New Era Philanthropy, an American pyramid scheme created in order "to change the world for the glory of God," succeeded in persuading 500 nonprofit organizations, Christian colleges, and Ivy League universities to invest $354 million—this on the promise of doubling their money in six months through matching contributions ("Charity Pyramid" 1997).[18] So much for rational economics. And for the disenchantment of modernity.[19]

The stories of witchcraft, body parts, zombies, and the brutalization of children—in which generational antagonisms and curious creatures like the baboon-witch are recurrent motifs—are not peculiarly South African. Everywhere the confident contours and boundaries of the human are being called more and more into question; hence the assertion of animal rights, the fear of invasion by aliens clothed in humdrum bodily form, the dangerous promise of cloning and genetic mutation. Postcolonial Africa is replete with accounts of the rich and powerful appropriating the life force of their lesser compatriots through monstrous means and freakish familiars, in order to strengthen themselves, to realize their ambitions, or to satisfy consuming passions.[20] Similarly, Latin America has, throughout the 1990s, witnessed mass panics about the theft and sale of human organs, especially those of infants and youths.[21] There, and in other parts of the world, the global body shop, like the international commerce in adoption and mail-order matrimony, is seen as a new form of colonialism, the affluent West siphoning off the essence, even appropriating the offspring, of impoverished others for ends both occult and ordinary. All of which gives ample evidence to those at the nether end of the planetary distribution of wealth, of insidious forces, of potent magical technologies and mysterious means of accumulation, of sorcery of one or another sort. That evidence reaches into the heart of Europe itself—note the recent scares there about the satanic abuse of children (La Fontaine 1998),[22] also reports in British broadsheets of a transnational trade in people, again particularly young people.[23] There's the story of the Sado Hangman and the Leather Witch arraigned in Berlin for offering Czech girls on the net to be used in torture, sexual slavery, or whatever—pick-up and disposal of bodies included—at DM 15,000 each (Staunton 1997). This case is neither fanciful nor singular.[24] It reached the Bavarian courts as one of a number of such incidents, many of them implicating the world wide web, that are leaving the pages of the yellow press and entering into the arena of serious social concern.

Precisely because they are at once profoundly parochial and so obviously translocal, these fragments, and innumerable others like them, raise the same conundrums, all of them distilling down to one order of question. As Peter Geschiere (n.d.) recently asked of African and East Asian occult economies: Why now? Why, at this particular point in time, does there appear to be a dramatic intensification—none of these things is new, of course—of appeals to enchantment, to magical means for material ends, to the use of the bodies of some for the empowerment of others?[25] Why now the acute moral panics? And why, in them, do generational antinomies loom so large? What, if anything, has any of this to do with processes of globalization and the forms of capitalism associated with it? With postcoloniality? Or with the sociology of postrevolutionary social worlds? We pose the problem both as a general matter of anthropological concern and, more specifically, of concern to contemporary South Africa. Is it not extraordinary, for example, that the hyper-rationalist, deeply Eurocentric African National Congress saw it necessary, among its first gestures in government, to appoint a commission of inquiry into witchcraft and ritual murder in one of the new provinces (Ralushai et al. 1996)? That it found itself presiding over an ostensible epidemic of mystical evil? That this epidemic, far from abating with the end of apartheid, is on the increase?[26] According to the head of the Occult-Related Crimes Unit of the South African Police Services—itself a somewhat curious creature—the devil himself seems to be making a "revolutionary re-appearance" here?[27]

Finally, what might these things have to do with the memory of Max Gluckman? Or with the present and future of the discipline of anthropology, about which he had such strong ideas?

II

Let us take the last question first. Our memories of Max Gluckman go back to the early 1970s, toward the start of our professional careers, toward the end of his. We came to Manchester having read and heard a great deal of debate about his work, and not a few critiques—most of them emanating from certain institutions south of the Watford Gap.[28] None of this, however, prepared us for our encounter with his charisma, Mancunian-style. Or with conflict structural-functionalism as propounded, in the flesh, by Gluckman himself, a formidable interlocutor if there ever was one. "Marxism," it is true, was not quite Marxism. Very much a creature of its day, many of its founding principles are now dated. But the principles of Marxism were essayed with vigor, certitude, and a bold sense of possibility. Anthropology, for Gluckman, was both a mission and an invitation to an argument; though, in point of fact, he was always easier to argue with when not actually present, or, more permanently, when dead. His combative, creative spirit lives on in our consciousness by two principles above all else.

One was his emphatically pre-postmodern insistence on discerning de-sign in, and abstracting order from, an "illogical assortment" of disparate de-tails, minutiae, even trivia; recall his introduction to *Order and Rebellion*, which notes, with approval, how a coherent anthropology grew out of "the study of oddments by eccentrics" (1963, 1).[29] Max, of course, was not lacking in oddness or eccentricity himself. And coherence is no longer valued all that much. But so be it. The serious, if simple, corollary is that our skills and sen-sibilities ought to be put to the effort of detecting—from diverse, discordant acts and facts—emergent social processes and patterns. The sacred charter of the discipline of anthropology is to explain the existence of such partly obscured, barely audible, often nascent phenomena in the world. Sometimes these phe-nomena, like the unruly events so memorably described in his *Analysis of a Social Situation in Modern Zululand* (1940), bring into sharp focus, and serve to bridge, cultural and material forces of dramatically different magnitude or scale. As they do, they compel us to address the evanescent, ever present connections between local concerns and world-historical movements. Herein lie the essen-tial distillate and challenge of the Gluckman heritage.

The second principle is more specific. Max Gluckman is justifiably famed for his work in legal anthropology, for his studies of political and social processes and the like. Amidst his lesser-quoted essays, however, is one which warrants special attention today. "The Magic of Despair" (see n.1) tries to make sense of the ritual practices of Mau Mau, and those practices are run up against Central African witchcraft movements (Richards 1935), millennial cults of the Middle Ages (Cohn 1957), Melanesian cargo cults (Worsley 1957), Zionist prophets in South Africa (Sundkler 1948), and various forms of social banditry (Hobsbawm 1959). The point? To explain why Africans should seek recourse in the occult in situations of rapid social transformation—under historical conditions, that is, which yield an ambiguous mix of possibility and powerlessness, of desire and despair, of mass joblessness and hunger amidst the accumulation by some of great amounts of new wealth (Gluckman 1963). These circumstances, added Gluckman (145) presciently, do not elicit a "reversion to pagan ritual." Just the opposite. "New situations," he says, citing Evans-Pritchard (1937, 513), "demand new magic."

Put these various pieces together—Gluckman's concern to decipher patterns-in-the-making from oddments and fragments, his insistence on seeing connections among phenomena of widely different scale, and his interest in mystical responses to contradictory historical situations—and the argument of this essay begins to take shape—so, too, do our answers to the "Big Questions."

The essence of our narrative, to sketch it out in a few bold lines, goes like this. The Howick monster and the pyramid schemes, the epidemic of witchcraft and the killing of those suspected of magical evil, the moral panic about markets in body parts, the idea that zombies roam the country in ever larger numbers—all are symptoms of an occult economy welling up behind the civil surfaces of the "new" South Africa. This economy is an odd fusion of the modern and the postmodern, of hope and hopelessness, of utility and futility, of promise and its perversions. Its roots, we have already hinted, do not lie simply in poverty or material deprivation, however cruel and unrelenting. This occult economy has a double origin, the very doubling spoken of by Gluckman in "The Magic of Despair." On one hand is a perception—authenticated by glimpses of the vast wealth that passes through most postcolonial societies and into the hands of a very few of their citizens—that the mysterious mechanisms of the market hold the key to hitherto unknown riches and to capital amassed by the ever more rapid flow of value across time and space into the intersecting sites where the local meets the global. In South Africa, after all, the end of apartheid held out the prospect that everyone would be set free to accumulate, to consume, to indulge repressed desires. On the other hand is the dawning sense of permanent dispossession, of chill desperation, attendant on being left out of the promise of progress, out of the discourse of development, and out of the logos of liberation. The millennial moment has come and gone without palpable payback.

The implication? That everything would be set to rights if only there were some real income redistribution; if, as we were told repeatedly by poor people in the rural northwest, there were enough jobs to go around and a fair wage to be had. But there are not. Or if the alluring world of business were more open. It is not. Why? Because, as they have done since time immemorial, evil technicians of the arcane regularly intervene to divert the flow of value for their own immoral, antisocial ends. This, in turn, underlies the essential paradox of occult economies, the fact that they operate on two inimical fronts at once. The first is the constant pursuit of new, magical means for otherwise unattainable ends. The second is the effort to eradicate people who enrich themselves by those very means: through the illegitimate appropriation, not just of the bodies and things of others, but also of the forces of production themselves.

Partly because of the nature of the struggle to end apartheid, partly because of the legacy of apartheid itself, partly because of the dawning of a new epoch in the history of production, most of the men and women who experience postcoloniality here as privation, and who enter the commerce in enchantment, are young. It is they who held out the greatest expectations for "the revolution." They are the repressed for whom the promise of postcolonial return of wealth and well-being long denied is most obviously blocked by the hardening materialities of life at this coordinate on the map of global capital. As a result, rather than the more familiar axes of social division—class, race, gender, ethnicity, status—the dominant line of cleavage here has become generational. Postapartheid South Africa, to put it bluntly, is trying to construct a modernist nation-state under postmodern conditions, a historical endeavor fraught with contradictions. Black underclass youths embody those contradictions most tangibly. It is they, more than anyone else, who have to face up to the apparent impossibility of the current situation; to the difficulties of social reproduction in an age that once held out fervent hopes of rebirth. But it is not only they. Traffic in the occult—itself multiplied by the triumphal march of the market, by the rapid expansion of entrepreneurial enterprise everywhere—transects color, culture, age, and sex.

We have argued before (1993) that the practice of mystical arts in postcolonial Africa, witchcraft among them, does not imply an iteration of, or a retreat into, tradition.[30] Per contra, it is often a mode of producing new forms of consciousness, of expressing discontent with modernity and dealing with its deformities, in short, of retooling culturally familiar technologies as new means for new ends—new magic for new situations. On a global scale, enchantment abounds; yet, in some scholarly circles, there is a reluctance to allow that the Africa of the 1990s is still home to such arcane ideas. The fact is, as Geschiere (n.d.) has said, there is a lot of witchcraft around now. And "natives" do speak about it; for many, it is an ontological given in this age of rapidly shifting realities (see Ashforth 1997, 2). It is also a pressing practical problem that needs to be dealt with. For our own part, we do not see enchantment as an isolated, even as an African, phenomenon. It is just one element in a surging, implosive economy of means and ends; an economy which is popping up all over the planet, albeit in a wide variety of local guises. As it does, it posits fresh (or refashioned) ways of producing immense wealth and power without regular work—against all odds, at supernatural speed, and with striking ingenuity.

We have claimed that the things of which we speak have to do with global processes, or more precisely, with specific intersections in the here and now between the global and the local. And we have said there is a lesson here for the future of anthropology. Before we can give either claim any credence, however, it is necessary to focus on a particular ethnographic setting, one in which realities appear more fragile, fluid, fragmentary, and contested than usual. We turn to the northerly provinces of the "new" South Africa just before and after the close of the epoch of apartheid.

III

The Commission of Inquiry into Witchcraft Violence and Ritual Murders in the Northern Province was established by the new provincial government in March 1995 in response to a mounting sense of emergency in the countryside. Official commissions were the stock-in-trade of colonial rule (Ashforth 1990). But these are postcolonial times, times in which politics often masquerades as culture. This post-apartheid inquiry was an unprecedented hybrid of government and ethnography.[31] An effort both to regain control over a runaway world and to grasp persistent cultural realities, its terms of reference drew both from the tropes of scientific universalism and from the language of difference. Chaired by Professor N. V. Ralushai, a retired Professor of Social Anthropology and Ethnomusicology, the commission was comprised of nine members, all but one of them Africans.[32] Their report is a rich, if barely analyzed, amalgam of informant accounts, case records, and firsthand observation, which adds up to a number of recommendations, revealing a clear tension between two poles: (i) civic rationalism, expressed in a call for liberation through education and for more rigorous control of witch-related violence, including a possible reinstatement of the death penalty;[33] and (ii) frank, even assertive, relativism. Large numbers of Africans, says the report, regard magical attacks as "normal events of everyday life" (61), a reality incompatible with the legacy of European law, which criminalizes witch-finding. It also notes that most black police believe in witchcraft, making them reluctant to intervene when suspects are attacked (63). And it concludes that there is "no clear-cut" solution to the legal problem. The commissioners advocate various means of stemming the brute force with which accused witches are hunted down, but they do not question the actuality of witchcraft itself.

On the contrary. The urgent tone of the commission, the sense of existential and constitutional crisis to which it speaks, is underscored by a rising demography of violence. According to the report, between 1985 and 1995 there occurred over 300 recorded cases of witch-related killings in the Province (31); in the first half of 1996 there were 676 ("Northern Province" 1996). (In the Northwest Province, the rate was lower, but also increased over the decade.) Little wonder that many people, here as in other parts of Africa, fear that witchcraft is "running wild." The mood of alarm is well captured in the opening remarks of the report: "As the Province continued to burn, [as] witchcraft violence and ritual murder" was becoming endemic, "something had to be done, and very fast" (i).

The countryside was burning alright. But there were lots of ironies in the fire. For one thing, this was a moment, much heralded and celebrated, of exodus from colonial bondage, a moment of transition to mass enfranchisement. And yet, as our research in the Northwest Province indicates, rural populations were convinced that their neighborhoods harbored trenchant human evil; that their familiar landscapes were alive with phantasmic forces of unprecedented power and danger; that the state had failed to shield ordinary citizens from malignity, leaving them little recourse but to protect themselves. For another thing, it was young men, not people in authority, who felt most moved to execute "instant justice." They marked Nelson Mandela's release from prison, viewed by the world as a sign that reason and right had triumphed at last, with a furious spate of witch burnings—often to the august chanting of freedom songs (Ralushai et al. 1996, 244). All this was accompanied by a burgeoning fear, in the rural north, that some people, usually old people, were turning others into zombies—into a vast army of ghost workers, whose lifeblood fueled a vibrant, immoral economy pulsing beneath the sluggish rhythm of country life in this, the poorest province of South Africa. The margin between the human and the inhuman had become ever more permeable, transgressed by the living dead and their monstrous owners. Along with disconcerting evidence of a grisly national market in human body parts, these zombies bore testimony to a mounting confusion of people with things.

As we have said, none of this is entirely new. It is now clear that, at least in Africa, the colonial encounter magnified preexisting enchantments. And it multiplied the sorts of frictions that ignite witch hunts (see Comaroff and Comaroff 1993; Fisiy and Geschiere 1991). Witchcraft has proven to be every bit as expansive and protean as modernity itself—thriving on its contradictions and its silences, usurping its media, puncturing its pretensions by revealing that the primordial lives on in its midst (Jean Comaroff 1994). Yet, as Geschiere reminds us, longevity does not imply continuity (2). Whatever their putative powers, witches cannot escape history. Neither is their flexibility infinite or random. Shifts in their form often register the impact of large-scale transformations on local worlds.[34] Indeed, the uncanny durability of the figure of the witch seems to stem from a genius for making the language of intimate, interpersonal affect speak of more abstract and expansive social forces. It is this articulation, in both senses of the term, that underlies the sudden intensification of witch-finding in postcolonial South Africa, and, despite its very local nuances, throughout the continent at large (Geschiere, 1). The parochialism of witches, it seems, is an increasingly global phenomenon.

Because witches distill complex material and social forces into palpable human motives, they tend to figure in narratives which tie translocal processes to local events, which map translocal scenes onto local landscapes, and which translate translocal discourses into local vocabularies of cause and effect. In rural South Africa, the recent rise in witch finding and exorcisms has coincided with an efflorescence of other magical technologies which link the occult and the ordinary by thoroughly modern, even postmodern, means—means that evoke, often parody, and sometimes contort the mechanisms of the neoliberal "free" market. These technologies have opened up a range of novel productive possibilities which appear titillating, auspicious, dangerous, and stunningly susceptible to the workings of global capitalism, creatively conceived.

Thus ritual murder is said to have become big business across the northern reaches of South Africa. In 1995, for example, stories spread widely about the discovery of dismembered corpses in the freezer of a casino in Mmabatho in the Northwest Province. The casino was built for tourists during the apartheid years, when betting and interracial sex were illegal in South Africa but not in the ethnic "homelands." Here, over the border, in the grey interstices of the transnational, white South Africans came to purchase sexual services and to gamble, itself a morally ambiguous mode of generating wealth without toil. In the "new" South Africa, black bodies were again for sale but in different form; the macabre trade now nested comfortably within the orbit of everyday commerce, circulating human organs to whoever had the liquid cash to invest in them (they are, after all, a materialized form of cultural capital) in order to strengthen themselves and their undertakings. Much the same thing was apparent in the burgeoning suspicion that some local entrepreneurs had taken to turning their fellows into working zombies, a practice which intensifies and distends a foundational law of capitalism; namely, that rates of profit are inversely related to labor costs. But the most fabulous narratives were about Satanism in the Northwest, where it became a popular fixation in the mid-1990s, to be the most lucrative, most global of all occult enterprises. Less a matter of awesome ritual than of mundane human greed, dabbling in the diabolical was said to be especially captivating to the young. In 1996, a talk show on the Setswana network, Mmabatho TV, broadcast two programs on the subject, and the "reformed" ex-Satanists who were featured, along with their "spiritual councillor," were all juveniles. As they took calls from the public they told in flat, prosaic terms of the translocal power of the black arts—among them, an uncanny ability to travel to distant cities at miraculous speed, where they garnered great riches at will. Such devilish dealings were associated, if inchoately, with a new evangelical movement of Brazilian origin (see n.15). This church advertised almost instantaneous material reward for professions of faith. It was also rumored to issue charmed credit cards, which registered no debt whatsoever.

We shall return to the substance of these concerns in due course. Here we note merely that what is at issue is an expanded array of enchanted, often unnervingly visceral, means of producing value. Visceral, yet also strangely banal. In colonial times, divination involved a discrete consultation with an expert; now, anxieties about witchcraft, money magic, ritual murder, and Satanism are ventilated in churches and comic strips, on the radio, TV, and the internet. The public, multi-mediated quality of this communication is neatly captured in innovative ritual technologies—for example, divining by "mirror" or "television," recently developed in the Northern Province (Ralushai et al. 1996, 6, 148, 177). An electronic update of such longstanding practices is found in reading oracular designs in a water bowl (Comaroff and Comaroff 1997, 97–98); this procedure requires clients to imbibe a fermented drink and seat themselves before a white cloth mounted in a darkened screenroom inside the practitioner's house.[35] Figures of miscreants—both human and bestial—take shape on the screen; they are transmitted by the same modes of productive compression that permit satellite dishes, broadcast networks, and the long-distance magic of witches to materialize images, objects, and sounds from afar.[36] While the adept might assist in unscrambling the magical pictures, these are received directly by his customers, who sit in the archetypal posture of family viewing and listening.

Who are the protagonists in these theaters of the banal, these mundane magical dramas? Who are the witches? And who takes responsibility for killing them? The witchcraft commission asked a large number of respondents. Their answer: "In general the community is responsible . . . but the youth who are called 'comrades' are in the forefront. *Note: ages of the accused ranges* (sic) *between 14–38 years*" (15; emphasis mine).[37] Not only were young men the most identifiable perpetrators of witch-related violence, but they seem often to have forced neighbors and ritual experts to do their bidding. Few women were actually involved in the killings or in the destruction of property that accompanied them (Ralushai et al. 1996, 50). The purported malevolents, on the other hand, were limited neither by gender nor age, although the evidence, from both the North and the Northwest, suggests that those who were physically attacked were overwhelmingly advanced in years.

Let us take a closer look at the most extended case presented in the report of the witchcraft commission, the Ha-Madura Witch-Hunt (Ralushai et al. 1996, 193).[38] The defendants, who ranged from fourteen to thirty-five years old, were charged with having murdered an elderly woman, one Nyamavholisa Madura, by necklacing. They were also accused of brutally attacking two others, both of advanced age, and of burning down a pair of homesteads. Witnesses recounted that, late in the afternoon of 21 March 1990, "the majority of the youths" of the town of Madura gathered under a tree near the primary school. After a couple of speakers had urged the need to exterminate the known witches in their midst, the crowd moved off along the road in search of their suspects, the accused at the head (202). Neither of their first two intended victims was home, so they torched their property, grievously assaulting a man whom they suspected of raising the alarm. They then moved on to the yard of the deceased. When they found her, they doused her with petrol, and set her alight. She fled across her maize field and crawled through a fence, where the crowd, wielding sticks and stones, caught up with her. At this point she wailed, "Why are you killing me, my grandchildren?" To which the assailants responded, "Die, die you witch. We can't get work because of you!" (195, 206, 212). Garlanding her with a rubber tire, they applied more petrol and ignited her one final time.

There could hardly be a more vivid expression of intergenerational struggle, or a more profound statement of its stark zero-sum logic. For rural youth, millennial "mass action" might have delivered the vote, but it had brought them no nearer to the wealth and empowerment that the overthrow of apartheid was supposed to yield. Quite the reverse: Economic sanctions had dramatically increased unemployment, especially among the unskilled in the countryside. The cruel irony of contemporary South Africa is that, as one of the world's last colonies, it won its right to secular modern nationhood just as global economic processes were seriously compromising the sovereignty and material integrity of the nation-state, sui generis. Multinational capital is capricious, its patronage shifting, and once apartheid had ended, it found cheaper, more tractable labor—with less violence—elsewhere. As a result, many corporations did not return and money flowed in other directions. The new era *has* raised the living standards for sections of the African middle class, both rural and urban, very visibly. But overall, industrial and agricultural work is harder to come by and poverty is still dire, which is why some places remain so incendiary well into the late 1990s (Ralushai et al. 1996, 15).

It is no coincidence that the most spirited witch-finding occurs where conditions are most straitened, where raw inequality is blatant: throughout the Northern Province and the remote reaches of the Northwest.[39] In small towns like Madura, new material distinctions, apparently inexplicable in origin, have become palpable among close neighbors. Such differences are made incarnate, personified even, in prized commodities: in houses, automobiles, televisions, cell phones. Said one man, Abraham Maharala, a pensioner forced to flee his village by evil-seeking neighbors, "the trouble began with the arrival of a radio" ("Outcasts" 1995). The alleged witch of Madura was the occasional employer of several of her attackers, and sometimes let them watch her TV (Ralushai et al. 1996, 212). The petrol that consumed her was seized from the few local men who could afford cars.

There is a good deal of evidence, both from the report and from our own observations in the Northwest in 1994 to 96, of widespread anxiety about the production and reproduction of wealth; it is an anxiety that frequently translates into bitter generational opposition. Witch-hunting youth in the Northern Province acted as an age cohort, almost like an age-regiment in Sotho-Tswana society of old. Ridding the countryside of *baloi* (witches) was all of a piece with the other forms of mass action that had sought to subvert an oppressive social order; urban "comrades," it should be noted, demonized the parental generation as passive "sellouts" to colonial oppression. Indeed, the war against mystical evil fused, in a hybrid of set of practices, political and ritual means of both recent and older vintage. In addition to singing songs of freedom as they carried out their exorcisms, comrades in Venda and Giyani also intoned one of the best known local circumcision chants, a chant associated with soccer matches, drinking parties, and other sites of male age-grade formation (Ralushai et al. 1996, 50, 179, 244).

Age, of course, is a relational principle. The youthful comrades forged their assertive identity against the foil of a sinister, secretive, and often gendered gerontocracy; significantly, those attacked were often referred to as "the old ladies," even when they were elderly men (Ralushai et al. 1996, 211). But, if it was the weak and defenseless who were actually assaulted, a more robust and predictable array of suspects tended to be accused, including the usual suspects of African witch-finding: men and women of conspicuous, unshared wealth (219, 253). The antisocial greed of these mature predators was epitomized in the idea of unnatural production and reproduction, in images of debauched, ungenerative sexuality. The commission, for example, makes repeated references to the inability of witches to bear natural children, to their red vaginas, and to their lethal, "rotten" sperm (141, 150, 158, 168); attacks upon them were accompanied by the cursing of their genitalia, and sometimes those of their mothers or their offspring (139, 144, 155, 158). Killing these "perverts" by fire—itself a vehicle of simultaneous destruction and rebirth—bespoke the effort to engender a more propitious, socially constructive, mode of reproduction.

Threats to local viability were also associated with the shadowy creation of a zombie work force. Thus the following verbatim case record: "On a certain day as [the complainant] was chopping firewood the accused arrived. They shouted from the street that she is a witch with a shrinked vagina. They further said that she had killed people by means of lightning and that she has a drum full of zombies. They also said that her son 'Zero' has no male seed and that he could not impregnate a woman" (50; see also 158). It is hard to imagine a more pointedly transparent portrait of perversion, of the zero-sum, immoral economy of witchcraft and its negation of life-giving material, sexual, and social exchange. In place of fertile procreation and the forms of wealth that benefit a wider community, the witch makes ghost workers out of the able-bodied. She prospers by cannibalizing others in a way that robs the rising generation, even her own offspring, of legitimate income and the means of natural increase.

Precisely this sense of illegitimate production and reproduction pervades youthful discourses of witchcraft in much of South Africa. Many young blacks explicitly blame their incapacity to ensure a future for themselves on an all-consuming, aged elite that controls the means of producing wealth without working, of accumulation without effort. Their concern is especially clear in the preoccupation with the figure of the zombie (*setlotlwane*, Northern Sotho; *sethotsela*, Tswana), long a feature of Caribbean *vodoun* but relatively new in rural South Africa (as elsewhere on the continent; see also Geschiere n.d., 14). Testimony to a diasporic flow of occult images (Appadurai 1990)—but evocative of a state of "living-death" or social nonbeing (*sefifi*) described by nineteenth-century missionaries to the Tswana (Comaroff and Comaroff 1991: 143)—zombies have been spliced into local mystical economies and have taken on the color of their surroundings. As one of our opening fragments suggests, they are missing persons, usually reported by close kin or affines, who are thought to have been killed and revived by witchcraft. These living dead exist only to toil for their creators—generally, in the South African context, unrelated neighbors.[40] As Ralushai et al. (1996, 5) note in the report, they are believed to work after dark, primarily in agrarian production. A woman suspected of profiting from phantom labor was accused, for example, of having a "tractor that makes a lot of noise during the night" (166). Ghost workers can also be magically transported to urban centers, indeed, to any place where they might accrue riches on behalf of their owners. And, in an era of increasingly impermanent employment, there are even what one young man described as "part-time zombies" (224–25): people who wake up exhausted in the morning, having served unwittingly in the nocturnal economy to feed the greed of a malign master.

Although they have no tongues, zombies speak of a particular time and place. The end of apartheid, as we have said, was in large part the product of a global moment, one in which the machinations of multinational capital and the fall of the Soviet Union had drastically restructured older polarities. When black South Africans at last threw off their colonial constraints, much of the rest of the continent had already learned the harsh truth about the postcolonial predicament, having experienced unprecedented marginalization and economic hardship—or, at the very least, striking new distinctions of wealth and privation. Such conditions disrupt grand narratives of progress and development (Roitman n.d., 20; see also Jean Comaroff 1994). But they do not necessarily dispel their animating desires; to the contrary, they may feed them—hence the situation that Roitman, writing of the Cameroon, describes as "negotiat[ing] modernity in a time of austerity" (20). In these circumstances there tends to be an expansion, both in techniques of producing value and in the "discursive field" in which wealth itself is figured. It is an expansion which often breaks the bounds of legality, making crime, as well as magic, a mode of production open to those who lack other means. This is why violence, as an instrument of income redistribution, is such a ubiquitous feature of postcolonial economies in Africa and elsewhere.

The zombie is the nightmare citizen of this parallel, refracted modernity. Reduced from humanity to raw labor power by means of magical violence, he is the creature of his maker, stored up in petrol drums or sheds like other inanimate tools. His absent presence accounts for otherwise inexplicable accumulation. Being solely for the benefit of its owner, the toil of the living dead is pure surplus value: it has "all the charms of something created out of nothing" (Marx 1976, 325). Zombie production is thus an apt image of the inflating occult economies of postcolonial Africa, of their ever more brutal forms of extraction. As spectral capital, it will be evident why these forms of extraction are typically associated, as is witchcraft in general, with older people of apparent means; why they are thought to have multiplied as wage work becomes scarce among the young and unskilled. Not only does the rise of a phantom proletariat consume the life force of others. By yielding profit without cost, it destroys the labor market and the legitimate prospects of "the community" at large. This, in essence, was the point made by striking workers on an Eastern Transvaal coffee plantation in 1995: they demanded the dismissal of three supervisors accused of killing employees to gain control of their jobs and, even worse, of keeping zombies for their private enrichment ("Spirits Strike" 1995).

But zombie production is merely one means among several. Evidence also abounds of a significant increase in the incidence of so-called "ritual murder," of killing for the purpose of harvesting body parts. Recall, again, our opening fragment about the eyes for sale in a Johannesburg shopping mall. As Ralushai et al. explain: "These body parts are used for the preparation of magic potions. Parts of the body may be used to secure certain advantages from the ancestors. A skull may, for instance, be built into the foundation of a new building to ensure a good business, or a brew containing human parts may be buried where it will ensure a good harvest" (1996, 255). A victim's hands, they assert, are "symbols of possession." Eyes imply vision, genitals fertility. As we know from elsewhere in South Africa, humans are thought to enhance their lifeforce by draining the vitality diffused in the organs of others, preferably cut out while the body is still warm (271)[41]—and, best of all, if they are taken from children under twelve.[42]

While they have long been part of the ritual repertoire of indigenous southern African societies, these practices were relatively rare in the past (Ralushai et al. 1996, 255). But now a great deal of gruesome evidence confirms that, in this domain too, market forces have stimulated production. In addition to horrifying accounts of mutilated remains, newspapers publish the going rate for various parts: R5,000 for testicles or gallbladders, R1,000 for a kidney, R2,000 for a heart ($1=R4.90).[43] Ordinary people, as we discovered in the Northwest in 1996, are obsessed with such facts; also with tales of butchered bodies turning up in places where they look just like raw meat. Hence the popular preoccupation—part fear, part fascination—with those corpses in the freezer of the Mmabatho casino and with any number of other, equally murky tales.

This commerce in the corporeal seems to be eroding conventional social, cultural, and moral margins. In December 1994, a white policeman was charged with having removed the insides of a cadaver at the Braamfontein state mortuary in Johannesburg for retailing as medicine (Khoza 1994). Meanwhile, in different parts of the country, two young couples, both jobless and expecting babies, confessed in court to slaying young girls for their organs—in order to make ends meet.[44] In each case, an older male ritual practitioner was implicated. It appears that these young people acted on the understanding that the occult economy feeds the malevolent ambitions of their elders, to whom the purloined parts were to be retailed. Already in 1988 it was noted that, in the Northern Province, any disappearance of persons, especially children, was "immediately linked to businessmen and politicians" by young activists (Ralushai et al. 1996, 271). It was consternation about a string of such killings in the former homeland of Venda that caused its government to fall in the same year;[45] while, across the border at Mochudi, Botswana, public discontent over the handling of a girl's ritual murder in 1994—allegedly by three local entrepreneurs, abetted by her father—brought youth onto the streets of the capital, prompting the Office of the President to call in Scotland Yard to help solve the crime (Deborah Durham, personal communication).

We reiterate that the traffic in human organs is neither new nor confined to South Africa. It has become commonplace to note that there is now a global economy in body parts (see Frow 1997, White 1997, 334, Scheper-Hughes 1996), which flow from poor to rich countries, from south to north, east to west, young to old. As rumors circulate to the effect that some national governments raise revenue by farming corneas and kidneys for export, popular apprehensions grow. From the Andes through Africa to Albania, mysterious malevolents are believed to extract fat, blood, members, and living offspring from unsuspecting local communities to feed an insatiable foreign demand. What these panics share with Western misgivings about corporeal free enterprise is a fear of the creeping commodification of life itself, a relentless process that erodes the inalienable aspects of persons and renders them susceptible to the long reach of the market.

Notice the emphasis on distance. The long-range, translocal dimension of dealings in the occult economy is crucial to the way in which its workings are understood in rural South Africa. Throughout the northerly provinces, people ponder the interplay of mobility and compression in the production of new forms of wealth. These forms appear to be a consequence of the capacity to siphon goods, people, and images across space in no time at all. By what means and through what vectors? Movement, especially instant movement, adds value. But how? How are its mechanics to be mastered? How, to use the idiom of an earlier era, is it possible to make cargo planes from far away places land on nearby runways? As postcolonial South Africa casts off its pariah status and seeks ever greater integration into world markets, the growing velocity of long-range transaction is discernible all around. In the rural Northwest, as we observed earlier, its impact is traceable in, among other things, a growing interest in Satanism—which is manifesting itself as a feature of the millennial moment everywhere, from the east coast of Africa to the west coast of America (La Fontaine 1998; Meyer 1995).[46]

Once more, however, translocal phenomena take on a strikingly particular local form. Among rural Tswana, discourses of the diabolical center widely, if not exclusively, upon the most recent in a long line of missions from overseas, the Universal Church of the Kingdom of God (*Igreja Universal do Reino de Deus*) of Brazil. Highly controversial in its country of origin, this new Protestant denomination promises instant goods and gratification to those who embrace Christ and denounce Satan; although, as the local pastor put it, believers have also to "make their faith practical" by publicly "sacrificing" as much cash as they can to the movement.[47] Here Pentecostalism meets neoliberal enterprise: the chapel is, literally, a storefront in a shopping precinct. It holds services for all manner of passers-by during business hours, appealing frankly to mercenary motives, mostly among the young. Tabloids in its windows feature radiant, well-clad witnesses, from all over Central and Southern Africa, speaking of the gainful employment, health, and wealth that followed their entry into the Church—eloquent testimonies to rapid material returns on a limited spiritual investment (see n.15). The ability to deliver in the here and now, again a potent form of space-time compression, is offered as the measure of a truly global God. Bold color advertisements for quality cars and lottery winnings adorn the altar, under the legend: "Delight in the Lord and he will give you the desires of your heart" (Psalms 37: 4). The immediacy of this, of religion at its most robustly concrete, resonates with the pragmatic strain long evident in black Christianity in South Africa (Comaroff and Comaroff 1997, ch. 2).

For those middle-class Tswana schooled in a more ascetic brand of Protestantism, the hordes that pack the storefront in hope and curiosity are being lured by the devil. Others are less sure, however. With the radical reorientation of local contours of desire and despair, of wealth and inequality, the diabolical has been invested with provocative and ambiguous powers. Its intervention into everyday moral and material life is hotly debated. We were ourselves witness to an intriguing argument among history graduate students at the University of the Northwest: Is the Universal Church the work of the Antichrist or a vindication of Max Weber?[48] To be sure, if Satan did not exist, crusading Christianity would have had to invent him; in order to assume its global mandate, neo-Pentecostalism summons up, perhaps as a condition of its possibility, a worthy, world-endangering antagonist to conquer. Like the Universal Church—which, by contrast to most other denominations, conducts much of its proceedings in English—Satanism is a globalizing discourse: "The devil and his demons," says its web page (see n.15), "have been deceiving people all over the world."

Remember, in this respect, the television programs we mentioned earlier: the ones in which "reformed" devil worshippers answered questions from callers. When asked by the show host to explain the relationship of the diabolical to *boloi* (witchcraft), one young man said, in a mix of Setswana and English: "Satanism is high-octane witchcraft. It is more international."[49] By such means are novel tropes domesticated, and the scope of older constructs extended to meet altered conditions.[50] Satanists, significantly, were said predominantly to be youthful. "It is we," offered another young ex-practitioner, "who really go for material things. We love the power of speeding around in fast cars." The devil's disciples were rumored to travel far and wide, fueling their accumulation of riches with human blood. As the "high-octane" petrochemical image suggests, the basis of their potency was, again, the capacity to condense space and time, to move instantly and seamlessly between the parochial and the translocal, thus weaving the connections of cause and effect that hold the key to the mysteries of this new, postcolonial epoch.

IV

Perhaps the overriding irony of the contemporary age—the "Age of Futilitarianism," we called it, in which the rampant promises of late capitalism run up against a thoroughly postmodern pessimism—is how unanticipated it was. None of the grand narratives of the orthodox social sciences came anywhere near predicting the sudden collapse of the twentieth-century international order, the fall of the Soviet Union, the crisis of the nation-state, the deterritorialization of culture and society, the ascendance of a neoliberal global economy. The surprising recent past of South Africa is one instance of this irony, one refraction of this world-historical process. Here too, notwithstanding an intense struggle, the end came unexpectedly both in its timing and in its manner. And more peaceably, perhaps, than anyone had a right to expect.

Apartheid might not have ended in a bloodbath, in a race war between colonial state and oppressed masses. But the birth of the "new" nation has nonetheless been tempestuous. Most perplexing, to many, is the apparently post-political character of the turbulence. Violence, by common agreement, is epidemic; it is widely said to be throttling the embryonic democracy. Almost none of it, however, is clothed in an ideological agenda, a social vision, a political program. Not yet. Which is why, perhaps, it is traumatizing the populace at large. The new nightmare is of street terror run amok; of a state in retreat; of crime as a routinized means of production; of police unwilling to protect ordinary citizens, preferring to profit from corruption, from the privatization of force, and from the sale of arms; of "faction fights" in KwaZulu and on the Witwatersrand that, having outrun their original bipartisan logic, take on a ferocious life of their own; of a new topography of public space to replace the geography of apartheid, marked by few zones of safety and many of danger; of gated communities and razor-fenced houses; of uncivil city scapes vigorously contested by youth gangs, Islamic vigilantes, drug dealers, carjackers, and other distinctly unromantic social bandits; of an economy, as much underground as aboveboard, in which "new" black bureaucrats and businessmen, politicians and property speculators, celebrities and criminals, grow rich while the rest struggle to survive.[51]

This, we stress, is a popular nightmare, a fast materializing mythos for the postrevolutionary moment. Sociological reality, as always, is much more complex, much less coherent. Not all is apocalypse. Nor does everyone participate in the scare scenario. In the wake of apartheid, all sorts of legitimate new ventures flourish, especially among people of color. From the quiet backyards of rural homesteads, through the teeming taxi ranks of large townships to sedate urban corporate quarters, inventive entrepreneurs seek creatively to do business. Postcolonial commerce ruptures and dissolves old racial lines in its millennial pursuit of virgin markets. And many whites continue to live in great physical comfort. A politics of optimism is actively purveyed by the ANC, not altogether in vain; refreshingly, the broadcast media envisage a future in which black is not bleak. What is more, some forms of cultural production—often exhilaratingly experimental, spirited, intense—thrive off the mean streets. Still, the fright nightmare persists. Indeed, it grows increasingly baroque, medieval almost, as it is represented with ever greater facticity, ever greater statistical certainty.[52]

Reports of escalating witchcraft and ritual murder, of zombies and satanism, must be situated on this restless terrain. The specter of mystical violence run amok is a monstrous caricature of post-apartheid "liberty"—the liberty to transgress and consume in an unfettered world of desire, cut loose from former political, spatial, moral, sexual, and material constraints. Socialist imaginings (utopian ideas of a new society), falter under the impact of global capital and its policy-oriented institutions. In their place reigns the rhetoric of the market, of freedom as the right to exercise choice through spending or voting or whatever, of personhood as constructed largely through consumption. Talk in the public sphere about violence—in official commissions and the press, on television talk shows and in "people's" courts, in artistic representation, and radio debate— gives voice to a pent-up lust for all that apartheid denied—from iconic objects (notably, the BMW) and an omnivorous sexuality unbound by Calvinist stricture, to extravagant self-fashionings and the ostentatious sense of independence communicated by the cell phone. But it also evokes a world in which ends far outstrip means, in which the will to consume is not matched by the opportunity to earn, in which there is a high velocity of exchange and a relatively low volume of production. And yet, we repeat, it is a world in which the possibility of rapid enrichment, of amassing a fortune by largely invisible means, is always palpably present.

The preoccupation with the occult is closely connected to all this. It depicts a macabre, visceral economy, an immoral economy, an economy founded on the violence of extraction and abstraction (1) in which the majority are kept poor by the mystical machinations of the few; (2) in which employment has dwindled because of the creation of a virtual labor force from the living dead;[53] (3) in which profit depends on learning the secret of compressing space and time, on cannibalizing bodies, and on making production into the spectral province of people of the night; (4) in which the old are accused of aborting the natural process of social reproduction by preventing the next generation from insuring the means of its material and social existence—and youth, reciprocally, are demonized. The fact that none of this is truly new, that it is an intensification of familiar practices, does not make it any the less significant or easily explained by those for whom it has become an existential reality.

In no small part, witch hunts are instruments of social divination— dramatic discourses of discovery in the public sphere—whose unspoken object it is to yield explanations, to impress clarity on bodies and persons, and to reduce the moral ambiguity of the moment (see Appadurai 1995). That ambiguity concerns many aspects of the new South Africa: the rights of citizens, the role of the state, the significance of cultural identity and of social difference, the meaning and the point of post-apartheid politics, the infinitely complex articulations of race, class, and ethnicity—the legitimacy of an economic order that has sanctioned dramatic polarities of wealth and caused intense jealousy among neighbors. But, most of all, there is perplexity—in this increasingly Hobbesian universe where social and moral anchors seem to be aweigh, where everything appears at once possible and impossible—about the very nature of human subjects, about their perverse secret appetites, and about dark practices of the heart that show themselves in spectacular new fortunes and orgies of consumption.

Here, then, are the answers to our questions. It will be clear now why, in the South African postcolony, there has been such a dramatic intensification of appeals to enchantment, to magical means for material ends. And why it is, in a world alleged to be filled increasingly with witches and ritual murders and zombies, that generational antagonisms loom so large. The rise of occult economies here and elsewhere in postcolonial, postrevolutionary societies, be they in Europe or Africa, seems overdetermined. For one thing, these tend to be societies in which the neoliberal promise of the free market runs up against the realities of scarcity and deregulation; of unpredictable shifts in centers of production and labor markets; of the difficulties of exercising stable control over space, time, or the flow of money; of an equivocal role for the state; of an end to old political alignments without any clear lines beyond pure interest along which new ones take shape; of uncertainty surrounding the proper nature of civil society and the postmodern subject. Such are the corollaries of the rise of millennial capitalism as they are felt in much of the contemporary world. Perhaps they will turn out to be entirely transitory, a mere passing moment, in the *longue dureé*. But this makes them no less momentous.

Which takes us to our final question, our final point. What about the present and future of anthropology in the global age? "Globalism" and "globalization," as everyone knows, have become tropes for our times. Like all catchwords and clichés, they are cheapened by overuse and under-specification. As a result, much of what is currently being written about them in the social sciences is "Anthropology Lite," fact-free ethnography whose realities are more virtual than its virtues are real. This is unfortunate, since the processes involved in the rise of novel forms of planetary integration and compression—especially in the electronic economy, in mass communications, in "flextime" flows of labor and capital, in the instantaneous circulation of signs and images, in the translocal commodification of culture, in the diasporic politics of identity—raise critical challenges for us (J. L. Comaroff 1996; J. Comaroff 1997).

Among those challenges is not, as some anthropologists would have it, to defend the local, to affirm, above all else, the capacity of "native" cultures to remain assertively intact, determinedly different, in the face of a triumphal, homogenizing world capitalism. Apart from being empirically questionable, this romance gestures back to an old form of anthropological patronization.

Even worse, it conjures up an anachronistic, ahistorical idea of culture transfixed in opposition to capitalism—as if capitalism were not itself cultural to the core, as if culture has not been commodified under the impact of the market. In any case, to reduce the history of the here and now to a contest between the parochial and the universal, between sameness and distinction, is to reinscribe the very dualism on which the colonizing discourse of early modernist social science was erected. It is also to misrepresent the hybrid, dialectical, historically evanescent character of all contemporary social and cultural designs.

Here lies the future of anthropology, its primary challenge, at least, as the discipline looks from the vantage point of the postcolony: to interrogate the production, in imaginative and material practice, of those compound political, economic, and cultural forms by which human beings create community and locality and identity—in terms of which they fabricate social realities and power relations and impose themselves upon their lived environments, through which, space and time are made and remade, and the boundaries of the local and the global (of here, there, elsewhere and everywhere) are actualized. Even the most overdetermined, most potent, most complex, most inchoate of world-historical forces—colonialism, the global market, cyberspace, "late" capitalism—take shape in sociocultural processes that come to rest at particular places during particular periods in particular personae. Without human agents, without specified locations and moments and actions, realities are not realized, objects not objectified, nothing "takes place," the social is not socialized, the present has no presence.

It is these locations and moments, people and places, events and actions, to return to Max Gluckman, that comprise the fragments from which an anthropology of the "new world order," of millennial capitalism, and of the culture of neoliberalism, is to be constructed. Out of this new anthropology we may recuperate, by positing imaginative sociologies and legible processes, the mechanisms by which the local is globalized and the global localized. For in these processes lies an explanation for the most parochial of things, like the new occult economy in South Africa, and also for the most universal, like the fact that enchantment, far from slipping away with the resolute march of modernity, is everywhere on the rise.

Notes

Our warmest thanks go to Richard and Pnina Werbner for inviting us to give the Max Gluckman Memorial Lecture, and also for having made all the necessary arrangements with consummate patience and kindness. We owe two further debts of collegial gratitude, both to unknowing recipients. One is to Derek Sayer, whose book, *The Violence of Abstraction* (1987), gives us part of our present title—although we use the phrase in a rather different way and for different ends, than does he. The other is to Peter Geschiere, whose recent work cross-cuts our own in significant ways and bears directly on the topic of this essay. We find his writings a constant source of inspiration. Finally, our son, Joshua Comaroff, read the penultimate draft with extraordinarily mature insight and intelligence, and made a number of important critical suggestions.

1   This line, from *Witchcraft, Oracles and Magic* (1937, 513), is contained in a passage quoted by Gluckman at the opening of his radio broadcast on Mau Mau, published as "The Magic of Despair" in *The Listener* (1959) and as Chapter 4 of *Order and Rebellion in Tribal Africa* (1963).

2   The story was carried by the Johannesburg *Sunday Times* on 16 March 1996. We read it from a Reuters report, "S. African villagers kill 'witch disguised as baboon'." Necklacing, notoriously, involved putting an old rubber tire drenched in petrol around the suspect and setting it alight.

   The incident occurred near the Kruger National Park, a celebrated (now controversial) game reserve which has drawn innumerable tourists over the years. Note that the animal at the center of the story seems neither to have come from the park nor to have had an owner. Interestingly, a state witchcraft commission (Ralushai et al. 1996, 17), discussed below, was told by its informants in the Northern Province that witches "should be kept with wild animals in the Kruger National Park!"

3   See Hammond-Tooke (1981, 98) on the Kgaga, a Northern Sotho people who live in the area. Elsewhere he adds that for Kgaga baboons are "disconcertingly like men"— and, hence, were not eaten (133).

4   The anthropologist mentioned in the piece is Sian Hall, a resident of Howick.

5   The notion that fearsome reptiles inhabit deep pools is a common one throughout rural southern Africa. In the 1820s, John Philip (1828, 117), Superintendent of the London Missionary Society in South Africa, remarked on the prevalence of this notion among Southern Tswana; David Livingstone (1857, 44), in fact, took it as evidence of the "remnants of serpent-worship" in this part of Africa. We encountered it ourselves in the 1960s and 1970s, as had Breutz (1956, 77), and, across the border in the Bechuanaland Protectorate (Schapera 1971, 35–6). The latter reports that rainmakers were thought able to charm enormous snakes, who could draw water from the heavens (Comaroff and Comaroff 1997, ch. 2, 4).

6   This fragment comes from a posting on the Nuafrica mailing list ⟨nuafrica@listserv. acns.nwu.edu⟩ centered at the Program of African Studies, Northwestern University. It was posted by Lumkile Mondi ⟨Lumkile_Mondi_at_DDT.ZA.JHB.MC@ dttus.com⟩ on 22 February 1996.

7   Here, though, the story becomes a little murky. Earlier in his account, Mondi says that "all but one [of the schemes had] closed down as the owners disappear[ed] with millions." But then he goes on to speak of "the scheme"—in the singular—and its successes. We assume he means to suggest that earlier pyramid operations had failed amidst corrupt practice, but that the most recent one, which features in the story, had survived and grown to its present scale.

8   These investors believed that state involvement posed a threat to their economic prospects: they told Mondi, quite explicitly, that "intervention by the authorities" promised to "push them back to poverty."

9   According to a 1997 report by Bruce Cameron for Independent Newspapers, "new get-rich-quick schemes are cropping up almost every week" in South Africa. Cameron mentions two more pyramids: Newport, run from a Netherlands address, and Balltron. "Some [of these schemes]," he adds, "are attached to other financial products like unit trusts, others have a magazine, while others like Rainbow [in South Africa] offer discounts on various products like airline fares. What most of the schemes have in common is that they depend on one or more layers of people being recruited to ensure the earlier entrants recover their money. When the stage of implosion is reached . . . many thousands of people [are] . . . left out of pocket."

10 This story tells of a case before the Bisho Supreme Court (Eastern Cape) in which the accused had been seen, by his "girlfriend," disemboweling an eight year old female in the bedroom of his home at Mdantsane (near East London) in July 1995 and packaging her organs for sale.

11 See Bohlen 1997; Andrews 1997; and "Violent Protests" 1997. This last report comments on the secretive operation of the funds and on the fact that, early on, protesters berated the government for intervening, believing that they would otherwise have been paid out (note shades here of our fragment from South Africa). For a left-wing analysis of the Albanian debacle, see Woods' "Revolution in Albania." According to Woods, "The spark which ignited the fire was the bankruptcy of the financial companies which were promising interest rates up to 100 per cent a month to people investing their savings [in pyramid schemes]. Tens of thousands of Albanians sold all their belongings, including their homes, in order to put their money in the accounts of the fraudsters. They have lost everything. The people responsible for this fraud they all belong to the clique around President [Sali] Berisha."

12 Large-scale scams have occurred in Russia, Romania, Bulgaria, Serbia, and almost every other formerly Communist countries (Andrews 1997).

13 Recall that, while operating in South Africa, Rainbow and Newport had administrative addresses in Liverpool and the Netherlands, respectively.

14 This type of swindle, says Leslie Eaton, works as follows: promoters take over a small company and issue its shares—most of which they own, and for which they paid little or nothing—at a public offering. Public relations operatives, market analysts, and brokers are then hired to drive up the price of these shares by championing the company and by selling its stocks to clients, often in return for secret commissions. But if stockholders try to sell, the conspiring traders fail to execute their orders. When the value of their paper has risen enough to make a substantial gain, the promoters sell, causing the price to plunge and leaving conned investors with large losses. There have recently been reports of soaring fraud of this kind in the United States—a result, it seems, of the fact that many investors are presently "predisposed to throw dollars at get-rich-quick schemes." While not new, such scams appear to be more elaborate and common than ever before. Six billion dollars was lost to them in 1996, a year in which complaints against brokers numbered 3,100 (40 percent over

the year before). This has been exacerbated "by the rise of low cost telecommunications and . . . the internet" (Eaton 1997, 1, 24).

15 See also the web page of the Universal Church in South Africa, http://www.surfnet. co.za/stop.suffering. In hypertext, under *Financial Testimonies*, it carries a story entitled "BMW and Business," in which one Lorraine Maila tells how, by joining the denomination, and by "making a chain of prayers" (echoes of the chain letter?) she "was blessed with a BMW 316 Dolphin and brand new equipment in [her] shop." By way of comparison with religion closer to home, there is in Annie Proulx's recent *Accordion Crimes*, a pointed portrait of an African American radio preacher, one Reverend Ike, whose Christianity speaks in similar terms: "I am telling you, get out of the ghetto and get into the get-mo. Get some money, honey. You and me, we are not interested in a harp tomorrow, we interested in a dollar today. We want it NOW. We want it in a big sack or a box or a railroad car but we WANT it. Stick with me. Nothing for free. Want to shake that money tree. There is something missing from that old proverb, you all know it, money is the root of all evil. I say LACK OF money is the root of all evil. The best thing you can do for poor folks is not be one of them. No way, don't stay. Don't stay poor, its pure manure, and that's for sure" (1996, 338).

16 One of the pyramid operators in Albania, Edmund Andrews notes, was "a gypsy fortune-teller, complete with crystal ball, who claimed to know the future" (1997).

17 We are not suggesting that get-rich-quick schemes of various kinds are new; patently, national lotteries, pyramid schemes, and the like have been around for a long time. What strikes us as remarkable are the widespread reports of their intensification and their integration into mainstream economic practice at this moment in history.

18 New Era was created by John Bennett Jr., who was sentenced to twelve years imprisonment in Philadelphia on 22 September 1997 for fraud. Bennett pleaded to having suffered "delusions that he was doing God's work." Interestingly, these delusions—which produced the "biggest charity scam in U.S. history" convinced a large number of philanthropic money managers to invest in the scheme in pursuit of unusually large returns ("Charity Pyramid" 1997).

19 It is striking quite how routinized, even commoditized, enchantment has become. Note, for example, the fact that tarot cards, once tools of the fortune-telling trade and of amateur new age afficionados, are "[n]o longer confined to emporiums of the occult. . . . [They] are now prominently displayed in major chain bookstores. There are also 15,000 tarot-related sites on the Internet. . . . Tarot readers are [now] the people next door." Some commentators go so far as to attribute all this to the fact that tarot cards have become a cheap, do-it-yourself alternative to psychiatry. See Lauerman 1997.

20 The play on the phrase "consuming passions" comes from Jean Comaroff (1997). For further discussion of the general point, see Bastian (1993), Schmoll (1993), White (1997), Comaroff and Comaroff (1993), and Geschiere (n.d.).

21 See Scheper-Hughes (1996). Daniel Rothenberg, a doctoral student at the University of Chicago, is currently doing an ethnographic study in Guatemala and Peru of "social panics" occasioned by the alleged activities of *sacaojos*, white Americans who were thought to steal the eyes of local children.

22 There have been countless stories in the British tabloid press about such matters. For one especially vivid one, see Brian Radford's article (1997). Its two subtitles—"Cult is cover for paedophile sex monsters" and "They breed tots to use at occult rites"— summarize aptly the content of the moral panic to which they speak.

23 Interestingly, in the United States there has been a recent spate of rumors, circulated through the internet, about the theft of kidneys from unsuspecting business travelers. According to this urban myth, the victim is offered a spiked drink at an airport—New Orleans appears to be a favorite—and awakes in a hotel bath, body submerged in ice. A note, taped to the wall, tells him not to move, but to call 911. He is instructed, by the operator on duty, to feel very carefully for a tube protruding from his back. If he finds one, he is told to remain absolutely still until paramedics arrive: both his kidneys have been harvested. We are grateful to Shane Greene (1997), a graduate student in the Department of Anthropology at the University of Chicago, for alerting us to this story—and to several email messages that attest to its "truth."

24 There is presently something of a moral panic in Central Europe about the "trafficking in women from Ukraine, Russia, and other nations of the former Soviet bloc" on the part of "slave traders" who force their victims into prostitution in Western Europe, the United States, Japan, China, and elsewhere (Isachenkov 1997).

25 Indeed, these phenomena go back a very long way. In 1888, to take just one example, a "Baby War" occurred in Korea. It began when rumors spread that "Europeans and Americans were stealing children and boiling them in kettles for food." These foreigners were also thought to capture women—rendering them insensible by means of a drug which became a powerful gas when blown out of the mouth—and cut off their breasts in order to extract "condensed milk," a commodity which the aliens somehow came to possess and consume even though they had no cows (Hulbert 1962, 2: 245).

26 See also Ashforth (1997) who also reports that, especially since 1994, "witchcraft is commonly thought to be rapidly increasing" (1). In Soweto, he adds, "there is a good deal of [popular] pressure" for the state to take a hand in solving this very serious problem (2).

27 Colonel Kobus Jonker, head of the Unit, is known by the nickname "Donker," the Afrikaans work for "dark" ("Donker Jonker's" 1995). Note that references to the *Weekly Mail and Guardian* here and elsewhere lack pagination, as they were taken from Internet editions.

28 Richard Werbner was kind enough to pass on to us a copy of the review by Stanley Tambiah (1966) of *Politics, Law and Ritual in Tribal Society* (1965); it offers an excellent example of the way in which Gluckman's work was received by British critics at the time.

29 Gluckman actually borrowed this phrase from the opening of Kluckhohn's *Mirror for Man* (1954).

30 We also argued, as have many anthropologists before us, that tradition is itself a chimera; that it is an ideological construct forged by teleological European narratives in contrast to modernity. Anthropological deconstructions notwithstanding, the concept retains its currency in Western discourses of otherness (1993, xii).

31 The *Report* of the Commission opens with a section on "Methods of Research" (Ralushai et al. 1996, 4). It defines vernacular terms, discusses "Unstructured Interviews" and "Problems Encountered in the Field," and ends with a bibliography of relevant scholarly publications, including one of our own (J. Comaroff 1985). Note that, from here on, to avoid cumbersome citation, we shall make reference to the content of the *Report* by page number alone; all of these references are to Ralushai et al. (1996).

32 The exception was J. A. van den Heever, Professor of Criminal Law and Procedure at the University of the North. The others were drawn from the judiciary and legal professions, churches and theological studies, traditional rulers, the Council of Traditional Healers, the South African Police, and the ANC (1–3).

33 The report begins its recommendations with a call to "liberate people mentally to refrain from participating in the killing . . . resulting from their belief in witchcraft" (6). It urges the government to sponsor mass workshops, rallies, media campaigns, and an international conference of traditional healers; and to bring "eminent local and international scholars"—for example, the anthropologist, Jean La Fontaine—to address the topic (60). As elsewhere in the document, Ralushai et al. are concerned here with ways of dissuading people from taking violent action against witches; they do not address the problem of eradicating beliefs in witchcraft itself.

34 This is especially evident in witch-finding campaigns in Central and Southern Africa, sparked in the past by a sense of momentous and economic change. Such campaigns have tended to give palpable expression in highly local terms to feelings of disempowerment in the face of exogenous forces (see Richards 1935; Auslander 1993).

35 In a story about the rise of witch-burnings in the Northern Province, the *Wall Street Journal* mentions a case involving the disappearance of Johannes Mashala; some of his kin, we are told, had kidnapped him in order to turn him into a zombie. The ritual specialist called in to divine his whereabouts "fed muti [medicine] to his mother, his sister, and three young male villagers and had them stare at a green cloth." (Note the cloth in this instance was green, not white, as reported by Ralushai et al. 1996.) The boys said they could see the kidnappers on the screen; shortly thereafter four of Mashala's relatives were found burned to death (Davidson 1994). As its title, "Apartheid is Over, But Other Old Evils Haunt South Africa: Witch-Burning on the Rise As Superstitious Villagers Sweep House of Spirits," suggests, this account is mired in stereotypic misunderstandings of "native" life in rural South Africa. But the basic facts of the story come from somewhat more reliable local sources.

36 An interesting parallel to this form of divination seems to have occurred in the celebrated case of the lost head of the Xhosa ruler, Hintsa. According to local tradition, Hintsa was shot and decapitated in 1835 by a member of the Highland Regiment; his head is said to have been taken to Scotland and buried in the regimental museum, although this version of the story has been widely disputed in the United Kingdom. When a Xhosa healer traveled to Britain in 1996 to bring the head home, Luise White (1997, 335) recalls, he "announced that a message from Hintsa's spirit scrawled on a blank television screen" told him where the missing skull was to be found.

37 Most respondents said that the youth were "manipulated" by adults and political cadres who wanted to render the country ungovernable. They added that young people were used in this way because as juveniles they would be treated lightly by the courts (15). While there might be some validity to this, it does not explain the broader phenomenon in question. Not only does it fail to make sense of the continuing escalation of witchcraft incidents in South Africa after the transition to majority government; it is also unable to account for the obvious passion that underlay youthful witch-hunting, a passion shared by most adult members of their communities. A similar criticism may be levelled at those who argue that the youth who led the popular resistance to apartheid in its final years were mere tools of adult instigators. Much more complex political and economic forces, parsed in intergenerational terms, were at issue.

38 State v. Mutshutshu Samuel Magoro and Others, case no. cc36/91, Supreme Court of Venda, heard 5–27 May 1992, delivered 3 June 1992.

39 On the ongoing incidence of witch-related violence in the Northern Province, see, once again, "Northern Province Targets 'Witch' Killers," 1996. Note, too, that this Province is the poorest in all of South Africa (see Davidson 1994). In the Northwest Province, as we observed in August 1997, orchestrated witch-finding tends to occur primarily in remote rural areas—such as those south of Taung and in the northeast Hurutshe district—which are quite far from the urban hub of Mafikeng-Mmabatho. We are grateful to Neil Roos of the Department of History, University of the Northwest (Roos 1997), whose insights on this pattern confirm our own.

40 Unlike the cases reported by Geschiere (n.d., 28), there is little evidence that zombies here are created by the sacrifice of close kin, although it seems largely to have been the immediate relatives of missing persons who voiced suspicions about their having been made into phantom workers. The one exception of which we are aware is the story, "Apartheid is Over," published in the Wall Street Journal, discussed in note 35.

41 Geschiere suggests that the rise of zombie-like beliefs in Cameroon implies that "witches see their fellow men no longer as meat to be eaten . . . as life to feed upon in order to strengthen one's own life force—but rather as laborers that have to be exploited" (n.d., 28). This shift is not born out in the South African material. Mounting evidence of a market in human body parts indicates that faith in the productive power of immoral consumption has strengthened along with other dimensions of the occult economy. Whereas most Africans insist that whites neither practice witchcraft nor are susceptible to it (23), there has long been evidence (as in the case of the blue eyes, mentioned above) that their bodies are especially effective sources of strengthening substances.

42 This is a preference attributed, speculatively, to ritual murderers and their putative clients. It derives largely from the "fact" that many victims of homicides alleged to have been committed for the culling of body parts have been young children (Khoza 1994). We have ourselves heard such speculations on countless occasions.

43 These were the given prices at the end of 1994 (see Khoza 1994). According to the Johannesburg Star, mentioned in the fourth of our opening fragments, the eyes of white children fetched $700 in April 1996.

44 One of these cases, cited above (n.10), was heard in the Bisho Supreme Court (Wright

1996). The other is State v. Edward Nkhumeleni and Others, Venda Supreme Court, case no. cc17/94, February 1995.

45 Dissatisfaction with the investigation into a clutch of murders in the territory led to protest on the part of the Northern Transvaal ANC Youth Congress, which organized stay-aways and a boycott of schools and local stores (Ralushai et al. 1996, 257). A local businessman, a former official of the Venda homeland government, and a ritual practitioner were finally convicted in these cases.

46 Also in white South Africa, where rising fears of the diabolical are part and parcel of an apocalyptic vision of the world after apartheid—and where the Occult-Related Crime Unit of the Police Service, mentioned above (n.27), wages "valiant battle" against "Satanic subcultures," said to be rampant among white teenagers ("Donker Jonker's" 1995).

47 The genealogy of the church can be traced back to the Pentecostal revival of the 1950s and 1960s in Brazil, and to the ideas of such proponents of the American "Prosperity Gospel" as Kenneth Hagin. For details, see Eric Kramer (1994), to whom we are grateful for sharing his extensive knowledge of this religious movement.

48 Kramer (see n.47) tells us that, in Brazil, the Universal Church denounces both the Catholic Church and Umbanda as "satanic," sometimes accusing Afro-Brazilian religions of such visceral practices as the sacrifice of children and the consumption of their organs. Kramer (personal communication; see also Pagels 1995), however, differentiates the satanic, itself an integral part of Christian history, from Satanism. This distinction is not relevant in South Africa, where it is the latter, unequivocally, that is invoked in the moral panic of the present.

49 *Metsweditswedi* ("Source of Sources"), Bophuthatswana TV (Mmabatho); broadcast on July 31, 1996.

50 In the Northwest Province the Universal Church holds special services for the victims of witchcraft, which it sees as the work of Satan; all over the world, it seems, the demonic must come to terms with local idioms of evil.

51 A report about neighboring Namibia gives a vivid example of just this imagery—and of much of what we have discussed here. According to the New York Times, "Popular anger is directed at the 43 members of Parliament who are Cabinet ministers or deputy ministers. They get $55,000 a year, plus allowances for housing, furniture, electricity, telephones and drivers. They also get free television satellite dishes, cellular phones, a Mercedes for weekdays, a Land Cruiser for weekends," overseas travel allowances and so on. Note, again, how these perquisites stress means of mobility, and of the transmission of signs and people across space and time. Interestingly, a national scandal has also occurred over the purchase of airplanes for President Sam Nujoma. Said an opposition politician, Mishake Muyongo, of a plan to spend $45m on a new plane with sufficient range to fly to Europe nonstop. "Planes are like toys Sam Nujoma has to play with. But we are holding out our left hands to beg while our rights are digging into our pockets to pay for his jet" (McNeil 1997).

52 We were struck, in 1996, by the confidence with which white Johannesburg residents told us, in the pseudoscientific argot of probability statistics, that they would fall victim to violent crime(s)—before the year 2000.

53 Ashforth also links growing anxieties over witchcraft with the problem of rising

unemployment and lack of jobs, which is seen in Soweto, apparently, as both a cause and an effect of mystical evil (1997, 2, 14). By way of comparison, in Thailand—where fortune-telling has been transformed by global technology and the rise of e-mail and dial-in divination—a "traditional" seer, auspiciously named Madam Luk, reports that her clients nowadays ask three questions to the exclusion of all else: " 'Is my company going broke?' 'Am I going to lose my job?' and 'Will I find another job?' " Clearly, in East Asia, too, the connections between global capitalism and occult practice are readily visible (Schmetzer 1997).

References

Andrews, Edmund L. 1997. "Behind the Scams: Desperate People, Easily Duped." *New York Times*, 29 January.

Appadurai, Arjun. 1990. "Disjuncture and Difference in the Global Cultural Economy." *Public Culture* 2: 1–24.

——. 1995. "Identity, Uncertainty, and Secret Agency: Ethnic Violence in the Era of Globalization." Public lecture at Chicago Humanities Institute, 28 November.

Ashforth, Adam. 1990. *The Politics of Official Discourse in Twentieth-Century South Africa*. Oxford: Clarendon Press.

——. 1997. " 'Witchcraft' and Democracy in the New South Africa: Sketches from a Political Ethnography of Soweto." Paper read at the annual meeting of the African Studies Association, November, at Columbus, Ohio.

Auslander, Mark. 1993. " 'Open the Wombs!': The Symbolic Politics of Modern Ngoni Witchfinding." In *Modernity and Its Malcontents: Ritual and Power in Postcolonial Africa*, edited by J. and J. L. Comaroff. Chicago: University of Chicago Press. 167–92.

Bastian, Misty L. 1993. " 'Bloodhounds Who Have No Friends': Witchcraft and Locality in the Nigerian Popular Press." In *Modernity and Its Malcontents: Ritual and Power in Postcolonial Africa*, edited by J. and J. L. Comaroff. Chicago: University of Chicago Press. 129–66.

Bohlen, Celestine. 1997. "Albanian Parties Trade Charges in the Pyramid Scandal." *New York Times*, 29 January.

Breutz, Paul-Lenert. 1956. *The Tribes of Mafeking District*. Union of South Africa, Department of Native Affairs, Ethnological Publication No. 32. Pretoria: Department of Native Affairs.

Cameron, Bruce. 1997. "Pyramid Schemes Under Fire, Yet in South Africa They are Flourishing Daily at Your Expense. *Independent Newspapers*. http://www.ifsin.com/indpfpyr.htm.

"Charity Pyramid Schemer Sentenced to 12 Years: New Era Organizer Collected $354 Million Soliciting 500 Groups." 1997. *Chicago Tribune*, 23 September.

Cohn, Norman Rufus Colin. 1957. *The Pursuit of the Millennium: Revolutionary Millenarians and Mystical Anarchists of the Middle Ages*. London: Secker and Warburg.

Comaroff, Jean. 1985. *Body of Power, Spirit of Resistance: the Culture and History of a South African People*. Chicago: University of Chicago Press.

——. 1994. "Contentious Subjects: Moral Being in the Modern World." *Suomen Antropologi*, 19, no. 2: 2–17.

—. 1997. "Consuming Passions: Child Abuse, Fetishism, and the 'New World Order.'" *Culture* 17: 7–19.

Comaroff, John L. 1996. "Ethnicity, Nationalism, and the Politics of Difference in an Age of Revolution." In *The Politics of Difference: Ethnic Premises in a World of Power*, edited by E. Wilmsen and P. MacAllister. Chicago: University of Chicago Press. 162–83.

Comaroff, Jean, and John L. Comaroff. 1991. *Of Revelation and Revolution*. Vol. 1. Chicago: University of Chicago Press.

—. 1993. "Introduction." In *Modernity and Its Malcontents: Ritual and Power in Postcolonial Africa*. Chicago: University of Chicago Press.

Comaroff, John L., and Jean Comaroff. 1997. *Of Revelation and Revolution: The Dialectics of Modernity on a South African Frontier*. Vol. 2. Chicago: University of Chicago Press.

Davidson, Joe. 1994. "Apartheid is Over, But Other Old Evils Haunt South Africa: Witch-Burning is on the Rise as Superstitious Villagers Sweep House of Spirits." *Wall Street Journal*, 20 June.

"Donker Jonker's Righteous Crusade." 1995. *Weekly Mail and Guardian*, 6 October.

Durham, Deborah. 1998. "Mankgodi Burns. Lost Youth In Botswana." Paper read to the African Studies Workshop, February, at the University of Chicago.

Eaton, Leslie. 1997. "Investment Fraud is Soaring with the Stock Market." *New York Times*, 30 November.

Eliot, George. 1994. *Silas Marner*. London: Penguin Books.

Evans-Pritchard, Sir Edward E. 1937. *Witchcraft, Oracles and Magic among the Azande of the Anglo-Egyptian Sudan*. Oxford: Clarendon Press.

Fisiy, Cyprian F., and Peter Geschiere. 1991. "Sorcery, Witchcraft and Accumulation—Regional Variations in South and West Cameroon." *Critique of Anthropology* 11: 251–78.

Frow, John. 1997. *Time and Commodity Culture: Essays on Cultural Theory and Postmodernity*. Oxford: Oxford University Press.

Geschiere, Peter. n.d. *Globalization and the Power of Indeterminate Meaning: Witchcraft and Spirit Cults in Africa and East Asia*. Ms.

Gluckman, Max. [1968] 1940. "Analysis of a Social Situation in Modern Zululand." *Bantu Studies*, 14: 1–30, 147–74.

—. 1959. "The Magic of Despair." In *The Listener* (29 April 1959). Republished in *Order and Rebellion in Tribal Africa* (1963): 137–145.

—. 1963. *Order and Rebellion in Tribal Africa*. London: Cohen & West.

—. 1965. *Politics, Law, and Ritual in Tribal Society*. Oxford: Basil Blackwell.

Greene, Shane. 1997. "Medical Appropriation, Embodied Economies, and Political Consciousness among the Awajun-Jivaro of Lowland Peru." Doctoral research proposal, Department of Anthropology, University of Chicago.

Hammond-Tooke, W. David. 1981. *Boundaries and Belief: The Structure of a Sotho Worldview*. Johannesburg: Witwatersrand University Press.

Hobsbawm, Eric. J. 1959. *Primitive Rebels*. Manchester: Manchester University Press.

Hulbert, Homer B. 1962. *Hulbert's History of Korea*, Volume 2. Edited by C. N. Weems. New York: Hilary House.

Isachenkov, Vladimir. 1997. "Enslaving Women from Former Soviet Bloc is Widespread." *Santa Barbara News-Press*, 8 November.

Khoza, Vusi, and Annie Mapoma. 1994. "The Human Parts that Heal." *Weekly Mail and Guardian*, 9 December.

Kluckhohn, Clyde. 1954. *Mirror for Man*. New York: McGraw-Hill.

Kramer, Eric W. 1994. *The Devil's Domains: "Conversion" and Everyday Life among Pentecostals in Urban Brazil*. Doctoral Research Proposal, Department of Anthropology, University of Chicago.

La Fontaine, Jean. 1998. *Speak of the Devil: Tales of Satanic Abuse in Contemporary England*. Cambridge: Cambridge University Press.

Lauerman, Connie. 1997. "Got a Problem? Pick a Card." *Chicago Tribune*, 4 December.

Livingstone, David. 1857. *Missionary Travels and Researches in South Africa, etc.* London: J. Murray.

Marx, Karl. 1976. *Capital: A Critique of Political Economy*, Volume I. Translated by Ben Fowkes. London: Penguin Books.

McNeil, Donald G., Jr. 1997. "Free Namibia Stumps the Naysayers." *New York Times*, 16 November.

Meyer, Birgit. 1995. *Translating the Devil: An African Appropriation of Pietist Protestantism—the Case of the Peki Ewe in Southeastern Ghana, 1847–1992*. Ph.D. diss., University of Amsterdam.

Mitchell, W. J. Thomas. 1998. *The Last Dinosaur book, or The Totem of Modern Culture*. Chicago: University of Chicago Press.

Mnyandu, Ellis. 1996. "Is it a Duck? No, it's the Howick Monster." *Reuters*, 10 June.

"Northern Province Targets 'Witch' Killers." 1996. *Weekly Mail and Guardian*, 27 September.

"Outcasts of the Witch Village of the North." 1995. *Weekly Mail and Guardian*, 3 November.

Pagels, Elaine. 1995. *The Origin of Satan*. New York: Vintage Books.

Philip, John. 1828. *Researches in South Africa; Illustrating the Civil, Moral, and Religious Condition of the Native Tribes*. 2 volumes. London: James Duncan.

Proulx, E. Annie. 1996. *Accordion Crimes*. London: Fourth Estate.

Radford, Brian. 1997. "Satanic Ghouls in Baby Sacrifice Horror." *News of the World*, 24 August.

Ralushai, N. V., M. G. Masingi, D. M. M. Madiba et al. 1996. "Report of the Commission of Inquiry into Witchcraft Violence and Ritual Murders in the Northern Province of the Republic of South Africa (To: His Excellency The Honourable Member of the Executive Council for Safety and Security, Northern Province)." No publisher given.

Richards, Audrey I. 1935. "A Modern Movement of Witch-Finders." *Africa* 8: 448–61.

Roitman, Janet. n.d. *The Garrison-Entrepôt*. Manus.

Roos, Neil. 1997. Conversation with author, 16 December.

Sayer, Derek. 1987. *The Violence of Abstraction: The Analytic Foundations of Historical Materialism*. Oxford: B. Blackwell.

Schapera, Isaac. 1971. *Rainmaking Rites of Tswana Tribes*. Leiden: Afrika-Studiecentrum.

Scheper-Hughes, Nancy. 1996. "Theft of Life: The Globalization of Organ Stealing Rumors." *Anthropology Today*, 12, no. 3: 11.

Schmetzer, Uli. 1997. "Letter from Bangkok: Thai Seers Dealt Reversal of Fortune." *Chicago Tribune*, 18 November.

Schmoll, Pamela G. 1993. "Black Stomachs, Beautiful Stones: Soul-Eating among Hausa in Niger." In *Modernity and Its Malcontents: Ritual and Power in Postcolonial Africa*, edited by J. and J. L. Comaroff. Chicago: University of Chicago Press.

Schneider, Jane. 1989. "Rumpelstiltskin's Bargain: Folklore and the Merchant Capitalist Intensification of Linen Manufacture in Early Modern Europe." In *Cloth and Human Experience*, edited by A. Weiner and J. Schneider. Washington: Smithsonian Institution Press.

"South African Arrested." 1996. *The Star*, 29 April.

"South African Villagers." 1996. *Johannesburg Sunday Times*, 16 March.

"South African Witches Accused of Abducting Dead Relatives. 1996. *Reuters*, 15 November.

"Spirits Strike at Labour Relations." 1995. *Weekly Mail and Guardian*, 27 December.

Staunton, Denis. 1997. "Couple on Trial for Child Torture Offer." *The Guardian*, 8 August.

Sundkler, Bengt G. M. 1961. *Bantu Prophets in South Africa*. London: Oxford University Press for the International African Institute.

Tambiah, Stanley J. 1966. "Tribal Society as Seen from Manchester." Review of *Politics, Law and Ritual in Tribal Society*, by M. Gluckman. *Nature* (5 March): 951.

"Violent Protests of Pyramid Schemes Spread in Albania." 1997. *New York Times*, 27 January.

White, Luise. 1997. "The Traffic in Heads: Bodies, Borders and the Articulation of Regional Histories." *Journal of Southern African Studies* 23: 325–38.

Woods, Alan. "Revolution in Albania." *http://easyweb.easynet.co.uk/zac/woodal.htm.*

Worsley, Peter M. 1957. *The Trumpet Shall Sound: A Study of "Cargo" Cults in Melanesia*. London: Macgibbon and Kate.

Wright, Steuart. 1996. "Girl Slit Open for Body Parts." *Johannesburg Sunday Times*, 11 August.

Contributors

BRIAN KEITH AXEL is an Academy Scholar of the Harvard Academy at the Weatherhead Center for International and Area Studies, Harvard University. He is the author of *The Nation's Tortured Body: Violence, Representation, and the Formation of a Sikh "Diaspora"* (2000).

TALAL ASAD teaches anthropology at the Graduate Center of the City University of New York. He was born in Saudi Arabia, spent his boyhood in India and Pakistan, and was educated in Britain where he lived for most of his adult life. His most recent book is entitled *Genealogies of Religion* (1993).

BERNARD S. COHN is Professor Emeritus of the Departments of Anthropology and History at the University of Chicago. His publications include *An Anthropologist Among the Historians and Other Essays* (1987) and *Colonialism and Its Forms of Knowledge: The British in India* (1996).

JEAN COMAROFF is Bernard E. and Ellen C. Sunny Distinguished Service Professor in the Department of Anthropology at the University of Chicago.

JOHN L. COMAROFF is Harold H. Swift Distinguished Service Professor in the Department of Anthropology at the University of Chicago and senior research fellow at the American Bar Foundation in Chicago. The Comaroffs' publications include *Of Revelation and Revolution*, Vol. 1 (1991) and Vol. 2 (1997), as well as the edited collection *Civil Society and the Political Imagination in Africa: Critical Perspectives* (1999).

NICHOLAS B. DIRKS is Franz Boas Professor of History and Anthropology at Columbia University. He is the author of *The Hollow Crown: Ethnohistory of an Indian Kingdom*, *Castes of Mind: Colonialism and the Making of Modern India*, editor of *Colonialism and Culture* and *In Near Ruins: Cultural Theory at the End of the Century*, co-editor of *Culture/Power/History: A Reader in Social Theory*, and has written numerous essays on South Asian history and historical anthropology.

IRENE SILVERBLATT is Professor of Cultural Anthropology at Duke University. Her publications include *Moon, Sun, and Witches: Gender Ideologies and Class in Inca and Colonial Peru* (1987) and "Imperial Dilemmas, the Politics of Kinship, and Inca Reconstructions of History" (1988).

PAUL A. SILVERSTEIN is an Assistant Professor of Anthropology at Reed College. He has done extensive research in France and North Africa, and is currently completing a book manuscript entitled *Trans-Politics: Islam, Berberity, and the French Nation-State.*

TERI SILVIO is Lecturer in Chinese and Indonesian Studies at the University of New South Wales, Sydney, Australia.

ANN LAURA STOLER is Professor of Anthropology and History at the University of Michigan. She is the author of *Capitalism and Confrontation in Sumatra's Plantation Belt, 1870–1979* (1985) and *Race and the Education of Desire: Foucault's* History of Sexuality *and the Colonial Order of Things* (1995), and coeditor, with Frederick Cooper, of *Tensions of Empire: Colonial Cultures in a Bourgeois World* (1997).

MICHEL-ROLPH TROUILLOT is Professor of Anthropology and of Social Sciences in the College at the University of Chicago. His publications include *Peasants and Capital: Dominica in the World Economy* (1988) and *Silencing the Past: Power and the Production of History* (1995).

Index

Freud, Sigmund, 24
Frontier context, 190, 197, 204
Frontier zone, 254
Functionalism, 6, 68

Galton, Francis, 80
Gandhi, Indira, 237, 248–49, 257–58n. 6
Gaze, the, 75, 87n. 13
Geertz, Clifford, 30, 35n. 9, 72, 73
Gellner, Ernest, 124
Genealogy, 32, 33–34n. 2
Genovese, Eugene D., 29–30
Geographic focus, 11
Germany, 125, 271
Geschiere, Peter, 271, 275, 277, 296n. 41
Gettysburg Address, 218, 220. *See also*
  Battle of Gettysburg
Glissant, Edouard, 196
Global economy, 26–28; creolization and,
  194–95; occult economies and, 273–78,
  286–90, 297–98n. 53
Gluckman, Max, 272–73
Golden Temple, 241, 246
Governmentality, 59–62
Grafton, Anthony, 63n. 1
Gramsci, Antonio, 113–14n. 8
Grand Army of the Republic, 225
Great Rebellion of 1857, 56–57, 60
Guaman Poma de Ayala, Felipe, 111–12
Guernier, Eugène, 146
Gunther, Charles F., 225–26
Gupta, Akhil, 235–36, 242

Hacking, Ian, 81
Haiti, 196, 204, 206–7n. 6, 207nn. 10, 11,
  12
Halbwachs, Maurice, 78–80
Ha-Madura Witch-Hunt, 279
Handler, Richard, 148n. 3
Henriques, Antonio Vaez (Moses Coen),
  101
Herzfeld, Michael, 123
Hierarchy, 256
Hintsa, 295n. 36
Historical anthropology, 1–12; analytical
  models, 1–2; Europe, 5–7; key decades,
  3–10; United States, 4–5; vicissitudes,
  28–33. *See also* Anthropology
Historical argument, 55, 57

Historiography, 75
Hobsbawm, Eric, 123, 124, 126
Holland, 100–101, 103
Hollywood Cemetery (Richmond), 219
Hollywood Memorial Association, 222
Holy Office of the Inquisition, 96
Homo Hierarchicus (Dumont), 256
Hope of Israel, The (Ben Israel), 105, 117n.
  40
Howick monster, 268, 269, 291n. 5

Identity politics, 71, 76
Image, 240
Imagined communities, 123
Imagined Communities (Anderson), 211–
  12
Imperial Acts (France), 130, 138
Incas, 105, 109
India, 15–16; cartography, 233–34, 236–40,
  242–44, 252–55, 257n. 2, 258n. 12; caste,
  57–58, 61; Cohn's view, 233–35, 237;
  Constitution, 244–45, 258n. 20; dynastic
  histories, 52–53; Great Rebellion of
  1857, 56–57, 60; internal threats, 248–
  49, 254; land records, 54–56; limitations
  on sovereignty, 240–44; national integration (rashtriya ekta), 233, 236–37, 243–
  45, 248–49, 257nn. 3, 4; nationalist discourse, 26, 32, 239; Patel Scheme, 244–
  45, 248; precolonial state and society,
  50–56; production of people, 233, 237,
  241, 247–48; regions, 233–35; Restricted
  Zone, 238–44, 253–56; settlement registers, 51, 54–55; social relations, 57–58;
  61; states, 244–47, 257–58n. 6, 258n. 20;
  Supreme Court, 248, 250–51, 260n. 36;
  Survey of India, 238–39, 252, 255; temples, 48–50; territorial sovereignty and
  integrity, 233, 238–44, 250–51, 254–56;
  terrorism, discourse of, 233, 239, 247–
  48, 259n. 24; totality and, 234–36, 251,
  256–57; unity in diversity, 234, 240–41,
  248, 250–53, 260nn. 36, 37
Indian Railways, 241–43
Indian Wars, 226–28
India Office Library (London), 50–51, 62
Indies Advisory Council, 168, 175–77
Indies Director of Education, 162, 173–74,
  177–78

Some of the material included in this book revises or
modifies what has been published elsewhere.
Talal Asad. 1994. "Ethnographic Representation, Statistics, and
Modern Power." *Social Research* 61, no. 1 (spring): 55–88.
John L. Comaroff and Jean Comaroff. 1999. "Occult Economies
and the Violence of Abstraction: Notes from the South African
Postcolony." *American Ethnologist* 26, no. 2: 279–303.
Michel-Rolph Trouillot. 1998. "Culture on the Edges: Creoli-
zation in the Plantation Context." *Plantation Society in the
Americas* 5, no. 1 (spring): 8–28.
Irene Silverblatt. 2000. "New Christians and New World Fears
in Seventeenth-Century Peru." *Comparative Studies in Soci-
ety and History* 42, no. 3: 524–46.

Library of Congress Cataloging-in-Publication Data
From the margins : historical anthropology and its futures /
edited by Brian Keith Axel.
Includes bibliographical references and index.
ISBN 0-8223-2861-5 (cloth : alk. paper) — ISBN 0-8223-2888-7
(pbk. : alk. paper)
1. Ethnohistory. 2. Social history. 3. Colonies.
4. Postcolonialism. I. Axel, Brian Keith
GN345.2 .F76 2002   909'.04—dc21   2001007054